Cut Loose

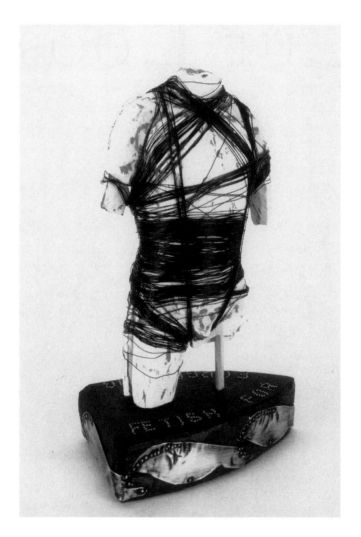

Louise Weinberg, *Fetish for Forgetting*, 1993, plaster, wood, wire, aluminum and acrylic. © Louise Weinberg.

CUT LOOSE

(MOSTLY) OLDER WOMEN TALK ABOUT THE END OF (MOSTLY) LONG-TERM RELATIONSHIPS

Edited by

Nan Bauer-Maglin

Rutgers University Press
New Brunswick, New Jersey, and London

Library of Congress Cataloging-in-Publication Data

Cut loose : (mostly) older women talk about the end of (mostly) long-term relationships / edited by Nan Bauer-Maglin.
    p. cm.
  Includes bibliographical references.
  ISBN-13: 978-0-8135-3846-4 (hardcover : alk. paper)
  ISBN-13: 978-0-8135-3847-1 (pbk. : alk. paper)
  1. Separation (Psychology)—Case studies.   2. Man-woman relationships—Case studies.   3. Women—Psychology—Case studies.   4. Middle-aged women—Psychology—Case studies. I. Maglin, Nan Bauer.
  HQ801.C86   2006
  306.89'3—dc22   2005028058

A British Cataloging-in-Publication record for this book is available from the British Library.

Design by Karolina Harris

Manufactured in the United States of America

Contents

Preface

Almost everyone in the world feels the agony of romantic rejection at some point in their lives. . . . Almost no one in the world escapes the feelings of emptiness, hopelessness, fear, and fury that rejection can create.

— HELEN FISHER, *Why We Love*

This book was born out of my own experience. As I was thinking about it I called it "The Dumped Book." Some people hated the title, finding the reference to garbage quite offensive. Other people felt the crudeness and harshness of the title were apt. These two perspectives are captured in Diane Raymond's exchange with a friend in this book: "Someone even told me to stop using the term 'dumped' to describe my experience; it's a way you've embraced victimhood, she told me. Yet I *was* dumped; to call it anything else seems disrespectful of my experience." The word is even more powerful in French, says Catherine Texier in her journal about the end of her eighteen-year relationship: "HOW DARE YOU??? Dump me for another woman. *Plaquer pour une autre femme*. In French the words sting worse, like the tip of a whiplash" (*Breakup: the End of a Love Story*, 46). As this book developed I played around with all sorts of words: jilted, unceremoniously left, thrown over, ditched, and dismissed. I was especially partial to "d" words: dislocations, departures, discardings, and other disruptions and disintegrations. And a new word has recently been coined that applies especially to celebrity dumping: "Cruised," meaning "jettisoned just before California's ten-year spousal support mark is reached," referring to the letting go of Nicole Kidman by Tom Cruise (Janet Maslin, discussing the book *The Starter Wife* in the *New York Times*, May 19, 2005).

In the end, I chose *cut loose*, as it seemed to have a double edge to it: that of being abandoned, let go, dropped, left to drift, unmoored, but also that of being no longer bound, freed and untethered or, more actively, of taking one's freedom or letting go. There is a violence to the word *cut* and an uninhibited, sexual, pleasurably frenetic implication to the word *loose*. *Cut loose* implies an afterlife that being dumped does not—and I do not want this very complex experience to be boxed in with the word *dumped*; at the same time I do not want to sanitize what is quite a horrible event in one's life.

I had hoped to include both men's and women's voices in this book. But the response from men was so meager that I decided to limit the project to women. Many women wrote me about their stories in response to either a call they read on various listserves on the Internet or being told about it through word of mouth. Many who first contacted me did not follow through by submitting an article: they usually said that it was too difficult, too depressing, they did not want to go back into that place of despair after having come so far, or they did not want their children exposed to the particulars of their pain. A few were afraid of retaliation or even legal action. So I am thankful to the women who did write with such grace, humor, and sometimes excruciatingly painful detail.

There are many, many people to thank; I will name only a few: Michelle Fine, Bill Fried, Bonnie Gitlin, Betsy McGee, Pam Trotman Reid, Barbara Rubin, Caroline Urvater, and Phyllis Van Slyck, who encouraged people to write their stories. Kathy Chamberlain, Ruth Cohen, Sam Eisenstein, Rochelle Fogel, Ellen Friedman, Gail Green-Anderson, Carole Langille, Lois Tigay, Sherryl Wilson, and others, who shared their writings with me. Merle Froschl, who helped me formulate the idea for the book and Neil Grill, who saw me through the first stage of the proposal. Lise Esdaile, Cheryl Fish, Linda Grasso, and Nancy Romer, among others, who led me to relevant reading material, and Marilyn Ogus Katz, Beth Kneller, Avis Lang, Jon-Christian Suggs, Florence Tager, and Sandy Weinbaum, who gave me editorial advice. Leslie Mitchner, Associate Director and Editor in Chief, Marilyn Campbell, Prepress Director, and other members of Rutgers University Press for their prompt and professional back-and-forths with me over two years from germ of an idea to the full production of *Cut Loose*. And to the careful copy editing of Susannah Driver-Barstow. My two women's groups and a number of new and old friends were a source of much food and emotional support during my personal travail and the making of this book. Certainly it is my husband who gets an ironic (or sardonic?) thank you; he and I have both learned a lot about loving, apart and together, but it is to Quin, my daughter, to whom I owe the most; her daily loving kept me and *Cut Loose* going.

CUT LOOSE

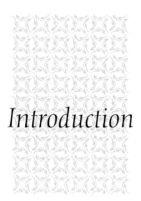

Introduction

Cast off the mooring lines.
Untie the wife.
—ANNA GAVALDA, *Someone I Loved*

Telling Our Secrets

Somewhere around age eleven or twelve, I became aware of the mothers, sitting around the side of the pool or in a game of canasta (yes, I grew up in the suburbs in the fifties), talking in hushed voices about women's stuff. Often they talked about hot flashes, sometimes about divorce. I heard comments such as "he left her with two babies" or "he waited until the kids were finished with college and then he dumped her for someone younger." I did not understand the implications of what I heard, but I knew they were tragic and secret.

Now more than fifty years later, neither menopause nor divorce is secret. Still, in almost those same hushed tones, my women friends and I report on yet another older woman whose husband has left her. When mine did so, all of a sudden, friends and friends of friends began sharing their own tales and secondhand stories. Several people gave me the e-mail addresses of women in the same boat—women who had been cut loose unexpectedly. They and I became e-mail pals, boosting each other up, sharing survival tips.

Nor has every woman in public life kept her own losses a secret. In *Madame Secretary*, Madeleine Albright has written about the end of her twenty-three-year marriage. It came upon her like a "thunderbolt," when she was forty-five. Her husband left her for a younger woman, telling Albright that she "was too old looking." Once out of the house, he began to waver, reporting daily how much he loved or did not love each of them: "'I love you 60 percent and her 40 percent. Or the next day I love her 70 percent and you 30 percent.'" Albright, her confidence shattered, said that if he "would have changed his mind," she "would have given up any thought of a career."[1]

Like Albright, I was shocked by the abruptness of it all. I felt so much pain, so much shame (I was to blame; I should have been more loving, more something . . .), as well as a heavy dose of fear and anxiety (I was sixty and would get sick and die alone). I was hungry to hear the stories of others; I did not want to feel alone. I wanted to figure out what my problem was and what the larger problem might be. I had the suspicion that I might not be alone in my grief, that this was an epidemic, not an episode. As Diane Raymond notes in her contribution here, once it happens to you, bundles of stories appear on your doorstep: "Since my relationship ended, I've heard hundreds of stories from other victims: from the women whose husbands left them for secretaries or students; from the colleague whose husband left a note on the kitchen table the day she arrived home from the hospital to recover from her mastectomy; from the friend whose partner moved in with her lover before she'd even told her." True to my experience in the women's movement, I believed that if we shared our stories, not only would we be comforted, but we might gain some insight into gendered behavior, into the cultural construction of marriage, aging, and happiness. So I organized this anthology: writings by older women who have been dumped or who did the dumping. I received very few selections by women who did the dumping (although who does what to whom and when is not so clear cut); it appears those in the victim position are more likely to turn to writing to purge themselves or at least are more willing to reveal themselves.

But personal confessional writing has been getting bad press lately. The title "We All Have a Life. Must We All Write about It?" succinctly sums up William Grimes's feeling that memoir writing is out of control, that every Tom, Dick, Harry, and Jane is spilling his or her guts. Why add to this overabundance of "navel-gazing"?[2] More specifically, why tell others about how you've been dumped? Why expose yourself to the world as someone unwanted? Why write about how miserable and vulnerable you felt—and the desperate places you have inhabited? Why allow yourself to re-experience some of the worst moments of your life? Why let your children in on all the sordid details? And if you did the dumping, why write about how you left someone in the lurch after many years of a committed relationship? Why show yourself to be a cad?

Several of the writers in this book—the majority of whom write from the dumped position—do question why they have embarked on such an enterprise, uncomfortable with their whining tone, uncomfortable portraying themselves as victims. Raymond ruminates: "If I were a stranger reading this, would I despise this pathetic, self-pitying writer? Would I snap, 'Enough. The world is going to rack and ruin and you're moaning over a relationship.' Would I remind the writer of world chaos, bombed-out Iraqi villages? . . . Yes, I know. I'm not proud of these feelings." Octavia Nevins's journal, " 'Chapter Four You Break Up,' " records her daily emotional temperature in great detail; at some point she hopes she will be able to "stop this total inward looking as it is exhausting, and especially since so much real violence and real suffering are out there to pay attention to." Telling one's story again and again in one's head or in one's journal or to a close friend is a very different thing from writing it for publication. Yet despite hesitations and doubts, the women in this collection have shared their stories of being cut loose.

Grimes suggests that our "storytelling urge may even be hard-wired," that creating self narratives is natural; in other words, that it "may be as fundamental as breathing."[3] Writing narratives about loss of love is a peculiarly gendered form of expression; girls and women do it more than boys and men. Helen Fisher ("Lost Love: The Nature of Romantic Rejection" in this collection) says that men are less likely to reveal their pain, whereas "rejected women sob, lose weight or eat too much, sleep too much or not at all, lose interest in sex, become unable to concentrate, have trouble remembering commonplace daily things, withdraw socially and contemplate suicide. *Some write out their grievances* [my italics]. And most women talk for hours on the phone with any sympathetic ear, retelling all. . . . As she dwells on the dead relationship, she can inadvertently retraumatize herself."[4]

And if telling or writing personal narratives is an act of being human, and particularly female, reading personal narratives is an extension of that impulse. Romance novelist Mary Bly explains why so many people enjoy romance novels or even bodice rippers (and I would add memoirs): "We are all interested in talking and reading about that difficult process of living with another person. . . . Many of my own books, in fact, have been about failing marriages: they are footnotes to that particular conversation."[5] Many of us consume adultery stories with relish, says Louise DeSalvo: "Adultery stories have a life of their own. They are passed from person to person. They are traded like precious baseball cards. People [or at least many women] would rather hear an adultery story than hear about the stock market, wars, drought, pestilence, plague, the destruction of the ecosystem."[6]

While writing about being cut loose may "retraumatize" a woman (and a number of women decided not to write for this volume because of that), there are many reasons not only to write one's story but also to publish it.[7] To get perspective on that story and therefore to get control of it is a major reason. In Nora Ephron's autobiographical novel *Heartburn*, Rachel first resists writing about what is happening—her husband is leaving her for another woman while she is her seventh month of pregnancy—because "to write it down was to give it permanence, to admit that something real had happened." But when she realizes that their separation is not going to be reversed, she decides to write a novel about it: "Because if I tell the story, I control the version. Because if I tell the story, I can make you laugh, and I would rather have you laugh at me than feel sorry for me. Because if I tell the story, it doesn't hurt as much. Because if I tell the story, I can get on with it."[8] Telling the story is a way to move forward, to move past the trauma. Jane Taylor McDonnell suggests in *Living to Tell the Tale* that "the very act of writing is part of recovery. In the telling, the writer becomes a survivor . . . These narratives . . . seek to constitute the lost self and reconceive the traumatizing experience as a survivor's story."[9] That is what Louise Weinberg's break-up art does for her: it keeps her alive. Writing for *Cut Loose*, she says: "Art making was a way into the raw emotion—a factory, some kind of mechanism to process human passions, not unlike a sewage treatment plant. Take the bad stuff; convert to innocuous mulch to make plants and trees grow better. . . . Each mark—I exist, I am, I am still here."

Weinberg also suggests that telling the story or making art is a way to release anger: "Shout, rant, drive the storm away with language, signs, and symbols." Certainly Susan Becker's "Unsent E-mails to an Ex" are gleeful expressions of anger; she rather revels in her "kinda bitchy tone." Feeling powerless and abused, Becker took to the computer: "Nasty, sarcastic accusations fell from my fingers . . . and I enjoyed every minute of it. . . . These after-the-fact e-mails allowed me to comment on the various facets of our relationship and to express my resentment and anger in a breezy, humorous way that helped me to transcend my saga." While writing unsent e-mails helps Becker defuse her pent-up anger, it also allows her to examine her thirty-year relationship: "Writing has enabled me to redefine our history together, . . . to deconstruct our relationship in an entirely new light. It has been transformational."

Many of the women in this book felt alone when they were cut loose—and older women who have been dumped feel particularly alone in as much as the bulk of our lives is largely invisible, or if visible is stereotyped. In the 1970s, women turned what they did in private (talking to each other) into something political (consciousness raising): by telling stories, what is private becomes understood in a social context. Many of the women in *Cut Loose* write to help others—explaining everything from the trough of despair to the steps to recovery, how they survived and, yes, how they even prospered. We reveal ourselves so we can be of use: Becker hopes her "divorce narrative is as therapeutic for others as it has been for me." Nevins asks herself if she should publish her journal: "Who will read this? Betrayed women? Older women? Men and women who struggle to remain in a relationship, a long-term relationship? People who are monogamous and/or nonmonogamous? There are personal questions and ethical questions I need to think about before and if I submit this for publication. And there are dreams of big money and fame. After all, all this suffering ought to be worth something. I have lost weight—and that is not nothing. Loss of weight and gain of money, not bad!" Nevins wants to be of use to others, but, in addition, she would not mind some payback for all the heartache. And publishing her journal is a form of revenge.

While a lot has been written about breakups, little has been written about women who are ditched or cut loose in their later years. This book is a mature version of *The Adventures of Breakup Girl*, a comic for younger women; call us "Break-up Women" or "Cut-Loose Women."[10] It is not that there are no books for women of a certain age; there are memoirs and self-help books such as *Dumped! A Survival Guide for the Woman Who's Been Left by the Man She Loved*. Based on interviews with more than one hundred women between the ages of twenty-four and fifty-four who were "unceremoniously left by the men with whom they expected to walk off into the sunset," *Dumped!* at least does not completely ignore older women.[11] *Cut Loose* extends the age range of the conversation: the majority of the women herein are over sixty.

This is a book about (mostly) long-term relationships that have come asunder; while some lasted eight to ten years, most had lasted over twenty years before the split. Each woman tells her own story. In journals, essays, poetry, stories, and art, the personal narratives of "leaking affections" and murdered plans are laid out: from Susan O'Sullivan who declares "no romance for me" to Phyllis Berman who says "I cannot return to what I have left" to Anne Simcock who asserts that "marriage comes and goes but sex is forever" to Margie Kaplan who after much pain has found "my own dance."

Cut Loose is divided into two major sections: "He/She Left Her/Him" and "Perspectives on Being Left and Leaving." All the pieces in the first section are personal narratives. Whereas Raymond and O'Sullivan write about being left by women, the other selections are about heterosexual dumping. The selection by Janice Stieber Rous is the only one in which the writer declares (in words that echo those that the male leavers use to explain their departures) that she must leave: to save herself, because she "was suffocating" and "trapped by the institution of marriage," because the marriage of thirty years has been robbing her of her "freedom, sexuality, and creativity." Zohra Saed's mother left her father for a younger man; if we could hear her mother's words they would probably be similar to Stieber Rous's. Mary Stuart describes how she has both been left and done the leaving: "I was dumped, I moved on to dumping, and at the end was dumped again. And then, in a very small way, I dumped my original dumper." But most of the women in this book find themselves in the abandoned position, even if, like Kaplan or Becker, they had to give the men a nudge to finally leave.

In the second section the contributors look at being left and leaving from a psychological, psychoanalytic, sociological, economic, sexual, medical, anthropological, or literary perspective, or they write as a representative of a specific class of women: Nancy Berke writes as a single woman and Merle Froschl writes as a widow. The distinction between the two sections, however, is not rigid; some of the pieces in each intermix the personal and the analytic. For example, in "Perspectives on Being Left and Leaving," Simcock uses her medical expertise to generalize about breakups in older-age relationships at the same time as she describes her own breakup. And Raymond's piece in "He/She Left Her/Him," while entirely personal, calls upon a feminist and psychoanalytic lens to explain why and how women and men throw each other over and why she and her female partner in particular acted as they did.

Cut Loose tells only one side of the story. Reading the selections, one wonders how the other partner (usually the male) might explain what appears to be such a seemingly immature act, an act that often comes after professions of love or after a joint household endeavor (such as moving to a new apartment) that might be expected to signify that the relationship has a future. Stieber Rous gives us a sense of that other side, of the feelings of the person who walks out. She is not without pain as she chooses to give up her history, wreck her family, and perhaps face a life alone. She feels a double pain: for what she has done to her partner and her children and for what she has suppressed in herself by staying in the relationship for so long. In some of the fiction I examine in "Splitsville: Break-up Literature," to alleviate the lopsidedness of a single account, more than one point of view is offered: in *Late Divorce*, for example, the husband, wife, and grown children each have a voice. In *Intimacy*, the narrator is not the abandoned woman but the man who is about to leave. Some of the writers in the present collection try to imagine how the partner would tell the story; for example, Raymond is concerned about not presenting a "balanced picture," that "I must be painting too positive a picture of my own behavior and too negative a picture of hers." Nevins includes some of her husband's e-mails. Saed presents the child's point of view. Nonetheless, in *Cut Loose* it is the adult woman's story of being left and leaving that is central.

Finally, I want to note that throughout this introduction I talk in sweeping generalities about men and women. I am aware that such broad categories need to be refined by class, race/ethnicity, sexual orientation, and other categories; nonetheless, for the purposes of this introduction I shall use a wide and general lens—the assumed categories are most often white, middle-class, heterosexual, and married.

An Epidemic?

Is there an epidemic of older men exiting their marriages with older women? Writing in 1998, Sally Warren certainly believes there is "a dumping epidemic" of men leaving women. She attributes this phenomenon to the shift in cultural acceptance: men used to have undercover affairs; now given that there is "no public embarrassment or ostracism attached to walking out on your wife, today's married dumper divorces number one and moves onto number two (or three) with relative ease."[12] But do the numbers warrant using the term *epidemic*?

One problem with the numbers is that in 1996, the National Center for Health Statistics stopped analyzing divorce statistics (in terms of age, income, education, and race). Nevertheless, from a variety of surveys and articles, some broad trends are evident. According to a 2001 Census Bureau report, there has been a slight decline in divorce rates as compared to the sharply rising rates of the 1970s. The highest rate of divorce in the survey was for older people: 41 percent for men who were between the ages of fifty and fifty-nine and 39 percent for women in the same age group.[13] And the statistics do tell us that "gray divorce" (ages fifty-five-plus to eighty-plus), as it is called by Alex Kuczynski, has increased; those sixty-five and older who divorced increased from 7 percent in 1999 to 10 percent in 2001.[14]

It is clear that more and more older women will enter their later years divorced: "At age 67, the proportion of the 1931–35 female birth cohort that is divorced is 12 percent. But for the birth cohort born just 20 years later in 1951–55, it is projected that 20 percent will be divorced at age 67. Moreover, many of the older women whose current status is not divorced will have experienced divorce at some point in their lives. In sum, the cohorts entering old age . . . in the coming years will have experienced a much different marital history than previous cohorts."[15] Nearly half of women over age sixty are "deserted by death and divorce," writes Froschl; "widows make up 38.6 percent of women over age sixty; divorced women make up 8.6 percent, and women who are separated, 1.2 percent." And from a financial viewpoint, to be divorced in later life is far worse than being widowed. "Among women 65 and older, widows have almost 50 percent higher average wealth holdings than divorcees" (see Nancy Dailey's "Divorce Is Economic Suicide"). The statistics in the article "Splitsville: A Special Report on Divorce" in *More,* a magazine aimed at women over forty, confirm that more older women are getting divorced and staying divorced. From 1970 to 1990, the divorce rate for women between the ages of forty and fifty increased 62 percent, and, according to the National Center for Health Statistics, the rate of remarriage has fallen over time: in the 1950s, women who divorced had a 65 percent chance of remarrying; in the 1980s, it dropped to 50 percent.[16] The probability of remarriage decreases according to age, says Dailey: "The younger you are at the time of divorce, the greater the probability of remarriage, most likely within three years. However, the inverse is also true . . . the older you are at the time of divorce, the less likely remarriage will occur. The probability of marriage or remarriage is less than 20 percent for women aged 50+."

Who Slams the Door?

Contrary to the notion that older men are exiting their marriages in huge numbers, it appears that more and more older women are leaving their marriages. Women are able to choose not to marry or to leave marriages they are dissatisfied with because of social changes fueled by feminism, the most important of which is that more women are in the work force (especially in the professions) and are able to support themselves. Articles like "The 37-Year Itch," "It's Cold on Mars," "Splitsville: A Special Report on Divorce," "Midlife Crisis? Bring It On!" and "Divorcing Mr. Nice Guy" indicate that in their twenties and thirties men seek divorce; in their fifties, women seem to be seeking it. The AARP article "A House Divided" (based on a larger 2004 study, *The Divorce Experience: A Study of Divorce at Midlife and Beyond,* of 1,147 men and women ages forty to seventy-nine) concludes that the majority of midlife divorces are initiated by women, that more women do the walking, and that the men are caught unawares: 66 percent of the women as compared to 41 percent of the men surveyed asked for divorce; 26 percent of the men reported that they were blindsided as compared with 14 percent of the women; 33 percent of these women over fifty said they did not act impulsively but had contemplated leaving for at least two years (21 percent of the men said the same); and one out of ten women ruminated for more than ten years before she bolted. The survey noted that women over sixty decided faster than boomers did. Of the 1,807 women who answered the *More* readership poll as reported in "Divorcing Mr. Nice Guy," 85 percent said they initiated the divorce. "Nearly 40 percent of wives who initiated a divorce when they were in their forties said they did so because they'd fallen out of love, they felt emotionally unfulfilled, or they felt like something was missing from their life. Among those who left between the ages of 55 and 60, more than 57 percent cited 'emotional unfulfillment' as the catalyst." According to the AARP study, the top three reasons women leave are physical or emotional abuse, infidelity, and drug or alcohol abuse—whereas men say that they "fell out of love" or had "different values or lifestyles."[17]

The practitioners Marilyn Katz interviewed for *Cut Loose* noted general differences in why men and women leave and under what conditions. One social worker said she had "never known a man to leave unless there was someone else in his life." In contrast older women seem to leave "because they have moved forward professionally and the marriage no longer satisfies them, or, if they are more traditional, once the children have grown, they would rather be alone than with someone they have come to despise." Explaining the contrast, a psychologist told Katz that "it is, after all, difficult for a woman to find another man. It is easier for men to leave; women have to be desperately unhappy." In *Marriage in Men's Lives*, Steven Nock states that "just being married appears to be more beneficial to men than to women, whereas the *quality* of the actual marriage appears more important to wives than to husbands. . . . Marriage is typically an asset for men, regardless of the quality of the marital union."[18] Amid all these different takes on gray divorce, two things appear to be true: men benefit from marriage regardless of the quality of the marriage and men have a wide range of choices for remarrying.

While it is interesting that divorce among men and women ages forty through seventy-nine is usually initiated by the wife, the numbers do not tell the whole story. It is almost impossible to unravel who actually leaves whom, when, and why. When does the leaving start? With the slamming of the door or way before that? With the announcement that there is another person in the picture or when the so-called aggrieved partner says she can't do it anymore, as in Marita Lopez-Mena's case? "When his lying, cheating self was finally confronted with the evidence of betrayal, I had an atomic meltdown and pitched him into the morning light to confront his very own dawn. I remember him saying, 'How like you to respond with anger.' . . . I felt fully entitled to being good and damn angry and went with that." For Lopez-Mena and Nevins there were many exits and returns as the relationship broke up and then broke up again. The seemingly abrupt act of leaving has an extensive prehistory: "Being dumped connotes being sacrificed to an unconscious drama, the last stage of a long and often unrecognized process of small withdrawals, emotional leakages, cuts into the fabric of a relationship bleeding to psychic death" (see Catherine Silver's "Leaking Affections").

So what does it mean to initiate a divorce? For example, Octavia Nevins was the one to consult a lawyer, but she was not the one to have the affair or to move out. So many of the women I have spoken to, and I myself, initiated the divorce proceedings, after their husbands left or after they said they were seeing another woman. Berman's husband, for instance, was having an affair, but he still wanted to remain in the marriage; however, when she returned from work abroad, she realized that she did not want the marriage any longer (see "Observing the Cormorant"). While the AARP study does try to get at the differences in motivation between men and women leading up to the divorce decision and does try to measure men's and women's seemingly different short-term and long-term reactions to the breakup, the numbers do not give us much nuance and texture. And what they surely never tell us about is the breakups of same-sex relationships and heterosexual unmarried relationships.

Most of the women in this collection differ in some notable ways from the 1,147 men and women in the AARP survey and perhaps from those in the *More* study as well. The women in *Cut Loose*, located mostly on the East Coast, are highly educated, most have always worked outside the home and at professional jobs, most are in the middle or upper-middle class. While calling themselves nonpracticing, many of these writers were born into Judaism, others list their religion of origin as Quaker, Assyrian Orthodox, Catholic, Protestant, and Congregational. In terms of ethnic heritage, the writers are of Irish, Dutch, Italian, English, Spanish, Czech, Middle Eastern, Mexican, and Turkish-Viennese background, among others. The similarity between these women and the AARP respondents is that most live in a metropolitan area. Some of the men and women in the AARP study list themselves as nonreligious, but in contrast about half are Protestants, Catholics and Baptists, and only 13 percent have college degrees. Seventy-three percent of those in the study were divorced in their forties; this book is looking at women who have been divorced at a much older age. And the women of *Cut Loose* have elected to write their stories, the biggest difference between them and the survey participants. So while I make generalizations here about men and women that may contradict the statistics, these generalizations arise from my own experience and from the specific stories in the collection. Even if the women writing for *Cut Loose* appear to represent a different cohort both in terms of demographics and experience (they were left, mainly, rather than having done the leaving) than the majority in the AARP survey, what they describe about the process of a relationship coming asunder and the after-effects would ring true to a broad base of women.

Cut Loose: The Stages of Suffering

The first two pieces in "He/She Left Her/Him" (Laurie Silver's and Nevins's) are the most immediate and raw: they describe the first moments of being left. In "What Was Home," a fictional story based on her own life, Silver's character tries to commit suicide after learning (through her own sleuthing) that her husband is seeing another woman and wants to move out. What comes across so vividly in many of these accounts is the shock over the abruptness of the partner's exit and the hurt involved in being left and losing a long-term relationship. Harriet Luria uses language that implies the destruction of the self: "I felt pretty much isolated, disconnected in so many areas of my life. When he left for good, it was for another woman. I was devastated. Broken. Shattered. . . . [N]o one really understood the depths of my devastation."

The description of the pain seems universal—even if the particulars are different. Luria, Caucasian, and her husband, an African American, were each other's mainstay as their marriage was disapproved of by both her family and the larger society; so for Luria losing the marriage felt like losing everything. Lopez-Mena says that she never slept and describes an obsessiveness known to many of the abandoned: "For eighteen months I lay in my bed, alternately crying or folding myself into or out of the fetal position. When the crying and sleeplessness just would not cease, I took myself off to a psychiatrist for an antidepressant and some counseling. The pill that all of America has discovered helped control the fits of weeping and allowed me to work. It also kept me from spending all my time when there in the bathroom sobbing or e-mailing friends with news of the latest revelation or outrage—'He was seen in the Grand Union standing by the eggplants, and he was holding hands with this scrawny waif. She had purple hair and an eyebrow ring.'" Becker, "anorexic and dysfunctional, and unable to carry out the most mundane tasks," likens her suffering to "some sort of post-traumatic stress syndrome." Older women who appear to have a heart attack often actually have a condition called stress cardiomyopathy, which is prompted by emotional or physical stress—the informal name of the condition is "broken-heart syndrome" since it is so often associated with being dumped.[19]

Being cut loose from a long-term relationship often means not knowing who you are and having to rebuild: the self, the home, the rhythms of life. Dismantling the family home, sifting through "all the discarded pieces / of the daily game we played / for twenty years" as Carol Burdick describes in the poem "Trashed," submerges us in loss and longing, as well as causing us to doubt the reality of that past.[20] Cora, interviewed by Naomi Woronov for *Cut Loose*, said that when her thirty-four year marriage broke up, she no longer knew who she was: "I was swamped with feelings of shame and failure, and I felt divorce would be the final failure. I never told my mother he had left because I was so ashamed. I had terrible nightmares. It wasn't fear of being alone as he used to go off for weeks at a time, but who was I except Jack's wife and the girls' mother? I had no other identity." And this sense of loss of identity can be true for women who have strong professional identities as well as for women who do not.

The stages of suffering after being left are mapped by the writers in this collection in various but similar ways. These stages, Froschl notes, are similar to the Elisabeth Kübler-Ross stages of mourning when a loved one dies, which "include denial and isolation, anger, bargaining, depression, and acceptance." O'Sullivan walks us through the stages that the "dumpee" will likely experience: "The first stage: shock, tears, and incomprehension. Much shit may be shoveled during this time and accusations may be vicious and hurtful. It's an interval which demands a great deal of patience from both the dumper and the dumpee, even while accusations fly, fury flays, or sullenness reigns." By the second stage, "most revengeful impulses have evaporated and the pull of maudlin pop songs and bad poetry is over." However, there is always the chance of "emotional recidivism." Kaplan, married to a man ten years younger than she, describes her three-year-plus recovery from her loss of self-esteem after the dissolution of their ten-year-plus relationship. In year one, she was numb. "I was nose to the grindstone with all I had to do—numb, not sad, not angry, just pushing forward. I don't remember thinking about romance, sex, partnering, et cetera. This meant I was alien even to myself." Year two was "the year of sad." And year three, approaching fifty, she began, with the help of therapy, to come out of her "morass." For Eva, interviewed by Woronov, it was a four-year recovery period after an eighteen-year marriage: "I think I've done really well at recovering. In *Crazy Time* [Abigail Trafford] says you're totally insane and do things you thought you'd never do, that it takes years. It does, so two years later I can see two more years of this. I still have all this anger; I would like to forgive him and let it go, but rage is still very much there."

While all the women describe searing pain and crippling depression, some, like Eva, are in touch with their rage. Rage comes out in language and sometimes in acts of fury as in the story "Access to the Children," mentioned in my review of break-up literature. To the wife, her husband is no less than a "murderer," having left her and the children for another woman. When he asks to

reconcile, "enraged, Elizabeth says no. 'He'd destroyed her as a wife, he'd insulted her, he left her to bleed.'" Saed calls her mother a "whore" because she
ran off to be with a younger man; her marriage to Zohra's father had been
arranged twenty-seven years prior in Afghanistan. Saed acts out both her own
rage and her father's over her mother's desertion: "The next day, I bring out
the family albums and rip apart every single picture of my mother. My father
finds me in the living room like this. He watches me as I take them out and rip
them up. He sits next to me, pulls out another album, and does the same. In
this way, we exorcize the house of her images. It helps express my father's
grief. For a moment, we are busy and the act of tearing makes things more
bearable."

Rage, says Lopez-Mena, "is a natural outcome of humiliation, betrayal, and
hurt. Unlike anger, it cannot be 'managed.' . . . I fantasized many atrocities . . .
with my favorite being the pure joy of running over his body repeatedly while
the corpse flopped around on the road. He was so dead he couldn't even . . .
beg for mercy."[21] Caught between almost equally frustrating tasks—accepting
her husband's declaration that he loves a much younger woman and trying to
admit some of her own faults in order to repair their marriage—Nevins writes
that her "intentions to be a loving companion keep going awry as my anger explodes out, eating us alive." And O'Sullivan composes fictional scenarios in
which revenge is "a creative act, one that had the power to cleanse the soul
and provide a kind of catharsis." A number of the women in this volume describe stalking their partner (such as Della in Woronov's interviews and Stuart).

While sometimes the anger has negative effects, often leading to drawn-out
and messy divorces, some of the therapists and counselors Katz interviewed
see being angry as productive, as opposed to stagnating in feelings of depression and shame. Anger can also turn antic and celebratory. Stuart threw a party
where no one except she and her "soon-to-be-ex" knew that it was a farewell
party. At the elaborate dinner party Rachel hosts in the novel *Heartburn*, the
husband is unaware that it is a good-bye party until dessert, when she throws
her homemade key lime pie in his face. In *Breakup: The End of a Love Story*,
Catherine Texier throws herself a "big blowout party" to "kickoff" her new
life, "to assert to the world that I wasn't a dejected/rejected ex-wife, but a free
single woman."[22] For jilted and betrayed lovers, a florist shop in Australia will
send a revenge pack (called "Drop Dead Flowers"), including everything from
a single dead rose to thirteen dead roses and a box of melted chocolates pack-
aged in black paper. They claim their customers, mainly divorcées, "find it
therapeutic to send a revenge pack because it means they can get on with their
lives and not think about their betrayer any more."[23] Indeed Fisher believes, as

she writes here, that abandonment rage has evolved for several purposes—an important one being "to drive disappointed lovers to *extricate* themselves" from a dead relationship.

Fisher has investigated the brain circuitry associated with romantic love and romantic rejection using functional magnetic resonance imaging (fMRI). Because early-stage intense romantic passion activates the ventral tegmental area (VTA) and caudate nucleus, rather than emotion centers of the brain, she has come to believe that romantic love is a fundamental drive: "And like all drives, romantic love is associated with elevated activity of dopamine in the brain." Fisher says that the psychological literature on rejection and some preliminary findings from her study suggest that soaring activity of dopamine and norepinephrine is also associated with the agony of lost love. "We humans are intricately wired to suffer when we have been spurned," she writes, and so the reactions exhibited by the rejected lover—frustration-attraction, separation anxiety, abandonment rage, melancholy, sadness, and depression—have a basis in biology.[24]

While there is no definitive study that measures and charts men's and women's pain and recovery after a breakup, the *More* report says that men and women seem to have different immediate reactions to a breakup. The AARP study, which weighs difficult midlife events against each other, concludes that "more women than men recall that their divorce was more emotionally difficult to handle than the death of a spouse or a major illness."[25] In contrast, after a long, unhappy first marriage, Festa describes how she felt liberated by divorce; whereas, upon the death of her second husband, she found it very hard to let go: "how to erase / his name at the entrance" ("The Chore"). Judith Wallerstein's work on divorce indicates that women, unlike men, look back on divorce "as a wrenching—even tragic—event." Sociologist Norval Glenn says that is understandable "since the older the woman is, the more likely she is to remain alone—and have plenty of time to feel those regrets."[26] Although 75 percent regret the decision initially, "by the second year, it's women—not men—who find they've evolved in the ways they wouldn't have without the divorce."[27] Fisher says that men (referring to men of all ages) are three to four times more likely than women to commit suicide after a love affair has decayed.

However, as *Cut Loose* emphasizes, how women and men react to the split and then view it over subsequent years depends on who initiated the split, for what reasons, and the economic situation and age of each of the partners. Being an older woman on one's own, after being in a couple for most of one's adulthood "ain't for sissies" asserts Stuart. "Dating? Help me. The entire singles' scene seems to be geared toward the younger set. . . . Maybe I'm pickier than I was at sixteen, maybe I'm more jaded, or maybe I'm not as desirable to the opposite sex as I once was." In the 1980s, the "fact" that a single woman over forty had a better chance of being killed by a terrorist than finding a husband was quoted in my circles with great consternation. Stephanie Coontz, in *Marriage, a History*, says this claim was wrong then and is wrong today; nonetheless, the odds are not in your favor if you are looking for a partner in midlife and later.[28]

Love, Sex, and Age

The reactions described above—the pain, the depression, the despair, the anger, the acts of revenge—are familiar to anyone whose love relationship has dissolved, especially unexpectedly and especially if it has been a relationship of some duration. A person's age and the length of the relationship add a heft to the loss that should not be overlooked.

This book is not a brief for preserving marriage; it is not meant to accuse all who leave long-term relationships or have affairs of being sinners.[29] Festa's poem "Unholy Matrimony" describes a twenty-two-year marriage that needed to end: "Look at the chain of / mountains around, the brittle / ice in our lives, impermeable / to sun and warmth." She asked to be cut loose from a relationship which she describes as a battlefield "where betrayal and emotional violence were daily occurrences." For Cora (interviewed by Woronov), whose husband left her after thirty-four years of marriage, "divorce wasn't in my vocabulary." It wasn't until sixteen years later, when her husband died, that she felt freed. Looking back at those sixteen "wasted" years, when "he continued to pull the strings," she wished she had taken the initiative to cut herself loose earlier.

What I believe often gets in the way of an honest evaluation of the marriage and of the breakup is the presence of the other person, the lover—usually another woman (and the two women described in this book who left women also had other women). What the man usually says is that even if he is having an affair, it is not about "her," and in many ways it is not; it is about what the marriage was and was not, did and did not provide, and could no longer be, and it is, of course, about him. Nevertheless, the fact of the other woman is devastating. The word *betrayal* is used over and over again in these selections. This betrayal is not primarily sexual, although that is what is often emphasized and what eats at the imagination; rather it is a betrayal of trust, of the couple's intimacy. It is about an emotional and affectional life that has been hidden and excludes the longtime partner.[30] It is about the loss of a planned future together and especially the hope that someone with whom you have been intimate will see you through old age — the decay of the body and the final stages to death. And finally it is about the somewhat unbelievable notion that the person leaving would rather give up a companionship constructed over years for a romantic attraction that always seems to be of the moment only.

The revelation that there is another woman is earthshaking; one becomes obsessed. Kaplan was bowled over upon learning of the other woman's existence from a friend's casual inquiry about whether her husband was "'still so smitten with that young, blond ingenue?'" Kaplan is not sure if she was upset because she now knew he left her for another woman or if she could not bear that she had been in the dark. Julie, in Laurie Silver's story, "imagined Tim with Lucy. She pictured her beautiful, smart, able to talk with Tim about neonates and spinal taps. Things that interested him. She imagined them in bed. And as if in a fistfight, Julie's arms and legs ached and failed, and the front of her fell over itself; her hands strong-armed her head as she rocked. Julie held the couch, soaking the cushions, trying to sink through them, to the other side of what it was." If it is a younger woman, as it is most often, the older woman cannot help but make a physical comparison, as Lopez-Mena does: "Young girl. Sob. She sails. Plays basketball. Sob. Skinny, she is. Sobbbbb. Hiccupping. Vomiting, dry heaves — sounds just like withdrawal, which it is."

Do men have a different sexuality, a different biology, a different psychology, different relational needs at fifty and sixty than women at those same ages? In Page Dougherty Delano's poem "If Not," the man claims biology as the cause: "If he hadn't wanted another woman so crudely / he'd not have screwed the woman next door, / some stupid satisfaction, a way not to stay / in my world — yet, as if it wasn't his fault, / yoked, he said, by biology." Medical doctor Simcock, writing in this book, and anthropologist Fisher, in her other writings, do not dispute the biological explanation, or at least they reason by analogy to animals, as Laura Zigman does in her novel *Animal Husbandry* (see my essay "Splitsville"). Zigman's main character, who has been dumped, comes up with the Old-Cow–New-Cow theory, about "the narcissistic behavior of the male species," in which the male moves from one mate to a new one over and over again, as each "New Cow" becomes, after a time, an "Old Cow." [31]

In "Marriage Comes and Goes but Sex Is Forever," Simcock suggests something similar to the Old-Cow–New-Cow theory, but does not limit it to the male species. "We are not a monogamous species. . . . We come from a primate line in which our nearest relatives are the chimpanzee and the bonobo (pygmy chimp). We share 98 percent of our DNA with them and both are promiscuous. . . . The social system we have evolved with the ideal of lifelong monogamy is rare in nature and probably unworkable because our strong inherited behavior patterns lead us toward more opportunistic mating, for both sexes."[32] Another animal, the vole, a rodent, can illuminate the genetic basis of sexual behavior: male prairie voles are monogamous whereas male meadow voles are not. To turn a meadow vole into a prairie vole, scientists have injected a gene from the "faithful" vole into the unfaithful. By analogy, Walter Kirn, in an article in the *New York Times Magazine*, "Curing Casanova," quizzically speculates about our own species: "By modifying the brain through simple genetic therapy—or, better, a pill—could Casanova-ism be cured, the incidence of male adultery reduced and thousands of troubled marriages repaired?"[33] But the biological explanation does not account for the increase in female adultery that Michele Weiner-Davis, who founded the Divorce Busting Center, has identified. Twenty years ago women committed just 10 percent of the infidelity; now, she believes, it is closer to 50 percent.[34] So maybe it is not about gender and biology after all, but more about culture, ideology—like feminism—and economics (for example, women who go to work have more opportunity).

As we age our sexuality changes. The alterations over time in sexual response and in the libido are not losses but adjustments, Simcock says. The changes beginning in one's fifties occur at a time when other changes—physical, social, occupational—are also occurring. Needless to say this concurrence of changes can produce anxiety in both sexes, but it is men's reactions that are most relevant here: "Men's reaction to all this varies. Some say, 'OK, my sex life is over.' Some accept what is happening and operate with what is available: 'So mostly it works and sometimes it doesn't but that's OK.' A few, quite a few, blame the resident woman: 'If you were younger, firmer, juicier, more passionate, more creative, more enthusiastic, indeed, not you, it would work.'" Viagra or a similar drug can help men with their sexual problems within their marriage; ironically enough, they can also assist in the aging man's search to affirm himself with an outside woman.

In addition, while there is the cultural assumption that men are sexual beings through the life course, no such assumption is made for women. Thus Berke's plaintive question: "What otherwise healthy, happy, and still horny middle-aged woman wouldn't feel discouraged by the cultural discourse on aging?" While the media claims that more older people are now shown in ads—after all they represent a huge market—these images are usually of sporty, youngish-looking, happily married couples (often in fields or on bicycles). Done as a broad comedy, the film *The First Wives Club* (1996) is good at depicting the older woman's sense that she is no longer attractive to men and cannot compete with younger, smoother-skinned, thinner women: Elsie, trying to hold on to her youth and sexiness after her husband has left her, has collagen pumped into her lips. Whereas the cult of the young and the beautiful affects both men and women, we are probably affected differently. A number of women I know have abashedly confided in me that they have contemplated face-lifts or the tightening of their arm flesh as they are quite self-conscious about their aging bodies.[35] While men deal with aging in numerous ways, some men do not transform themselves as much as they look for a younger partner to do that. In the film *Something's Gotta Give* (2003), after a lifetime of dating younger women, the older man, in a reversal of the norm, does choose the older woman, the mother of the young woman he had been dating.

Marriages age as well. They go through transitions which, as Katz notes, "often culminate at midlife with the departure of children or disappointment in them, the acceleration of untreated alcoholism, or the sudden loss of financial security." Catherine Silver describes the disappointments of "unfulfilled needs and unexpressed fears about not being loved, taken care of, or simply recognized enough. In the end these feelings turn into accusations, transforming the perception of the spouse/partner into a castrating and dangerous (M)Other." Often one partner is oblivious until the dissatisfied partner calls it quits. While one partner appears to be the actor and the other the victim, both of them, and their separate and joint histories, are being acted out: "Dumping," says Silver, "is the hidden psychic work of two people who have been in love, raised children, taken care of each other, and finally are confronted with a feeling of 'overproximity.' "

While the changes that Catherine Silver describes are gender neutral, she, Simcock, and Katz see specific gender-related reactions to aging that play themselves out with the dissolution of many long-term relationships. For instance, as Katz says, "many men feel threatened by evidence of their wives aging and harbor a fantasy that they will be able to attract someone else." The man "is scared to death of dying and keeps himself very fit. He thinks, if I don't do it now, it will be too late." Whereas men sometimes seem to become less self-assured, mellower, and more dependent as they age, Silver says that often "women develop greater independence and assertiveness," in what Margaret Mead has called "postmenopausal zest," and men "often perceive this change as a loss of increasingly needed attention and care." In addition, often it is the woman in the marriage who devotes herself not only to the children but to the aging parents (see both Lopez-Mena and Laurie Silver); the man may experience her focus on other people as a further loss. Some men then deal with the many changes in their marriages by cutting loose, dumping the losses into the older women's laps.

Looking Forward

It is hard to move on, hard to let go of the victim position, hard not to live in the past (especially if, as Fisher suggests, dopamine addicts you, as it were, to the past, to that lost romantic love), especially if you still have contact with your ex, as Mary Stuart describes it: "Although by that time I had moved away geographically, I realized that our every communication raised the specter of the marriage, a ghost that clung to me like the clutching vegetation of a swamp-thing seeking to drown unwary trespassers."

With the passage of time, however, the overwhelming sense of loss diminishes and instead the shortcomings of the relationship often come into focus as well as the positive aspects of being on one's own. Becker, in her biting irony, thanks Harry for cutting her loose, saying it "was the kindest thing he has ever done. . . . As our therapist has pointed out to me repeatedly, it is hard for a divorce to be better than the marriage. And frankly, Harry, our marriage sucked. . . . It appears that your betrayal and abandonment precipitated an emotional crisis which has expanded my spiritual horizons. So first of all, Harry, let me thank you. I couldn't have done it without you, and I like the person I have become very much." The present and the future need to be grappled with; the past needs to relinquished or at least placed in perspective. Dougherty Delano (in a personal communication) says that in her poetry she has tried working "to name the *present* I was experiencing, which seemed unfamiliar yet, somehow, thrilling."

Dougherty Delano has a friendship or a sexual relationship with her ex-husband as described in "I Give My Husband Fish Sausage." Octavia Nevins, it appears, has reconciled with her husband, but moving beyond the infidelity (if one wants to repair the relationship) is not easy. Using the language of the criminal justice system, Stuart says that both parties have different tasks: "In the case of the offender, getting over guilt was the hardest. With the offendee, anger and resentment were the barriers to successful re-engagement." Another tack is to do as Simcock has done: embrace nonmonogamy. Most of the women writing in this collection do not go back to former partners; some find other partners; all go forward.

For women who have had a long-term partner, to imagine the story of oneself without a partner is not easy. Berke, having always been single, knows the psychic energy it takes to embrace one's solo status against a society that sanctions only one version of the story:

> Friendships, community ties, and whatever other contributions a woman makes are subordinate to the story she might tell about her hot, new romance

(or the rekindling of a marriage about to go south). Talk of her career, artistic pursuits, and hobbies can never sustain a conversation the way her love life does. To put it another way, romantic attachments, especially with men, are considered the only kind of legitimate romance. The midlife single woman could have a romance with her work, with nature, with music, with her studies, but such romance is never given the same respect.

O'Sullivan wonders if she has had a somewhat easier time of it post breakup as lesbian culture is not couple obsessed: "It's true perhaps, that lesbians are less likely to think of those who are single with pity or as left on the shelf. Perhaps lesbian culture judges you less on whether you've got a partner and more on who you are?"

For most women, friendship has always been important; for many of the women in this book, friends saw them through the really dark days, so, like Berke, they truly value them. Many single women have "friendships that are far more intimate and enduring than the marriages of our parents, or a great number of the couples that surround us daily." The *New York Times* article "Older Women Team Up to Face Future" indicates that it is not just divorced or widowed women or women alone who are teaming up (for example, to design communal living arrangements), but women with male partners as well "because they trust their friends to be good caretakers."[36] The dialogue in *Cut Loose* between "Snow White" and "Rose Red," a k a Isabella Giovanni and Annie Peacock, describes the swift and unsavory breakup of a relationship each had to the same man via the Internet. What they gained out of it was their friendship, having not known each before this event. As they say: "Sometimes fairy tales end happily without a prince, especially when princesses learn two important lessons: they can overcome adversity without a prince and, second, a true friend is much better than a phony frog."

The titles of "From Buddy to Joe to Harriet" (Luria) and "My Own Dance" (Kaplan) affirm that one can get over the fact of being unceremoniously cut loose (set adrift) from a long-term relationship and that one can embrace the self who is now cut loose (free), seeing the limitations of that former relationship and allowing for a new and perhaps fuller chapter, even if it may be close to the last chapter. But let us not be pollyannaish. There is pain, lasting pain, or, at very best, distant echoes of pain and traces of loss even as one goes forward. Raymond catches this looking back/going forward bifurcated state: "I wonder what I can learn during this 'last chapter' (as a friend puts it) of my life and consider the possibility that, on one level anyway, not knowing where I'm going could be the most exhilarating, youthful feeling imaginable. But I still wish, more than anything, to be back in my earlier life with that sense of security and hope." It is hard not to look backward over one's shoulder and long for the known, for the used-to-be. Cut loose from the relationship ties that bind as pictured in this book's frontispiece, *The Fetish for Forgetting*, by Louise Weinberg, one may also find a new exuberance, an exuberance not of youth but enriched by age and experience. Dougherty Delano, like Becker, is in touch with "the celebratory aspects of having cut loose/having been cut loose"; as O'Sullivan describes it: "I discovered other areas of openness. I am finally able to love my mother in a way I hadn't been able to since my early teens. . . . I feel a kind of contentment—if you can leave aside my over-determined negativity about my body. I have regained energy and enthusiasm. . . . I feel connected to life and love on many levels. I've still got my fears and times of loneliness, but mostly I feel affection for the old bird I am becoming."

Notes

1. Madeline Albright with Bill Woodward, *Madame Secretary* (New York: Miramax Books, 2003). Articles about *Madame Secretary* have titles which focus on the "dumped" aspect of the story, such as "Divorce Drove Me to the White House," October 15, 2003, http://arts.telegraph.co.uk; "How Albright Joined the First Wives Club," September 20, 2003, *http://wwww.*the age.com.au; and "I Would Have Given Up My Career to Save My Marriage," Sharon Krum, *The Guardian*, September 18, 2003.

2. William Grimes, *New York Times*, March 25, 2005, http://www.nytimes .com/.

3. Ibid. Grimes refers to an article by John Eakins in the journal *Narrative*.

4. See also Helen Fisher, *Why We Love: The Nature and Chemistry of Romantic Love* (New York: Henry Holt, 2004). Sally Warren (with Andrea Thompson) in *Dumped! A Survival Guide for the Woman Who's Been Left by the Man She Loved* (New York: Harper Paperbacks, 1999), suggests that in order to cope in the early stages of having been cut loose, one should keep a journal or even write (an unsent) "hateful letter" (44–45). Anne Kingston, in *The Meaning of Wife* (New York: Farrar, Straus and Giroux, 2004, 179), dates the emergence of ex-wife memoirs as a literary genre to the 1990s.

5. Mary Bly, "A Fine Romance," *New York Times*, February 12, 2005, Op-Ed.

6. Louise DeSalvo, *Adultery* (Boston: Beacon Press, 1999), 23.

7. DeSalvo asserts that reading and writing about adultery is dangerous; in fact, she says that writing about it "might be deadly" (ibid., 11).

8. Nora Ephron, *Heartburn* (New York: Pocket Books, 1984), 150, 221. In *Anatomy of Love: The Natural History of Monogamy, Adultery, and Divorce* (New York: W. W. Norton, 1992), Helen Fisher says that "the dumped person creates

a narration of who did what to whom. At first the individual " fixates on the worst humiliations. But with time he or she builds a plot with a beginning, a middle, and an end. This account is a little like a description of an auto accident; perceptions are garbled. But the process is important. Once in place, the story can be addressed, worked on, and, eventually discarded" (170).

9. Jane Taylor McDonnell, *Living to Tell the Tale* (New York: Penguin Books, 1998), 14. Quoted by Susan Becker in "Dear Harry" in this collection.

10. See http://breakupgirl.net/. Breakup Girl was created by Lynn Harris and Chris Kalb.

11. Warren, *Dumped!*, xii.

12. Ibid., 148.

13. Dan Hurley, "Divorce Rate: It's Not as High as You Think," *New York Times*, April 19, 2005, Science.

14. Alex Kuczynski, "The 37-Year Itch," *New York Times*, August 8, 2004.

15. Steven J. Haider, Alison Jacknowitz, and Robert F. Schoeni, "The Economic Status of Elderly Divorced Women," Michigan Retirement Research Center, University of Michigan, May 2003, 4, quoting from Barbara A. Butrica and Howard M. Iams, "Divorced Women at Retirement: Projections of Economic Well-Being in the Near Future," *Social Security Bulletin* 63, no. 3, Fall 2000.

16. Sarah Mahoney, "Splitsville: A Special Report on Divorce," *More*, March 2004, 102–107.

17. Xenia P. Montenegro and Knowledge Networks, Inc., *The Divorce Experience: A Study of Divorce at Midlife and Beyond* (Washington, D.C.: AARP, May 2004); Elizabeth Enright, "A House Divided," *AARP*, July/August 2004, 60–67, 83–84; Kuczynski, "The 37-Year Itch"; Jane Gross, "It's Cold on Mars," *New York Times*, July 22, 2004; "Midlife Crisis? Bring It On!" *Time Magazine*, May 16, 2005; and Lynn Schnurnberger, "Divorcing Mr. Nice Guy," *More*, April 2005, 99–103, 179. Also see Nancy M. Better, "Midlife Crisis: How Women Cope," *More*, May 2005; "Splitsville at 71: Late-Age Divorce Growing American Trend," July 26, 2004, http://abcnews.go.com; and Lorraine Ali and Lisa Miller, "The Secret Lives of Wives," *Newsweek*, July 8, 2004, http://msnbc.msn.com. As Gail Sheehy puts it, middle-aged women choosing divorce are "causing another demographic lurch." "Passages Redux," *More*, July/August 2004, 62, 64–66.

18. Steven L. Nock, *Marriage in Men's Lives* (New York: Oxford University Press, 1998), 14.

19. Denise Grady, "Sudden Stress Breaks Hearts, a Report Says," *New York Times*, February 14, 2005. See also Ellen Barry, "Humiliation by a Cruel Ex-Lover Can Spark Depression," *Boston Globe*, August 13, 2003; and Kenneth Kendler et al., "Life Event Dimensions of Loss, Humiliation, Entrapment, and Danger in the Prediction of Onsets of Major Depression and Generalized Anxiety," *Archives of General Psychiatry* 6, no. 8, August 2003, 789–796.

20. In the memoir *Around the House and in the Garden: A Memoir of*

Heartbreak, Healing, and Home Improvement, Dominique Browning uses a musical analogy: "Perhaps I have spent the years of recuperation cleaning closets. There's been a strange tempo in the activity, and it feels almost as if it has proceeded in symphonic movements—first movement, putting away the shards of grief; second movement, sifting for clues in the debris; third movement, building a structure in which to fit everything, as if to contain emotional chaos with scaffolding. . . . Somehow it has all been about holding on, though, whether I'm holding on and hiding or holding on and seeking" (New York: Scribner, 2002, 195–196). Writing about the end of her eleven-year marriage, Theo Pauline Nestor also was counseled with the house simile: "Your grief is like a house. One day you'll be in the room of sorrow and the next you might be in anger." "The Chicken's in the Oven, My Husband's Out the Door," *New York Times,* November 21, 2004, Styles.

21. In "Learning to Drive" (*New Yorker,* July 22, 2002), Katha Pollitt, a fifty-two-year-old who takes driving lessons after her lover leaves her, fantasizes about running him and his new, young girlfriend down as they stand in the crosswalk. While she probably would go to jail since no jury would believe it had been an accident by a neophyte driver, at least her story would be made into a movie for a cable channel, she muses. And in "Webstalker" (*New Yorker,* January 19, 2004), Pollitt describes how she became a technological peeping tom: she "webstalked" her ex and everyone in his world. It was an addiction to fill in the void: "It is so terrible to go from living with someone to never seeing him, never even glimpsing the top of his head bent over the art magazines at Barnes & Noble or catching sight of him through the window at the meat counter at Citerella. It was as if he had vanished in a puff of smoke" (42). Despite how much she could learn about him on the Internet, the stalking did not answer her real question: why?

22. Catherine Texier, *Breakup: The End of a Love Story* (New York: Doubleday, 1998), 154–155.

23. Julie Fitness, "Betrayal, Rejection, Revenge and Forgiveness: An Interpersonal Script Approach" in *Interpersonal Rejection,* ed. Mark R Leary (London: Oxford University Press, 2001), 87.

24. See also Helen Fisher, "Dumped!" *New Scientist,* February 14, 2004, 41; Benedict Carey, "Watching New Love as It Sears the Brain," *New York Times,* May 31, 2005; and "The Heart of Love," *Elle,* February 2004, http://www.elle.com.

25. Montenegro and Knowledge Networks, *The Divorce Experience,* 26.

26. Wallerstein and Glenn are quoted in Mahoney, "Splitsville."

27. Mahoney, "Splitsville."

28. Stephanie Coontz, *Marriage, a History: From Obedience to Intimacy or How Love Conquered Marriage* (New York: Viking Penguin, 2005), 284. As to the odds, Warren says that "women who today are between the ages of thirty-five and fifty-five are at the mercy of numbers and the age-related pecking order: women typically marry older men, as men marry younger women. . . . Men have more to choose from the older they get, and women have fewer" (*Dumped!* 147). For a

history and cultural analysis of love and marriage, see, among others, Nock, *Marriage in Men's Lives*, and Nancy F. Cott, *Public Vows: A History of Marriage and the Nation* (Cambridge, Mass.: Harvard University Press, 2000).

29. Laura Kipnis, in *Against Love: A Polemic* (New York: Pantheon Books, 2003), argues against marriage and monogamy. She roots for desire; "mature love" in long-term relationships is in her view a form of settling and represents repression: "The question remaining unaddressed is whether cutting off other possibilities of romance and sexual attraction while there's still some dim chance of attaining them in favor of the more muted pleasures of 'mature love' isn't similar to voluntarily amputating a healthy limb. . . . But if it behooves a society to convince its citizenry that wanting change means personal failure, starting over is shameful, or wanting more satisfaction than you have is illegitimate, clearly grisly acts of self-mutilation will be required" (59).

30. Shirley Glass, who did research in the 1970s on infidelity, said that an affair does not necessarily signal "a problem in the marriage. Over half of the men and a third of the women who had affairs said they were happy with their spouses" (48). Nonetheless, that does not mean that the betrayed person does not feel severe emotional trauma. Quoted in Ira Glass, "The Doctor of the Dalliance," *New York Times Magazine*, December 28, 2003.

31. Laura Zigman, *Animal Husbandry*, 248–249.

32. We are hardwired for adultery: "Our human tendency toward extramarital liaisons seems to be the triumph of nature over culture. Like the stereotypic flirt, the smile, the brain physiology for infatuation, and our drive to bond with a single mate, philandering seems to be part of our ancient reproductive game." Helen Fisher, *Anatomy of Love*, 87.

33. Walter Kirn, "Curing Casanova," *New York Times Magazine*, July 18, 2004, 13–14. See also Nicholas Wade, "DNA of Deadbeat Voles May Hint at Why Some Fathers Turn Out to Be Rats," *New York Times*, June 10, 2005.

34. As quoted by Ali and Miller in "The Secret Lives of Wives."

35. An extreme example is that of Clara Harris, age forty-five, who testified at her trial that in order to save her marriage (her husband was having an affair), she planned to have liposuction and breast enlargements. Apparently either they did not work or she never had them: she instead ran over her husband with her Mercedes (Ellyn Spragins, "A Makeover Can Be More Than Skin Deep," *New York Times*, March 2, 2003, Business Section). Makeovers are no longer for women only. In "A Nose by Any Other Name," David L. Marc, at age forty-four, chose a nose job in response to his "marriage collapsing, my career in limbo, my hair thinning and my kids acting out" (*More*, July/August 2005, 76).

36. Jane Gross, "Older Women Team Up to Face Future," *New York Times*, February 27, 2004.

One

HE/SHE
LEFT HER/HIM

If Not

PAGE DOUGHERTY DELANO

I
f it hadn't been the next door neighbor
it'd have been someone else. We'd soured.
I'd unraveled things long back,
even if he didn't know. Fighting equaled
passion, the mending tenuous, our sorrow
for the rage brief & blindly sexed.
In fear of losing the light, one lashes out.

If it hadn't been the woman next door
I might have stayed.
I'd given up on fixing it, smelling
trouble in other women, taking risks
that didn't seem risky. Long enough
to keep me satisfied, or stupid, dazed
with the hollow sips of possibility.

If he hadn't screwed the woman next door
she'd have become my friend. Lately I catch her
at the elevator, the laundromat, she has a good
haircut—and silence. Still, she carts

that sheepish look as if she's free of blame.
Sorry for me, and more important, for
herself. Her half-glance mends nothing.

If he hadn't gone on to the woman next door
I thought we might have mended it. I blindly
thought he might want to work it out. As if.
My forgetting—that it couldn't work—
must be a sign of loneliness. Forgetting
I dislike his voice on his answering machine,
the way he takes a quip about his haircut.

I'd been seeking another flat, giving
little heed to finding another man,
I was sure that would come, but his taking knocked
the wind out of me, a hurried breach.
At times I'd like to slug her.
Now I can't get men to stay
long enough in my reach, my world.

Each waking is a long reach into the world.
I wonder why I slow so much for men.
If he hadn't wanted another woman so crudely
he'd not have screwed the woman next door,
some stupid satisfaction, a way not to stay
in my world—yet, as if it wasn't his fault,
yoked, he said, by biology.

If it hadn't been that woman,
he'd have picked apartment 26, or 44.
He just rose to the top. One night,
we made love on the roof of the couch,
my back arching to her wall. I say this
with my own shame of deceit walled
inside me, the screws of dead and want.

I Give My Husband Fish Sausage

PAGE DOUGHERTY DELANO

It fills his mouth with fish smell
so he is fishy when I near him.
He changes his mind
about coffee. We drink red wine
in the kitchen, so soon I forget
fishness, and touch his stomach.
For an hour we taste in ways
old lovers have of touching
the other's folds and places,
and we make V's and W's
with our legs, crooks of our elbows.
Then he's ready to go home
and I'm OK with his leaving,
for the sun, which had gloried
the red brick flats across Broadway
and the thousand windows, reflecting
light, now fails, and the earth-glow
brilliance fades to dusk. He knows
he will cook alone in his kitchen
where he lives apart. And I—

I've begun to chop carrots, stir
garlic into the pan, get dressed.

I have always loved this day.
It lies midweek, but begins
with W, toward the ragged
close of the alphabet, two
V's clinging to each other.
You say Wednesday by
swallowing whole a small part,
birds that fall from nests.

* * *

These poems are born out of the unworkable last stage of a twenty-five-year marriage, a marriage which had been, in its time, rich and full, and whose dissolution was more or less mutual. But, obviously, it was not without its painful moments. We shared two wonderful children, years of exciting political involvement, common joys, economic ordeals, and the sweet and sour of weathering a relationship. The poems concentrate experiences in the years of breakage. If there are moments that aren't entirely true, they could have been. I also try to touch on the celebratory aspects of having cut loose/having been cut loose from a relationship turned difficult, as well as to suggest the complexities of a long erotic life and a history of desire. The vocabulary problems that come in naming this liminal period are indicative of this new experience/ existential moment.

What Was Home

LAURIE SILVER

JULY 5TH

Julie tried to hold Tim's hand, but they were forced by circumstance to walk single file; Bloomingdale's was a traffic jam, people chest to back, stilettos digging randomly into toes, tossed hair a weapon.

They escalated to the linens section of the Home floor. Tim had suggested this, buying new bedding; their linens were beginning to wear thin, shred. Julie wandered among the forest of patterns.

"Tim, what about these? Or wait, this—what do you think?"

"I like it . . ."

"They're Ralph Lauren, they're really expensive . . ."

"Don't worry about it."

"Right. Because we never worry about money."

"No, get them, it's fine."

"The whole set?"

"Yes."

Something nonspecific startled her, the way a flapping bird can when it dives too close; this came and went, like an afterthought.

At home they made up the bed in silence, Tim pulling their down quilt into the new cover, Julie stretching first the fitted sheet and then the top sheet, stuffing the sham covers, covering the pillows. Tim's cell phone burbled, and he took it into another room. Julie hardly noticed, used to his obligations. She tried to get the comforter evenly spread, shaking out first one side, then another, but it remained lumpy here, smooth there. European goose down with a mind of its own. She stepped back to get a better view of their reinvented bed.

It looked like a photo in the sort of magazine she would never read.

JULY 8TH

Tim slid out of bed in the dark, collected his clothes, and dressed in the hallway. For the third day in a row.

Julie pulled his soft pillow, still warm, over to her side and wrapped her arms around it.

"God, Tim, I'm so impressed . . ."

"Get some more sleep."

The ceiling fan circled slowly, the one broken blade causing a blip, a hiccup.

Julie strained for consciousness. The predawn sky had thickened with rain: it was the wettest summer in years, and she thought of Alexandra at camp, stuck indoors, passing time in the crafts cabin, with waning supplies and mosquitoes hovering by the window screens. Tim was writing Alex letters; he had left two for Julie to stamp; by now, they were almost like father and daughter. He helped her with homework, had taught her to ride a bike. He was willing to go to movies with her that Julie refused to see.

Eyes closed, Julie silently reviewed her to-do list:

1. Clean out Alexandra's schoolwork from seventh grade to make room for eighth
2. Buy and send birthday card to Tim's father, get Tim to sign it first
3. Pick up Tim's shirts at dry cleaner; see if they misplaced a box; his shirts seem to be disappearing like socks in a dryer—ask if he's leaving some at the office?

Hank, the puppy, shuffled in his crate, and Julie sat up, stood up.

Julie shook her head at herself in the bathroom mirror. She wasn't unreasonable about her looks; her face, while still pretty, had fallen. Young men had started calling her "ma'am," holding doors open. Young women didn't notice her at all, as if she was simply a cipher they could pass through. Her skin reflected the color of the cracked walls of countless hospital recovery rooms; there were parentheses around her mouth like her mother's before the face-lifts.

Two days after the fourth surgery in four years, Julie's mother had had an aneurism and could have died quickly and painlessly, but a third-year resident had rushed her to the ER just in time. Doctors were not trained to let people die. So she lived four more months, ashen and bones, until Julie could get her home and have her disconnected, like an errant phone call. Only a year ago she had still had a mother.

Tim asked Julie to manage his new private practice after her mother died. He said he needed her help. The families that came to the office appreciated her, asked her advice, confided in her. They came from all over, bereft mothers with damaged infants in their arms, awkward toddlers in tow. They were in pain, and frightened, and they loved their new doctor's calm, comforting manner.

"He walks on water, your husband. On water. He's a saint."

Within six months the practice had grown so quickly that Tim leased a larger space on Park Avenue, and they prepared to move in. Julie hired movers, notified his referring physicians, the HMOs, the hospital. She picked out the wall color and hired the painters. And as a surprise, she had his degrees beautifully matted and framed, and meticulously hung each one on one wall of the consultation room. After thanking her, Tim removed them; this was his second career, he had started late and it was only the second year of his private practice. He wanted the illusion of having been practicing for years.

So Julie dressed the office as if it were an off-Broadway set; she bought a swiveling maroon leather chair, huge mahogany desk, mahogany credenza, matching book shelves, porcelain lamps. A maroon leather desk set—blotter, picture frame, pencil box, tissue holder.

She found original cartoon art to hang on the walls: framed *Bugs Bunny and Sylvester* color cels, Pooh Bear posters for the hallways, a cartoon clock for the examining room, signed *Cat in the Hat* sketches. Alexandra had gone with her to F.A.O. Schwartz to pick out books, trucks, wooden puzzles, and dolls for the toy chest in the waiting room. She bought and installed computers, found used file cabinets, opened an account with Staples. She ordered phone lines, implemented management software, hired and trained a receptionist. The move was expensive, but she had been investing in Tim for years, believed it was worth the cost.

Washed and brushed, Julie returned to the bedroom and slipped on one of Tim's polo shirts; she had heard once that men found it sexy when you wore their clothes. She recalled something she'd read long ago in *Cosmopolitan*: an article describing the perfect "man-trap apartment." The writer insisted that serving frozen green grapes to your date was a sure bet for snaring him. It's strange what you remember, she thought.

Julie heard the shower in the small bathroom; Tim was back from his run.

Julie wandered into the living room, wondering what she had meant to do next. Only three months ago her father had been found wandering through Mount Sinai hospital at four in the morning, losing his pants and searching for his internist. On the advice of the emergency room doctor, Julie had him admitted until she could arrange to get him help, someone to keep him from running out of his apartment and getting hit by a bus. By now his twenty-four-hour in-home care was devouring his stock portfolio like termites eating away at a Catskills motel.

Back in their bedroom, Julie found Tim in a towel, laying out clothes while on the phone to his service, balancing the receiver between his chin and neck. She studied his broad back, his thinning hair; she walked over and kissed his bare shoulder.

Letting the puppy out of his crate, Julie fell backward on the bed, and they rolled and rubbed; their morning ritual. He was a three-ring circus, madly wagging his tail, licking her face, jumping into her lap. Julie loved every love-able inch of him, every wholly joyous yap and yawn. Delicately pawing out of her arms, he scattered around the bed, head down, sniffing for treats.

"Could you get him off my jacket?"

Julie made Tim's lunch: tuna salad sandwich on whole wheat with lettuce and tomato (draining the tomato slices first on paper towels so they wouldn't sog the bread), a Bosc pear, small bottle of water. She folded and added the *New York Times* sports section to the bag.

Tweed sport coat over his arm, Tim half kissed Julie's forehead, said he would call later. He typically called twice a day: once from the hospital just to say hello, and once when close to leaving the office, to see if she or Alexandra needed anything. Tim had grown up in the Midwest, and politeness, calm, and orderly behavior came naturally to him. Once, years ago, they were strolling down Broadway, continuously bumped by the usual Sunday crowds.

"The problem is everyone is walking randomly, there's no order."

She smiled up at him, at his slight frown, his handsome face.

"Do you have a better idea?"

"If all these people just walked on the right side of the street, there wouldn't be an issue."

"Tim, this is New York! That's never going to happen."

"I know, but it should."

They had met at a party, one of the weekend parties. They were both eating raw baby carrots; Tim just came around and she liked the way he looked. She admired him, his size, his solid presence. He extended his hand.

"Tim."

"Julie."

They shook hands, a perfectly reasonable greeting that Julie found surprising, as if they were being graded for good manners. On their third date he spent the night in her room and they fit perfectly, wrapped together during sleep the way you dream you will when you dream of these things; arms and hands and legs all in the right places. They dated for almost a year.

But Tim went to medical school, and she didn't see him again until Alexandra was one year old. She and Alex moved in with him, and they had been together ever since; Tim signed birthday and anniversary cards *"To Julie, the love of my life"* and she believed in those words the way some people believe in an afterlife.

JULY 21ST

Alexandra came home from camp on a Saturday with a waistline and a new confidence that made Julie want to weep with pride.

At dinner, as Alex passed around Polaroids, told water-skiing stories and campfire tales, Julie noticed that Tim's eyes had glazed over. He must have patients on his mind, she thought, wishing he would put it aside, give tonight to Alexandra. She felt a sudden shiver at the small of her back, as if a salesgirl behind her was trying to get her attention.

That night Julie dreamt it was her job to make Thanksgiving dinner; her mother was still alive. But she had waited too long to shop and the stores were out of everything, no turkeys were left, no stuffing mix, fresh cranberries all gone. She ran frantically up and down, but there was nothing available anywhere. Trying to get home, the elevator she stepped into was her neighbor's apartment; the neighbor was wearing an apron and peeling vegetables at the sink, and didn't seem to mind that Julie was there or that her kitchen was now a passenger vehicle. Julie saw her parents and faceless guests seated at the empty dining table, waiting for nothing, her mother skeletal, fading.

Alexandra slept late the next morning, and then snuggled into her mother on the couch. It wasn't until she asked about him that Julie checked her watch, realized that he'd been gone for hours. Almost three hours. Her stomach fell, that escalator stumble-fall that is the beginning of what can become panic; she dialed his cell.

"Where are you?"

"God, I'm sorry, I should have called but I totally lost track of time. My clothes got soaked, so I came to the office to change and wound up doing some dictation. Totally lost track. I'll get in a cab and be home soon. Do you need anything?"

When Tim came through the door, Alexandra wrapped her arms around his waist and the puppy ran circles at his feet. While he made himself a drink and turned on the football game, Julie went to get his clothes for the dryer, and realized they weren't even slightly wet. Not his socks, not his pullover, not his running shorts. His Nikes were not damp inside.

Julie waited for a commercial.

"You didn't go to your office to dry off."

He frowned. "I'm sorry?"

"Tim, what's going on? Exactly what is going on?"

"What are you talking about?"

"Your clothes are completely dry. That's not what you did, that's not . . . could you please tell me what is going on?"

He sighed, muted the TV, rubbed his forehead.

"Jesus, Julie, you know me so well."

"Not at this moment. At this moment, I don't. You were gone for hours, Tim . . ."

"I suppose I need to . . . look, I've been wanting to talk to you. I've been feeling like I need, I don't know, some time, time alone, time to think."

"Think? Think about what?"

Preciseness, Julie imagined, could make everything all right. By eliminating her imagination. A PowerPoint slide show with headings and diagrams could do it. Yes, items numbered in order of importance. Proper spelling of proper nouns. She experienced an uncontrollable flutter, a rhythmic butter-knife heart stabbing.

"The truth is I haven't been—I haven't been happy. I realized that for the last few weeks, for the last few months even, I just—I just haven't been happy."

A drop, drop-fall, stomach-plunge, tossed over an inappropriately short wall. Julie was losing her skills.

"Tim, you're lying. I know when—I can tell when you're lying."

"Julie. Really. Don't make this harder."

"But I don't believe you. I don't. There's someone else. There has to be. You wouldn't be saying this if there wasn't."

"I swear to you, there is no one else. That's not it. That isn't it. I need—I just need some time. I've been realizing that I'm just not happy, that I don't want to come home at night."

There might be a thousand women with husbands saying the same thing all over the city, Julie thought, all the men just returned from invigorating love affairs around the reservoir, on their cell phones with their secretaries, their co-workers, their best friends' wives. Thank god Tim was not, had never been like those other men.

Every Christmas Tim and Alex would select an enormous fresh fir, and the branches were left to fall overnight. He was in charge of stringing the white lights, hundreds of them, and then they all would decorate, using their amazing collection of glass balls, bells, and wooden toys, every year four or five new ones found at flea markets, on weekend trips to country inns. Gifts from friends. Tim even had a collection of little houses, miniature skaters on a pond, fake snow, tiny streetlights, miniature white picket fences. Julie bought him a new part of town each year.

"Friends have told me I look—that I don't look happy, and I realize that they're right. I'm not."

"What friends?"

Tim frowns. He hasn't got any friends, as far as Julie knows.

"A doctor I work with at the hospital. Different people . . ."

Julie leaned against the stove because standing upright was not possible. For no reason at all she thought about the first time you use a wok, how you follow the directions you were told and nothing works the way they said it would.

"The thing is, you're my best friend."

"*Best friend? Best friends* don't do this, Tim. This isn't what *best friends* do. This is what men do. Because you can. This is what *men* do, they walk away."

If her crying moved him at all, he kept it to himself. He said that he hadn't really decided what he was going to do. He really hadn't, he said again. He loves me, Julie thought, and for weeks they played a game that she didn't catch on to. She didn't get it. Choked like a summer drought, she was a hick, a stupid, gap-toothed backwoods creature.

Determined to make Tim happier, Julie vowed to herself to change, immediately. It was her fault, of course it was; she'd been so difficult for so long, first losing her mother, then caretaking her father, she must have been hard to come home to. OK, she would change, be in a great mood, hopeful, cheerful.

She gave him space, and he took it. He didn't call twice a day any more, and Julie said nothing. He ran every morning. One night she curled up to him in bed, put her hand on his chest. He picked up her hand and moved it off. Still, she made his favorite foods, bought him gifts, kept Alexandra and the puppy quiet and out of the way. In a blaze of blindness she couldn't make out the blinking sign, didn't feel the Spanish moss creeping up the trees; she never heard the wail of the siren, instructions for an all-alert. Julie figured that Tim just needed time.

AUGUST 9TH

Alexandra is sleeping at Chloe's; the house is quiet except for rhythmic splattering of rain on the air conditioners. Hank is asleep on the coffee table. Finally paying a huge pile of bills, Julie sits at the desk, writing checks, licking envelopes: Tim's student loans, Con Ed, Saks, the mortgage, maintenance, the vet, Tim's cell phone bill. She spots something that makes her dizzy, and grips the sides of her chair. She stares, stares at the pale blue bills, piled with print.

Julie moves the lamp nearer. But the print jumps up and down, the way the ticking stripe wallpaper did in her room at her parents' house. She makes out hundreds of calls to the same number. Up and down each page, both sides. The calls were made at all hours, early in the morning, in the middle of the night.

The number is a Chicago number; Julie knows her area codes.

She strains for a clear thought. Tim had said *something* about Chicago, she remembered, but she hadn't thought much about it because the story made no sense. Some old students of his were going to fly him to Chicago to give a speech, and it was all going to be paid for. What students? He had never gone anywhere before, not because Julie wouldn't pay for it, but because he couldn't leave the hospital, had no one to cover for him. Chicago.

It takes her more than a moment to reach the second level to shutdown. Maybe this number was a hospital there? She dialed, not one inch of her touching one inch of anything else, no solids, only a liquid base.

"Hello?"

"Hi. Hi, who is this please?"

"It's Lucy!"

"Is this a home number?"

"Yes, it is."

"I'm so sorry; I've made a mistake."

Finally and endlessly, the ribbons untie, the gift paper unwraps itself, the crackling of unwrapping an unbearable sound.

Her chest cantering, Julie calls Tim at his office. He's with a patient, the receptionist says sternly. Julie says she'll hold.

"Who is Lucy, Tim?"

"Excuse me? Lucy? Well, the only Lucy I know is one of my medical students, *was* one of my students. Where did . . . why are you asking about Lucy?"

"You called her thousands of times, Tim. At night, at the crack of dawn, every weekend. She's the reason, isn't she?

"You want to tell me what you're doing going through my phone bills?"

"I *pay* the bills. I've *always* paid the bills."

"Look, this has absolutely nothing to do with her. She's just a friend, a sympathetic ear. And I may have had dinner with her once or twice."

The Sympathetic Ear: a vision, a solitary ear in flight. An uncontrollable soundtrack itches, scratches at the slowest speed. The Sympathetic Ear wafts in the chorus, high up in those clouds that cloud around, white, mesmerizing.

Julie's eyes were slammed shut, as if that would help. She pictured Jackie at Jack's funeral, pictured the veil she wore, black lace, a mantilla. Remembered how well behaved Caroline was. Stop, Julie murmured to herself, stop and get air. But there wasn't any air, and she knew there wouldn't be for some time.

When Tim arrived home late, very late, she waited for an apology, for shame, but there wasn't any shame and there wasn't going to be an apology. Unkiltered, Julie took her mother's leftover Percodan from a drawer, grabbed a bottle of vodka from the freezer, and drank down handfuls of pills, drinking from the bottle, a derelict, a lowlife at the lowest point in life.

"I'm not fine, am I?" Julie asked Tim, or what was Tim when he was still in front of her. She could no longer tell exactly what was in front of her. It could have been anything, a cave, a cartel, seven maids a-milking. The floor hit her head, rudely and without warning.

In the morning she held on to the puppy while she waited for Tim to leave and her friends to arrive. Surrounding her, *we understand*, they said, *but you have to think about Alex*. They sat on the king-sized bed, made limp jokes, and drank strong coffee. In her alcohol-drugged fog, Julie thought they were having a party.

Julie's friends arranged an intervention; she overheard their whispering, and didn't mind. There was a clever ruse to get her to the hospital; a handsome young doctor in a white coat was out in front, waiting to greet her, to calmly, quietly coax her inside. She actually tried to run, but he held on to her, almost hugged her, and she let him lead her through the rotating door. Once inside, the handsome young doctor disappeared, and the grey metal door slammed shut.

AUGUST 10TH

Julie is out of order, unable to think in sequence.

There is a pile of magazines on the table by the single bed, *O*, *People*, *Vanity Fair*, but she's not interested. Did Tim bring them? He was there earlier but did not say much, which is, of course, like Tim. Pulling the bed covers high, Julie is vaguely aware that she is not available at this time. She's not eating, but if you saw the food you would understand.

The day before, when she saw the white room with the stained floor and single chair, she lost control, began throwing up. Humiliated, she overheard the women in white uniforms: ". . . saved us the trouble of pumping her damn stomach."

She was on the private-insurance side of the wing. There were only two other patients on that side; Julie saw them when she used the pay phone. It was hard for her to keep thoughts for more than a moment, as if they were on short-term loan. One of the patients constantly mumbled; he was angry and frightened her. The other didn't speak.

She wore pajamas, and there was a robe, but Julie couldn't find the ends of the belt at the same time to tie them together. She would have liked to tell this to someone. She had visitors, but couldn't remember anything they said after they left. Julie could not understand how they knew where she was. The nurses gave her tiny blue pills and she slept. A two-person team woke her every few hours, checking her pulse and blood pressure. Vital signs, they called them.

Days later a pretty doctor told Julie she could go home, and yes, Julie told her, yes, she understood that home wasn't going to be the same, even though the keys would work and the mail would come. She was given a flurry of prescriptions and sent on her way.

Home, Julie imagined Tim with Lucy. She pictured her beautiful, smart, able to talk with Tim about neonates and spinal taps. Things that interested him. She imagined them in bed. And as if in a fistfight, Julie's arms and legs ached and failed, and the front of her fell over itself; her hands strong-armed her head as she rocked. Julie held the couch, soaking the cushions, trying to sink through them, to the other side of what this was.

Julie's friends and neighbors told her that she had to *be strong for Alex*. They told her that she was, deep inside, *a strong person*. They said *it will take time*, and that eventually she would come through this and *be fine*. Everyone had a suggestion, a helpful hint, a word of kindness; they encouraged her, said wise things. Julie understands that sometimes these things are thoughtful and true and kind; but sometimes, they are just things people say.

The large apartment is ghost empty, as if no one had ever moved in, adjusted lighting, considered the color of the walls. And this doesn't matter any more than startling noises, fire engines, cop cars splattering and wailing past, parsing out time. *I should have served frozen green grapes*, Julie said aloud to the mountainous echo of what was home.

"Chapter Four You Break Up"

A Journal

OCTAVIA NEVINS

Note: These are excerpts from a journal written at least once a week from September 23, 2002 until September 1, 2003. Brackets—[ ]—indicate events and emotions that I have summarized for the sake of space and so that the excerpted entries make sense.

I take the title from the song "Book of Love," written and recorded by the Monotones (peak Billboard position no. 5, in 1958):

> Chapter One says to love her, You love her with all your heart
> Chapter Two you tell her you're never, never, never, never, never gonna
>   part
> In Chapter Three remember the meaning of romance
> In Chapter Four you break up but you give her just one more chance

Over the year that I kept my journal, it took on several titles: I began with "The Husband, the Wife, and the Mistress: Journal from the First Year"; later I changed it to: "The Husband, the Wife, and the Young Woman or Aging Wife/Younger Woman." In the summer of 2003, "Can This Marriage Be Saved?/Should This Marriage Be Saved?" became the working title; it is taken from an advice column, "Can This Marriage Be Saved?" in the *Ladies' Home Journal*, which during the women's liberation sit-in at the magazine's offices in 1970 became revised to "Should This Marriage Be Saved?" And then as I excerpted it for publication in the fall of 2003, I settled on " 'Chapter Four You Break Up': A Journal."

I. Where He Tells His Wife That He Has a Twenty-five-Year-Old "Girl Friend"

SEPTEMBER 22, 2002

Our housewarming party [we had just moved permanently into San Francisco after living in Oakland for twenty years and renting in San Francisco for the last two years.]: Everyone says the apartment is fantastic and that I look happy/we look good. I was a little pissed off that I spent all the time in the kitchen and Jack seemed to be entertaining on the roof. Nonetheless, we cleaned up contentedly.

SEPTEMBER 23

Today we saw a couples' therapist. Why? Because Jack has been unhappy lately; we have fought; one evening he cried; he seemed disconsolate. It has been a stressful summer moving both out of the apartment in Pacific Heights where we had rented for two years and from Oakland, where we have lived most of our marriage.

At this first session, Jack announces that he is seeing Margaret Oyama [MO] and wants to continue and that he needs to do this for himself and "for us." Margaret is twenty-five, his student who has just graduated from the college where he teaches history; slim, Japanese, very smart, going to grad school in history, and seemingly in need of a father. She is married; he is away in the service. She has had an affair with another professor. Her father and mother divorced while she was young. I know about her (and I might have the details wrong since I was unaware that I should have been paying full attention to her particulars) because Jack has talked about her to me over the years, as he talks about all of his students—many of whom he is close to.

I cry; I have deep pain, fear, panic, shock; Jack is angry and clear that there are to be no negotiations about this relationship. That night I cry most of the night, sleeping just barely, curled up in the study. We talk a lot but none of it reaches into my panic.

The rest of that week: I go to work with sunglasses on since my eyes have black circles around them; I am shaking inside; I feel so alone and scared. The job is also falling apart. I cannot hold it together. I want to put my head on my desk and cry. An older woman laid off by another department comes for an interview; she is desperate for a position, a place; I so identify with her . . . an older woman, redundant, wants me to choose her. I reject her.

I do not know how to chronicle the other movement that is happening at the same time as this is wrenching me into pieces: our talking, our closeness, our intimacy. Our sexuality is very intense. Jack is quite concerned about me, very attentive, very loving but also saying that we have to live with this and we have to discuss the terms for his seeing MO. While he is saying he will not leave me, I keep thinking about how I can possibly live with this, that we will have to split up; I am trying to understand it, trying to see if we can have a full (better?) relationship around this other relationship. I hate his utter rationality and yet I am thinking in new (if painful) ways in response to aspects of it. Feeling silenced—don't want to call him on his cell as he might be with her, can't tell my friends/our friends/our children. Feeling powerless/a victim (he says he had to live with loneliness himself for so long in our marriage because he felt I did not love him, did not recognize his needs; I see a parallel in how I did or did not love Josie, my daughter, unconditionally; I am a failure in both relationships); feeling as if he has destroyed our new home, our old-age plans, the city for me, everything. . . .

Incredible unbearable love we have that I am finally feeling—too late? Is this love really just expression of my fear? My sense of self is slipping; I am no one if he does not love me. Also, we have three daughters [my daughter is twenty-five] already; I do not choose to have another who is also my husband's lover. Is he simply an old fool who is afraid of aging and death? His obsession with running is part of this.

I tape a note at 5:25 a.m. on the computer: I CANNOT DO IT! IT IS TOO PAINFUL.

Every time I get close to thinking I can do this . . . I sink into anxiety, loss, an immense pool of tears . . . I can't eat/can't sleep.

Jack goes out to spend some time with Margaret. I speak rationally to Emily [one of the few friends I tell] about staying in the relationship, somehow being able to handle this. . . . But later I break down. . . .

He argues with me: we love each other; he will not leave me; but I say I may have to leave him. Am I a "wimp" to stay or is this the mature thing to do? On Saturday and Sunday, we go back and forth between an ordinary weekend in Big Sur [our country house] of doing household things together to hard discussions to physical and emotional expressions of love to a total meltdown.

He suggests we write down "our" demands/"our" desires; he, of course, has this all planned out:

Jack wants: two nights a week with MO (but not necessarily staying over); Margaret can call the house and he can call Margaret from the house; Fri. night and Sat. morning with her

Octavia will agree to: one night over, one late night but not real late [later I change it to two nights out and DON'T come home on those evenings]; calls only of necessity; priority in long-range planning; no weekends; can't go away with Margaret

Of course, I do not really want to participate in this. None of these are my desires. I sit there calmly (stunned inside) as he says two nights a week overnight and a weekend sometimes. We also look at our finances. Again Jack has it all mapped out: if we stay together; if we separate, if we divorce. There it is—the harsh numbers.

We are running late and need to get back to the city, but we are hungry (I am not; I no longer eat much). We stop at the Ginger Café; I step in dog shit as I get out of the car. I order a glass of red wine. The owner insists I must taste four different red wines before I choose. I tell her I need her to go away as we are dealing with some serious stuff; she insists I do the tasting. I tell her we are talking about divorce; I am crying; she persists. I am never rude; now I was because I was just flabbergasted that she would not listen to my request, my plea.

Dear Octavia, I'm glad that at least you and Jack are going to therapy and trying to work things out. What hurt me most about my marriage breakup was that Henry wouldn't go to therapy or even admit that his point of view might be wrong (or partially wrong). I was desperately unhappy and cried for six months (also in public).

Coraggio, as the Italians say (take courage),

Love,

Elizabeth

OCTOBER 1

I did some research on Amazon.com. I need to think and read about my situation, but I do not want soppy advice books. I searched for "divorce" and "divorce memoirs." Two titles among hundreds strike me: *Should I Stay or Go?: How Controlled Separation Can Save Your Marriage* [by Lee Raffel and Jean Houston] and *Breaking Apart: A Memoir of Divorce* [by Wendy Swallow]. I have not searched under the key word "mistresses." Is that a category? What will I uncover? What other topics should I look under: "open marriage"? "old men and young women"?

OCTOBER 25

I have not written for some time. I will have to look over my journal to figure out when I stopped, but it must have been right after Jack withdrew his proposal that he have a weekend morning with MO, etc., etc. He withdrew it because he understood (finally) that I could not do it and thus our marriage could not withstand it. Instead he reduced his request to dinner with her once a week. He however still remains interested in his original proposal and believes we (I) should have been able or should be able to do it at some point.

Well, I should be happy and thankful—and I am! I know it would have destroyed me in many ways, but unfortunately I cannot let go of my fears, my sadness, my sense of loss, my inability to stand the competition. Yes, he says there is no competition, but he always refers to us as Margaret AND Octavia as in "I get pleasure out of Margaret and you." I ask if he cannot formulate it differently, but he keeps forgetting and equates us; he tells me I am not supposed to fantasize about this equation; I am not supposed to feel jealous or in competition with. On the one hand, I want to let go of these obsessive thoughts that keep me awake and choke me in the pit of my stomach: I feel like I am weak and not able to handle this well, that I spoil our evenings with my frequent tears, that I cannot seem to live in the moment, in our relationship but am always evoking, invoking "her." On the other hand, I wonder why I have to go through this, why Jack is cruelly making me live with this; why he thinks he can tell me she loves him and he loves her and I can listen and function with this burden.

Typing an e-mail Monday night, accidentally I was thrown into his e-mail message to Margaret: it is signed "I love you Jack." That night was horrible, the next day was horrible (for both of us; Jack appears to be having a temporary breakdown) and I continue to see that message emblazoned in front of me. . . . What am I to do with this? How does one live with this (and do I want to?) and most seriously how can I be a loving person knowing their love is active, alive, verbalized, and constant? How do I make these words (I love you) my own anymore?—he has given them to Margaret. I feel unloved and un-given-to. Ours is not a courtship; this is a twenty-two-year relationship, a relationship where I am equal; I am not subordinate; I do not look up to him and hang on his every word; he cannot buy me dinner; he cannot give to me in that same way. Ours is a relationship that often seems dominated by the leak in the Big Sur roof and not by intimate love talk or by my loving admiration.

Well of course we have talked about this and there is much I can learn in all of this of my desire to control, my inabilities to permit any boundaries between us and any differences between us, of how I feel that there is only so much love to go around and then it gets used up. I can learn but still the pain sometimes is unbearable.

I have reached out to a few friends to support me in all of this; I have great love for my women friends: Miriam, Alys, Michelle, and Emily; and for

Edward for his thoughtfulness; he established a phone tree—so I would get a phone call from a friend every evening. Emily sends me an e-mail every Tuesday to help me emotionally manage the evening [his dinner night with Margaret]; sometimes she just chats or tells me to do something for myself or sometimes she challenges my attempts to handle this arrangement. I say that Jack hopes I can be in good cheer when he returns from his outing with MO:

> cheerful and sweet—what a joke. i would find that really infuriating and kinda—hm—humiliating. i guess i feel he should recognize the pain and sadness if he wants something as difficult, impossible?, intense as this. it asks so much from you. all this is to say I'm sorry that he's being so dense, insensitive, self-absorbed. maybe that's the point of all of this.
>
> Do you feel you have any bargaining power?

There is so much tension in the household with me wafting off into sadness tinged with anger often and Jack not understanding this at all—like we live on two different planets; we cannot find common ground here. My intentions to be a loving companion keep going awry as my anger explodes out, eating us alive. 3:45 a.m.: he finds me downstairs reading, gathers me up. I fall asleep in our bed in his arms.

NOVEMBER 15
At 4:00 I awake and see (in my mind's eye) him calling her every day, e-mailing her, knowing her life in such an intimate way, worrying about her, consoling her, loving her; she is before my eyes—in my waking dreams. . . . I can't stop crying; he wants to sleep; he says I am pushing him away and is that what I want? . . . He goes down to the couch to sleep. He tells me I am the one obsessed by her, not he; I am putting her in the center of our lives, not he. He also tells me of her unease, how she feels dishonest with other graduate students; like she is a spy among them since she has a relationship with a professor. He tells her that her life as a graduate student will eventually take over and she will move away from him. He is so passive in this; he could separate from her, tamp down the interaction, change the constancy of their communication for her good and for my good especially. Yes, for my sake, he has pulled back from the arrangement he had originally desired; but he is still having his pleasure and hurting two women in different ways. How greedy of him . . . how mean, how hurtful. Would Margaret say that as well? She must want more. She is probably grateful for what this older man is giving her and does not feel empowered to ask for more.

NOVEMBER 16

I understood [I am seeing a therapist] then (I have known this all along but it hit me in a more powerful way at that moment) that what has occurred (Jack with Margaret) plays into my deep-seated feeling of not being loved or not being able to abide a triangle [with my younger sister, Janine, and my parents]. And that it is psychologically impossible (almost) for me not to feel despair (he has kicked me out of Eden; I will never be able to feel loved in a secure and unambiguous way by him which I had finally come to believe in—unless he can stop seeing Margaret—and even then I doubt I will ever again feel secure and I will be unable not to feel over and over again pain and not to fantasize his romance with her . . .). I cannot bear it; I will just opt out. I want out of this horrible, hurtful interaction we are trapped in.

DECEMBER 15

Candida Wilton takes to writing a diary [in *The Seven Sisters* by Margaret Drabble] when at around age sixty her husband leaves her for another woman. She thinks back to her earlier girlish diaries:

> I am going to write some kind of a diary. I haven't kept a diary since I was in school. *En effet*, we all used to keep them then. Julia, Janet and I, and all the other girls. It was the fashion, at St. Anne's, in the Fourth Form. Nothing much happened to us, but we all wrote about it nonetheless. We wrote about our young, trivial, daily hopes, our likes and our dislikes, our friends and our enemies, our hockey games and our blackheads and our crushes and our faith in God. We wrote about what we thought about Emily Brontë and the dissection of frogs. I don't think we were very honest in our diaries. Blackheads and acne were as far as we got in our truth-telling in those days. (3)

I too kept a diary when I was a teenager; now I am a sixty-one-year-old married professional leftist woman, but my diary sounds a lot like the one I kept so many years ago: does he love me or does he not? Most of the writing since September 23 has been an outpouring of anxieties and a reporting of my day-to-day doings in terms of the central issue: Jack is dating/loving/being loved by Margaret.

A third of the way into her story, Candida promises to go through the diary and delete the passages of self-pity: "Self-pity is a seductive emotion. One day soon I'm going to read through this diary and weed out all the passages contaminated by self-pity. If I recognize it for what it is. Which, of course, I may not. It deludes as well as seduces" (111). I suppose I would have to blank out, white out, block and delete most of my diary: all the whining, all the repetitious wails of pain would have to go.

And when I get to the end of this obsessive recording of my life, how will I feel about the diary? I have not looked back to read it; I madly and blindly go forward, adding entry upon entry. My words are probably boringly the same, repeated over and over since I am perpetually being thrown into the same primitive scary place that has prompted the writing of the first and subsequent entries, just as Jack and I repeat ourselves helplessly, trying but failing to find new ways to talk about the "situation." When I finally read through it, will I feel turned off by the person I present as myself? Will I have recorded that which is good, positive, happy or will it only be about pain and loss? Will I feel that I have been unfair to Jack and to Margaret? Will I have managed to step back and draw any insights that will be useful to myself and to another reader? Candida, who has determined to take control of her life, is about to go on a journey, a journey that reproduces that of Virgil's *Aeneid*; she is going with six women: "I have just reread the whole of this diary. I am not proud of it. What a mean, self-righteous, self-pitying voice is mine. Shall I learn to speak in other tones and other tongues when I leave these shores? Do I still have it in me to find some happiness? . . . Let me write this down. I am happy now" (160–161).

"Shall I learn to speak in other tones and other tongues when I leave these shores?" Can I speak in other tones and tongues? Can I leave these shores? Can I recreate myself? My questions are similar to hers, but I have additional questions: ones about revealing my story to the world; unlike Candida, I am not a fictional character, nor are the people in and around my life fictional. Will I try to get this published? Will any of this be worth reading? Who will read this? Betrayed women? Older women? Men and women who struggle to remain in a relationship, a long-term relationship? People who are monogamous and/or nonmonogamous? There are personal questions and ethical questions I need to think about before and if I submit this for publication. And there are dreams of big money and fame. After all, all this suffering ought to be worth something. I have lost weight—and that is not nothing. Loss of weight and gain of money, not bad! But would I rather turn back the clock to the summer, and not have Jack lay the bombshell on me about Margaret, his twenty-five-year-old student?

DECEMBER 23

References to affairs and marriage dissolution keep bombarding me; e.g., from "Two Questions That Could Change Your Life" [by Raphael Cushnir] in *O: The Oprah Magazine*:

"My wife's voice on the phone was panicked. 'What's wrong? I asked. . . . Is it bad?' 'Yes, it's bad. . . . I am having an affair . . . I don't think I can stop.' . . . For the next three months, as we separated, I was utterly lost. Every moment felt like a punch in the gut. I knew there was something I needed to do with my pain, but what? [He gets advice from an ex-Zen monk, who essentially says live in it.] I decided to try it, to just sit in the soup of my suffering. I lived that way for three more months." (113)

We started this on September 23; have I lived in it for three months? Can I come to some Zen place of peace about it?

DECEMBER 26

After Christmas dinner was over, Coretta [my stepson, Kevin's, mother-in-law, Mama Walker as they call her, who is a beautiful, stately almost-eighty-year-old African American woman with Native American "blood"], Blanche (Jack's mother, in her eighties), and I sat around the dining room table, while Jack and Kevin talked and Dora (his wife) read. Our conversation was about bodies: how Coretta cannot seem to eat, about the arthritis in her hand, about how Blanche has to pee all the time and could not get out of the bed after she broke her leg to do so, on and on. I felt uncomfortable. I am closer to them in age and experience than to Kevin and Dora, yet I did not want to be identified by myself or anyone else as an old woman, as belonging to them. Who do we identify with when we walk down the street, on the subways, in the movies; who do we watch to see how like or unlike we are to her? I find that older women talk to me. That may be one of the benefits of aging; a free and easy exchange between older women feels possible, unlike that usual isolation in the city.

Also, Blanche and Coretta, like so many older women, are alone. They negotiate their homes, their pains and sicknesses alone. Coretta's husband is now dead; they had divorced way before that. Blanche's husband (Jack's father) died a few years ago; they had been married sixty years. Apparently the loss Blanche feels poignantly now is that of their dog Checkers; she had to give him up as she was no longer able to walk him.

Loss of touching ("skin hunger"), loss of sexual interaction, loss of the significant other ("Unplanned Obsolescence: Some Reflections on Aging" [Sandra Bartky]): these losses loom down the road for me and my older women friends. In response, I have often contemplated turning to women. I love my women friends. Could I live with them? Could I be with them in a more intimate way? These observations resonate and sting so much as I am not rehearsing Jack's death but rather his leaving me for "the other woman."

JANUARY 5, 2003

Yesterday at around 4 p.m. Jack said he wanted to talk about our relationship. I reluctantly sat down in a chair opposite the couch where he was in the living room. I expected him to tell me that he wanted to have dinner with her the evening before we left for Guadeloupe; I also expected he would tell me what more he wanted in terms of seeing and being with her when we got back. Instead he said he decided not to see her anymore. After my initial shock and a kind of disorientation, I felt both fear and a tremendous sense of relief: fear that he will blame me for having to give up what he wanted for himself; fear that I failed him in not being able to do this with and for him; fear that now there is nothing between him and me—no Margaret to blame for our problems. Nonetheless, I did feel happy and my body felt as if a great weight had been removed.

Besides crying and being quietly ecstatic, I felt like I wanted to sleep for a long time, I felt that I had not really slept since this all began. I also felt a sense of giddiness; my heart was beating so fast as I was so relieved not to be in this soap opera anymore (the word soap opera does not mean that it was not serious and is not serious). We go off for a week in Guadeloupe starting anew!

II. Where He Tells His Wife That He Is Moving Out

JANUARY 12

(This entry is written on the back pages of Maryse Condé's novel *Winward Heights* while sitting on the beach Le Grand Anse two days before my sixty-first birthday.)

Jack says he needs to/wants to live alone, to figure out this new person he has become, is becoming, to not have to respond/serve/negotiate with me/with any other woman . . . He needs to go away in order to return to me/us. I am beside myself with fear and despair—fear of being alone, despair at giving up a man I truly love. I feel as if I have worked so hard in the past months to be a more loving, less neurotic, less controlling person—clearly my work was too late, too late. I am sitting under a palm tree, the Caribbean blue as far as the eye can see, people in groups on towels talking French, couples putting suntan lotion on each other. I begin this moment of my life alone; I begin my life alone, my last 10/15/20 years.

JANUARY 15

The plane ride home fills me with dread. I do not want to face the hard reality of splitting up. Being separated in Guadeloupe is all talk and theory; living alone in San Francisco at age sixty-one is quite something else.

Together we write two lists as we sit flying toward the city:

TO REMEMBER

1. Whatever we experience, exercise some control, keeping "it" within the range/bounds of our desire to come back together.

2. Being alone will be the first, major experience.

3. We are not closing doors, especially Jack.

4. It may be good that this extreme "taking stock" takes place *before* we also face the restructuring of our joint life at retirement.

5. Jack thinks he would benefit by taking a break from the marriage. Octavia sees the separation in those terms, trusting that Jack means "break" and not "end."

6. Two sets of reasons *not* to end our marriage:

ROMANTIC	PRAGMATIC
20 years of love and care and rich times and humor (despite pain & anger)	20 years of work, growth, investment Property
Genuine love even now	Children and grandchildren
Desire to care into old age	Tastes and interests in common
	Shared politics

Great mutual respect

LET'S TRY TO (ALL ARE AMENABLE TO NECESSARY MODIFICATION)

1. Phone every day during business hours.

2. E-mail once a day at least.

3. Jack will declare himself by June 20; schedule a session with Adam (couples' therapist) for that day.

4. Do common tasks regularly.

5. Avoid letting money poison our attempts to be loving and supportive during this period.

6. Say "I miss you." and "I love you."

7. On phone and in e-mail, use humor if possible.

JANUARY 16

Jack began his search for an apartment and immediately goes to see Margaret. My journal is turning into letters and e-mails to Jack (rather than letters to myself and to the reader).

JANUARY 20

From Jack, the day he moved out: Dearest Octavia, I am so reluctant to start this "trip" into myself without you. You have defined my life for 22 years.

I guess it's time for me to do some of that alone, tho' I really don't want to—at one level at least. Remember I love you and am working for us. I'll call and e-mail—Your husband J

JANUARY 21

From Jack: You know, over the long course of a thing like a marriage, one ought not to be surprised at how uneven the "terrain" looks. I think we have been pretty lucky in that we have saved our children from the real disasters out there, haven't driven one or the other of us into alcoholism or addiction (I'm sure, in fact, that because of you I drink less and am all the better for it), and are reasonably solvent. This moment is the worst for us because it hints at structural change, and will probably result in at least some of that. But it should be understood as a *necessary* perturbation of that "terrain," a big bump in the landscape of our lives that shows up on radar as a blip. If then, we have a topography, we both want it to be navigable and even pleasant to stroll across. I'm sorry that our wanderings have led us down this difficult track, but there have been and will be plenty of Provences [refers to our walking vacation in France] of the heart to walk.

JANUARY 28

J: Hey—this is so hard—I feel so pressed to get everything [meaning his emotional work and his writing] done at once, but I just can't. Hope you are ok and are not struggling too much on the upslope of this blip.

We e-mail each other about the "blip."

O: Dear, I would not worry about the bowls leaving a hole [bowls he took for his apartment], it is you who have left a hole—quite a gaping one at that. As to the upside of the blip, I am not a great climber: it looks too high and icy for me; I keep slipping back down.

J: Don't slip back—just hold on if you can't climb.

JANUARY 23

I need sleeping pills!

What is the correct formulation for what we are doing?

1. We are separating and may come back together again or may not (therefore divorce).
2. We are separating and will come back together again (June 20?).
3. Another formulation?

I cannot send this list to J so sent it to Bettina, my therapist.

JANUARY 24

Jack just called; he went to the country with Margaret to look at our Big Sur house. E-mail to Jack: What torture . . . you really expect we can come back somehow, get from here to there, get to a good place as loving partners? Did you move out to replace me? I AM now in Margaret's position, getting my dole from you of calls and e-mails. I feel like a jerk trying somehow to maintain a loving relationship with you. While you have two women . . .

Give me your vision again of where this (us) is going because I do not see it. Please speak honestly to me. If you left me to come to terms with all sorts of things (your work, me and anger, your relationship to women), I could live with this separation ok. But if you left me to be primarily with Margaret, then I do not see much reason for hope.

[The next few months, I write of the extreme difficulties I am encountering facing my aloneness. The winter is particularly harsh as if to underscore my inner realities. Jack tells the children (Josie [my daughter from my first marriage], Kathleen, Lynne, and Kevin [the children from Jack's first marriage]); I reach out to old friends and make some new friends (single women); we write and talk back and forth sometimes lovingly and sometimes angrily; we meet about once a month to take care of all sorts of bills and joint commitments; sometimes he stops by my office to see me (we both work at the same college). I go to yoga, walk a lot, try meditation, work hard at the book I am writing, and somehow try to fill up my time. Josie, my daughter, calls every morning and every evening—a life saver! This has brought us closer together.]

FEBRUARY 5

Jack gets alternately upset and angry about how he feels isolated and judged by both the children and our friends. He gets angry at my constant need for reassurance and pleads for some time away from me and my needs; he desperately wants unmediated time.

FEBRUARY 6

On jury duty began reading *The Dying Animal* by Philip Roth. I sit in the main jury room with tears streaming down my face; it is about a love affair between the narrator, David Kepesh, age sixty-two, and a twenty-four-year-old Cuban student, Consuela. I visualize Jack and MO at events out in the world together; this feels harder on me almost than imagining their sexual encounters. Kepesh's anger at the institution of marriage echoes Jack's: "Coupled life and family life bring out everything that's childish in everyone involved. Why do they have to sleep night after night in the same bed? Why must they be on the phone to each other five times a day? Why are they always *with* each other? . . .

But deferring, deferring, deferring? Appeasing, appeasing, appeasing? Every other day dreaming of leaving? No, its not a dignified way to be a man. . . . Or . . . to be a woman" (110 and 112).

Jack does not seem to acknowledge what role aging has in his decision to leave and be with Margaret: can he own up to this fear and therefore see his desire for a young girl in this light? "In every calm and reasonable person there is a hidden second person scared witless about death. . . . Yet what do you do if you're sixty-two and believe you'll never have a claim on something so perfect again? What do you do if you're sixty-two and the urge to take whatever is still takable couldn't be stronger? . . . It's like playing baseball with a bunch of twenty-year-olds. It isn't that you feel twenty because you're playing with them. You note the difference every second of the game. But at least you're not sitting on the sidelines." For David Kepesh, sex—especially with a twenty-four-year-old—is viewed "as revenge on death." (153, 33–34, and 69).

FEBRUARY 12

I am so depressed; had about an hour telephone conversation with Jack. He feels he is living his separate life in terms of me, thinking about how his work could or could not be done in our new study, reassuring me, not going down certain paths because he is afraid of frightening me. He fears he will waste this time, that he is a coward, maybe he should not speak to me every day; he does not want to feel compelled to reassure me every day. He has so much anger, anger at himself, at me, his frustrations at facing or not facing life, death, work, relationships; he is flailing around and meanwhile I have to give up my hopes, either for a quick return or for any return. Oh I hurt so much!

Later he called to apologize, but I do not trust him anymore, meaning he is so driven by his own psychology, I do not think he will ever find peace back in the marriage.

FEBRUARY 19

I am having such a hard time. Jack and I have pulled back from each other; I cannot ask him for reassurances. Somehow I have to live alone in these silences, without someone watching over me (in this time of duct tape and three days' supply of water in case of gas attacks and the horrendous war on Iraq), without someone reflecting love of me, concern for me. . . . How does one do it? Will I have to do it only until June 20 or beyond that? And what can I learn from this time? Is self-love bullshit, just like feminism feels like bullshit to me now as I have to live without the male gaze. Am I just a sixty-one-year-old reject? Well that is a bit much, but I seriously do not know how one feels good about oneself without love. Also, the loss of this specific relationship feels tragic so it feels doubly hard to figure out how to go on. I realize even with J's love I have had a very shaky sense of self . . . think about this and my jealousy of others . . .

MARCH 1

I read *Feminist Accused of Sexual Harassment* by Jane Gallop in order to get insight about love and sex between teacher and student, both from the teacher's point of view and the student's. Gallop writes from both positions. As a student she says: "I felt that in their eyes I was both a desirable woman and a serious scholar. . . . Lots of other smart, ambitious young women, many of them like-wise feminist academics today, have felt powerful because they seduced their teachers" (43). As a teacher, she has collected stories of student/teacher sexual interaction, noting that "In every instance, it was the student who made the first move; it was always the student who initiated sexual activity" (49). Jack said Margaret came into his office and offered herself to him. Why did she offer herself and why could he not refuse? Out on the narrow "edge of trans-gression," Gallop slept "with students for essentially the same reason [she] slept with other people—because they engaged me as human beings, because a spark of possibility lit between us" (51).

MARCH 2

I go out for dinner to Kevin's restaurant; I feel the need to assert my place in the family. Josie and Dominic [her partner] go with me; I have always re-lated to Kathleen, Lynne, and Kevin through Jack so this is not easy. While it was awkward at times, the children were warm to me; I am pleased that I pushed myself to go.

[We go through a month of anger on J's part and me trying to apologize for all the big and little ways I hurt him. I do this because he needs to hear it and also because I do think I was hurtful to him, critical and unloving in many ways. I do not think I did not love him, however, but he cannot seem to see that right now. Then, I get a voice message from him asking for good words about our relationship. We start telling each other good memories. I am hopeful. Jack plans to go to Scotland to a retreat-like New Age community for two weeks (Findhorn) where an old high school friend has lived for many years. When he returns on April 15, we agree that we shall talk seriously about how to slowly come together. He writes me on March 28, the day before he leaves for Scotland: "I wanted to write to you in case anything happens to me on this trip. I want you to know how much I love you and that this has been a very hard time for me but I know it has been so very painful to you. If I don't get back for some reason (acts of war or "God"—whatever), please try to think of us as still having been married and together. I don't expect anything to happen, but this is the kind of note I think we need to have between us at this time." For me, I am anxious to begin the work of coming together and want finally to stop this total inward looking as it is exhausting, and especially since so much real violence and real suffering are out there to pay attention to. I do go to some antiwar marches and vigils during this time—at least! I hang on hungrily to all his phone calls, e-mails, and postcards while he is in Scotland.]

APRIL 2

From Jack at Findhorn: No emotional news here—that is, it should not be news to you that I miss you. I am beginning to think there are no more insights; now must be the time for summing up and moving on. I am trying to write about it but don't seem to know much more than I did weeks ago. I don't know how you want to proceed when I get back—nor do I really—I mean what it is we want to do and how to do it and on what kind of schedule, if any. I think I'll spend some time here trying to formulate what I think we should look for—from me, from you, as a couple. This is a change for me because I somehow thought I'd find some revelation out of unfiltered experience that would make everything clear and ideal. I think it all can be clear, but only if I work at it instead of waiting for revelation. Looking back at this I see it sounds more somber than I mean it to be—I mean I'm looking forward to finding out how to do this. I love you and will be glad to be home.

APRIL 16

Jack returns home from Scotland, bearing gifts but telling me that he loves Margaret (and myself) and wishes he could have two wives. I am shocked; I had no sense that she was in his life like that given all his loving words to me. I cry; he cries. He goes to his apartment in Oakland and tells her it is over, but she asks if she can stay with him until June 20, the day he must move out of this sublet. He says yes. Two days later he returns to see me; he is an emotional wreck; I beg him to go into therapy. I tell him that I know this is hard for him, but it is impossible for me and that I cannot accept this June 20 arrangement he has made with MO.

APRIL 18

Such a very hard night, when I did sleep I dreamt that a crippled man with no legs in a wheelchair, wearing a pinstripe suit, fired me. I begged him; told him I am sixty-one and my husband just left me; he said he could find part-time people to replace me—it was cheaper.

When I awoke, I thought it was about my job as my contract is expiring and they want to cut my salary. Jack called around nine in the morning (was not sure if he would); I innocently told him the dream; as soon as I said it, I realized it was him. When he came over yesterday he was wearing wool pinstripe pants; I noticed them because I like them and noted in my head that he looks good and he probably is going to meet Margaret afterward.

[Jack extricates himself from his promise to MO of being with her through June. We spend two weekends together. Very unsure of myself around him, I am nevertheless happy; he seems loving. On May 17, he tells me the marriage is permanently over.]

MAY 18

An e-mail to Jack: Josie called and she could hear in my voice that something was wrong. I could not not say anything to her. I told her we were not going to live together and you did not want the marriage. I did say that you loved me and you wanted to figure out a way for us to have some sort of a relationship (probably I would say no to such a thing). I knew she would be very upset for me; what I somehow forgot is that she considers you her second father and she now feels totally abandoned by you. I am not telling you this to make you feel guilty; I am not asking you to do anything about her; I do not think there is anything to be done.

Yes I know you would have preferred if I said nothing to her right now while we think about all of this. I am sorry if I cannot do it as you wish.

She is one of the sad fallouts of all of this.

III. Where He Tells His Wife That He Made a Terrible Mistake

[The weeks after May 17 are ones of such pain and anxiety that I can hardly stand up; I am not eating nor sleeping. I finally see a psychiatrist and get a prescription for anti-anxiety pills. Somehow I manage to do a number of radio interviews and public presentations for my book and conduct graduation for the students in my program. Dazed, nonetheless I begin to gather our financial documents together and gather names of mediators and divorce lawyers. Even still I cannot believe what I have refused to believe all along (and what so many people said I should have faced from the beginning): that he is leaving me for a twenty-five-year-old, that he was abandoning what I had believed was a rich and vital intellectual and emotional partnership. I had held to the mantra that he meant what he said when he left on January 20 and that this was a temporary blip in what would be a long and loving companionship.

When I do talk or write to Jack, seldom now, I express amazement at this turn of events. He keeps reiterating that the marriage is dead for him, although he holds out the desire for some continued contact.]

JUNE 13

E-mail from Jack: You know—it was not a matter of keeping my word. I struggled with that in therapy—I stayed so long because I did not want to be a man who does not "keep his word." Every day until the day I said "it," I intended for us to live out our lives as husband and wife. None of this changes the impact of that day on you, I know, but I did not betray you. Nor did I fail you. I did lose you and our marriage—and I feel that loss. If it could be rebuilt as a marriage I would be happy—and if it gets rebuilt as loving but parallel lives, that, too, is acceptable. But not to have our joint consciousness of a life in some way—that is not to be desired.

[I get comfort from friends and from Josie—asking me to dinner or to sleep over at their house, calling me— but there is no comfort for the emptiness. I begin to face the enormity of the loss. I realize that I will lose this family of twenty-two years, given that the step kids are silent (except for Lynne). I hold tight to Josie and even call my sister, whom I have not spoken to in years. I force myself to think about dating, knowing that it will be near impossible to find an older man who could take Jack's place. I fiddle with an advertisement for myself: I write the basic text but then add and subtract according to what friends think describes me better or is more catchy; I have fun with this editing process but am not comfortable with the ad as my age gets lower and my image gets sexier: "Vibrant, stylish, diminutive college teacher, now an administrator and writer of biographies. Late fifties. Passionate about many things, from injustice to good movies; especially likes to walk the city and read novels. San Franciscan with 2nd house in Big Sur, grown children, a terrific laugh (according to my friends)." Edward feels I have to insert more of a come-on tone. I abandon the project.

[Unexpectedly I meet a man, a few years older than me, whom I had known slightly; we have much in common, including the fact that we are both recently out of long-term marriages. The more we talk, the more I am taken with him—he has a great love of literature and he is very open with his feelings. We begin to go out and soon spend the night together; I am told to go slowly but how do two intense people at our age go slowly? I let him know that I am still very attached to my husband and that I expect the process of letting go to take a long time; in contrast he seems kind of distant from his wife and the act of uncoupling. Often I identify with and think of his wife. We have some wonderful times together and I begin to believe that this could be another round for me — that the loss of Jack is not a death knell.]

JUNE 21

[Addressed to Jack in my journal:] During this weekend, the first weekend Stephen and I have spent together, at one point I wanted to lie on the floor and weep loudly knowing that as nice as it is with him I miss you so deeply and that you have forced me down a road I would not have taken.

[And then sometime toward the beginning of July, Jack begins to communicate with me, by phone and e-mail; he is panicked, saying that he has made a grave mistake and wants the marriage back. He writes: "I am so moved and horrified by what we have done to each other, each in our own blind ways." I hear him but do not trust him emotionally any more. But things begin to change: he sees a therapist and is much more aware of what has been driving him; since June 20, we have been sharing our living spaces (he in the country and me in the city apartment and vice versa since his sublet is up and his next sublet does not begin until September), forcing him to confront the physical presence of our lives together; and, he, with the introduction of Stephen into my life, realizes that he will lose me forever. What is also new is that he has broken his isolation (which was the case from January through May), e-mailing our friends asking for their advice as to what he can do to win me back, admitting his mistake and saying he loves me. The weekend of July 21, while on a trip to Oregon visiting some colleagues of his, he breaks up with Margaret. Pleased but wary, I express anger about his treatment of me and his treatment of her.]

JUNE 29

E-mail to Jack: I just want to go back to us sitting at our tin table [San Francisco] and us at the long wood table [Big Sur] and clever plays on words and wine and bread and talk of people and books and tenderness. . . . I feel like you keep making that unlikely as you flail around between Margaret and myself.

[I go for a week's vacation to London with Miriam, who wanted me to have a break from all of this; I am grateful for her thoughtfulness. Jack calls and e-mails every day: "I am glad you are coming home. I have read some of our correspondence and I see your love and patience and courage and grace in pain and I wonder if I can match it over the next few months while I take over the role you had to assume at my insistence. (He is referring to being alone while I will continue to see Stephen.) I can do the love part but I have little respect for the rest of my abilities. But I've got it coming. This has been a lonely but productive few days for me, waiting for you. I'll be glad to see your face at the terminal. I love you. J"

[On July 27, I return, expecting to tiptoe into a relationship with Jack (that is, talk with and date Jack while further getting to know Stephen). But I cannot do such a juggling act nor is Stephen interested in such an arrangement, so I tearfully say goodbye to Stephen; and, with fear and hope, Jack and I begin the mending: "In Chapter Four you break up but you give [him] just one more chance."]

SEPTEMBER 1, 2003

The story does not end with Chapter Four. On August 23, Jack has a semi-breakdown and tearfully tells me he just cannot stay in the marriage, that coming back was a mistake. He leaves, returns to Margaret. There are no other chances. End of story.

Well, sometimes there are second acts and fifth chapters. In February 2004, a year and a half after the beginning of this journal, we started seriously talking (although we had started divorce proceedings) to each other; by June we moved in together, and now after almost a year, we have a solid and loving (and more respectful) relationship—not without scars and not without hurting some innocent people in the process.

Works Cited

Bartky, Sandra. "Unplanned Obsolescence: Some Reflections on Aging." In *Mother Time: Women, Aging, and Ethics*, ed. Margaret Urban Walker. Lanham, Md.: Rowman and Littlefield, 1999, 61–74.

Condé, Maryse. *Winward Heights*. New York: Soho Press, 2000.

Cushnir, Raphael. "Two Questions That Could Change Your Life." *O: The Oprah Magazine*, November 2002, 113.

Drabble, Margaret. *The Seven Sisters*. New York: Harcourt, 2002.

Gallop, Jane. *Feminist Accused of Sexual Harassment*. Durham, N.C.: Duke University Press, 1997.

Raffel, Lee, and Jean Houston. *Should I Stay or Go?: How Controlled Separation (CS) Can Save Your Marriage*. New York: McGraw-Hill, 1998.

Roth, Philip. *The Dying Animal*. New York: Vintage International/Random House, 2001/2002.

Swallow, Wendy. *Breaking Apart: A Memoir of Divorce*. New York: Hyperion, 2001.

Growing Up Middle Aged

MARITA LOPEZ-MENA

> Your lover or spouse may leave you without warning after years of trusting companionship. You may recover your crushed sense of worth, not by proving that you are not to blame, but by finding renewal in that dark night.
> — THOMAS MOORE, *Dark Nights of the Soul: A Guide to Finding Your Way Through Life's Ordeals*

I was fifty-four and my husband fifty when he had an affair with a young woman in her twenties and left our marriage, declaring that he no longer loved me "that way." And, incidentally, I was too fat, too bossy, and *difficult*. All true. He forgot to remember, however, that I was also honest, loyal, and steadfast during the times when he needed me to be that. During a year of massive dissembling, struggling to believe his every denial about having a girlfriend, eventually even I could not deny what my heart already knew. When his lying, cheating self was finally confronted with the evidence of betrayal, I had an atomic meltdown and pitched him into the morning light to confront his very own dawn. I remember him saying, "How like you to respond with anger." I thought, "How like you to be clearly in the wrong and somehow I am deficient." I felt fully entitled to being good and damn angry and went with that. And, just so you will not mistake me for a brave and heroic female, I subsequently blubbered and begged him to come back for a very long while. Alas, I noticed he clicked his heels together as he skidded down the driveway and out of sight.

Any teenager knows how rotten it feels to have your heart broken after a few weeks or months of surrendering to the overwhelming vulnerability of love. Multiply that by decades—leaf piles of memories, spooning the cold winter nights away, raising children and witnessing the births of grandchildren, and finally the satisfaction of newlywed poverty that eases into almost financial comfort. There is a terrible jolt when waking into an empty house after years of having a husband, children and their friends, and dogs and cats littering the rooms. Dreams worked toward so hard evaporated like the morning fog over the river outside my kitchen window. One day, and it happens in one day, one hour, one minute, one heart-stopping second . . . it all goes away, just like life itself. The rooms contract with a deepening silence. The last child has left for college. The ailing mothers and fathers have all recently died in a cluster of loss and pain. The older children are married or have moved away. And your beloved, the sun god, has packed up his new wardrobe and running shoes. He is giddily on the way to a "new life" while justifying his abandonment by alluding to your more negative qualities—a tendency to point out his faults, a certain rigidity during arguments, a desire to be right more of the time than not, and a wicked case of PMS during the fertility years. I cannot dispute his claims, but as in any good divorce, I have a few of my own. Yeah, I was angry.

After anger comes sensational rage. A perfectly normal, peaceable woman told me about an incident that occurred on a sunny afternoon when her philandering ex-husband returned home to pick up his fishing rods after leaving her for a younger woman. Yep, he had caught himself a nice, sleek new trout, my friend thought. She was outdoors working on the farm, repairing a fence, when he arrived. He was sitting outside in his car, probably trying to gather up his pitiful courage. After she had finished hammering another nail into the post, she stood to get a better look at him. Without a thought she threw the hammer—hand-rage coordination, I call it. The weapon left her grip easily and after it sailed over the broken fence it glided right on through the open car window, clipping him a good one. She walked closer and leaned down to peer in at him and saw a trickle of blood on the face of her torturer. She grinned. The tiny rivulet was inching toward his chin while he cursed and slammed the car into a forward gear, loudly gaining traction. She remembers no feelings of gratitude for not killing him, of being spared the trial and the gurney and the heart-stopping injection, but only relief that her children had not been there to witness her frenzy of hatred and violence. Rage is a natural outcome of humiliation, betrayal, and hurt. Unlike anger, it cannot be "managed."

I have often found myself thinking about *him*, the sun god (SG), cheerfully letting loose his warm rays upon decades of women from their twenties to their forties, where he finally settled unsuccessfully for a while. I fantasized many atrocities, as well, with my favorite being the pure joy of running over his body repeatedly while the corpse flopped around on the road. He was so dead he couldn't even raise one finger to beg for mercy. And then, before I bloodied up my nice sports car any more, I would transport myself to the funeral. After a lot of maybe this, maybe that, I would finally settle on a Jackie Kennedy look—an elegant, simple A-line dress with three-quarter sleeves that covered the flabby upper arms. I was dignified, dabbing an occasional tear from glittering, slitted eyes underneath the black, embroidered veil. This fantasy would continue through the prayers and the eulogy only to lurch back into a rage-filled frenzy as I threw myself at his coffin in the privacy of the hearse, banging on the lid, screaming, "I hate your stinking guts."

We had been married for twenty-three years, and he had adopted my two children from an earlier youthful, short-lived foray into wedded hell with the maniac boy next door who almost resembled James Dean. After two years of living together to make sure this one wasn't a closet crazy also we married, and then three years later had a child—the tiny sun goddess. We were very much in love, and young, but we also had lives that put huge stresses on our relationship. As a mother of two by the age of twenty-one I felt much more mature than he when we got together. I was serious and anxious about life and my responsibilities (James Dean wasn't paying child support), and tended to get overwhelmed at times by the weight of it all. Because we were both college dropouts in the sixties, making a living was not easy. I had a job and also struggled through a two-year nursing degree program while he built the first of three promising, but ultimately failed, businesses. Psychiatric nursing, where I settled professionally, while fascinating and perfect for the woman who to this day wears a Wonder Woman cuff bracelet on her arm, was not the best career choice during pregnancy. So, when the happy event came along, a temporary leave from working on the locked ward seemed prudent. The decision came when I strolled through the key-coded door onto the psych unit one day and was taken aside by my nursing supervisor. There had been an "incident" that morning. One of the paranoid patients had been found with a hypodermic needle in his possession. When asked what he planned to do with that big, fat baby, he replied calmly that he planned to plunge it through my heart when next I came in to work.

The SG knew I was bored at home post childbirth and suggested I volunteer at an upstart little museum that he was already involved with. He was working as a boat designer and builder in the young museum's industrial building where he set up an amalgamation boat-shop-business-cum-living-history-exhibit. The museum was still in a formative stage and in a short time I became its first executive director, launching an unexpected career. It was exhausting work but we were having fun, and the baby was passed back and forth between office and boat shop to spend time with whichever parent was available. Our little family of two budding teens, a baby, an Airedale terrier, and a Siamese cat were smashed together in a romantic, way-too-small home overlooking the river. The view was lovely and suited our nautical lifestyle, but allowed us no matrimonial privacy. The place was constantly in need of repair and expansion, and each spring we lived in some hellish construction site. There was never enough money no matter how hard we worked. My salary, however ridiculous at first, was reliable, and his income, while greater, fluctuated wildly depending on how well the business was going.

I can safely say that we still loved each other madly at the ten-year mark. I remember sitting with him on the end of a dock overlooking a lake as the sun set on that anniversary. He raised a glass of champagne, as the evening bat patrol swooped overhead, and toasted me saying that I was the best thing that had ever happened to him. He paused for a fond smile, and then said with a cracking voice that he would do it all over again in a minute. That was probably the very minute that bonded me to him forever. He was sincere and eloquent and I knew that he was surely the love of my life. Whatever difficulties came our way we would cope . . . somehow.

He left thirteen years later after a year of leaving and then returning and leaving and returning—the terrifying roller coaster of fear and indecision. I was in shock, but the minute the shock started to wear off, the crying began. I cried and cried. I could not stop crying. Water seeped and bubbled from some broken faucet behind my eye sockets. I cried so much that the tears didn't even taste salty after a while. They came in huge downpours, soaking the bed, the pillows, making the floors slippery I imagined. My eyes puffed up awfully. When I looked in the mirror I did not recognize the ugly frog staring back from the heretofore magic glass. Every time a friend called, I would start weeping anew as I related the horror of it all. Young girl. Sob. She sails. Plays basketball. Sob. Skinny, she is. Sobbbbb. Hiccupping. Vomiting, dry heaves— sounds just like withdrawal, which it is.

Sleeplessness sets in after these exertions. For eighteen months I lay in my bed, alternately crying or folding myself into or out of the fetal position. When the crying and sleeplessness just would not cease, I took myself off to a psychiatrist for an antidepressant and some counseling. The pill that all of America has discovered helped control the fits of weeping and allowed me to work. It also kept me from spending all my time when there in the bathroom sobbing or e-mailing friends with news of the latest revelation or outrage—"He was seen in the Grand Union standing by the eggplants, and he was holding hands with this scrawny waif. She had purple hair and an eyebrow ring."

I thought a lot about the years after we toasted each other on the end of the dock. We continued on our hard path, with successes and failures for both of us. I enrolled in night school and five years later got a bachelor's degree in literature while working full time. During that period I developed endometriosis, which was undiagnosed for three years, and then deteriorated into intractable pain for two more until I finally submitted to a hysterectomy and what I feared would be the end of my femininity. I was ragged from the pain, and he had grown very weary from holidays spent with me crouched on the couch while he tried to help get the big meals to the table and maintain some cheer. Also trying was rubbing my back faithfully during the long nights of stabbing pain. He said he never slept soundly anyway anticipating a sudden scream from the nightmares I suffered. I was definitely a burden, and yes, I was edgy. But, contributing to the edginess may have been the loss of two businesses, the over-a-million-dollar lawsuit that hauled him into court for trial while I quaked and fretted, trying to be supportive. I remember walking down the driveway one day during that interval, mail in hand, and opening a letter from the IRS. It informed us that our house had a lien on it. I stood suddenly rooted to the spot in a mixture of rage, because he had told me only the day before that there were no problems, and terror . . . that we would lose our home.

Despite the demands of his business he managed to get in some sailing trips when delivering boats, and spent the better part of two summers in a catamaran racing series he organized that ran up and down the East Coast. I was envious when he went on a four-day jaunt to France to a catamaran race, but mollified when he came home smelling like salty water with a hinged, beautiful mother-of-pearl hollow egg from the second Napoleonic era in his hand for me. But the sad loss of the last business propelled me into a higher paying job and he went to work for the reincarnation of his old boat-building company, which was not easy for him.

He had always been a carefree and adventurous guy, coming from a slightly privileged background, and even he admitted that fiscal responsibility was not his strong suit. In the early years our marriage and family grounded him, I believe, and certainly he brought fun and excitement into my life. There was a good balance. However, as the decades of raising children and running in place reeled by, doubtless he began to feel that I dragged him down, and I began to feel that he endangered my security—a precarious change in the balance. The teenagers were off to college but came home on and off as kids do, and the little one was in private day school—thank heaven for a generous grandmother. One day he quit his job, without any prior discussion with me, and announced that he was going to make a career change. He also informed me that he had enrolled in college that very day and would be going after his bachelor's degree.

For the next five years he went to school full time and then wrote a book while I worked, which made me resentful. I desperately needed creative time also and it was always just out of reach. He exercised and got buff and flatly refused to cut back on what he termed his minimal lifestyle requirements. When he hired a cleaning woman so that he had plenty of time to study and take long walks, I felt very pissy indeed. After all, I had gone to school nights for five years while working full-time—and did most of the house cleaning also. I began to view him as a rather spoiled fellow and myself as a drone. I suspect that he believed that all the years he had slaved away in business and worked on the house had kept him from having any kind of life, and he felt like a drone too.

He finished the undergraduate degree and we enjoyed the book-signing parties. Finally he got a new job, and then decided, correctly, that he needed a master's degree. By then I had an even more high-powered position, making more money than he did. I was now able to pay all of our bills combined. I started feeling independent. In some ways this was beneficial as I felt more secure, but in others it was not as he felt less the provider. Our culture may pay lip service to how it is all right for wives to earn more than husbands, but men seem to have a need for the biological big-guy role even if it is buried somewhere deep in the reptilian part of their brains.

The other outcome of my fatter paycheck and diminished fears about money was that I began asserting myself more. I wanted him to be financially responsible and initiated more confrontations on this, his least favorite of subjects. Rather than examine himself in any depth or mend his ways, he felt attacked by what had admittedly become my open hostility. I recall quite a number of monthly sessions with me waving copies of the credit card bills and getting angry when I found five more books and twenty CDs charged. We all cope in different ways when attacked, and he went underground. He defied my anger and entreaties by quietly going off to do whatever he felt was reasonable with his money and his credit cards. When I smelled the silent threat of his anger, my confidence would shrivel and I would back down. I was starting to dislike myself.

Once he left me that underlying lack-of-confidence problem came roaring right around the corner to knock me down. I wondered if I had dreamed the whole experience of love. How long had I been in love with him and he not with me? Moreover, if I did not see what was going on with the person sleeping next to me in bed, what else in my life was inauthentic? Did my friends find me as unbearable as he obviously had? My co-workers? As my self-esteem took a nosedive in tandem with my confidence, I also questioned if I was the decent person I thought I was.

This is where being in therapy is very helpful. We went over my history and examined my response to early traumas and how patterns developed then informed my daily life as an adult. We sorted out what was a useful response and where I was just battling the shadows. The experience in therapy helped me to remember the intelligent, capable, daring, fun, and outrageous person I used to believe was me. I thought it would have been generous of my husband to balance these good qualities against also being your average garden-variety shrew of a wife. Good therapy is a tricky juggling act. The therapist had to help me sneak up on my outdated defenses in order to expose them. Simultaneously, the infrastructure of what was terrific about me had to be supported as a new incarnation of myself developed and emerged. Therapy was reassuring, at times enlightening, difficult as hell, and helped me to balance many conflicting emotions while focusing on the only person I could change—myself.

Outside of therapy and medication I sought the comfort of my friends. During the course of a breakup that is not mutually agreed upon, I have noticed, the tongues on the most stoic and well-mannered of us get loosened, and I was neither. I not only wore out my friends, but even found myself discussing the pain of divorce with a hired driver when we were careening across the desert in California to visit Taliesen West. Fifteen years earlier the poor guy had caught his wife cheating and threw her out. He was still so overcome thinking about it that even so many years later he had to pull over the big car and sit by the side of the road to cry. He said that he had never told anyone about it before. I had to hop from the back to the front seat to put an arm around his shoulder and give comfort. Here's a tip—it's better when wearing a skirt to open the door and go around. I have also shared divorce tragedies with massage therapists as we blubbered in unison, old women in nursing homes, sales clerks—strangers I would never see again. There are some other-than-emotional benefits to sharing betrayal tales with your own sex. I got an ultra-generous insurance payment after a hurricane blew down a lot of trees on my property. We bonded when the adjuster told me she had caught her husband cheating by reading his e-mails. After a while I got worn out by all this drama, but given that seemingly half of Americans can expect a divorce, one is guaranteed to find (or give) a sympathetic ear at some point.

Of course everyone you know wants you to be over with the whole mess and "get on with your life." That is what I thought I was doing. It is not as though the most important relationship in your life ends and you simply sniffle and whine a little, and, like Scarlett, declare, "Tomarrah is anutha day." The last time someone said the thing about getting on with it, I hissed, "What the hell do you think I am doing?" After that, the word was out, and the new, safer mantra was "It's not about you, it is about him. He left you because he was really (you can fill in the blank here) immature or selfish or confused or narcissistic, et cetera." My self-loathing and grief made some people uncomfortable, but I knew that my friends loved me and would see me through until I could lasso my galloping tongue. We must heal ourselves in the manner and amount of time it takes.

I can only wish that my husband had been talking more about what was on his mind during the marriage, but he was a quiet kind of guy. His father became ill and increasingly dependent on him, and on me to a lesser degree. Then my favorite aunt had a recurrence of cancer and became terminally ill. When two years of driving three hours to attend to her needs a weekend or two a month escalated to every weekend, we had to make some choices. At the same time his aged cousin, for whom he was the closest relative, developed Alzheimer's, and my mother who also lived three hours away needed more and more assistance. We were surrounded by illness and death. His father died, we built an addition on our home and moved my aunt in only to die eleven months later, his cousin died, and my mother developed uterine cancer and came to live with us for a while. And, my best friend was dying of breast cancer.

He became tired of reassuring me that everything someday would turn out right if only I could hang in there and not be depressed. I no longer believed anything would ever be better. I wanted to pick the fleas off our relationship, and he wanted to stay away from being blamed and brought to task. Why did we not see what was coming? He was in graduate school getting adoring eyes from a very young woman. She was slim where I had grown plump. She was young and energetic, whereas I was middle aged and pooped. I had become "corporate" and she was fresh and idealistic. She admired him—an older man, intelligent and adventurous. I was temporarily out of admiration. He began to retreat from me. On our twentieth wedding anniversary, over dinner in a crowded restaurant he announced that he no longer felt "the same" and that he already had "one foot out the door." He swore there was no one else. I simply went into shock and denial. Despite all that we had been through I firmly believed in our love and his loyalty.

As he backed away, I became increasingly anxious. He finally left me. He returned in ten days. He left again after a couple of months. We spent many months in couples therapy while separated. He still vehemently denied having another relationship. I wanted to believe him. He returned again promising that the storm had passed, that he would never leave me again, and even produced a real engagement ring. I was wary, devastated, and exhausted. Each time when he came back I hoped it was because he loved me still—that there was something left in the marriage to sustain him and to sustain us. In the six years that he has now been gone I have had lots of time to think not only about why men have affairs with younger women and leave, but also why they return, even if only briefly. I believe that he loved me in a habitual way, and probably felt very badly about leaving. No one wants to risk their children's wrath and disappointment. But he also could not stay. He could not confront the growing problems he had, much less the ones we had as a couple, unless he intended to make some serious changes in himself. He was having an internal crisis, of which the young girlfriend was only a sad manifestation. She, poor thing, served a purpose of which she was completely unaware. She boosted his ego and was also the fulcrum upon which he could pry himself from a marriage he could not deal with.

I have come to believe that marriages fall apart for complex reasons, never for this or that reason, or something someone did or did not do. It happens because there is a convergence of inner conflicts and outer pressures that seemingly cannot be resolved without an explosion or implosion. Feelings of pent-up anger and resentment toward the partner, unresolved conflicts with parents that suddenly loom large when the parent dies, fears of growing old and dying all play a part. He probably kept wending his way home like a lost dog because he could not himself believe what he was doing. He was also afraid. Afraid of being outside his family, afraid of the anger and disapproval of friends and children, afraid of being out in the world alone after twenty-three years; all this would bring him to heel. He may even have been afraid of never again being in the home he loved, despite the fact that he hated pounding nails as he witnessed life slipping through his fingers. He was wise to be afraid because all that he feared would come true.

I have often wondered what I might have done differently when I found out about the cheating. A friend took another tack than mine altogether when her husband was threatening to leave her for their dental hygienist (how could a dental pro even want a man twenty-five years older who was suffering from gingivitis?). She got as calm as the eye of a hurricane. Against anything that a therapist would condone, she called in their twin teenaged daughters and told them what was going on. I can hear the psychologists and family counselors gasping at this bold triangulation involving "the children." Then she asked that they meet as a family to discuss openly how they felt about what he was doing, and what life was going to be like if he chose this foolhardy path in a house full of women.

During this time she lost twenty pounds, had her eyebrows shaped, got a new wardrobe and basically blew the doors off her rival even if the latter was wearing a white nurse's uniform. And, incidentally, she spent a lot of time convincing her husband that they needed to work together to keep the marriage intact despite this periodontal escapade. She was hurt and it showed, but she refrained from death threats and assaults on his character. They became partners again in defeating something that could destroy their family. It must be noted that she also made sure he was never out of her sight for long, at least until the worst of her anxiety had passed. She persevered, and eventually he felt it was a case of temporary insanity that had caused the depraved behavior. Maybe it was the midlife male brain awash one last time in a sea of testosterone. They are still married many years later, their children have forgiven him, and one more family has avoided the statistical horror of divorce in America.

Eventually, after three years of therapy, I was able to acknowledge that although my personality might not be to every man's taste, it was not all that scary either. And, I was not the cause of the marriage ending. Nor was he. We undid it together and just did not see it coming unraveled. Once that was clearer, my confidence began to return. Instead of agonizing over why he left, I could address the more relevant questions that were crawling out of the old mind swamp in my head. What does it mean to be a mature woman? What will life bring me now? Am I still attractive and interesting enough for someone wonderful to desire again? How do I furnish a home that reflects *me*, not *us*? Everything becomes a choice, particularly those that reflect image. For instance, my daughters insisted that I stop wearing old, formless clothes made of that nasty flax material. The sun goddess, index finger on chin, said "Mumsy, if you think those big shirts cover the fat . . . they don't. They just make it worse. Accept that you are voluptuous until you can fit into smaller clothes." How did she get so smart so young?

I was excited about looking good again as the divorce diet did its magic. This woman was sick of black—she wanted color, form fitting, and a little glam. I also decided to do what so many others have done before me. I made the pilgrimage to the plastic surgeon. Convinced that the sorrow I felt had been writ permanently on my face, I resented the idea of being "marked" that way. After the coward's version of the mini-lift, I don't think there was any big change, which is the way it is supposed to go anyhow. People are supposed to lilt, "My, my, you must have just returned from a wonderful vacation—you look so rested." I kept insisting to the lawsuit-wary surgeon that I only wanted an itty, bitty snipping to help lift my sagging neck and that is what I got. I was not about to hit the dance floor doing the turkey wattle. I was thinking more about tango. The psychological lift I got when friends who learned about the surgery declared there had been an amazing transformation was worth the terror of going under the knife.

A short-lived relationship with a tall, dark, handsome, charming, and intelligent European man fortunately came along during this period. Definitely worth the nips and tucks. I may have been mourning, but I was not resigning myself to any funeral pyres either and so I decided to enjoy the experience. After the initial rush of romance, things degenerated into the usual monotony of desultory dinners, working, and discovering each other's flaws. And we weren't even living together. I was aghast when he told me in a moment of unwelcome candor how opinionated and bossy he found me. Sputter, sputter. *Moi?* Well, yes, now I had to recognize that he was the second male sharing this bad news with me. After the usual defensive postures—a predictable going after him about *his* faults—I decided it might be better to focus on me and mine.

The relationship was not to be for many reasons, but it was, as they say, validating to see my new self in action—slightly more evolved and eyes wide open. When it was over I moped around for a couple of days, shed a crocodile tear or two, and then congratulated myself for sticking to new attitudes and behaviors. Subsequently, I dated another man for a more extended period but it didn't feel right. I surprised myself by not trying to cover it all with papier-mâché and gold paint and declare it a beautiful thing. I fired his butt.

Dating also helps one regain a sense of humor. If I did not laugh at what incredible messes I could get myself involved in as a middle-aged adolescent, I would have been very upset. After hearing lots of urban legends about great husbands snared through a skinny cable on your laptop, I entered the enticing world of online love. Internet dating is a whole book in itself and not for the faint of heart. Filling out those awful forms about yourself and checking off those terrible, little boxes that reveal what you are looking for in another person, however, is valuable even if you never post the information on a Web site. In the course of a few months I met a very nice man online. However, he expressed serious concerns that I had resorted to antidepressants when my marriage broke up. I guess he was into stoics. So I fired him too. Then there was some other woman's maniac ex-husband who revealed his psychotic self in a down-home bar one night. I excused myself mid-tirade and took a powder through a large screened window in the ladies room. Cleverly, I had parked my little car nearby in the parking lot making for a fast getaway. Sprinting across the gravel in my girl shoes I thought about how I had always, foolishly, sworn I would never wear Birkenstocks. I met his ex-wife at a party one night a few months later and she told me that I was lucky to escape unharmed. She had a restraining order. Then there was the guy who showed up in a cape and I think you can figure out he was not Batman. And we must not forget the fellow who took me on a boat cruise around Manhattan, going below decks for a couple of big beers before delving into his briefcase for a handy bottle of gin. These are the times when you start rethinking why you got all upset with your husband for having an affair with a young woman. Hey, maybe you should have let the midlife hurricane blow over and been more conciliatory. Most intriguing to me are the women who simply ignore their husband's affairs. They look the other way, often over and over, while the man becomes increasingly desperate to drive his wife into throwing him out. The escalating and outrageous behaviors involve shoving the girlfriend right into her face, and sometimes even into her home. It is like "Mommy, mommy . . . look at me. Look at how bad I can be. Don't you want to stop me? Or punish me?" Sometimes these men just age out and their wives plod onward.

The big, underlying fear driving all my dating activity was growing old alone. Our upbringing, culture, and biology insist upon finding and keeping a mate. We go from the protection of family life into solo young adulthood. While there is excitement about exploring the world at that time, there is also a huge fear of being unattached to anything or anyone. As adults we recoil from the memory of sitting home hovering by the phone on Saturday nights or the agony of waiting on the gym floor for some doofy guy to ask for a dance. Facing this again in middle age is nothing anyone wants to do. But, if forced, it can be exciting again in some twisted way. I used to hate hearing women in my position saying that after a few years of being alone they realized they would never want to be married again. They claimed to like being on their own, eating solitary low-cal dinners, cramming the closets full of clothes and shoes with greedy enthusiasm, taking up the whole damn bed themselves or sharing it with a smelly dog. I do not think I am cut out for a single life as I enjoy sharing the bed and eating chocolate bars with a mate. But I will admit that it gets easier and easier to come and go as I wish, spend however much I like, and make no accommodation to another person's schedule or weird ideas.

It is still not clear how much I trust myself to become involved with a new mate, even if there is one out there interested in a somewhat reformed, aging neurotic. I have renewed questions about what love is, and whether it even exists in the form I once believed in. Before I was dropped into this black hole in space, I thought I knew all about love. Love was a feeling. An emotion. It came upon you like a fever with a cold. It was not a choice made. It just was. It was magic. It was unconditional. Soul mates. Once conjured up, it stayed forever. Clearly, I should not have been walking the streets alone. All I have left is a rock solid belief that there is a chemical attraction between people . . . love at first smell . . . the biology business.

Lots of new research leans in the direction of love being an addiction. The same pathways of the brain are activated in love by the *amor* chemicals as by heroin, according to this theory. I admit that I read this in a fashion magazine while lolling about one night, with the poodle curled up on the rug next to the bed where he belongs. When the source of love is removed, accompanied by the misery of betrayal, we supposedly suffer the withdrawal not only emotionally, but also physically in the same way an addict does. Our dutiful brain gets imprinted with the trauma, and each time we see or think about the no-good creep who betrayed us we feel the original pain. This is why it sometimes takes years to "get over" someone. The pain that I had in the area surrounding my heart for so long was real. Yes, it was. It is always reassuring to learn that what was considered surefire insanity or lack of strength is only brain damage.

Middle-aged women can still seek love that has room for chemical attraction, but also something more sustaining for the remainder of our lives. In other words, yeah, it's still possible to enjoy sex if we don't mind slathering on the Astroglide and wrecking the sheets. However, we should think a little more clearly as we are making choices in the mate department, and those choices are not altogether about the other person. What a pleasure to think it really may have more to do with ourselves. We can ask, secure that we will find an answer to the question, why we are choosing this person right now? Do I have a need that feels very familiar, but might better be met in some other way? If I am only attracted to big, strong bearish men maybe the real issue is a need for feeling protected. This may sound harsh, but a new alarm system and a well-trained dog could be an acceptable solution. I don't have to marry Godzilla. If only adventuresome guys appeal, maybe it is time to strap on those tango shoes and go have some adventures of my own. And, as our therapists, those secular purveyors of the new religion, are wont to tell us—if the love we feel seems very familiar, maybe it is because we have been here before. We do tend to repeat patterns in our lives with ritualistic frequency. What we may mistake for love, however, may be only the unfortunate revisiting of a not-so-good relationship with one or both of our parents. Just because it feels familiar does not make it beneficial. Eventually, the other person in this scenario may also begin to wonder what co-dependent hell he has just stumbled into.

Another apparent fallacy I used to believe is that love during a long marriage becomes unconditional. It does not matter if you feel love for your partner every minute of the day. Love is a deep well that occasionally gets dangerously low for a spell, but always tops up again. I had not heard of the "love bank" theory at that point. Yes, another shallow fashion magazine article. Some people believe that in a marriage there is a given amount of love banked, and that if you withdraw more than you deposit, it goes bankrupt and there is no Chapter 11. Love dies. That truly had never occurred to me. I thought that love depended on the strength of connectedness—time spent together, good sex, vicious arguments, children conceived, and all the other family ties that strangle. I also thought that love was protected over the long years of marriage by the strength of each partner's character. I believed that what I would never do to him (abandon or betray), he would never do to me—a sort of reverse Golden Rule. I thought these promises were codified in the marriage vows, certainly not subject to renegotiation. But, as my husband said, "things change," and indeed they do.

The Benedictine order of nuns, for whom I once worked and whom I admire a good deal, has as one of their tenets that change is inherently good. I do not believe that there is anything good about being fired by a spouse or lover. It is a terrible experience not even to be wished upon your ex-husband. Death yes, dismissed no. However, while you have no control over what another person does or feels or believes, you do have control over what you make of your personal mess. I decided, after sanity had reasserted itself, that whether I wanted change or not, it was here. I had fought and screamed and wept and bargained, and the universe simply refused to let me have my way. One person can tolerate only so much suffering, and a blessed weariness sets in. In that time of exhaustion comes surrender. And, all the obsessive mulling and picking over the past and poking at one's self eventually begins to yield some answers. Forget that you ever will understand fully what the hell happened. But you can explore and find answers to other questions. Who am I? What do I believe in? What do I want out of the life that remains to me? As those answers begin to be revealed, life starts to happen again.

This is the damnable "getting on with your life" that my earnest friends kept talking about. An old Scorpio pal who is usually right said, "Once you really discover yourself after a marital trauma or break you never give it all away

again. You always reserve a place deep inside where no one gets to go but you."
There will always be pain from the death of a marriage, being left by the side
of the road like a dead horse, but change really can be good. Renewal does
come out of the dark nights of our soul. Mature love, if we are fortunate
enough to find it again, seems to demand, well, maturity. Oh no. Oh yes.
Responsible choices. Grown-up behavior. What will I bring to this person's
life, not just what will they bring to mine. I choose to still love my old husband
in some way, if only a little, because ceasing to do so would diminish me in
some way. We are each the betrayer and the betrayed in any life that progresses
beyond the age of five. It would have been a miraculous event if he could have
joined me in the adventure of refashioning a badly tattered union, but he
chose not to. In this world there are the people who toss out the broken lawn-
mowers and the people who read about small engine repair and fix the damn
things. Had I only acknowledged this basic difference in temperament early in
the relationship I might have spared myself a lot of heartache. But then there
would have been no long, delicious marriage filled with twinkle light
Christmas eves, babies that morphed into teenagers overnight, Saturday morning furtive sex when the kids were still sleeping, and all else wonderful and terrible that goes with the futile attempt to mesh souls with another human
being. Occasionally I feel a small twinge that he may be missing what a terrific
woman I have become with his unwitting help, but grownups must deal with
what is, not with what one wishes might have been.

Reflections on April Fool's Day

DIANE RAYMOND

B eing dumped is, by definition, one-sided and abrupt. So my story will not be any different from those of the hundreds of others who have had such experiences. I wish I could tell the reader that my story has a happy ending. Or at least that I might impart some edifying messages to those in these same straits or to help others avoid my fate. Though I might wish for this, an upbeat ending with useful tips on how to weather such an experience is not forthcoming here. Personal narratives, unlike the narratives of fiction, do not lend themselves to tidy closure. Any lessons we glean from our experiences are fictions we create to push us on, to give us a reason to get dressed in the morning, to convince ourselves of some ultimate purpose. To trick ourselves into meaning. I'm too much the child of postmodernism to fall for such consolation. I am without consolation. I do push on and I do get dressed in the morning. But I never stop wondering why and I never doubt that my life would have been better had none of this happened.

Since my relationship ended, I've heard hundreds of stories from other victims: from the women whose husbands left them for secretaries or students; from the colleague whose husband left a note on the kitchen table the day she arrived home from the hospital to recover from her mastectomy; from the friend whose partner moved in with her lover before she'd even told her. I can testify as well to having heard almost every possible variant on every possible cliché: that some day I'll look back and see why all this happened, that time heals all, that I'm better off alone, that everyone bounces back, that something better is on the horizon. Generally I nod passively in the face of such attempts to reassure. I know many people do move on, but I wonder at what cost. I recognize that, with the passage of time, the pain subsides; but the numbness that replaces the despair is a constant reminder of how empty my life is. Someone even told me to stop using the term *dumped* to describe my experience; it's a way you've embraced victimhood, she told me. Yet I *was* dumped; to call it anything else seems disrespectful of my experience.

It happened on April 1, 2002. April Fool's Day. No joke. Whether or not she deliberately chose that day, I'll never know. We were driving to our condo on Cape Cod, and she turned to me and said, "I have something to tell you and there are cigarettes for you in the glove compartment." I'd been a social smoker who had an occasional cigarette with a drink or when extremely depressed. So I knew this was bad. My mind raced to sort out what news might be forthcoming. I thought perhaps she'd decided to move temporarily to Florida to take care of her parents who had just had surgery. I thought that she had decided to leave teaching. I started to spiral. But of all the possibilities that ran through my mind, the thought that she'd fallen for someone else never occurred to me. "I have feelings for Michelle," she said to me. "I don't understand how it happened, but we've kissed."

We never made it to the Cape. I cried; she alternated between anger and numbness. She told me they'd "only" kissed. I asked her to ask for my forgiveness, to tell me it was just a stupid mistake, but she refused. She told me she wanted to "pursue these feelings," feelings that were new to her. She told me that they'd gotten close over the last couple of weeks, weeks that I'd been busy at work. She told me that they'd kissed at our Cape house. I couldn't shake the feeling of utter contamination. I wanted and didn't want details. Inane questions bounced around in my head: *Where* in our home? How long was the kiss? Who initiated it? But she would hardly talk with me. She left the house that night—she drove to the Cape and I stayed. I immediately regretted letting her leave and tried all night to reach her by telephone. Busy signal. Six hours of busy. She'd been talking with Michelle the entire time. Yet another betrayal. How could she not know I'd need to reconnect? How could she so quickly choose her over me?

We took a couple of days apart and set up an appointment with a couples therapist. Over the next several weeks her story changed constantly. At one point, she needed to be single. At another, that she'd always love me and always want me in her life. Once she even e-mailed Michelle (at my prodding) to tell her she couldn't see her again and was going to work on the relationship with me. At other times, she wanted to follow through on her feelings for this new woman, wherever that might take her. She stayed with her aunt and was almost never in touch unless I initiated the contact. I assumed that she was in touch with Michelle on a more regular basis.

We'd been together for nearly eight years. Not so long, given stories of women being dumped after thirty or more years of marriage. But I was fifty-two at the time, she thirty-three. I saw the relationship as forever. Only the weekend before, I'd suggested a ten-year commitment ceremony, something I'd resisted before that. Our families were intertwined. On her own, Annie frequently visited my daughter in New York. She was close to both my nieces and only the year before we'd traveled to Ireland with my brother and his family. Her entire family had come up from Florida and stayed with us for weeks when her grandmother died. We bought the condo on the Cape together, though at the time she was a graduate student earning a small teaching assistantship. Only a year or two into the relationship I'd put her name on the home I'd owned for more than fifteen years before we ever met. I'd never done that with anyone; I knew I could trust her. We had matching rings. I'd been married once, many years before, but I'd never felt committed to anyone before Annie. She used to say the same thing about me.

If I were reading this story, I'd think exactly what you're now thinking: it was the age difference. Yet all our friends and family members were as shocked by this as I was. No one ever said to me, "How did you miss this? The signs were all there." Annie was, everyone thought, an old soul. She was the conservative one in our relationship, always trying to get me to save money, to buy in bulk. She loved to buy Christmas presents for the coming year at day-after Christmas sales. She liked to go to bed early—I was a night person, but with her I learned to savor the mornings. She worried about everything; she unplugged all the appliances when we left the house for the day. She installed smoke alarms, bought a fireproof safety box, never let the gas tank in the car get below half full.

Yet it worked, or so I thought. We balanced each other—with her, I became more settled. I felt a passion that endured during our entire relationship, that surprised me about myself. When she entered the room, I felt—how unexpected for someone who loved existentialism and was writing wills at age ten—happy. I felt loved *and* seen. With her, I felt sexy. I felt cared for. I felt that even my worst qualities were loveable. She was also the kindest person I'd ever known. She made sure that we saw my parents on a regular basis. She daily e-mailed my fragile teenage niece; she drove me to work and picked me up. She used to joke that rush hour traffic just "gives us more time to be together."

And I took care of her. I loved to cook, and I treated her to wonderful meals and desserts she loved. I read her work as she struggled through a Ph.D. program in literature. I encouraged her to visit her parents in Florida when she resisted because of the cost. Perhaps it was all an illusion, but it felt equal to me. We learned to read each other's signals, to know when it was time to leave a dinner party. We knew each other's insecurities—for me, my age; for her, her intelligence. We were proud of each other's accomplishments; there was never even a hint of the jealousy and competitiveness I'd felt so often with other women. Instead of obsessing about dying, as I'd done for as long as I could remember, I used to feel content knowing she'd be taken care of if anything happened to me.

Given how the relationship ended, this description cannot be accurate. I struggle to remind myself that the relationship would not have ended if what I believed it to be was real. But even our closest friends remind me how loving she was. "She adored you," they say. "She lit up when you came into a room." A colleague remembers the time she saw Annie videotaping me onstage during our college's commencement ceremony. When she asked Annie what she was doing, she replied: "I'm going to surprise Diane with this at the sixtieth birthday party I'm going to throw her."

What happened? We saw the couples therapist only once; Annie refused to go again. She said she wanted to be single; "liberated" was the term she used. She felt that the therapist was against her and on my side. When the therapist asked Annie, "Why now?" after Annie announced that she'd never been happy in the relationship, Annie said she had no idea, but that perhaps having her Ph.D. and being able to "stand on my own two feet" gave her the foundation to make the decision. Abruptness and shock are part of being left, and my experience was no different. But to go from having someone who called or e-mailed me at work several times a day just to let me know she was missing me to the total emptiness I experienced at the breakup was devastating.

I have never believed, even in my wildest glory days of feminist fervor and sisterly solidarity, that women are more nurturing or less individualistic than men. Perhaps it's the men with whom I've been involved. They've tended to be underachievers—men who would certainly pose no threat to my father (yes, I've been in therapy), but who nonetheless were kind and loving to me. Ultimately, those relationships did not satisfy me; sex had nothing to do with that discontent. Rather, for me, those relationships left me with a form of control that frightened and, finally, bored me. I used to like to put it in the following way: "In relationships with men, I felt *loved* but not seen." I'd never been left by a man, but I take no "credit" for that. I *chose* men who couldn't possibly imagine leaving me.

Women were a whole different story. "Deciding" to join the lesbian sisterhood at age thirty, I jumped in with gusto. I prepared my family before I'd even actually slept with a woman. I joined a women's karate school. I let it be known that I was switching teams and that I was looking for a relationship. I read coming out stories and cut my hair. But my relationships with women had none of those mystical, life-transforming qualities I'd read about in lesbian novels and short stories. They were embattled relationships where nothing ever seemed easy. They involved constant processing, constant attention to hurt feelings; inevitably, someone's feelings were always hurt. I wondered about gender differences and about my own choices. I refused to identify as bisexual; I liked to say that I was heterosexual with men and lesbian with women. But where were those feelings I thought I should be having? I came to think that I couldn't have a healthy, committed relationship. That I didn't know how to love. Until I met Annie and I began to feel that my relationships to that point had been a training ground for this one.

The sheer experience of being left abruptly subjects one to incredible psychic cruelty. So often I've asked myself how I might have done things differently, what I did wrong, how I'll ever trust another person again. In my case, though, the psychic cruelty was matched by Annie's actual behavior. The kind, loving Annie I had known became transformed into a person I didn't know. "I have to be selfish," she informed me, and she more than exceeded her goal. The woman who told me that she'd take care of me in my old age told me that I was "too old to change" when I offered to go to therapy with her. The woman who swore she'd take only her bicycle and her cat if we ever broke up challenged me on every penny and ultimately won a large settlement from me, despite the fact that I'd supported her through graduate school. The woman who insisted she could never be attracted to someone her own age began living with her new girlfriend (only one year older) just two months after the breakup. In an e-mail recounting all the wrongs I had committed, she listed as one of her examples a surprise party I had thrown her five years before. "How could you have been so selfish?" she asked, rhetorically I assume. "The party was about *you* and had nothing to do with me." She told me that she'd been "acting" the entire relationship and that she'd never been happy. I returned home one night after the breakup to discover that my alarm clock was gone; she had taken it, along with all the other clocks in the house. One day she called me at work and demanded to know where was the metal spatula I'd promised her. I hang on to those little moments in the complete absence of any ability to synthesize this experience.

It's difficult not to become all "meta-" here and reflect on what I've written.

I can't be a victim in this; I'm responsible for my choices. I must be painting too positive a picture of my own behavior and too negative a picture of hers. There's got to be a more balanced picture. She changed. She needed something or someone different. She grew up and didn't want the same dynamic. She felt threatened by my success, including a recent and much-debated promotion at work. She didn't have the courage to ask for what she needed. She was guilt-ridden over her infidelity and as a result had to be cruel and ostensibly unambivalent with me.

But she's thriving and I'm not. I hear occasional tidbits of news about her. She bought a house (refusing, wisely, I suppose, to put her new girlfriend's name on the deed); she got a tenure-track position (something we'd hoped for over the years); she travels (something she claimed she hated that I'd always wanted to do); she married. I still fantasize about her calling to tell me she's made a terrible mistake. I still wonder whether I might have done something differently, both during and after the relationship. I wonder whether, if I'd maintained contact with her, she'd have started to remember all the things she loved about me. I still miss her, the relationship, how I felt around her and with her. I tell myself it's not being single that's so hard; it's being without her. I can't/won't date—what's the point? I don't want to start all over, meet new family members, deal with new baggage, explain the differences between Syrian and Assyrian. I don't want to risk the hurt again. I don't know how to trust another person. I know I don't trust myself.

I've stopped seeing my therapist. There's nothing she can say to me that I can't say to myself. I have an untouched bottle of antidepressants in my medicine cabinet; why medicate the pain when I know its source? I am highly functional on the outside and numb on the inside. I have no illusions to keep me going. The future I had happily anticipated is gone. At one point Annie assured me that "one day" I'd see that this breakup was the right thing for both of us. More than three years later I've yet to come to that realization.

It was my mother's reaction that I cherish above all else. She allowed me, for what was probably the first time in our shared lives, to be sad. As a parent myself, I know how difficult that is. After the relationship ended, she reached out to me in ways that let me know she understood. She said at one point, "I see so many little things around the house that remind me of her. I can only imagine how you must feel." How precious that simple statement was to me. That she missed her, too, meant so much. But, more than that, that she did not presume to know how I felt, but that she might begin to imagine. That she did not urge me to move on, did not appropriate my pain as hers, did not tell me about a brighter future, did not berate me for not seeing the end coming.

If I were a stranger reading this, would I despise this pathetic, self-pitying writer? Would I snap, "Enough. The world is going to rack and ruin and you're moaning over a relationship." Would I remind the writer of world chaos, bombed-out Iraqi villages, starving children, the homeless and the maimed? Yes, I know. I'm not proud of these feelings. And there's a part of me that recognizes that I'm choosing to embrace my pain, that I am consciously refusing to move on. Too much Sartre, perhaps.

Is it different to be left by a woman? With men, I've been the one to end the relationships, though the endings were never abrupt (now I wonder whether they seemed abrupt to *him*) and the signs were always there. With women, I've always been the one left. Don't think I haven't wondered about that. I joked about that with Annie (she loved, for example, to hear the story of an ex of mine who'd wake me at five in the morning to tell me that she was sad that I "just wasn't it" for her), believing I had picked differently, wisely this time. When I told my kindly therapist some of the things Annie said and did during the breakup, she said, "There are times when I can't even believe that she's a woman." Please! Did this so-called therapist never go to junior high school? Women are complex and can be cruel in complex ways. They know our secret fears. They don't just cheat. They explain why their infidelity is really *your fault*. They tell you how much happier they are without you; they even tell you *why*. And, even with all that, they are *angry* with you.

I've often puzzled over Annie's anger at me. I've often referred to it through a variety of clichés, including "rubbing salt in the wound." I remember back to an old acquaintance of mind who—like Annie—fell in love with someone else and left her then- partner as abruptly. I recall that at the time I was mystified not by the fact that she could fall in love with someone else—after all, I could be as "romantic" as the next person—but at how furious she was at the woman she was leaving. "Isn't that forgetting who's been left?" I asked her. "Isn't that rubbing salt in the wound?" (I was good at clichés even then.) "No," she replied, confident of her response (she was a therapist, by the way). "I'm angry at Maggie because she's not the person I need to be with." How does one even begin to respond?

Well, here's a perhaps overly intellectualized, overly generalized response. I'll get to the point eventually, but allow me for a moment a theoretical digression. Many academics, all feminists, and some lay people know of the work of psychologist Carol Gilligan. She studied with Harvard psychologist Arthur Kohlberg and was troubled by his stages of moral theory and the research that led to the development of that theory. Partly because the theory itself was a completely linear one—six stages, in a neat hierarchical order, where stage six was the nearly unreachable stage of universality, a stage reserved for the likes of Gandhi, Martin Luther King, Jr., and Socrates (yes, all men, but I'm getting to that). Partly because the stages were mutually exclusive and discrete—once one reached stage four, for example, there was no going back. Stages that seemed to reify and privilege western moral codes—sympathy, for example, falls in lower stages; acting out of a fear of punishment identifies one as a primitive, childlike moral agent. But, most importantly for Gilligan, Kohlberg's stages seemed not to speak to women's moral experience. Indeed, Kohlberg's research seemed to suggest that women never achieved anything past stage three and a half (Kohlberg has since rejected that interpretation, but never mind about that).

Gilligan, in theoretical protest, studied women's moral reasoning and hypothesized that gender "themes" (she was careful, notwithstanding later feminist interpretations of her work, not to make these differences global or essential) emerged in the work she had done with female subjects. These women, she noted, moved between and among types of moral reasoning. They frequently took into account the feelings of others (something the highly evolved, justice-oriented stage six actors of Kohlbergian theory rarely if ever do), and they seemed to focus less on autonomy and rights and universality and more on responsibility. All of this seemed to lead to a notion of morality that Gilligan identified as "a different voice"—the voice of "care."

One aspect of Gilligan's research intrigues me in this context. In one study, she showed men and women pictures and asked them to tell a story about the picture they were observing. The pictures showed people coming together (e.g. two trapeze artists about to connect in midair) or people separating (e.g. two people appearing to part near a park bench). She noted an interesting difference in the male and female subjects: the women told stories of love and romance when shown pictures of connection; they told stories of loss and abandonment, even violence, when faced with pictures suggesting separation. In contrast, the men Gilligan studied recited stories of violence and betrayal when describing the pictures depicting connection; their stories about separation were banal and nonthreatening. She inferred from these results that both women and men share a fear of certain aspects of relationships, but that gender differences result in very different sorts of fears. Men, she hypothesized, fear connection; women, in contrast, fear separation.

I won't belabor the evidence Gilligan cites in defense of this hypothesis or the ordinary experiences that seem to support it ("Mom," my daughter always asks me, "why is it so hard for you to say good-bye and hang up the phone when we talk?"). Suffice it to say, Gilligan (and other feminist psychoanalytic and psychological theorists before her) invokes gender socialization to explain the origins of these differences. Women—in order to become "women"—must identify with their primary caretaker, namely Mom. Such gender identification, Gilligan believes, is part of human development. But men, to become "men," must separate from the Mother—they stay connected at great social and psychological peril to themselves. This gendered dynamic may, then, account for women's and men's different emotional responses to connection *and* disconnection.

I promised I would return to my point, and perhaps by now it's obvious. A woman who leaves another woman violates all of the gender role socialization she has been taught—not only because it's not "nice" but also because she is, on a deep psychic level, rejecting her mother. The anger she feels may be anger at the original mother (who must, after all, inevitably fail us if we are ever to become autonomous, individuated selves), but it may also mask the guilt of leaving the mother. For Annie, who had never really separated from her own mother, that anger had to have been all the more intense. And our age difference, I assume, made those feelings all the more "original" and primal.

Please don't misunderstand: I'm certainly aware of the fact that men get angry during breakups. But my sense is that men who leave relationships are angry over *something*, some situation or event or loss: being denied custody or visitation, being refused access to a home or a savings account, being threatened with reprisals of some sort. And my sense is that men move on easily, often have overlapping relationships, and sever their previous connection when they create a new one. They let go, in other words. I used to think that that ability to let go so easily was a character flaw. I still do. But as much as letting go may be symptomatic of a failure in the male psyche, the egregious nastiness that typifies women's breakups strikes me as a different sort of pathology. I'll leave it to the reader of this collection of narratives to determine whether these hypothetical conclusions resonate in any way at all.

There comes a point after the breakup of a long-term relationship where one must deal with the Dividing of the Property. When one person has clearly moved on and the other has not, the deck is stacked in favor of the less vulnerable party. To put it mildly, I was a mess. Annie wanted things to move quickly and she demonstrated frustration and anger at anything she perceived to be decelerating the process. She consistently refused to respond when I asked for help (for example, about financial information or computer files), but she demanded that I respond to her questions immediately. Friends urged me to seek out a lawyer, and so I did. But my lawyer—an acquaintance from years before—had a counseling background and was more focused on feelings than on things. In retrospect, I should have looked for someone more aggressive. In retrospect, I shouldn't have gone in with my best offer. Let's just say I did everything wrong.

Annie seemed to be operating under three unspoken principles for how to Divide the Property:

First, anything of which we had two, she took one.
Second, anything her parents had given us, she took.
Third, anything I asked for, she refused.

These principles led to some fairly bizarre behavior on both our parts. Because we owned two houses together, we of course had duplicates of many, perhaps most, items. "You have two couches," she screamed at me at one point. At another point, I noticed she had packed up one of the Kitchenaid mixers; both had been gifts to me that I'd received over the years. When I showed some rare spine and refused to let her take one, she became furious. My reasoning was as follows: because her cooking skills were limited, she'd never miss the mixer. On the other hand, I did a lot of cooking and would have had to replace the mixer. But instead of saying that, I stupidly said, "You don't even cook!" And she quite rightly responded, "Logically, that means I shouldn't get *any* kitchen supplies." But I held my ground and won that battle. That may have been my only "victory." And she never let me forget that I had denied her. "Materialist," she called me. To give her her due, she did offer to let me stay in the house while she packed up her stuff. I knew, though, that I'd be incapable of observing her moving out without collapsing in a heap. I also knew that my inevitable behavior including my atypical passivity would only exacerbate her anger toward me. So I stayed away. I still don't know if that was the right decision.

She took things that I had rescued when her parents had planned to donate them to charity or toss them. She took half a bag of potting soil. She took one of two matched bowls my brother and sister-in-law had brought us back from France. She took my favorite sauté pan. She took a popcorn popper that was on its last legs. She took one of the two pillows we'd bought for the couch; I could even imagine that she'd congratulated herself on her restraint in taking the smaller of the two. I admit to my own pettiness as well. We had two beautiful white bath sheets that we'd bought on sale at a pricey boutique in Provincetown. I had no doubt that she'd take one and knew that one unmatched bath sheet would drive me crazy. So I hid both in my car, brought them back and forth to work with me every day until she'd completed her move so that she couldn't take one.

But the one-of-two principle didn't always apply. She took, for example, all of our clocks. I tried to remember if, seven years before, she had brought those clocks into the relationship. Perhaps she had. It amazed me that she could remember such things; had she always had a property tally in her mind? Was she consulting with her new girlfriend to take those items needed to fill in the gaps in their new trousseau? I assumed that the things she did *not* take were those she didn't need and not a result of any compassion toward me.

I asked her for the laptop I'd bought for our shared use. She refused and never gave any explanation. I then asked to borrow the laptop so that I could recover my files. Again, she refused. Finally, I asked her if she'd send me any files I had on the computer. That time she didn't even respond. She packed the printer, all of our files, and even novels that I was in the middle of reading. At times it seemed that her packing was completely calculated and cold-blooded; at other times, it felt like some sort of frenzy where everything in her path was swept up and carted away.

Through it all I continued to doubt the reality of what was happening. I couldn't convince myself of it. I'd dream about her and they'd be dreams of normalcy. I kept thinking it was a mistake, that there would be a moment when she'd realize that she wanted me and our old life back. In one e-mail message to me, she wrote, "You need to treat me fairly financially if there's to be any hope of salvaging our relationship." I obsessed over that statement, thinking that perhaps she only needed a little time apart. I now think it was a horribly manipulative thing to say, given my vulnerability and my desire for her. She e-mailed my parents at one point because she needed some files of hers that my father had; in that message, she told my mother that things "had turned ugly," despite her best efforts. I think she really believed that she had made "efforts," but I have no idea what examples she could invoke as evidence. In another e-mail to me, she wrote: "Somehow I thought our foundation of love and trust would get us through this. But I see now that I was wrong and that you can't be trusted." I marveled at her self-deception and her blindness to the painful irony of statements like that.

For me, that worst part of it all was her intense anger. I suspect that the anger was motivated not only by her guilt but also by her desire to distance herself from me. I became the reason for her leaving, for her turning to someone else. She told me that I'd silenced her in the relationship. She told me that I was too old to change. She insisted that she felt no ambivalence about her decision; never a math whiz, she told me at one point that she was "150 percent sure of her decision." She told me that she felt a sense of liberation when she thought about her life without me. From where had this cruelty emerged?

Before all this, if someone had asked me to describe Annie in one word, I think I would have said "kind." But there was no kindness for me. While she made love with her new girlfriend and I fought to stay afloat, she took every opportunity to make herself the righteous one and to make clear that she was faultless.

Having been in relationships with both men and women, I've thought a lot about the differences, including differences in how these relationships end. Perhaps there's always more trauma when lesbian relationships end. The lesbian community seems to have an unspoken law that women stay friends with the exes after a breakup; I've never been able to do that, though I know many who have and I believe that it does work for some. Perhaps I've always been more invested in my same-sex relationships, and that's resulted in more pain when they end. I would never want to "rank" pain, mine or anyone else's. But I do know that when one loses a lesbian partner, one also loses a best friend as well as a partner. I know some women are savvy enough not to put all their eggs into one girlfriend, but I've tended to throw myself into these relationships; women tend to be intense and consuming, so it's difficult not to. But losing Annie meant losing my buddy, my confidant, my audience, my sounding board. I've thought a lot about how to create this in my single life. And, so far, I've been unsuccessful doing it. Instead, I feel miserable and I think: "Whom to call?" And my answer is that there's no one in my life who fulfills that best-buddy-I'm-always-here-for-you kind of role. I recognize that we're probably too old for that anyway. But it's still painful and feels like a tremendous loss.

On the off chance that the reader has failed to glean this from my ramblings, I should point out that I recognize that I possess a powerful streak of masochism. So, perhaps from a psychoanalytic perspective, the end of a relationship with a woman may evoke the trauma of the lost mother. In my case, though, as the older woman, the loss feels more like the loss of myself as a mother. I went from being adored to being demonized. From the good, omnipotent mother to the evil, all-consuming mother. Annie was the first woman I'd ever been with who was close to her own mother. In fact, after a series of mismatched relationships with WASPy women, all of whom had distant mothers, I had resolved to be with someone who was not ambivalent about intimacy. Annie's mother adored and smothered her, lived vicariously through her; perhaps Annie dumped me rather than separate from her. I know this to be true as much as I know anything. There were several times at the end when Annie accused me of some misdeed or other. Once she said, "You hate my biceps." I was confused by those accusations because I didn't remember saying or doing the things she threw at me. Later, though, I realized that they were in fact things her mother had said or done. So perhaps lesbians are caught between the Scylla of the absent, cold mother and the Charybdis of the dominant, voracious mother.

I have tremendous admiration for that young woman who went back to surfing only weeks after a shark ripped off her arm. My favorite film character—Ripley in *Aliens*—returns to the alien monster's lair to rescue a child under conditions I know I could never manage. I lack courage. I am a highly functional, professional woman with lots of loving friends and a wonderful family and I don't want my future. I try to imagine "happy," but it just does not compute.

I learned recently that Annie and her partner (the very same woman she left me for) got married. I think back to all of my friends who told me: "It won't last." "These rebound relationships never survive." "I give it a year." Et cetera, et cetera. Clearly, they were wrong. And I think to myself that Annie was right to leave me because she has found someone she wants to spend her life with. And that I was simply not the right person for her. I confess that my first reaction when I found out about the marriage was my usual: denial. In fact, I thought "Michelle must be pressuring Annie into marrying. I'm sure Annie won't go through with it." Still dysfunctional after all these years!

Postscript

Because this essay was written over a fairly long period of time, some things have changed in my life. I'm now dating. Men, in case you're wondering. I've decided that whatever it is that draws me to women (and to certain types of women) is dangerous and to be avoided at all costs. So I'm seeing men. But I continue to struggle with trust. On one date a man admired my home; "don't think your name is going on the deed," was my first thought. I don't know where any of this is going. I try not to obsess over patterns, healthy or otherwise.

Perhaps if I choose someone closer to my own age, there's less of a chance of being left. Perhaps I should choose someone who's too needy to leave (uh oh, there's that old pattern again). Perhaps I should just have affairs and be the one in control. I just don't look at the world in the same way any more; can one experience change one's world view so dramatically? Is this a new me or the me who was always there, dormant? The other day, walking on the beach, I met a lovely young family—father, mother, two beautiful boys—who were enjoying the sunny day and skipping rocks in the water. As I chatted with them, all I could think was "Do you really believe you'll always be like this? Do you really think you can stay happy?" I wondered if one was already cheating on the other, and, if not yet, when that would begin. I miss my romantic innocence, I miss my hopefulness.

And here's what I fantasize about as I think about whether I'll ever be with anyone: I want to feel that I've met someone who makes me believe that it was all worth it. That my pain and suffering were not in vain. I know and I'm sure my readers know how ridiculous those fantasies are. They suggest a magical belief (very un-postmodern!) in a just and fair world where it all, ultimately, makes sense and works out. They also imply a passivity, a lack of agency, where one has no responsibility for making that meaning for oneself.

Yet, even as I recognize that that desire is completely absurd and self-defeating, I still yearn for it. I judge everyone I meet against that standard. I worry that I'm no longer a romantic and I fear that I may be too romantic. I worry about my growing narcissism as I turn increasingly inward. I want to be head over heels. I know that head over heels is not to be trusted. I wonder what I can learn during this "last chapter" (as a friend puts it) of my life and consider the possibility that, on one level anyway, not knowing where I'm going could be the most exhilarating, youthful feeling imaginable. But I still wish, more than anything, to be back in my earlier life with that sense of security and hope. Knowing that it was all false doesn't help to make the desire go away. How ironic to write about an ending without knowing how it all ends.

Talaq, *Divorce*

Zohra Saed

*B*leach is my alternative to crying. I have made white countertops and windowsills sparkle each time I had the urge to weep and I have wept every time I sniffed some bleach at a surprising place. My sorrow and anger are so interwoven in the smell of bleach that at any point when my sorrow is exposed, I become suffused with the scent of bleach.

Once, while listening to a friend's story of betrayal, the phantom bleach scent returned to me as we stood online at a health food store. The sharp scent pervaded my body so quickly that I was nauseous from the urge to weep and this weeping, in turn, helped me unlock the door to remembering my mother.

JANUARY 10, 2003

Dream: She is sleeping next to me. I wake up to the warmth of her breath. There is no furniture. We sleep on the floor. Her body writhes closer to me like a snake. My father walks by the door. I try screaming out to my father, warning him that she has invaded my room and stolen the furniture while I slept, but I can't get my voice out. She leans over me, ready to bite. She is the vampire I used to hide from under my blanket when I was a little girl. I am frozen with fear. Then, something happens, and I realize that I am not a child anymore. So I stick both hands into her mouth and pull apart her jaw. My fingers reach to the back of her teeth and then I crack open her mouth. She transforms into a skeleton. I crush her animal-like skull and it shatters into gray dust.

JUNE 21, 2002

She calls me while I am watching a show on royal couples on the WE Channel. She is calling from a pay phone. My mother, who said she was going out for some vegetables on Avenue U, calling me from a payphone is a strange thing. I was already getting worried because it was getting dark out and she never stayed out late. My father would be home soon and we had a habit of eating our family meals together. Now it was an hour till dinner and she was calling me.

"Zohra, I'm not coming home." At first I think she means that she still wants to shop. I tell her that I will do the rest of her shopping tomorrow.

She is in a panic, cuts me off and says, "I'm leaving! You take care of your father and brother. I'm finished. I'm leaving with your sister."

At first, I don't believe it, so I laugh. It is only when she cries that the reality of what she says sinks in. I say, "Okay," and hang up on her.

I tell my brother, who is just coming out of the shower. He is confused and starts yelling at me, "How could you not know where she is? You were together every day. How could you not know?"

After the yelling and the rushing around the apartment checking closets, we realize that she must have cleared everything out earlier in the day while I was at work. Silent, we wait together for my father. I tell my father while my brother sits with his head between his hands. My father knows something is wrong as soon as we open the door. He is stunned. He hardly blinks. I have to shake him to make him look at me. When he understands, it is my turn to un-ravel. I sob uncontrollably all night. He sits by my bed, puts his hand on my forehead and tells me stories of when I was born to soothe me to sleep. He sits over me all night and each time I awake, I sob as if I hadn't slept at all, and he puts me back to sleep again in this way.

This is the last night I cry for her.

The next day, I bring out the family albums and rip apart every single pic-ture of my mother. My father finds me in the living room like this. He watches me as I take them out and rip them up. He sits next to me, pulls out another album, and does the same. In this way, we exorcise the house of her images. It helps express my father's grief. For a moment, we are busy and the act of tear-ing makes things more bearable.

After two weeks, my father begins to speak again. Each night, I empty out my ears to have them ready to listen to the story again the next day. I don't mind the repetition of his story. Sometimes, I take a tape recorder out so he can narrate his entire life story. It feels different, telling this story with the ap-pendages of microphone and headphones. His story comes out like a novel.

His details are cinematic. We must keep telling this story and keep listening as if it is brand new; otherwise, we'll be buried in the happening itself.

SEPTEMBER 21, 2001

The divorce is finalized. She had asked for a divorce and had taken my father's money to arrange all of the papers. He was very gentle with her. My parents were in an arranged marriage. They grew apart. The children were grown and living their own lives. My father worked very hard and my mother stayed home a lot. We had no family in the area to keep her busy. Her friends were beginning to irk her, so she broke many of her friendships and for the past two years kept us isolated. My grandmother was giving her a guilt trip because my father could no longer fund my mother's entire extended family like he used to. He sold our vacation house in New Jersey to pay what was due to her after their divorce. In all Muslim marriages, the *Haq Mahr* is what the woman is given after the divorce. The Mahr is settled within the marriage contract, sort of like a prenuptial agreement. My father gave her $30,000 Haq Mahr and she continued living at our home and everything seemed normal. She led my father and her children to believe that it was her mother who wanted divorce papers, because my father had not been sending the family money in Saudi Arabia. My grandmother had stopped talking to my father years ago. She was adamant about arranging my marriage to my first cousin in Saudi Arabia. My father prevented this from even being a topic of conversation.

There were many arguments before the divorce, a year of arguments. Mainly the arguments were over money and about bringing over her brother, who did not work, to come live with us in the States with his wife and children. After the divorce papers were signed, everything was calm and they were getting along amicably. My mother jested that we should have a second wedding for them. *She lived with us like this for nine months. When she left, she had cleared out my father's bank account of his entire savings.*

My mother couldn't read or write in English, so it was my younger sister, twenty years old, who did all of this for her and emptied us all out. They live in the States, but I don't know where. Since they left, I haven't heard from either one; I have only heard about them.

THE KITCHEN, 2002

I am trying to create Afghan dishes so it can ease the pain. My friend tells me how she finds herself becoming her own mother now that she has moved out of her house. Sometimes in the mirror, she says, she sees her mother looking back at her. My neighbor Dawn says that when I stand near the kitchen window like this with my hand on my hip stirring a pot, I look like my mother. She laughs at me. She says I am turning matronly. I do not like her and want her out of my home. But I am too polite to ask her to leave and I'm still not used to the place being so quiet. I also don't look into mirrors. I don't wear black *surma*. I don't speak Uzbeki, opting for Dari instead.

My brother feels the same about our "mother" language. He says he hates Uzbeki and hates the way it sounds. We both find ourselves turning belligerent around short, heavy-set women who speak Uzbeki. When my brother reveals his new hatred of Uzbek women, we are walking to the car and stepping on cracks on the sidewalk to break our mother's back. He says, "I never want to marry an Uzbek girl because she will turn into a short, round old lady." I laugh and say, "I never want to be a mother because I may turn into a short, round Uzbek woman." My brother stops and turns back to hug me, which for him means to put me in a headlock. "No, don't say that. Just don't get fat!" And we both laugh.

Around my father, I hear another language more frequently, Pashto— a language that we didn't hear so much when she was around. She had somehow dried up that winding stream of language from my father's throat from the day she married. Now he sings sorrowful songs in Pashto and asks for things in Pashto. I don't really understand but I know his routine, so I know what he is asking for. An unseen door within my father has opened up for me.

One day after work, my father looks at me struggling with the fried onions that start off a *korma* dish. I had never been the domestic type before. I smile and make jokes about eating something burnt for another night.

But he is serious faced. He says, "I took care of my father, washed his clothes, cooked dinner, and then studied late at night using the light from my neighbor's window because my uncle's wife did not want to waste her money giving me light."

My father's mother had divorced my grandfather after he had been left partially paralyzed by a stroke. She left my father when he was two years old. My father grew up taking care of his father. He came over to the stove and his eyes welled up with tears. "Please don't worry so much about taking care of me."

OCTOBER 2002

The thin lady, who is always walking around the neighborhood, pushing a thin shopping cart, and who always smiles and refers to herself as a girl, stops me to congratulate me on my mother's wedding. She sees my expression and stops smiling. Didn't I know that she had married a Pakistani man who was twenty years younger than her? My mother was forty-six.

How do I tell my father this? Why am I left to clean up her mess? What is this woman's name? Karen? Kate? She tells me that she always suspected my mother was a liar because we seemed so different than how my mother saw us. She has a list of questions for me: Was it true that I was a pharmacist who never gave my mother any money?

No, I'm a poet.

Did I try to strangle my mother because she wanted the keys to my house (apparently I had bought one and wouldn't let her in)?

I live with my parents.

Was my brother left at his wedding by his rich Saudi fiancée and did he have a nervous breakdown?

My brother is twenty-four and has refused to have children because of all this.

Did my father have another wife that he kept in his house in New Jersey?

Laughter.

My mother played up some of the stereotypes about Muslims to garner some strange sympathy among the little old people who lived on our block. These were the same women who refused to call my father by his name and referred to him as Mohammad. Lying is nothing new to my mother. When we first come to America, she tells Anna, our neighbor, that I am not her daughter. My mother has fair skin and light brown hair. Her face is slim with high cheekbones. My skin is a dark olive, hair jet black, and eyes almond shaped. I look just like my father. I am known as the "darkie" of the family. Anna always pinched me when I got too playful at her home and then would complain to my mother that I was a bad influence on my brother.

My friends' mothers in elementary school believed this. My mother was a magnanimous stepmother in their eyes. I remember a cluster of women sitting with my mother in the playground watching how my brother and I played together and commenting, "It is good that they don't know."

KABUL, 1974

My parents are both renamed, given a *laqab*, and married. Each calls the other by their married name. They move into my dad's home in Jalalabad, a two-hour ride from the city and a resort town. There is an album full of photos of them in bell bottoms and dark rectangular sunglasses. They are the modern couple. My mother is eighteen years old. My father is twenty-eight. My mother was the third daughter in a family of seven daughters. She was kept home by her father after she finished grade school because they needed someone to care for the children.

JALALABAD, 1975

I am born on the rooftop at dawn. My father delivers me because the doctor couldn't come soon enough. In a culture of midwives, Afghans say that the one who delivers the baby is a second mother. So by delivering me, my father is both parents for me. Later, when I am three years old, I jump up on the coffee table, put my hands on my hips, and proclaim that I was born out of my father's mouth!

SAUDI ARABIA, 1978

In a place like Saudi Arabia, my mother had an affair. We are at an amusement park. She is wearing a black veil. I try to have her hold me. I slip on all of the black silk that covers her. She keeps pushing me away. I am whisked up by my father and taken to a bumper car. It is always like this, I am alone in my room for hours and hours. I am left with a crate of tangerines and this is all I eat until she returns.

She asks for a divorce. My father calls his friend, the one she is having an affair with, to tell him to take her then and marry her. But he doesn't come. He is a coward. She is left in despair. My father sends plane tickets for her father to come from Afghanistan to take her home. He is a poor man, my grandfather says, he doesn't want his daughter. There is nothing for my father to do. They try again to make the marriage work. *My brother is born in 1979. In 1980, we arrive in New Jersey, then come to live in Brooklyn.*

JUNE 2004

At a gallery, I am cornered by the women of our community. Afghan Uzbeks reeking of powdery perfume and blushed up to make their round cheeks even rounder. They ask me what happened with my mother. They are so eager to hear this story they have crowded around me. It makes my stomach sick to tell it. But I tell it with all the details. I have developed an aversion to sentimentality. In the end they say, poor you, all alone and getting older. You should marry, the one in a peach suit says. Another begins, "My son . . ." I stop the clucking hens. I say, glibly, "No, I'm never going to marry because my honor's been besmirched by my whore of a mother." I smile at them and walk away, imitating that condescending look these women are infamous for. It shocks them. But I know what they call my mother when I am not there. So I just tell them to their faces and stomp on their phony etiquette.

Yes, I am still belligerent around older Uzbek women who remind me of my mother.

MOTHER'S DAY 2003

My brother and I buy our father balloons, flowers, and a card for Mother's Day. We do the same for him on Father's Day. It makes my father's eyes sparkle with tears that never seem to roll out.

FEBRUARY 2005

There is no news of my mother. It has been almost three years. My father finds a tape of my brother's graduation. I see myself and another woman next to me. It takes me a few minutes before I realize that it is my mother. I had erased from my mind what she looked like.

It is an eight-minute tape. My father rewinds it and watches it once more. Then he shuts off the TV to sleep early.

What Dawn had said to me stayed with me for a long time. I stopped looking into mirrors in case I caught her ghost grinning at me when I was applying mascara or a hint of blush. I cut my long, permed hair that we had all three had done together at the local hair salon. They hair stylist asked in Brooklyn drawl, "Wanna go for a drastic change, huh?" And I nodded my head. I came out with short cropped hair.

Even months after I banned Dawn and other matronly mother-substitutes posing as friends, her comment lingered inside me. Even after the haircut, I dreaded mirrors. I became hypersensitive about this idea of her growing in me as a ghost. My father and I threw out everything in the apartment that belonged to our past life. The apartment was redone. Ancient coins he kept in a small jar were put on display. We spent an entire summer at Ikea. We put up photos I had enlarged of the paternal side of my family. Photos of my father as a young man were professionally framed and put up in the entrance area. In this way, we reclaimed the blank white walls of our apartment. But even still with all these changes, this idea of her growing in me as a ghost affected every decision I made. Her character became the meter to judge everything I did not want to be.

On my thirtieth birthday, I looked in the mirror and analyzed every facial feature that I had inherited from my parents. I squinted hard. I did not see her surfacing from inside my face as if I was molten and she was the ghost trapped inside it. Nothing, just Zohra. Zohra with a few gray hairs (which I pulled out). I sighed, pleased with my face after a very long time of fighting with it. Even if I had inherited her chin and jawline, I said in relief, "I'm not her."

No More Romance for Me

Sue O'Sullivan

When I was dumped in my mid-fifties by my lover, it was not the first time I'd been ditched by a woman. It set into motion familiar emotional upheavals around betrayal and rejection, hurt, anger, surprise, and noncomprehension. In fact the repetition of the emotions was in itself depressing—despite the predictability, I was unable to disrupt them. I had hoped that were I ever to face the chop again, I would cope better, having learned from previous experiences and with the added benefit of maturity. But aging only added new dimensions to my last breakup.

I spent just under eight years with my last ex, Jen, the longest lesbian liaison I've managed and still a shorter time span than that with my long-ago husband (who I am still very close to). I am a little embarrassed that I have not been able to come up with a full understanding as to why lesbian rejection has proved particularly difficult for me even after time in analytic therapy. After all, the notion that relationships are a failure if they don't last forever has been widely critiqued and I tend to agree. So why have rejection and perceived betrayal felt like a series of emotional time bombs, leading, in fits and starts, deeper and deeper into emotional chaos? Particularly when in the midst of it all, I knew that ultimately it was not all to do with my spurning lover and much more to do with older personal psychic patterns. Nevertheless, Jen became the focus of my anger and despair. She was the person I hurled endless litanies of "why?" at. Recognizing that I too was not happy with how we were didn't stop my emotional meltdown when she pulled the plug.

My girlfriends, with the exception of one, fell somewhere on the butch continuum. They were also all younger than me. A friend commented early on in my lesbian life, "You like a bit of rough trade." This wasn't true. But what I did like was a bit of the tough stuff—handsome or not, masculine girls. What I adored was the tension between a butch persona and a woman's body—and they all had very womanly bodies.

I wonder about the cradle-snatching element. In a heterosexual relationship, if the man were older, the age difference would have been unremarkable—they were never more than a dozen or so years younger than me. With women, I had plunged head first into a kind of adolescent sexuality I'd not experienced before. Even though I was in my mid-thirties and the mother of two young boys when I first started a liaison with a woman, I felt like a romantic teenager. A friend asked if there was a something of a mother/daughter dynamic in my relationships with younger women, but this did not resonate for me. Having been asked myself, I in turn questioned my younger girlfriends and they all assured me, perhaps unsurprisingly, that no, they were not looking for a mother figure. Still, it was not altogether comfortable.

Some friends also felt my relationships with particular butch girlfriends contained aspects of inequality. It seemed as if some of them believed I had the power to confer happiness and confidence. Of course, in the end I always disappointed them. But finally when I got together with Jen, I felt I had found an equal, someone who had plans and self-confidence, who could do as much looking after me as I could of her. My friends approved and were relieved I had found someone as solid and smart and handsomely butch as Jen. This was a woman to depend on.

When Jen announced eight years later that she wanted to sever our bond, it came out of the blue. But of course it hadn't: it was clear even then that she had been depressed for months and that contrary to what she had told me, being together was part of the problem, even if we had easily presented a contented front to the wider world. Once the words were out, our partnership unraveled with amazing speed.

I do not want to go into any "she said this, and I said that" litany of accusations. I analyzed Jen's personality with endless compulsion for the first couple of years, but it now holds no interest for me. What I do want to settle on is the dividing line between a breakup, its inevitable fallout and recovery, and the much longer process of how you pick up the sloppy mess and wrestle with it. A wrestling (to the death, in jest, with rules or without, against, alone, together) that might ultimately include the *positive* winding up of a relationship. Which might even lead to a reconciliation via a kind of friendship with an ex;

or perhaps a peculiar but warm connection, exactly because it is based on an almost forgotten intimacy; or a special tie which acknowledges a past love *and* painful breakup. Regretfully for me all that remained was the growing realization that dragging something new and positive out of the wreck of our relationship would never be possible.

The First Stage

Shock, tears, and incomprehension. Much shit may be shoveled during this time and accusations may be vicious and hurtful. It's an interval which demands a great deal of patience from both the dumper and the dumpee, even while accusations fly, fury flays, or sullenness reigns. In one way or another, this stage (weeks, months, or years) in all its variations is inevitable and often boringly repetitive, but it *will* end.

During the first stage in the break with Jen, I derived a great deal of gleeful enjoyment from hearing about acts of nonviolent revenge by spurned lovers. Some years later I wrote a short story weaving together aspects of a friend's tale of revenge and my own real-life, lower-key version. I called myself Stella, Deanne was my bona fide friend Deborah, and Ruth was Jen. When Deborah originally related her story of vengeance, we doubled up with laughter during one of our regular "Ladies Who Laugh" lunches. Writing much later, I called the story "Gold Among the Ruins." The excerpt here illustrates how symbolic or literal revenge can confer a strange sort of comfort. Perhaps revenge is not always best served perfectly cold.

Deanne was by far the more daring of the two and Stella obtained comfort from her stories. As Deanne told it, when Barbara gave her the axe, she took to her bed and only got up to pee or make tea and toast. This state of affairs went on, she claimed, for several months. Finally she emerged with renewed vigor and a deep well of anger. Taking all Barbara's love letters and little notes—the protestations of love and fidelity, some written only days before she left—she went to work in her studio, blowing them up to poster size, printing out dozens and dozens of them. She explained to Stella that she had developed a theory of revenge as a creative act, one that had the power to cleanse the soul and provide a kind of catharsis. If you treated it as an art form it would never rebound on you. One day while Barbara was out at work, Deanne took a large bucket of poster glue, a brush, and the stack of blown up letters, and loaded up the car. At Barbara's house she proceeded to plaster the entire front of the building with evidence of her duplicity, until windows, walls, and the door were completely obliterated.

Stella wondered if she regretted it at all, now that it was so long ago, and Deanne said no, not a bit of it. "I loved doing it. I loved the way it looked. I loved the thought of her finding her house in such a state. No, I have not a shred of regret, quite the opposite." Stella remarked then that she didn't know if she could create something as fulfilling. . . .

Stella moved into a friend's place until she organized her return to New York. The day before she left she went to the house on Bridge Street. In silence she walked slowly through the rooms. Her mouth was tight and set. There were no tears. She sat in the kitchen and made herself a last cup of tea in one of Ruth's cups. She ran her hand through her dyed blond hair and pulled. Once, twice, until she had pulled out more than a dozen strands.

Abandoning her tea, she moved across the kitchen, opened a cupboard and placed one strand at the back of a shelf of food. A dreamy state of well-being spread through her body. She pushed another deep into a bag of rice. In the bathroom the multicolored tiles they had chosen together glowed in the late afternoon light. Stella arranged single hairs between towels, sheets, and deep into the center of a duvet cover, which rested in the cupboard. She paused and took a deep breath. In the bedroom she insinuated a golden hair into the pocket of one of Ruth's favorite jackets and shoved one under the mattress. In the study at the end of the hall, more hair went into the middle pages of several books, including the one she'd given Ruth for her birthday a few months ago. With one hair left, she walked out into the long hall with its polished wooden floor. Approaching the low bookcase, and then taking great care, she wrapped it around the base of a large, prickly cactus they had bought together. She stretched slowly and her lips curled. Stella was ready to leave.

The Second Stage

In my experience, the second stage is less predictable and more complex, although eventually it holds the richest potential for a positive outcome to the sorry event. By the second stage, most revengeful impulses have evaporated and the pull of maudlin pop songs and bad poetry is over. Projection onto the ex-lover is less likely, and there's more possibility to dig deep in one's own psyche. Generally, a clearer head prevails although emotional recidivism lurks around many corners. How many times did I cautiously, yet with growing conviction, congratulate myself for being on the road to recovery, when blow me, I was felled by a single image, one memory, or a searing resurgence of the big unfathomable "why?" Nevertheless, periods of calm and contentment grew longer in relation to the raw hurt of rejection.

UTOPIAN SECOND STAGE

During this ongoing and dynamic stage, ex-lovers may reapproach each other, offering a hand, recalling good times, making self-criticisms or reparations which relate to the relationship or breakup. It doesn't matter who starts this uneven process because in its most ideal form, what one starts, the other continues. It is now, in the months or years which follow, that no matter how banal, awkward, or uneven, the basis for some kind of new closeness can be established.

STAGE TWO DYSTOPIA

Ironically, it has been with my ex-husband and then with other serious lesbian lovers, none of whom were so solid, dependable, together, mature, or loyal as Jen, that I have achieved some form of what I've described above. With Jen, none of this has proved possible. A friend of both of us said to me years ago that only when you stopped caring about someone who had hurt you in a relationship could you become friends again. I replied, "But if I didn't care about her anymore, why would I want to be friends?" What I do still care about is what the loss of reconciliation with Jen has meant to me in relation to my sense of self, or my ability to look for or be open to another lesbian sexual relationship (forget heterosexual; I know sexuality is fluid, but I also know I'm not interested). Jen and I had totally different approaches to the wreckage of our relationship. Whereas I wanted to struggle with it, hoping eventually to extricate some understanding of why it happened and what might be built out of it in order to inform my future and retain something positive from the past, it seemed she wanted to withdraw, recover, and set her back to it in order to walk determinedly into the future. No moral imperative attaches to either approach, but for me, at my age in particular, the total failure of stage two has been too scary to allow it ever to happen again.

My Aging Body

Being dumped in my mid-fifties and having made no meaningful reconciliation with Jen after an inevitable first long stage of fury and unhappiness left me warped in matters of love. When I tried tentatively to suggest possibilities of some sort of friendship she turned and ran as fast as she could. In many ways this hurt more and had more lasting negative consequences than the initial banal brutality of the breakup. I'd had total confidence in Jen. Our relationship covered the time I passed through my late forties and into my mid-fifties. I went through my menopause while I was with her. I was utterly convinced that she loved me and that we would be in some sort of relationship for the rest of our lives. It was not about believing we would be together as a traditional couple forever. But I trusted we would stay connected because of love, if not passion. I knew we were not in great shape sexually and increasingly recognized that something was going to have to give or change in that area. However, *whatever* happened, we would be deep and loving friends. Long after the event, without a glimmer friendship on the horizon, the harsh break healed, but without much flexibility or softness left. My confidence was battered and I doubted my ability to discern reality in a relationship.

Now, looking down at my body, seeing it reflected in the mirror, blurred but lumpy through a steamed-up shower door, rubbing cream into legs which sport spreading, faded, inky webs, kneading loose tummy flesh, avoiding the waves and dips of cellulite, seeing the wrinkling parchment which is the back of my hands—I see my aging body and do not like it at all.

I cannot separate my body's inevitable demise, its slow but easily discerned motion toward death, from how I have reacted to being let down by someone I trusted would always be in my life in one way or another. Something so inevitable as bodily aging has become the emotional repository of my own fears and the detritus of an unresolved but no longer meaningful betrayal. I know these are things I "shouldn't" feel but I've long recognized that "should nots" don't work very well on any level. I can be sweet on myself when I masturbate— I feel soft skin, touch sensitive places, give myself orgasms, which resonate for minutes. I love my feet. I enjoy my face. New wrinkles are now the object of amusement and interest. I try them out in the mirror, quickly get used to them. But my body has snared me. And I have returned its negative embrace, creating a wall against any other relationships—and other rejections, other slides down slippery slopes of drawn-out recovery. No way would I take that chance.

It's such a contradiction, but as I've lived most of my adult life celebrating contradictions, I'll have to learn how to celebrate this one too: I can love myself and know that other friends and family love me. I can accept my body for myself and find it pleasurable. But I cannot bear to contemplate someone else "seeing" me naked and inevitably, as I imagine it, reacting in disgust. It sounds so trite, so simple, as if all that's needed is someone to say, "Sue, stop this silliness immediately."

Of course there is no logical connection between the state of my body and the possibility of lust and love with someone else, no matter how the chances reduce or the difficulties of meeting someone new increase the older you get. Nevertheless, irrationality wins. Eight years after my girlfriend dumped me, and I still have not had one single mildly or mediumly serious relationship, nor have I been struck by overwhelming desire for any woman. Only one delightful fling with a highly desirable old friend very soon after I returned to my old home from the country where Jen and I lived, for which I am grateful. At least Jen was not my last lover. At least our desultory lovemaking wasn't the last lovemaking I took part in. In bed with my old friend turned passionate temporary lover and after fucking our brains out, I sighed with satisfaction. Later I thought, "Thank god my sex life didn't end on a boring note." But now I don't have the nerve, the energy—or the desire. Where has it gone? All dried up and run away in fear.

Lighten Up, Girl, Life's Worth Living

My good life, my friendships, connections with grown children and ex-partners, these—and work, writing, and political activism and cooking, making a lovely home, holidays, and meeting up with dear ones around the world—must not disappear in a story of losing a lover in my mid-fifties. I won't let that happen.

My overly mournful tale of breakups blurs all the pleasures of living alone and being single. Someone said to me recently, "But Sue, you could have a relationship where you saw someone one or two nights a week." I nodded, and having imagined it, blurted out, "Oh my god, *one or two nights a week? No way.*" I couldn't handle having to deal with someone in my home or be in hers that often. It filled me with visceral dread. What I wouldn't mind, but can't imagine doing, is serial no-strings-attached sex with women in dark rooms. Anyway, I do maintain an orgasmic sex life, helped along by a satchel of creative sex toys, an active imagination, and a responsive body. Ironically, I have more sex (with myself) now than I did with Jen in over eight years together.

I appreciate the freedom I have to do as I like in my home, including sex when I feel like it. I revel in being alone. I get excited about seeing friends and loved ones. I love silence and music. I enjoy my colleagues, being social in groups, going out, meeting new people, returning home. The way I'm living my life now is not lonely or sad. I deeply resent any implication that if you don't have a partner you are missing intimacy in your life, especially if you are old. As if partners always achieve intimacy. Bullshit. I am intimate in different ways with a number of different people. I am quieter than I used to be, with a smaller network of friends, and this suits me well.

I actively don't want to take into account a new lover's demands, desires, practicalities, whims. My various and very different friendships have endured way beyond any relationship. I'm still part, if not "on the scene," of lesbian life and culture. Lots of us old dykes are around—some in increasingly long relationships and others single—we do things together and laugh a lot. It's true, perhaps, that lesbians are less likely to think of those who are single with pity or as left on the shelf. Perhaps lesbian culture judges you less on whether you've got a partner and more on who you are?

I look at the blue sky and moving clouds out of my study window and experience a sweep of happiness. I fantasize more about the possibly too-near ghastliness of dementia and physical disasters than I do of lost romance or a girlfriend's betrayal. I rage at the ongoing destruction of war, famine, and fulminate against the neocons and fundamentalists who are currently devastating the world. I march and sign petitions. I continue to work around HIV/AIDS as I have for years. But sometimes I opt out and do nothing. I refuse to watch the news on TV with any regularity. I read, I know what is happening. I don't need to have images burnt into my brain in order to understand or care. It's a confusing time to live in. I wonder if it's right to feel sorry for my children and younger people in general, living without much optimism that the world can be a better place, when for much of my life I have believed so passionately in change.

In the end, being dumped by Jen took up too much of my time and energy, robbed me for too long of my joie de vivre and sapped my confidence at a time when I didn't have the resilience I might have had before. It wasn't her fault, and she wasn't to know, but she activated ancient psychic spots, which let it all ooze forth. I've tried, but how can I know for sure if I've defused those tender, vulnerable places?

I'm sixty-four. I contemplate my death and suddenly realize the obvious: I'll never die young. I've reached that stage. I measure the rest of my life in maybe two or two and half decades if I'm lucky and maintain I'd rather go sooner than later, if later means dementia and major physical pain and/or incapacity. I prefer to remain free for as long as I can—in order to take on work and responsibilities, delights and difficulties, solitude and companionship, which will not lead me into despair. Over the last thirty years or so, lesbian relationships have brought me much happiness and, overall, fantastic sexual enjoyment. But they have also resulted in unexpected levels of emotional upheaval. I prefer to celebrate my lesbian identity in other ways now. My heart may have hardened against romantic love, but in the process of healing I discovered other areas of openness. I am finally able to love my mother in a way I hadn't been able to since my early teens. Now, as she dozes toward the end, I rejoice that I have been able to feel unconditional love for her. I feel a kind of contentment—if you can leave aside my over-determined negativity about my body. I have regained energy and enthusiasm. I experience pleasure, laughter, occasional bursts of wild abandon. I've joined a workshop for creative and improvisational dance, which is something I hadn't done for decades. I feel connected to life and love on many levels. I've still got my fears and times of loneliness, but mostly I feel affection for the old bird I am becoming.

From Buddy
to Joe to Harriet

Harriet Luria

W hen you're sixteen and you're dumped, dropped by a boyfriend you are madly in love with, it's devastating. For me, it came as a shock. We were at a New Year's Eve party and I had had too much to drink, something I was a novice at. I was from a hard working, working-class, movin' on up Jewish family that had moved from Kinsman Road, down in the city of Cleveland, up to Shaker Heights, a wealthy enclave. We lived in a two-family house in Shaker, renting out the top floor to a series of tenants. I didn't have firsthand experience with alcohol and parties. My family drank wine at religious dinners like Passover or had "schnapps" when my grandfather stopped over, or when an old friend of my parents, one of the few people they socialized with outside the family, came for dinner.

I was an outstanding student in high school, determined to go to a "good"— no, outstanding—college, preferably in New York City. So to that end, I studied, was on the student council, was active in many clubs, and inwardly lamented my social status. I wasn't from a rich or well-connected Jewish family: No country clubs, no trips to Florida at Christmas or spring break, no posh camps in the summer for me. Instead, we went to Miami in August because of my father's hay fever; I went to Camp Vladeck, a Workman's Circle "Der Arbeiter Ring" camp in Ohio where we listened to Yiddish stories, met holocaust survivors, swam, and ate. We were not part of the vanguard of assimilation.

With my kinky hair, short stature, unadorned clothes, abundance of ideas, and determined aspirations, I didn't fit. I loved books and reading. But I also wanted to be beautiful, be part of the social scene, have boyfriends, and wear gorgeous clothes. I had a glimpse of this life through some of my friends, through dancing school—stories for another time. Then I met Buddy at one of the student clubs I was in—tall, dark, handsome, Jewish, not a serious student then, but a great dancer and really sensual. I fell hard. I was the daughter of a "junkman"; he was the son of a photographer who through his store did wedding, bar mitzvah, and graduation pictures. Buddy and I would often go to the events in his old jalopy, take the pictures, and then hang out with his friends and make out in his car. I was in heaven.

When I got sick at the New Year's Party, he drove me home. I was so apologetic, sorry I was ruining his evening, blah, blah, blah. Not to worry, he said. I'll call you tomorrow. He never called again. He had gone back to the party, taken up with Charlene, a tall, blond, gorgeous WASP, and they became an item. I dragged myself through the rest of the school year. My grades plummeted, I lost weight, and really fell apart. My family didn't have a clue how to help me. Like Lily Bart in Edith Wharton's *House of Mirth*, I was left to my own devices in navigating the social waters.

Somehow I made it through high school. My grades went back up; I had lots of friends, but none I confided in about my broken heart. I dated guys who thought I was the cat's meow but I had learned a complicated lesson from getting dumped by Buddy: you're not one of these people, you want out, you don't let yourself get hurt like that again. I got myself into Barnard College in New York City, and never went back to Cleveland except for weddings, to be with my parents near the ends of their lives, and for funerals.

What happened with Buddy was to continue to be my pattern in all the major love affairs of my life: I would take up with a charismatic, tall, dark, handsome (although usually not Jewish) guy and be completely "shocked" when I was dropped. That there were plenty of guys I dated who were really taken with me and who I brushed off didn't register on my self-esteem scale; only the negative pattern stuck. Which brings me to my marriage. I give this brief background to show how it was both connected to the whole and yet different because of time, place, and circumstance.

I met Joe in 1966 at an anti–Vietnam War march in Central Park in New York City. I had gone to the march with an interracial couple I met somewhere, somehow, a light-skinned Black guy and his White girlfriend whose names escape me. They knew Joe. He was tall, at least 6'2", with dark brown skin with a reddish cast (I came to notice later), tight black kinky hair, a black mustache, a very thin, lanky guy with big brown eyes. His manner was both intense and inviting at the same time. Intellectual. Brilliant. Dazzling. That evening, I went to a party on the Lower East Side. Although my mother had been born on Hester Street (or was it Grand?—she couldn't remember; they had moved to Cleveland by the time she was four or five years old), I had rarely been that far downtown since coming to New York in 1959. A run-down tenement building, crowds of people mashed into a railroad apartment, lots of life, noise, dancing. Joe was there and he was attentive, helpful. We talked endlessly and danced, Joe towering over me.

I noted details, but as is usually my way, set them aside, didn't let them influence the course of my actions. There was a pay phone on the wall in the living room—Joe used it to make a phone call. I should have known. As I discovered much later, the phone call was to the woman he was living with, a relationship he neglected to mention until we had been together for about six months. And in the ultimate of ironies, when we parted over twenty-one years later, it was to her he returned.

I was getting my first master's at the time, taking a course called "The Negro Novel" with the White guru of the field, Robert Bone. Bone was writing a book on contemporary Black poets and used us as researchers. My chosen poet was Calvin Hernton. Of course, when Joe told me he was a poet, I asked him about Hernton. Turned out he knew him well, had access to his written work, and would gladly send it to me. What luck! I gave Joe my address and he never even asked me for my phone number. Such a gentleman, part of his elusive, non-pushy charm. I was hooked.

A powerful combination for me: politics and study—obsessions of my life then (as well as now) when I wasn't out looking for guys, moving through a series of "relationships." When I met Joe, I was coming out of a three-year affair with a thirty-ish, White, working-class, hard-luck film editor, a good person, but not someone I envisioned spending a lifetime with. The attraction had worn off and I wanted to move on. When you establish the pattern of being the "abandoned one," it's difficult to play the role of the heavy. My method of choice in those situations has been to make myself so nasty, remote, and unattractive that the guy can't help but "break my heart." I jumped at Joe as a lifeline out of the film-editor dilemma, out of the series of unfortunate, brief, going-nowhere affairs, out of a sense that nothing much was happening in my life—other than work, study, politics, friends! But when you're young, romantic, and passionate, love and sex are at the top of the survival list.

You definitely wake up when you enter into an interracial Black/Jewish affair. The city was our frame, and as we moved through it, public response to our coupling was, shall I say, electrifying? Even when we weren't openly ogled, we were observed. I wasn't used to that kind of scrutiny and the gaze that settled on us was not kind. This was 1966. Antimiscegenation laws were still on the books in parts of the United States. By the time Joe and I married, the last of the laws against interracial marriage was finally struck down. But though the law was finally on our side, opinion and practice weren't. I thought I was prepared for what was to come. But I really didn't have a clue. I didn't know how racism seeps into every crevice of everyday and everynight living. I went from being Harriet Luria (who are you? Are you Italian? Hispanic?) to being Harriet Johnson (you don't look WASP! What did your father do? What part of England is your family from?). I moved from being a sensitized-to-any-indication-of-anti-Semitism Jew, to having to deal with people thinking I was WASP, only "you don't look WASP," to the shock, anger, and sense of betrayal "they" felt finding out I was a Johnson because I was married to an African American. Oh my God, I've hurt *their* fucking feelings. Friends, strangers, therapists asked, "Why have you made your life so difficult?" It took me thirty years to understand that the real question they were asking was "Why have you made our lives so difficult?" Joe's and my very existence was both titillating and confrontational to their sense of the proper order of things. We were a living transgression to the racial hierarchy in the good ol' classless, egalitarian U.S. of A. Do I sound bitter? I don't want to and I don't feel bitter. I suppose the person I am most angry at is myself. Because the racism and its manifestations got to me.

Finding a place to live as an interracial couple wasn't easy. African Americans deal with the inequities of shelter all the time; I wasn't used to it. The public scrutiny on the streets, in restaurants, movie houses, parks constrained me. I didn't want to be openly affectionate for fear of the possible consequences. Friends, Black and White, were curious about my choice. Family support wasn't available. I had invited my parents to our wedding, but they wouldn't come. For the twenty years of our marriage, my mother pretended that she didn't know our anniversary date. She never acknowledged it.

So when things started to go bad between Joe and me, I felt pretty much isolated, disconnected in so many areas of my life. When he left for good, it was for another woman. I was devastated. Broken. Shattered. I really loved Joe. I had married my whole life to him, and remained only tangentially connected to my family, marginally connected to my religion. My close friends were supportive, my therapist sympathetic, but no one really understood the depths of my devastation. Being secretive had been part of my growing up; being in a marriage disapproved of by both my family and the larger society reinforced my inclination to keep my life private. Plenty of people wanted to know what had happened. We had seemed like such a close couple, so happy together. From some, I detected a sense of "Well, what did you expect?" Those who had found my standoffishness arrogant were almost pleased at my public "downfall." Others, White, had a more openly prurient interest. They could finally ask me what I guess they had wanted to know all along. What was sex like with a Black man? They were furious when I wouldn't comply in providing a vicarious accounting for them.

I dropped the veil, letting it cover my whole being. While I had been sexually betrayed by Joe, the worst possible transgression in my book, I wasn't about to join the prurient, racist interrogation and discussion. But the most important reason for me to keep as quiet and dignified as I could was my son. My father's advice to me at the time determined the direction I would take. The only important thing for you now, he said, is to raise your son. When I balked at Joe's taking my son to his girlfriend's, my Old World father said, "That's his father. Never say anything against him. Make sure he sees him all the time."

So writing about being dumped is fraught with restraints for me: Wanting to protect my son, even though he is grown and on his own now, lifelong habits of secrecy, the masks and veils I got used to wearing as part of an interracial life in a society that punishes women, especially, for crossing boundaries, and residual feelings of misplaced loyalty and a sense of failure.

Being cut loose is never easy. On one level, the MO was the same with Buddy as it was with Joe: young girl/woman falls in love with a tall, dark, handsome, elusive guy. The guy seems to adore her, ultimately leaves her for a tall, blond WASP. But the early dumping experience occurred within a Jewish community in Cleveland. I was young, resilient, and although devastated, hopeful. The experience was part of a class and social disaster, part of an ambivalence and rebellion against marrying up, taking my place in the grand upper middle class of bright, well-turned-out, cared-for Jewish women. It was what my mother wanted for me, perhaps so desperately because she hadn't married that way. While always urging me to work and make a living so I wouldn't have to depend on a man, she also warned me not to let men know how smart I was, to marry a man who loved me more than I loved him, and to get myself a Jewish husband who could give me the world.

I concentrated on the working and making a living—the independence—part and ignored the rest of her advice. The ultimate rejection by an idealized husband, who walked out on a forty-seven-year-old woman and an adoring son, occurred within a totally different context, richer, yet more complicated.

It was only late in her life, nearing death at ninety-four, that my mother finally acknowledged my struggle. She said I had done all the things she would have liked to do. She left me with three pieces of advice: Take care of your son, have a happy life, and, she said, find a nice man. What more is there to say?

So Much for
"Happily Ever After"

NAOMI WORONOV

We were having breakfast—I don't know why he chose that moment. His words were, "Our daughter tells me I should tell you that I'm moving out." He said it would be a while because his place wasn't ready yet. This was June 1st—by September, he said, he'd move out. We'd been married thirty-four years, and I had no idea he was building a "place."

— CORA, seventy-five

I didn't believe him at first. After eighteen years I had totally taken him for granted, and it was like a bomb going off.

— EVA, sixty-one

I remember sitting at the table, and he patted me on the shoulder, and I was shocked. I was terrified of losing him. The three years we were together were the happiest in my whole life; I felt my life was complete, nothing was lacking. He had a weekend trip planned with the guys, and he just went ahead with it.

— DELLA, thirty-four

Cora, Eva, and Della are neither friends nor acquaintances, but they would recognize one another on the street in their rural town in upstate New York. They know one another's stories. Everyone does in a small town. They don't think about how much they have in common:

Three generations, but shock is a common theme of their stories.

Three levels of education, but shame is a central theme of their stories.

Three layers of vocational achievement, but financial upheaval—or chaos—is an enduring theme of their stories.

Three couples spanning five decades, yet the inability to communicate is at the heart of all their stories.

What follows are the women's stories, because that is what I have. But whatever the other side of each story may be, the sudden, blunt announcements of imminent departure by these men created the sort of emotional, social, and financial havoc that is never entirely erased from a woman's being. It can, if she lets it, define her life.

What differs? The women's responses differ, and are, to some degree, typical of their generations. Cora never divorced her husband, now deceased, and regrets it to this day. Eva wavers between intermittent tears and a fun new sex life. Della has found a "safe" man to "date" and travel with.

The stories below come from interviews conducted in August 2004. As I talked to each woman, I typed her words directly into my computer, so the voices below are their own. However, for clarity and fluency, I have reorganized, cut, and edited, and I have changed all their names.

Cora was born and raised on a farm, went on scholarship to college, taught school for four years, then married, and has lived in the same house ever since.

Jack died last week. He had some sort of internal bleeding and in a few days he was dead. What a surprise! The girls didn't want me to visit him in the hospital because, they said, "He'll turn blue if he sees you."

Sixteen years ago he told me he was leaving. We were having breakfast—I don't know why he chose that moment. His words were, "Our daughter tells me I should tell you that I'm moving out." He indicated it would be a while because his place wasn't ready yet. This was June 1; by September, he said, he'd move out. We'd been married thirty-four years, and I had no idea he was building a "place."

This was shortly after the birth of our first grandchild. I'd been helping [my daughter] Janet a lot as her husband was away on a job. I took her to the hospital and brought her home and stayed with her. While I was there he'd gone through all the preparation, arranged to have the house built, bought all the stuff for it while I was busy helping Janet, so to have him say that Janet told him to tell me still sticks in my craw. She knew all that time and she didn't say a word. The transaction was done in another county so it wouldn't be in the local paper. I found the deed recently; it said on top "DO NOT PUBLISH" so I wouldn't catch on.

He used to tell me that when the kids were grown he was going to leave me, but he said it a lot and I didn't pay much attention. So that morning I still didn't believe him. Can't we work this out? He didn't say why he was unhappy with me, but he was retired and had been depressed for a long time. He spent most of his time in the basement. He hated noise. If I did laundry or mowed the lawn or vacuumed, he would leave the house. If he went down to the mailbox, I'd rush to get out the vacuum before he came back.

Things were not easy, but I felt this was extreme and wanted us to see a therapist. "No," he said, "you go." I did. I went for therapy, but it was pretty painful and I didn't stick to it. Unfortunately. I really regret that.

He always talked a lot about politics and business and music and many other things, but he was totally noncommunicative about personal things. We went together for five years before we married; he kept asking me to marry him and I said "no" because I had a sense he was so controlling. I can remember our first disagreements in those years before we married. He would be in tears; he shared his early family life, all his feelings, everything—before we married, but not after.

There was no other woman involved, as far as I know. I think his retirement did it. He had been Mr. Somebody, an important, successful businessman, and now he was nobody.

After that day I was busy with Janet and the new baby, and I was in total denial—I was not going to break down and cry. I've always been self-sufficient and I kept singing that little song: "Got along without y' before I met y', gonna get along without you now."

After Jack left, Janet called often, was concerned. My son-in-law said, "We won't let him do anything to hurt you." But over the years it changed. He sided with Jack. We once tried a Thanksgiving with all of us, but they ended up ganging up against me; I figured I didn't need that.

Our other daughter, Sarah, was also married, but that lasted about a year. She stayed in the town where she was teaching. She was having her own problems and she's not so easy to talk to; she hides her feelings like Jack.

I never sought a divorce. I was afraid. When I first married Jack said, "I'll teach you to be a widow," in other words, to handle all our financial affairs. I had lived by myself and taught school for four years after college, but in fact he kept the checkbook for our joint account (though he also had his own account separate from ours). He'd give me a check for immediate household needs, and then he'd give me another. He took care of all finances, did the taxes, and handed them to me to sign. He was licensed in insurance and in financial advising, so I was convinced I wouldn't be able to handle all these things.

He had to control everything. I remember when the kids were teens I felt I needed to learn how to talk to them about sex, to change some of the attitudes I'd grown up with—even though I grew up on a farm. At Albany Medical Center there was a sex ed course for students that was open to the public. It was six or eight sessions of lectures and discussions. Jack felt threatened. I was apparently too aggressive and he was afraid of what I would know or do, that I might have some control over some aspect of our daughters' lives and maybe even my own.

Divorce wasn't in my vocabulary. My mother and father didn't have a great relationship, but they had a "you make your bed and you lie in it" attitude. Of course if I were divorced, I'd have to consider another relationship. That scared me half to death.

I was chagrinned to be left, and in a sense it was more hurtful that there wasn't somebody else. It took me a very long time to be able to walk on Main Street, to talk to people. I was swamped with feelings of shame and failure, and I felt divorce would be the final failure. I never told my mother he had left because I was so ashamed. I had terrible nightmares. It wasn't fear of being alone as he used to go off for weeks at a time, but who was I except Jack's wife and the girls' mother? I had no other identity.

He indicated that I could stay in the house and he'd pay the expenses. The day he left he handed me a typewritten statement of what he would and would not pay for. He would cover my medical expenses, for instance, but wouldn't pay for hearing aids or false teeth. I had to laugh. He certainly did plan ahead and he certainly wasn't going to take care of me.

Of course I had a role in all of this too. From childhood, I was never able to say what I wanted or even needed. I was insecure about so many things. I always tried to save money. Instead, we should have had a woman in to clean the house while we went out for lunch and had some fun.

When he was in the hospital I discovered that I still hoped for some kind of reconciliation or forgiveness, but the girls said he didn't want to see me. With his death a big black cloud of fear disappeared, fear of what was going to happen next because he continued to pull the strings all those years, and I felt there was nobody who disliked me as much as he did. On the other hand, I had that sense of "He's gone, now I'm next," which surprised me a little. But then my brother died only a few months ago too.

I'm so sorry I didn't divorce him there and then. I wasted sixteen years living on the end of a fishing pole, and even now that he's dead there are still family issues: I said I need a new car badly and would take his, but the girls said he wouldn't want me to be driving his car. And the house? Well, I've lived almost all my life in this house. It's all I have. And if I sell it, I only get a third of the money as the girls each get one third. So they're pressuring me to sell it and move. Everything would be much easier now if we'd been divorced then because I would have gotten the house—I think.

Most of all I wonder what my grandchildren think about what they've seen all these years. They're all girls, ranging from nine to sixteen, and I worry about the scars on yet another generation.

Eva, sixty-one, is a freelance writer living in upstate New York with her now five-year-old daughter, Ellie.

It was Christmas Eve, 2002. Adam had been uncharacteristically distant in the last few weeks—he was usually overbearing and intrusive. But my birthday is on Christmas, so I was looking forward to our having a good time together.

He was so quiet on Christmas Eve I asked him if something was wrong. "Well, I'm in love with somebody else and I want to leave you." I didn't believe him at first. After eighteen years I had totally taken him for granted, and it was like a bomb going off. I was very dependent on him emotionally, and couldn't conceive of being left alone with no money in the middle of the woods on a dirt road unplowed in winter with a two-year-old child.

So I asked who is it, and it was Laura, who was his best friend at work for eight years. I just wasn't suspicious; it never even occurred to me. They used to go to lunch with a friend, and then they went alone, and then about a month earlier they went to New York City together and they declared their love. That's why he'd been so silent this last month.

He said he'd never wanted to adopt Ellie—even though he was the primary caregiver. She adored him, and all my friends talked about how much he adored her.

I tried to hold on to him. My friend Nancy was to visit us, but I went to her place instead. I left him with Ellie, and Nancy took care of me for the weekend. She rescued me and was giving me lectures on divorce. But I didn't want to face it all. I kept saying "Oh, no, Adam wouldn't do this, et cetera, he's my best friend, my comforter, my supporter—he wouldn't do this to me."

We'd been together for eighteen years, married for fifteen. He's fourteen years younger than me. My wise therapist said that the problem with a young man is someday he'll grow up and leave home. He did grow up to the extent he could. The marriage was always unbalanced because I rescued him. He was a wreck—no job, no place to stay. I rescued him from destitution or moving in with his parents.

When I came back from Nancy's, we made up. I talked him into staying even though I really knew he was seeing her—even though he denied it. He didn't have the nerve to leave, and we stayed together for a miserable year after that. We went to counseling, and talked and talked and eventually I thought things were OK.

Two years earlier, when I was fifty-six and Adam forty-two, we adopted a newborn. She was a half-Jewish, half-Cuban crack baby. Our marriage was shaky then, one of these "have a child to save the marriage" deals. We'd had a fourteen-year-old foster child, and we were really happy then; she was a sun-shine person, and she was neater than we were and took care of herself and was a joy. But she went back to her mother who finally got out of jail. I wanted to re-create that time. I made huge attempts for an older child. We were matched with a seven-year-old, but after three months her existing foster parents adopted her. That was a devastating loss. I was willing to adopt a teenager, but Adam refused. He didn't want a kid already formed. I had many misgivings about an infant, but Adam seemed really enthusiastic. I looked on the Net and found her very quickly, so we flew down to Florida and adopted Ellie.

Then things went downhill rapidly. Later when I was reading *Crazy Time* by Abigail Trafford, I saw how power balances in marriages can be in deadlock for years until some event throws off the balance. Often it's retirement. "My god! I have to spend the rest of my life with this person?"

When Ellie came I felt I'd always been taking care of him, and it was he who wanted an infant, so I handed her to him and basically said, "You take care of her." Of course he was furious. Why aren't you the traditional woman, in essence, taking care of me *and* Ellie? She became the scapegoat; we used her to punish one another. We had huge battles over supervision; I'm ex-tremely permissive, and he's totally overprotective. He was angry all the time and would go into rages. Our sex life disappeared. One day we were picking up Ellie and he threw his jacket in the car. I found a love letter, and that was it. He knew that would do it and it did. He couldn't get out fast enough. All of a sudden he had a furnished apartment—overnight and all fixed up.

From the moment he left it was like having a poison gas cloud out of the house. I was free and alone with Ellie and not being constantly criticized. I could parent her any way I wanted. But for a year I was a wreck, severely de-pressed, crying constantly, wanting him to love me. I never wanted a man again in my life. I just grieved—which I give myself credit for. But I still cried a lot and had fantasies we'd get back together.

Then things started to happen: I sold a book and got a big check I so des-perately needed. I found a great therapist who charged me almost nothing, and a great divorce lawyer. Now if that isn't the universe providing, I don't know what is.

I think I've done really well at recovering. In *Crazy Time* she says you're totally insane and do things you thought you'd never do, that it takes years. It does, so two years later I can see two more years of this. I still have all this anger; I would like to forgive him and let it go, but rage is still very much there.

My parents are dead and I have no siblings, so Adam was my only family and I felt abandoned. But in reality I have Ellie and friends and a whole support system to guide me through the postmarriage landscape. And now I even have a social life and a sex life. Not so bad, huh?

Della, thirty-four, was born and raised in a working-class home in a small town in upstate New York. Her mother returned to school for an M.A. in education after she divorced Della's alcoholic father, and she saw Della through law school.

It was one year ago, this date exactly, August 4th. After dinner we were supposed to go to a public hearing on taxes for the town. Bill said he didn't want to go. We started talking, and he said he wanted out. I was staggered! This continued for two days while I wept and tried to get him to stay. Two days later, he packed and left.

This was the second time. In May he had said he wanted out, and I thought, "What the hell is he talking about?" I remember sitting at the table, and he patted me on the shoulder, and I was shocked. I was terrified of losing him. The three years we were together were the happiest in my whole life; I felt my life was complete, nothing was lacking.

He had a weekend trip planned with the guys, and he just went ahead with it. He said he would think about whether to give it another chance, so I was left the whole Memorial Day weekend wondering if I would have something or not. I didn't tell anyone — I just couldn't believe it was happening.

All this time he'd said nothing, and harbored all these grudges. He felt we'd tried everything, but in fact he'd kept all this stuff to himself. He never told me before that he felt suffocated, hemmed in because he believed he was my whole life. But he spent lots of time with the guys. I knew that was important to him; it was a freedom I'd have wanted for myself if my health had been better.

I'd been bleeding heavily on and off for three years, but he never said it bothered him, never said it interfered with our sex life. Then my gynecologist left, so I had to start all over with the same surgery I'd had three years before. He was great during the surgery. Now he says he's sick and tired of hearing about the bleeding — but at the time he sat there and held me and comforted me, and I felt so lucky and so loved, so how was I supposed to know?

When he returned he said he owed it to our relationship to give it another shot. From May to August 4th I thought things were getting better. God, I remember what I did that day: I bought a set of pots and pans for us, and he didn't tell me not to. He kissed me and said he loved me. The night before we had made a week's menus, and before that we'd hosted my family reunion together. My mother had said, "Gee, Bill, we're so lucky we found you."

From May to August I worked hard on the things that were bothering him. He refused to acknowledge my efforts. When I was home after surgery I tried looking for another job because he said my job made me miserable. He thought I should just quit, and I began to see that it bugged him that I'm a lawyer. I thought we were intellectually equal; though he has no professional degree, he's educated, has special training in his field. He's licensed by the state and has a good job assessing house values for banks.

Soon after May he says, "Why don't we sell the house and move into an apartment because the house is too much to take care of." But I think he was afraid when the house was finished I'd be looking for marriage. He had an agent out to value the house. He had nothing, whereas I have some funds to fall back on. He owned only his truck and snowmobile. He had just paid off his debts before he left me in August. When we sold the house later he put $100,000 in his pocket. He wants no responsibility. He just wants a roommate, not a mate. He was upset if I asked him what time he'd be home for dinner!

Other women? I'm conflicted about it. I noticed that he started whitening his teeth, running again, doing sit-ups, and often came home late. He denied all that and continues to, though maybe his boss set him up in an apartment he owns above their office. He lives there now with a buddy—not another woman. I had him followed last fall because it was driving me crazy, but nothing turned up. I don't think he's dating now, but maybe that's just my hope. I moved in with my mother for a while, and then I found my own place.

He never asked me to marry him. He was twenty-seven when we met and I was thirty-three. He turned thirty last August. Then at Christmas his pal Nate died riding a snowmobile in the dark—he rammed into a tree. Nate was thirty and dead, so he starts thinking, "I'm thirty living in this house with this woman who will soon want to get married." He had never lived with a woman before. After we'd dated only six months, he invited me to move in with him. We rented a house for a while, then bought this great house at auction; we spent all our time and money remodeling, and it was just about perfect. Nate dies, he's freaked out, wants to be alone and starts blaming me.

His mother is an alcoholic, so he left home when he was thirteen, when his older sisters left the house. He left every woman he's ever been with, though I was the only one he'd actually lived with. You know, I was the seventh woman he'd left by age thirty.

My father was also an alcoholic. Bill drank and I was always concerned that it could all deteriorate, but I'm hypersensitive and have no gauge of normal drinking. As an adult child of an alcoholic he was living on the edge, trying to control everything because he had no control growing up. He never looked at any of this, and would never talk about it or get any help. I try to. My first boyfriend had addictive habits, and he, too, was as noncommunicative as my father.

But the breakup was far worse than what I went through in childhood because it was more personal and direct. The worst part was that I was so happy. I appreciated him more because of the ways he wasn't like my father: he was never violent, he treated me with respect, and I felt that we worked together as equals.

It all affected me horribly, physically and emotionally. I couldn't eat or sleep and was severely depressed. I lost my best friend, my lover, and my home—my escape, my retreat—all in one day. He destroyed my ability to trust and believe in anyone, male or female. I still have a long way to go to gain confidence, but I'm doing better. I have a friend now, a man I can go out with and travel with who understands what I'm still going through, and is willing to accept just friendship until I'm ready for something more. Am I happy? No. But I can enjoy some things, like traveling. The thing is I still love Bill and care about him. After all, can I just dismiss those happy years?

Work Cited

Trafford, Abigail. *Crazy Time: Surviving Divorce and Building a New Life*. Rev. ed. New York: HarperCollins, 1992.

Dear Harry

Unsent E-mails to an Ex

SUSAN BECKER

At the age of fifty-one, after a thirty-year relationship and early retirement from an academic career in conjunction with moving to a new country, I was suddenly dumped for a much younger woman. It took me nearly six months to actually absorb the reality of what was happening. This was complicated by the fact that my husband refused to move out, saying that there was no reason that we should not remain friends and continue to share a household even though the marriage was over. He argued that the house was big enough for all of us and that it would be "better for the children" if he didn't leave right away. Neither did he want to incur the additional costs of a third household. We already owned an expensive apartment in Manhattan which he used as his base for business abroad, and, as I now discovered, various other activities. For the sake of good will and the children, I did what I suppose I usually did. I repressed my natural instincts and my anger, and tried to be accommodating. He was traveling abroad more and more frequently, but when he was home he attempted to maintain the semblance of a normal family life. Although we were sleeping separately, he persisted in continuing a social life with me. I am embarrassed to admit that, confused and devastated, I allowed it. He pressured me into maintaining the status quo "for the sake of the children," but it became increasingly bizarre and painful. When I finally had the strength to insist that his unusual divorce agenda was untenable, requesting that he move out sooner rather than later, he became very nasty and flew into a rage, screaming, "I knew you would be like this." "Be like what?" I asked him quite innocently. "You know. Get angry. Refuse to be friends just because I left you," he yelled indignantly. My mouth is still hanging open. I was beginning to see my abandoning spouse in a whole new light, not to mention myself.

A few months after his announcement, before he moved out, I was cruising the bookstore for pop books on relationships and divorce and I came across an interesting study on emotional and verbal abuse by Patricia Evans titled *The Verbally Abusive Relationship*. I wasn't even sure why I picked it up, but it stopped me in my tracks. I stood reading in the bookstore for some time and was shocked to find that I could identify so closely with the author's case studies. Her descriptions of the experiences of emotionally abused women conveyed a perfect depiction of my own marriage, even though I had never thought of myself in this way. It was such an overwhelming realization that I became dizzy and nearly fainted in the Barnes and Noble. Suddenly I understood that I had been married to an uncaring, hostile control freak. What was worse, the abuse was continuing during the separation. Of course, this too should have come as no surprise, as my therapist later explained. "We should not expect someone to be different in the divorce than they were in the marriage," she told me toward the end of our therapy, hoping to prepare me for the difficult work ahead. I also learned that divorce may end the marriage, but it does not end the relationship. Even though my husband no longer wanted to be married to me, he continued to be controlling and invasive in my personal and professional life. Other than sleeping in a separate room, he offered me little privacy in my own home, barging into my study when I was visiting with friends or working and entering the bathroom when I was already there. When I complained about the latter, he responded with "What's your problem? I've seen you naked for years." I was beginning to feel invisible in my own house. Maybe I always had been.

Finally, some six months after D-day, he moved to an apartment just two blocks away, presumably to be close to the children. He left most of his personal effects in the family house, claiming that his new apartment was too small to receive them, and giving him a convenient justification to reenter the family home on a regular basis. He refused to return his key. I knew that had I gone to the expense of changing the locks, he would have merely manipulated the children to get use of their keys. He was determined to assert his legal conjugal presence. Sometimes he would enter the house unannounced and make phone calls from his old office. Once I overheard him speaking long distance to "the other woman." I complained about it in couple's therapy and he agreed to stop, but he reneged time and time again, and I was hesitant to take legal measures, still adopting my lifelong policy of appeasement. Even more bizarre, although he lived around the corner, he would use the bathroom when he dropped by, like a dog marking territory. While the marital/divorce therapy which I initiated at the time of his original announcement had concluded, and it was clear that our marriage was not salvageable, he refused to abdicate his power over the family household. At one point, I attempted to rent space in the house in order to generate some income, but he threatened me with a legal suit since he was still joint owner. He claimed that it was "detrimental to the children." For tax and business reasons our funds had always been parked offshore, and I had no access to our savings, which he brought into the country on a monthly basis, thereby exercising total financial control of our lives, even refusing to buy a second car, so that we were forced to communicate about logistics on a daily basis. He also attempted to confide in me about his new, volatile relationship and requested that I continue giving him his regular massage treatments.

As the harsh reality of my thirty-year relationship began to sink in, I entered into an incapacitating depression that came to a head some nine months after D-day. It was a horrendous emotional abyss, or what Carl Jung has called the "dark night of the soul." But I was still not in touch with my anger. Like so many women, I turned my rage inside, becoming anorexic and dysfunctional, and unable to carry out the most mundane daily tasks. In retrospect, I assume that I was suffering from some sort of posttraumatic stress syndrome. Noises startled me, nighttime terrified me, and I became increasingly agoraphobic. I was also anxious whenever I reentered the family home, even after my ex moved out. When I finally emerged from my breakdown, after several weeks on antidepressants, I was able to begin the therapeutic work necessary to find out how I came to be in my current situation, a long and painful journey. My new partner used to ask me how I could have stayed so long in such a detrimental relationship. In truth, I am still working on this question. This is my ongoing journey and indeed the impetus to write about my experience. What I do know is that my husband's final gesture of cutting me loose was the kindest thing he has ever done. As to my previous lack of awareness, Evans likens the emotionally abusive relationship to a scientific experiment with a frog: "A scientist conducted an experiment. She put frog number one into a pan of very hot water. The frog jumped right out. Then she placed frog number two in a pan of cool water. This frog didn't jump out. Very gradually, the scientist raised the temperature of the water. The frog gradually adapted until it boiled to death."[1]

Two years after D-day, my new life was taking shape, and I filed for divorce so that I could negotiate the financial settlement I needed to be independent of my ex and support myself and my children. This enraged him since he was used to being the initiator. However, he eventually acquiesced to an out-of-court settlement because he was terrified of financial disclosure in court. I had also been advised by lawyers that his obvious financial adeptness and cunning meant that any attempt at formal litigation on my part would be fraught with enormous fees and could take many years to resolve. It wasn't a great deal, but my partner, children, and friends all encouraged me to finish with him because they could see the detrimental effect of the lack of closure. While I got the primary family home free and clear and the first installment of his marital "buyout," he ultimately defaulted on his further financial obligations to me and the children. After several skirmishes in court, he left the country illegally to avoid further payment. He did not even say good-bye to his children for fear that they would alert me to his activities.

One day when I was working on my legal case and I was particularly livid over his failure to pay me and support the children, a close friend of mine said "Why don't you write him a letter and tell him what a schmuck he is! Not to send, just for catharsis!" To date I had maintained my composure in all our negotiations, never expressing my true feelings when we communicated about legal matters by e-mail, something I was all too adept at doing. Evans's book legitimated my strategy because she explains that part of the abuser's rush comes from successful provocation. So I took my friend's advice and started writing the truth in a series of unsent e-mails. I wrote *to* him, but not *for* him. Nasty, sarcastic accusations fell from my fingers on to the computer keys and I enjoyed every minute of it, sometimes laughing so hard I could barely type. These after-the-fact e-mails allowed me to comment on the various facets of our relationship and to express my resentment and anger in a breezy, humorous way that helped me to transcend my saga. When other friends ask me why I don't send the letters, I tell them that he doesn't need to hear it, I do! Writing has enabled me to redefine our history together, to make order out of years of marital chaos, and to deconstruct our relationship in an entirely new light. It has been transformational.

Natalie Goldberg, author of the now famous *Writing Down the Bones* and one of the leaders of the new "writing about writing" movement, tells us that "Writers end up writing about their obsessions. Things that haunt them; things they can't forget; stories they carry in their bodies waiting to be released."[2] Currently, there is a splendid burgeoning literature on memoir writing that deals with the therapeutic function of writing about personal trauma, sometimes referred to as "crisis memoir." Many authors, like Jane Taylor McDonnell, argue for the therapeutic aspect of writing: "The very act of writing is part of the recovery. In the telling, the writer becomes the survivor—one who has changed, but lived to tell the tale. These narratives . . . seek to reconstitute the lost self and reconceive the traumatizing experience as a survivor's story."[3] Susan Zimmerman talks about letters in particular. "There are love letters, and there are the other kind. There are those letters we need to write because we are so angry, so fed up, so frustrated, so sad."[4] Nancy Slonim Aronie describes one woman who goes to her computer every night and "writes a nasty letter to her ex-husband, which she never mails, but in doing this she now feels free to work on her new novel."[5] Last but not least, my favorite memoirist, Anne Lamott, instructs us that contrary to popular wisdom, "you should always write out of vengeance, as long as you do it nicely."[6]

These unsent e-mails are meant to follow in this fine tradition. I hope that my divorce narrative is as therapeutic for others as it has been for me. As the saying goes: Revenge is a meal best served cold. *Bon appetit*!

The X Files
DEDICATION AND INTRODUCTION

These e-mails are dedicated to Harry, my partner and mentor of thirty years, who taught me everything about life that I would rather not have known. First, there is nothing more important than money and power. (I'm not so clear about the order here. I think Harry would find this a tough call.) Second, there is nothing so sacred that we can't joke about it. Third, and more important, you should always aim with great precision, right below the belt. Thanks, honey.

Apologetic caveat: To all the nice Harrys in the world. Sorry, guys, but I had to pick a name. I humbly apologize. I have nothing against you, or men in general for that matter, just one in particular whose real name must go unmentioned for obvious legal reasons.

I hope these e-mails do not offend my readers. Especially men. I understand that some people might think they go beyond the boundaries of good taste. And some men might feel a tad defensive. But I want to assure you that there is no cause for concern here, because these letters are addressed to Harry and Harry alone. Furthermore, I promise you that Harry has a simply fabulous sense of humor, albeit a little warped, so I can practically guarantee that he won't have a problem with any of this.

As to the kinda bitchy tone. Harry always told me I wasn't competitive or ambitious enough. Although I have a Ph.D. and I used to be somewhat of a local celebrity during the heyday of the women's movement, I never made much money from it, and I'm certain that Harry would say I failed to capitalize on my reputation and charisma. He always thought I should hustle more and be more aggressive, especially in bed, although I have to admit I never understood that one. He thought I needed more of an "edge." Well, this should do the trick!

As to the privacy thing, the notion that confidences between intimates should be respected even after the relationship is terminated, this is a much more serious issue. And I have deferred to Harry on this one time and time again, especially on the very delicate matter of financial disclosure. Truth is I haven't a clue how much money he has and my pockets aren't deep enough to undertake a proper investigation. My first lawyer told me that I should hire a "forensic accountant," whatever that is, to get the goods on someone like Harry. I realize that some people think Harry is a little "shady," but I try to avoid this term, because I know how much it presses his button. I understand that all those foreign bank accounts, offshore trusts, and brass plate companies leave him no choice. A guy's got to protect himself.

If, in spite of these caveats, anyone is still offended by my e-mails, I can only say two things. First, anger is therapeutic. Second, laughter is the best medicine. Oh, I almost forgot. She who laughs last, laughs best! Finally, I humbly apologize for all the clichés. They just seem to go with the territory.

REGRETTABLE E-MAIL

Dear Harry,

I probably should have been furious when I received your curt little e-mail. "Regrettably, market conditions preclude a payment at this time." But instead it sent me into incredible cascades of laughter. Your syntax is so predictable. You completely avoid the pronoun "I" as in "Sorry I can't pay you" or "Sorry I lost all your money dicking around in the stock market." Not to mention the possibility of "Sorry I lost the kids' university funds," etc. I mean really, Harry, there were so many options. But your message is so utterly blameless. It is reminiscent of a neutral announcement over a PA system which might report: "Due to rain, the picnic has been cancelled." And let me tell you this, Harry, there are no picnics ahead! The gloves are off. Just who do you think you are? We had a contract. It was a court order. You can keep on repeating your "financial woes" mantra, but, frankly, I don't believe you and neither does anyone else. So maybe I can't get blood from a turnip, but I can squeeze real hard. Yes, I laughed for a long time after receiving your little note, sweetheart, because it was so quintessentially you. But then I got real angry. And, Harry, if you wanted me to be sympathetic to the falling stock market and your failing financial circumstances you might have tried sounding a little vulnerable or pathetic, and you could have had the decency to warn me that my money wasn't going to be deposited in the bank as we agreed. Instead I kept calling the bank repeatedly like an idiot and asking them about my funds, to which they replied "what funds?" That was tacky, Harry. Very tacky.

Regrettably yours,

S.

THE BRACELET

Dear Harry,

I know that this thank-you note is a little belated, but I was just looking down at the bracelet you bought me only a few months before you dumped me. It was rather amusing, because a close mutual friend (whose name will go unmentioned because you know how much I hate gossip) received a similar bracelet from Tiffany's from her husband when he was having an affair a few years back. What can I say? Great minds think alike. Anyway, I was just thinking to myself how much I adore this bracelet. You always did have excellent taste. And I want you to know that I wear it every day, even though some of my friends think it's a bit weird since you later confided that you bought the same bracelet for your "twinkie." Did you get a bulk discount? Since it is the only piece of jewelry that you didn't ask to have returned, I also like to think it has some sentimental value. My booby prize, so to speak. Truthfully, I almost threw it in the trash several times, but I just didn't have the heart. Besides, the one positive thing you can say about us as a couple is that we were very "consumer compatible," a "résumé marriage." However, the real reason I love wearing this bracelet is that it reminds me that I am a survivor, one of the walking wounded, a dumped, middle-aged woman, cut loose in the prime of life. And although you always found me pretty hard to take in this regard, I believe in calling a spade a spade. So tell me, Harry, does your twinkie wear her bracelet every day like I do? I hope she appreciates your elegant taste as much as I always did. By the by, does she know you bought one for me? I am worried that we might end up at some family function like a kid's wedding wearing our matching bracelets and it could be embarrassing for everyone.

Sensitively yours, as always,

Susie

NASTY MAIL

Dear Harry,

I heard via the grapevine that you received a nasty little legal document today and that you are not a happy camper. Please accept my apology. I never

dreamed that the courts would deliver on a Friday and ruin your whole weekend.

Mea Culpa

THE OTHER WOMAN

Dear Harry,

You know many of our friends think I was quite strange for being so disinter-
ested in the "other woman." But frankly, I have never held much stock in the
notion that other people break up marriages. It's always been pretty clear to me
that we get involved with other people because there is something wrong with
the marriage in the first place. Since I have been so excruciatingly ignorant
about so many issues, it is rather remarkable that I have been so clearheaded
about this one. That's why I never pried into the identity of your twinkie. I did-
n't really care. Besides, you told me from the onset that she was "much
younger," and it all made good sense to me. Aging-businessman-fails-and-
reinvents-himself-with-much-younger-devoted-deferential-female-looking-for-
a-father-figure. My biggest embarrassment was that I felt like I was in a
Hallmark afternoon movie. Okay, so I'm a walking cliché. Whatever. But I can
no longer ignore the fact that I have heard various tidbits about "her," and
there is a particular detail that I just can't get my head around. Well, actually
there are two. The first is that I know her, and that she had been to our house
for dinner, since she used to date a friend of ours who confided to me that he
broke up with her because she was too neurotic. As I recall, I liked her. She
was rather charming in a frenetic sort of way. Which reminds me, Harry. Did
you know that they actually met at a stoplight where she picked him up because he was driving a cute little sports car? And then they went back to her
place, or was it his, to do the nasty? So tell me, how did you guys meet up
again? I just love romantic anecdotes. The other thing I just can't get out of
mind is the fact that everyone says she is FAT. Listen, honey, I don't have a
problem with this. Each to his own. But I seem to recall that you always did.
Aren't you the guy who harassed me all those years about my weight? And the
truth of the matter is that I have never been what anyone would call fat. Yet
you persisted in making rude remarks about my body. Of course, when I said
I didn't like it, you invoked your favorite verbally abusive defense tactic,
"You're too sensitive. Where's your sense of humor? Can't you take a joke?"
Then you would wonder why I wasn't "in the mood." I hope that these e-mails
demonstrate that you were dead wrong. I have a great sense of humor. I just
wasn't in the mood for YOU. So Harry, what is this fat thing really about?
Maybe I got it all wrong. Are you really wild about fat women and you were

actually trying to provoke me to eat more? It wouldn't surprise me one bit to find out that you are one of those fetishist types that likes to dive into mounds of flesh. It goes with your other kinky proclivities. Come to think of it, your mother was pretty chunky, may she rest in peace. And one of your sisters is downright obese. I think I'm finally starting to get the picture. Unfortunately, I must confess that I am just as thin as ever, even though I eat like a teenager. Your stunning daughter and I still share clothes and so does my lover. We all wear the same size jeans and I can never keep the laundry straight. You always said I would never change! You were right about so many things. So if fat is your thing, honey, go for it. As your mother always used to say, "There's someone for everyone!" And it certainly sounds like your twinkie enjoys your gourmet cooking even more than I did.

Bon appetit!

NOT A ROCKET SCIENTIST

Dear Harry,

I am shocked and dismayed to hear that you are telling everyone I should stop sitting around the house playing the piano and get out of retirement instead of going after you in court. Harry, I'm fifty-eight and it is pretty hard to start up again. Besides, what have I got to feel guilty about? I paid my dues. I worked professionally full time and was primary caretaker, cook, and chief bottle washer during our many years together. Besides, I'm too busy for a full-time job. I have barely touched the piano for weeks. I've been too busy preparing my case with lawyers. But I have managed to get in some tennis. And a good thing too. If I couldn't get my endorphins moving on the court I might inflict bodily harm on SOMEbody. What do you mean I don't work? When I'm not dealing with the kids, and looking after your white-elephant house, I spend full time, just like you used to do, taking care of family money and managing lawsuits. I am also a landlady since I have been forced to rent space in a house I can't sell. In fact, the whole scene is rather ironic, me sitting at the computer in your beautiful office, a monument to greed and narcissism. While I don't really enjoy messing around with this investment stuff, I am learning fast. (sorry, honey, not fast enough to let you off the hook) and I am hoping that my new legal ventures pay off because we need the eggs. It hasn't been easy, but I have finally accepted the way things turned out, and I keep my nose to the grindstone. Harry dear, for years we built our life around your travel, your work, your financial decisions. And you buried yourself in the office poking around on the Internet doing God knows what. By the by, from the looks of our investments during the flush '90s I must tell you that I was shocked to see that you were a lot less successful than I assumed. Maybe you were just distracted by all the porn. In short, the one thing you always claimed with pride is that you provided me and the kids with financial security. What a joke! Although it is still hard to believe that you actually lost all your family money, my money, my mother's gift money and even the kids' university funds. If your woe-is-me-mantra is true, then prove it in court. If it's not true, and you were successful or at least less than a total failure, then you've ripped us off royally. So which is it? You don't have to be a rocket scientist.

Speaking of rocket scientists, I have to admit that I used to be in awe of all your fancy financial footwork. What is unfamiliar is always a bit mysterious and impressive. I recall the words of my shrink, who told me that she has seen many mid-life women blossom in their competency skills after a traumatic divorce. She was so right. This money stuff is pretty empowering. It may be time consuming, uncreative, and a bit boring at times, but it is strangely satisfying. Maybe in part because it has revealed the insignificance of your contribution to the family. Sad, but true. Listen, Harry, I know that you did what you could. But in retrospect it wasn't really all that much. I could only know that now.

Sue

THE GOOD DIVORCE

Harry,

About that book which you insisted I just had to read, *The Good Divorce*, by whoever.[7] I don't buy it. It's downright wrong. Maybe it applies to a small segment of the population, but certainly not to us. Remember US? We were not a mutually separating couple. You had a long-term affair and didn't tell me until you dumped me without warning. In the book, some couples remain friends because the split was a mutual proposition, negotiated over time, and third parties were not involved. Did you really read the book or did you just like the sound of the title? Harry, of all the insulting and dishonest things you said and did during our painful separation, insisting that I read this book and arguing with me about its validity was probably the most offensive. I understand that you must have felt guilty about our one-sided breakup, and that you would dearly love to pin our estrangement on someone other than yourself. But did you really think you could convince me that we should remain friends after you left me the way you did? And trying to confide in me about your twinkie and your long-distance relationship really takes the cake. I mean, tell me about it! You and I had a long-distance relationship for thirty years, and I am not referring to your business trips. Actually, my therapist thinks that we probably would have split years ago if you hadn't traveled so much.

Back to the book. Quite frankly, the whole premise of the study, if you can call it that, is a little bizarre. But what do I know, I'm only a social scientist. If a couple can communicate so well during and after a divorce as to remains good friends, you have to wonder why they split in the first place. As our therapist has pointed out to me repeatedly, it is hard for a divorce to be better than the marriage. And frankly, Harry, our marriage sucked. On a scale of one to ten this book gets a zero. Thanks for your generous offer to buy an extra copy, but don't bother. Besides, as you can see, I am writing my own book on divorce. Let me know if you want an autographed copy. God knows you deserve one!

BUYING A BARRACUDA

Hi Harry,

The other day I was cleaning out some office drawers and I found one of your humorous cartoon notepads. Remember this one: "My lawyer can beat up your lawyer." I'm into my third divorce lawyer, and I don't mind telling you they are getting more expensive and of course more aggressive. I like my new one. He has a fabulous, all-glass, corner office looking out over Park Avenue. He apologized for his high fees, but says he's worth it, and I believe him. Besides you always said I was a cheapskate and that you get what you pay for. And you said a lawyer should be a barracuda. Naturally, when it comes to business matters and lawsuits I always defer to your good judgment. Which reminds me. Remember that day when we had lunch together to sort out a couple of bureaucratic matters, and I was right in the middle of my horrendous depression? I had the distinct feeling that you were starting to worry that I might actually wake up and start giving you a hard time instead of flagellating myself. I recall that in the middle of lunch you took a piece of paper out of your pocket and got so excited that your eyes started to bulge out of your head the way they do when you're agitated. You proudly announced that you had the names of the toughest divorce lawyers in town. You said that if I hired one of these guys then you would too, and we would only escalate the cost of litigation and make things very unpleasant for everyone. I think I nodded in agreement because it was too late to do anything else. I feel badly, Harry, because I sorta lied that day. I had already hired number two on your list. But I was inscrutable just like you taught me. I mean I may have been depressed, Harry, but I wasn't lobotomized! By the way, you will no doubt be flattered to hear that when I told my latest Park Avenue lawyer about you and all your financial hanky-panky, he was suitably impressed. He even said to me, "Smart guy, eh?" But I have a gut feeling that he may be just a little bit smarter. See you in court, sweetheart.

Your star student—Sue

THE DIAMOND

Dear Harry,

I know that there is no love lost between you and my mom. But I really must let you know that she was really irked by the fact that you took back that very expensive emerald-cut diamond engagement ring. Of course, she was delighted to hear that we split, as were all of my family members and some of our friends. But you know how moms are, so conventional about etiquette and protocol. I tried to explain to her that I really didn't give a hoot about the diamond, except of course for the resale value. Diamonds were really your thing, not mine. Not that you ever paid for it since it was part of the booty you inherited from your family along with various other silver spoons. But what the heck, you seemed to want it so much. Frankly, I was happier to keep the appliances. Which reminds me, when are you and your twinkie tying the knot and why isn't she wearing it? It is also worth mentioning that before I gave it back to you, my mom and I put a curse on it, so that any future recipient will become instantly repulsed by the sight of your "magic wand" and you in turn will become permanently impotent. So Harry, guard the ring carefully, and don't forget to keep up the insurance!

Ta-ta

SEX

Dear Harry,

I heard a great line the other day and I thought of you immediately. It was about your favorite topic, or rather your second favorite topic after the green stuff. (Of course, I don't mean grass. How could I possibly forget how paranoid it makes you?) So here's the quote: When sex is good it's about 10 percent of the relationship. When its bad its 90 percent. Now isn't that a beaut? Do you think it could have helped us if we had heard it a few years back? Whatever . . . I could never understand why you were so obsessed with our sex life. In retrospect, it seems to have been the least of our problems. But with you it was always "never enough" and never the "right kind." It reminds me of the famous Woody Allen line in *Annie Hall* about the food at a summer resort: "The food was terrible, and the portions were too small." But I am digressing here, as usual. Harry, I scarcely knew what to do with all that sleazy lingerie like the crotchless pantyhose and the weird leather paraphernalia you insisted on collecting. I put most of it in a used-clothing box, because truthfully I don't know another living soul who would wear it other than perhaps your twinkie, but decided it would be too weird to send it to her. Then I thought about putting together an installation exhibit on women and coercive sexuality, but I had second thoughts. You see I have stopped being that angry, male-hating, feminist bitch you always accused me of being. Instead I am putting all my eggs in one basket, so to speak, where they rightfully belong. Sweetie, don't think for a second that I don't know that I am at least partly to blame. I know that I withdrew sexually. I'm sorry, but I just couldn't help it. After all, you know better than anyone that we have to go with our bodies. And mine wanted out big time. I was just too unconscious to realize what was happening. However, I was more than a little irked to hear that you have been telling some people that I was frigid. For someone as private as you wasn't that a teensy insensitive? Furthermore, just to set the record straight, if I ever was, which I wasn't, I sure as hell ain't now. Maybe it's true what they say about midlife women coming into their sexual prime. Maybe you should have waited, Harry. Anyway, I would dearly love to hear from you regarding the quote. Do you get it? I must have your answer by Thursday.

Your *petit chou*

P.S. I have been meaning to tell you that I have finally got rid of those nasty late-night headaches. Probably just a change in diet.

OOPS

Oh my God Harry,

I am so embarrassed. I must have hit the wrong line on my computer address book. The problem is that your name happens to be right next to my lover's name, just the way the alphabet goes, so please don't read into it. I am soooo sorry. I never meant to subject you to our mushy e-mails. It's just that we like to write to each other first thing in the morning and sometimes before we go to sleep. It's one of the romantic features of not living together. Remember how you always used to quip that "familiarity breeds contempt." So tell me, Harry, how are you and your live-in doing?

Sue

WHAT YOU MEAN "WE"?

At the risk of sounding repetitive, Harry, exactly when do you intend to pay me? As I am sure you are aware, your grace period is almost up and you are about to be in deep legal doo-doo. And please stop sending me revised proposals with new payment schedules. Your strategy may work with your fellow "suits," but remember me? I'm the idiot who lived with you for thirty years, and although I am a slow learner, I finally get the picture. You are a psychopath, a liar, and a thief. And you are up the proverbial creek without a paddle. Sorry if I sound harsh, honey. I don't mean to, because our marital therapist has convinced me that you are not actually evil, but more likely psychotic and delusional, and a few other technical diagnostic labels which I won't bore you with. But under no circumstances do I accept the position of your last e-mail in which you say that you are sorry you can't pay now and that further legal pressure would merely be "counterproductive and detrimental to the children." How could it be detrimental for a guy to support his own kids? Funny, since you always accused me of psychobabble! Although I must admit that I am really impressed with how often you mention your deep concern for the children in your e-mails. Maybe it is true that some divorced men become better, more active, caring fathers. On the other hand, why don't you just pay them their paltry allowance and shut the f—k up! Bottom line, I definitely do not agree with your assertion that "Like it or not, we are all in the same boat." Remember the joke about the Lone Ranger and Tonto who are out riding on the plains when they are suddenly surrounded by a tribe of hostile Indians? So the Lone Ranger says to Tonto, "What do we do now?" And Tonto quips back, "What you mean WE, white man?" Harry, we are not a "we" anymore. I'm not on your team. I don't have to be nice. I don't have to be understanding. And I sure don't have to accept your meaningless I.O.U.s and cover for your financial fiascoes.

Yours (Not)

MIDLIFE CRISES

Harry,

Please forgive me. I know how much you hate too much introspection. Actually I used to be a little resistant myself until you dumped me and I slipped into a major clinical depression. It appears that your betrayal and abandonment precipitated an emotional crisis which has expanded my spiritual horizons. So first of all, let me thank you. I couldn't have done it without you, and I like the person I have become very much. I am especially intrigued by this whole issue of midlife crises and the notion that as we age and move toward death, all sorts of material comes up, unfinished business, dreams, failures, and we come face to face with the essence of our being. Pretty scary thought for you, eh, Harry? I always assumed that this meant taking a harsh inventory of things and getting one's act together for the final round. I figured that if divorce was so traumatic, the upshot should be a new and improved, more authentic quality of life. Or else why bother? I mentioned my assumption to a friend/therapist the other day and she looked at me aghast, as in how could I possibly be so naive. She said that while crises help some people rise to their higher selves, others go the other way. So tell me, Harry, how is it down there? Authentic enough for ya? Thank God and bless you for not taking me with you.

Gratefully Yours

P.S. Was it Freud who said that the purpose of psychotherapy is to replace real pain and suffering with neurotic pain and suffering?

TROPHY WIFE
Dear Harry,

Wow, this is a tough one, and I won't be surprised if you don't get it right away, since it has taken me a long time to figure it out myself. I mean who can believe it, I was a trophy wife! So I may not be blonde or gorgeous. And I have never been into makeup and clothes. And I didn't exactly hang on your every word. But I'm reasonably nice looking and pretty personable. Plus I have a damn good résumé! Only in retrospect did I realize how much mileage you got off my academic status and my local celebrity. Perhaps you liked my "fringiness" since it complemented your dry, uptight suit mentality. Let's face it, Harry, we must have both enjoyed our archetypal division of labor with me as the intellectual, hippie-earth-mother and you as the big-chief-hunter-venture-capitalist. And it worked until it didn't. Do you recall when my unconventional charisma started to aggravate rather than to excite? Exactly when did you sour on our *Dharma and Greg* [a sitcom about the New-Age daughter of aging hippies and her upper-class, lawyer husband] arrangement? Just the other day a new acquaintance of mine, who happens to be a shrink, asked me about our relationship. So I gave her the five-minute *Dharma and Greg* synopsis, even though it barely did you justice. When I was finished she proclaimed with great excitement, "Oh I get it. You married him to rein you in!" Smart lady. Why didn't I think of that! Well, I don't need reining in anymore. I'm single. I'm middle aged. I feel great. I love being me. And *I'm-nobody's-trophy-wife-now.* (Sing it!)

MY LITTLE ADDICTION
Dear Harry,

I know you were shocked the other day when I lit up after our "business" lunch. I used to be such an avid antismoker. I am embarrassed to admit that the stress of the divorce and litigation seems to have precipitated my newly acquired habit, which is way out of control. I have decided that I must do something about it ASAP. Last night a friend of our son's dropped by, and I bummed a ciggie from him. It was terrible, one of those really cheap third-world brands. So I had this great idea. I will only buy the cheapest, worst-tasting cigarettes that I can find. Do you think this could cure my addiction? It worked for marriage.

COMPUTER COMPETENCY
Harry dear,

I miss you and I need you. Urgently. You know how hopeless I am with machines. I got a new laptop, but until recently I didn't use it for very much except some surfing, e-mail, and a few business letters, mostly to lawyers. Suddenly I find myself writing this book about us and I need to know how to forward attachments, how to format, and all sorts of stuff. I know perfectly well that I drove you crazy all those years asking you for your help since I was always such a technophobe. And you always helped. IF you were in the country. IF you were in the mood. Or IF you thought it would help to get me in the mood! Even though you always made me feel like an idiot and you never really had the patience to show me how to do things, you just did them for me, and I am sorry to say, Harry, not very graciously. You will be proud to hear that I am getting a lot better. You wouldn't believe all the mechanical maintenance I do now, taking care of the house, electricity, plumbing, and the car all by myself. The computer is my last remaining nemesis. Oh well, you know what they say about necessity being the mother of invention. This book is a great motivator on so many fronts. For one crazy moment I actually thought about e-mailing you for computer help, before realizing how absurd it was since you use IBM and I use Macintosh. Am I right in presuming you are still a PC kinda guy? Then it would never work.

Susie

The apple of your eye

THE THIRTY-YEAR MISTAKE

Dearest Harry,

I apologize for writing so many letters, but I just can't seem to stop. I suppose it's not so surprising that after so many years together I still have so much I long to share with you. There is still such a lack of closure, and I have so many questions. Mainly, WHAT THE HELL HAPPENED TO YOU? Although some people tell me that you didn't change at all, i.e. I just never saw you clearly. In one of our final conversations you asserted two things quite adamantly. First, you swore that you "never really loved me." Second, you insisted that you were never really a "family" man. In short, it was all a great mistake. Well that's some mistake, sweetheart. The odd thing is that you were the one who wanted more kids. Maybe that's not so surprising since I was the primary caretaker and you traveled so much. But when you were home and the kids were little, you seemed to be doing a good job. You seemed to be involved. But then again, you seemed to be a lot of things which you obviously weren't. Do you have any idea how many birthday parties you missed? The kids never complained. Neither did I. We had some fabulous times without you. Frankly, I feel sorry for you. You missed so much, and you still are. Our kids have turned into spectacular young adults, in spite of the mess you made. Harry, how on earth did you manage to screw up your life like this? Makes me wonder who made the thirty-year mistake.

As to the "never loved me" bit. This is just plain ridiculous. Only a few years before you left you gave me a very thoughtful birthday gift, something I had been wanting for a long time, an etymological dictionary. And you inscribed it "To the love of my life." You even presented it to me in front of friends which was very touching considering how undemonstrative you always were, especially in public. At first I was so stunned by the inscription that I thought it was a used book, but then I realized that the handwriting was definitely yours. Which reminds me. After you moved out I noticed that the book was missing. Really, Harry, it's one thing to take back a diamond ring, but stealing a book! Besides, what if your twinkie opens it and sees the inscription, or did you rip out the cover page? Does she even know what an etymological dictionary is?

It is one thing to say that you fell out of love with me, or that you started to hate my guts, but at least be truthful about the past. You used to adore me and I must have loved you too, even though right now it's hard to imagine. So stop with the revisionist history. It doesn't sit well with someone of your educational stature.

Mistakenly yours,

S.

DEATH THREATS

Dear Harry

I hear that you are making death threats against me, and I am curious if you are planning to do it yourself or hire out. Although I can't understand how you can afford to contract someone since you claim to be so financially limited. I consulted a few mental-health care professionals on the matter to see if I should be concerned, and they agreed that you might be capable of doing something really bizarre. It must be comforting to know that someone believes in you. Anyway, I want you to know that I am leaving the manuscript with a friend to be published in my absence in case anything should happen to me.

Posthumously yours,

S.

Notes

1. Patricia Evans, *The Verbally Abusive Relationship* (Avon, Mass.: Adams Media Corporation, 1992), 111.

2. Natalie Goldberg, *Writing Down the Bones* (Boston: Shambhala Publications, 1986), 38.

3. Jane Taylor McDonnell, *Living to Tell the Tale* (New York: Penguin Books, 1998), 14.

4. Susan Zimmerman, *Writing to Heal the Soul* (New York: Three Rivers Press, 2002), 119.

5. Nancy Slonim Aronie, *Writing from the Heart* (New York: Hyperion, 1988), 107.

6. Anne Lamott, *Bird by Bird* (New York: Anchor Books, 1994), 224.

7. Constance Ahrons, *The Good Divorce* (New York: HarperCollins, 1995).

My Own Dance

MARGIE KAPLAN

Even though Ted had said that he wanted to leave, I was frantically working on being perfect, loving, and the woman no one would want to leave, so frantically that I really hadn't even considered the actual reality until the night I was lying flat on my back on my bed and Ted was STANDING, legs veed on either side of my waist, shrieking down at me that he hated me. It was scary, I'll admit, and that was when I decided that my "wait until after the holiday" plan was unacceptable, and he should GET THE FUCK OUT AS FAST AS POSSIBLE. Pieces of mental health crept out periodically from my behaviors long before I had the slightest understanding of what I or life was about. I think I was somewhere in the middle of that path that night, much further along than when, twenty-six years before, I'd decided not to have children to infuse excitement into a one-year-old marriage that had already been boring before the wedding day.

This was a very different time and story. Ted and I had been married more than ten years. We had two great kids. Since it was a second marriage for me (if you consider that year of playing house when I was nineteen a marriage), and I'd spent almost fifteen years living a very "socially active" life, this commitment was nothing I took lightly. I didn't feel our relationship was made in heaven, but I certainly was in it for the long haul, and I did love Ted and would have worked indefatigably at keeping us together. I never thought I was an easy person, but working out my kinks, especially in relation to those I care about, was (and continues to be) my main agenda. I may be a difficult pain in the ass at times, but a valuable, life-affirming force nonetheless. I think those who really are close and know me, know that. Having Ted not thinking I was "worth it" probably has been the hardest part of this whole experience. He had my best (as well as my worst), my love and fun and energy and support. He didn't feel it, though.

Anyway, if I'm going to reenact it, you'll need some background. I think we had quite a love affair. We met in a bar/restaurant on the Upper West Side in New York City. After conversation and a lot of "energy exchange," he walked me back to my office/weeknight apartment, and so it began. We were very different people. I was just short of thirty-five and Ted was twenty-five. I was a therapist in private practice wanting to connect with a life-mate after years of serial monogamous relationships, none of which I wanted to continue. I was always the leaver. He was a wannabe musical theater lyricist earning his income through actuarial work. We were driven people, though in different directions. Writing was the energy source for Ted; people were for me. One oddity was that I was the third relationship in his life and his third older woman. Before Ted, the men I dated were never much more than a couple of years in either direction of my age.

We clicked, good repartee, chemical energy, and we were off. I should have known four months into our relationship that we were a mismatch. My dog, my thirteen-year life companion, died, and Ted accompanied me and a dear friend to my country place upstate to bury him. We did that deed and celebrated his life in a mini service. I was bereft driving back into the city but Ted said, "I don't get it, being so emotional about a *dog*." Why I didn't realize that this person was from another planet than mine I don't know, but there is a lot to be said for chemistry.

Ted is from an Italian/Irish Catholic Connecticut family and I am a New York City "cultural Jew" (to use words he put into a song). My family is inappropriately intrusive and loud, hostile, warm, and competitive, and always together for the standard occasions, birthdays, holidays, et cetera. His is repressed, church attending, and not close or loving toward each other. His mom was a wonderful exception to this description, but unfortunately for us all, she died much too soon to have an impact on the families' interactions apart from her communicated love of music, which was so important to us all. Those harmonizing dishwashing moments we all shared are forever with us. She embraced me, the older, divorced, New York Jewish woman, and I loved her back.

So Ted and I moved forward, merged friends, had fun, became partners, and then time pressured us. I wanted children, as did Ted, but our ages and where we were on our paths were quite different. He was waiting for his break, success in the musical theater world, and writing was his "raison d'être." Having a family, he felt, would limit his time for going after what he wanted. I defended the "having a stable environment as a seedbed for moving forward" proposition. Before meeting me, he partied, drank a lot, and felt lonely. With "us," he could feel secure and have a warm place to work. I'd keep the kids while he worked and wrote. About a year and a half later when we both cried at the disparity of our places in life and agreed to part, Ted called the next day and asked me to meet him for dinner. I arrived to champagne and a very romantic proposal. We were married shortly thereafter.

Our first daughter was born fourteen months later, and our second, four years after that. Our marriage wasn't made in heaven, but, I think, I never questioned my decision. I know I loved and cared for Ted. I adored my girls. I felt that I had choreographed our lives to keep my part of our bargain. I've often wondered about that, as one of the things Ted yelled down at me as he straddled me that night on the bed was that I was "totally selfish" and only thought about myself. Reality checks with family and friends revealed that Ted was always writing and we had to give him the time and space. Even vacations in the Caribbean, we'd all beach frolic, shop, and sightsee. Ted would be in the hotel writing, only joining us at dinner time.

Don't get me wrong. Ted always loved the girls and was adoring and clearly happy with them and they with him. His writing, however, needed to be respected, number one, and we all did that. I felt that I was a cheerleader and enthusiastic support for all his forays into the musical theater world. We never missed a showcase of his work and I don't think he could have had a more encouraging mate or family, but he felt differently.

Life went on with its ups and downs. I parented, was very school active, started a Brownie troop, and let my practice dwindle some. Ted studied for actuarial exams (another big time-consumer that needed to be, and I felt was, respected), spent other time writing (of course), and probably was let down by the years passing with only very limited acknowledgment for all his creative effort.

But we persevered. Ted can be a very loving, expressive (usually with written words) person. We had fun, fought, had fewer "chemical juices" flowing, but it seemed to me, and I think to him as well, that we were OK. I remember my fortieth birthday, before our second daughter was conceived, feeling very lucky and grateful to have work I loved, a husband I loved, and a beautiful daughter as well. Our second daughter was a thrill, completing our family. We used to laugh hysterically remembering the cab ride to the hospital—between contractions I noticed the meter flying way too fast ahead. I alternately moaned about the severe cramping and was in a fury at getting screwed by our driver. We lucked into a good apartment, Ted was financially successful, I had a small practice and life continued on.

But I wasn't delusional. Ted was an uninspiring lover and I'm sure I walled myself off from deeper levels of intimacy (as is my way). At the end of the day, I liked to blob out in front of the boob tube for an hour of inane entertainment. I think I was letting Ted down, as when he was finished with his writing he would have wanted us to share music or reading together and I was already "gone" for the day. Suffice it to say I fell far short of being the perfect loving wife, and I do have a big mouth to boot.

I can be terribly critical, especially if I feel threatened and turn to people, as others use Valium, when anxious. Ted is a considerably less social person. I think this fact (as it always is) was one of our attractions to each other and a cause of ongoing dissatisfaction. As an example, we had rented the next-door apartment for a niece of mine who would walk into our apartment with her key, head to the kitchen, pour a glass of orange juice, and head home. I loved the connection. Ted told me, "I didn't know when we married that I'd be living in a commune!" We were different people.

The years passed. I don't remember anything gigantic, no major upheaval. I think my big mouth was experienced by Ted as he experienced his berating father, and I think he fell into accepting my loudness as law, and his resentment grew. Through all those years he never learned that all he needed to do was stand firm and I would defer, sound and fury signifying nothing but fear and insecurity.

Somehow, there was love and caring and we shared wonderful times both as a family and as a couple. We enjoyed singing together, working out harmonies, and getting a repertoire. We appreciated each other, all along. His ranting that he had hated me for years contradicted the Valentine's Day card of a few months before, where he hand wrote "Here's to a continued loving and rewarding life together. We're really lucky to have so much, and even if I'm too busy or too tired or too hysterical or too whatever to realize it all the time, I *do* realize it and I do feel it deep down in my heart." A part of me is frustrated that I keep this card, but it is a reality touchstone for me.

In June 1992 Ted had raised the issue of our separating, and I panicked and got us into couples' counseling and tried to be perfect in the ways I thought he wanted me to be. We were like cement blocks sleeping together over those months. The tension was so thick. All I knew then was that he wanted to leave *me*. He was staying because of the agreement, but not really present in any way, so that night in September as he tyrannically towered over me, with his lifetime of rage focused, laserlike, down on me, I broke through the fear of rejection that had been with me since my father died when I was six and said "GET THE FUCK OUT NOW."

This was the beginning of a new life. I think I actually felt better, though terrified about working out the arrangements, telling the kids, et cetera. How were we going to do this? Ted went out and got a sublet and we planned the family discussion.

The kids were nine and five that fall. I was forty-seven. We gathered in the living room for a family meeting and explained (I think mainly Ted), that we hadn't been getting along and that Daddy was going to move out and get another place. Our oldest immediately began wailing, crouched in the corner of our living room. We explained that they had nothing to do with this, we loved them dearly, we would both always be their parents, yada, yada, yada. We did it "the right way."

Though I don't think our youngest got it. When she saw her sister sobbing, she too began crying and asking questions. Only now do I realize the amazing similarity to what I experienced as the youngest child in 1952, at age six, sitting with my family of two sisters in a car as my mother explained to us that Poppy, our father, had "gone away on a long trip" (talk about euphemisms). My oldest sister began crying and I, like *my* youngest, lacking the cognitive development, but astute in emotions, joined in the sob fest. Words were irrelevant. Tragedy was present.

As painful as that grueling evening was, I felt the tension lifted, and though life was heavy, it was beginning anew instead of being a day-to-day experience in anxiety and fear. This was true for my kids as well. Words need not be spoken for dissension and anger to permeate an environment. This was finally over and we moved on.

Ted took the kids to see his/their new place and he and I "lawyered up" for the nightmare of the next year of sorting out our arrangements. He left in late September never to return overnight again.

I would describe year one as *numb*. My job as I saw it was to keep my kids' lives as unaltered as possible—in practical ways, obviously. Luckily I had a wonderful circle of friends who supported me and dished Ted. Several said they felt this was going to be great for me as I had become eclipsed, even with my big personality, by his life and needs. These friends made a big difference.

I began a push to increase my practice which I had let dwindle as PTA and Brownie troop had absorbed my time. I knew I was going to need money. That's what our two lady lawyers haggled over. It took one year for us to resolve a separation agreement, which later became incorporated into our divorce. To comment simply on that, Ted felt he paid too much and I felt not enough, so it is probably a somewhat appropriate settlement plan. His income was more than twice mine at that time.

There was no disagreement about the kids. They were living with me and Ted had dinners twice weekly and overnight visits to his apartment every other weekend. I think this was more than enough for him at the time. I will never forget that first weekend at Daddy's. He got the kids at about ten on a Saturday morning. I wandered around the apartment from room to room crying, feeling so forlorn. With the exception of a professional conference or something scheduled well ahead for Ted to take care of the kids, I had not had a day alone, to say nothing of an overnight, for years. I will admit it didn't take long for me to savor the new experience.

The year passed, I worked at my practice, I began teaching at a college, I oversaw my kids' activities and care and food and home love. They were/are my family and they were the biggest support I had. I was nose to the grindstone with all I had to do—numb, not sad, not angry, just pushing forward. I don't remember thinking about romance, sex, partnering, et cetera. This meant I was alien even to myself.

Things went generally well. The kids continued to seem happy, doing well in school, having friends, parties, normal life. Ted and I did "together" well in those days—parent-teacher conferences, birthday parties, school productions, et cetera. Our kids had two parents who loved them and were there for them.

I didn't know what Ted was involved in and I believed it wasn't another woman, as he had asserted that while telling me how he hated me that evening months before. So I was quite shaken about three or for months after he moved out when I ran into a well-known entertainer at Barnes and Noble. She had sung some of Ted's work in her cabaret performance and had rehearsed quite a bit at our apartment. She expressed how upset she was at hearing about our breakup and "Was Ted still so smitten with that young, blond ingenue?" I mumbled that I didn't know and got away from her feeling struck. I'm not sure if it was knowing that he left *because* of another woman or if I couldn't bear that I didn't know. I was out of the loop. This is an aspect of life that has been hard for me to accept. Then, it couldn't be OK that I didn't know it all. It's still not a pleasant feeling for me to be outside of the "secret," but now my substance is solid enough to understand and let it be. It also explained the frequent schedule changes Ted made regarding his time with the girls and probably his interest in more stylish dress and presentation. Whatever, she dumped him shortly thereafter and he became the single man-about-town.

Year two was the year of sad. We'd survived and it seemed we'd continue surviving, so I could let go a little and feel, and sad was what was there. Even though I'd been a divorcée at age twenty, my marriage to Ted was what I'd grown up believing life was to be about, raising our children, growing old together, and sharing a life on off into the sunset. I teach the marriage statistics in my psych courses so I am aware that a large 41 percent do not succeed, but I'd not contemplated that on any emotional level. The reality that my life to come had no preexisting fantasy to guide it forward was startling and painful. I was a failure at the way it was supposed to be. I was sad, but scared too.

I cried a lot that year and remembered all the wonderful times Ted and I had shared and felt somewhat desperate about myself and "my failure." I was doomed to be dumped and alone. First Poppy and now Ted. I was not lovable—too many hard edges. I got back into therapy and bemoaned my plight for a while.

Year three, approaching fifty and hadn't had sex since Ted's departure. Obviously I was coming out of my morass. Thinking about sex and closeness is always a healthy sign. Being back out there physically was scary as my naked presentation, two C-sections and a gall bladder removal later, wasn't as secure as when I'd been a tight thirty-five-year-old, but I was determined basically to live on, and this was part of it.

The first icebreaker was not anyone I was interested in. He was a secure test balloon for me and a good reentry. I remember telling myself I *had* to be OK as is. I would not cover up or turn out the lights to protect myself, and walking away from the bed, headed for the bathroom, backside out there in the light after we'd "done the deed," was a noteworthy character builder. I'd be OK. That intimate aspect of my life has been too. I'm lucky and grateful and I work hard at it. I think all three play a part.

The years have continued on, ten more to be exact. The kids have grown. The kids *are* grown and again they're good too. Ted, though always a caring, if distracted, father, went on and continues to be a wannabe lyricist, disgruntled (as the girls tell me) with his work. He has remarried and we have very little to do with each other now. In all these years he has never admitted that we shared many loving, wonderful times together. Last year our youngest sang in a concert. I had given her money to get the lowest-priced tickets for myself, a friend, and my mother. Those seats were sold out so she used a credit card of her dad's to get the next-lowest-priced tickets. I had the extra money in an envelope for him at the concert. My daughter saw him first in the crowd after the performance. I saw him say something into her ear as she came over to us for hugs and accolades about the concert. The first thing she said was "Do you have the money for Dad?" I pulled out the envelope and handed it to her, feeling the raw chill of his disdain. I have never owed him fifty cents over all these years! I don't need to share those earlier memories anymore. I genuinely believe it's his loss.

I still do not (age fifty-eight) have any set future fantasy to strive toward. I've got lots of ideas and each day moves me more toward one, or creates a new possibility. I see life in blocks of time and activities now, not the "young and then married forever" scenario. It continues to be sometimes sad, sometimes scary, but also exciting. I feel much more the creator of my destiny and I know me so much more intimately than I did as Ted's wife, the choreographer for his dance. This life is *my* dance and getting dumped was one of the basic exercises that has built up my strength in creating life, growth, and loving.

Event Horizon

Mary Stuart

Astronomers and astrophysicists have a flair for the dramatic. They created the phrase *event horizon* to describe the region near a black hole's center, an area where light and matter have no chance to escape the beyond-imagining gravitational forces that gobble up whatever comes close to that perilous edge. At that inevitable point everything is irretrievably sucked into the center and transformed.

Transformation is an interesting process. In science, physics in particular, it means to change one form of energy into another. In psychology it speaks to the change the psyche undergoes as a result of insight. In the spiritual world, transformation leads to enlightenment. In the mundane world, however, the process of transformation can be hell on wheels.

I've had more than a few of my own event horizons, times in my life when I fell into the black hole and transformed in ways I had neither imagined nor, in many instances, desired. One of the earliest events was the first time my heart splintered because of romantic rejection. I was sixteen, he was eighteen, and he was my first love, a high school student who had transferred in from another state in our junior year. We made goo-goo eyes at each other, experienced teen angst, and had phone conversations that went on for hours. It was love forever more . . . he was my one, my all, my everything. When he cut me loose just before we graduated I was astounded, demoralized, shocked—and surprised. I hadn't yet learned to look for the subtle signs that presage romantic disaster. Although we were going to attend different colleges, it was a nasty learning experience to discover that he wasn't on board with my plans for our future—weekend visits, proms, spring breaks, summers at home, the works. He had a plan, too, but it involved a previous girlfriend from his home state where he was planning to attend college.

The girlfriend was news to me. The first I heard about her was the evening he pushed me over into the black hole where I lived for a while in a state of suspended shock. Since I hadn't realized we were already at the event horizon, it took a while of swimming in that utter darkness to figure out the girlfriend and he must have been in touch all through our two-year, hot and heavy, panting, teen-drama courtship.

But all bleeding stops eventually . . . one way or another. When I emerged from that temporal blind spot into the light, my whole approach to relationships had changed. It wasn't a conscious plan. I simply evolved into a Dumper, and I did the job well. It wasn't until thirty-six years later that I lost focus and let my guard down, and whop! It happened again. By then, I'd successfully navigated through a first marriage, a divorce, and into subsequent relationships which I thought were, once again, going to be my one, my all, my everything. When I married the second time, at the age of thirty-eight, I was convinced it was going to be the last—and lasting—relationship.

He was the salt of the earth, stable as they come. He was learning the details of running his family business (and later became the business owner). He adored me. He had never been married, a fact at the time I thought was positive, but which I later realized was a problem for us because I rode the adjustment period with much less concern than he did. He had principles. I know he had principles because he told me all about them. I was in awe. He had more ethics and values than I did. He thought so, too, because he told me quite clearly the third week after our wedding that if I ever cheated on him I could expect to be put out onto the front lawn with nothing but my toothbrush. Maybe not even the toothbrush. He was quite firm about this point because he felt I might cheat on him. We'd had a couple of rough spots during our dating years and once, when we broke up, I had dated others. There was some overlap when we started to see each other again, which he had considered cheating. Back then, I fancied myself a fairly intelligent woman. The thought did cross my mind that I wasn't the one we needed to worry about because his intensity on the subject was so over the top. Of course, I pushed that thought aside and became Mrs. Goody Two-Shoes for the next sixteen years. Like Caesar's wife, I was so above reproach I bored even me. Along the way I failed to notice the adoration's slow disappearance. My husband told me often that I didn't know what I was talking about, that I was opinionated, that other people didn't like my opinions, and he gave me the impression I should just shut up. So I did. With his constant reminders of all my faults on a regular basis over the years, I managed to lose my voice and sink into despair. I gave up all my opinions. I deferred and demurred and otherwise backed off. Later he complained that I never had an opinion about anything and that I left all decisions up to him, which he felt was burdensome.

Can we talk? How crazy making is that?

Let me back up a bit. First of all, my ex-husband is not a bad man. He and I simply became embroiled in a horrible möbius loop of a marriage that twisted and snaked around on itself in such intricacy that neither one of us could figure out how to exit the morass we'd created. Lack of effective communication leads to such messes. And how could a "fairly intelligent" woman who had a career (as a therapist, for God's sake), and a life, sink into such a pit of despair, and how could she abdicate all her power?

Good question. I've given that a lot of thought since the breakup some ten years ago. I've come to the conclusion that it was very like Chinese water torture—drip drip drip—and day after day, week after week, year after year, I gave up chunks of myself. I hardly noticed the pieces falling off until one morning, about nine or ten years into the marriage, I didn't want to get out of bed because I couldn't find myself; I rolled over and didn't feel my body on the sheets. I thought for one wild moment that I had disappeared and become a disembodied mind lost somewhere in the ether, but no, I was only having a massive anxiety attack. So I did what any red-blooded American, depressed and anxious woman would do. I turned over, pulled the sheet over my head, and went back to sleep. I had great hopes that when I woke up I would somehow reincarnate into my late and sorely missed self.

That craziness went on for some time. I didn't tell my then-husband what was happening to me because I was afraid of his withering contempt, or at least what I perceived as such. I figured if I told him I was depressed and anxious he would think I was crazy, and he did not like "crazy" people, so I had to avoid that label at all costs. In fact, I wasn't crazy, but I *was* crazed, like a clay pot with cracks deep in its infrastructure. Crazed. Cracked. Commensurate behavior was about to ensue.

I felt that his attentions had been directed away from our marriage for some time, but whenever I asked about his new behavior he asked, "What new behavior?" I hunkered down and thought about his new clothes (he hated to shop) and the fact that he left the house every morning with a quart of after-shave splashed into every available pore. Then there was the way his face lit up whenever he was around a certain woman in his office, and how warm his voice became on the phone whenever they spoke. I calculated she was only about five years younger than I, and lulled myself into thinking she couldn't possibly be the typical younger, other woman. There were also the clichéd evening absences due to "work" and other oddities, but I remembered that conversation about infidelity three weeks into our marriage and thought there was no way he would be unfaithful. He might want to leave, he might not want to go to marriage counseling (he didn't believe in psychology), but he wouldn't cheat. He had values. How was I to know he'd forgotten the very conversation he initiated? And I mean *completely* forgotten, as if it had been erased from his memory. It seemed he had his own black hole to deal with.

By now you must be asking yourself what the hell was wrong with me. Was I too stupid to live? In a word, yes. I chose to ignore what Oprah calls "the pebbles" that fall on you long before the rocks and the big boulder squash you flat.

But wait! There was more stupidity! He sent me off on a trip (by myself) that I had wanted to take (with him) for a long time. He convinced me that I would enjoy this trip by myself because he wasn't interested in my destination, and when I came back he would take his own vacation to a place I wasn't interested in. I knew by then that something was up and I was frantic to reconnect, but I was floating down that famous river in Egypt, De Nial, and I shut off any notion that he might be unfaithful. I hoped the time apart would help us (that was the stupid part). When we both returned from our trips, the distance between us had grown colder and larger. I couldn't stand it anymore, so I asked for an explanation. We made a date to talk. He took me to a restaurant and commenced the Big Dump. In public. I suppose that was so I wouldn't create a scene. He needn't have worried. In the dutiful habit of being Mrs. Goody Two-Shoes, I bit my lip, fought back tears, and listened as he explained he "needed some space" (I swear, that's what he said). He told me he was thinking about leaving, which I interpreted to mean that he hadn't yet decided, so while I took an out-of-body trip somewhere way past Jupiter, Mrs. Goody Two-Shoes took over and told him that I respected his need for "space." It was an oh-so-civilized meeting, and he sighed in relief and moved out to our summer cabin the next day.

However, a niggling little voice in the back of my head was scratching on the walls of its jail where I'd consigned it years ago in the hope it would go away. I felt the scratch, ignored it. Then I heard faint sounds. I tried to ignore the whole sorry mess I called my mind, but soon I had a full-blown harpy in my head screaming at me that I was about to be done in and I'd better by God get out of my pit of despair, back away from the event horizon of that yawning black hole, and get my butt in gear so as to save said butt from ruin.

So what about that cracked behavior? For a long time I couldn't tell anyone except my closest friends just how crazy I was about to become, but from the distance of some years I look back and have to laugh. However serious I thought it was at that time, I see now how utterly comical it really was. Not to mention banal.

Danger causes the brain to flood itself and the body with feel-good natural drugs, and they produce a high second to none. They also produce feelings of empowerment and strength. For the next four months, before I moved out of our house, I felt like Wonder Woman. My behavior was still cracked, as I will relate below, but I felt great. I had The Power, baby, because by then I'd found proof of his other relationship, a discovery I kept to myself. My rationale for that was twofold: one, I hoped the whole mess would blow over, no harm, no foul; and two, if I kept my own counsel he would not have to face the fact every time he looked at me that I knew what he'd done. From my experience counseling others I had observed that some couples survived the initial infidelity but that the offending party, statistically equal between men and women, often couldn't get past his/her guilt and the relationship broke up anyway. I wanted to avoid that particular pitfall. In counseling couples, I knew each case was unique, but the one outstanding piece of behavior that seemed to appear in all of them was that for a couple to successfully get past infidelity both of them had to rise above their own flaws. In the case of the offender, getting over guilt was the hardest. With the offendee, anger and resentment were the barriers to successful re-engagement.

In the sixteen years we were married I had done the unthinkable, the one thing I always advised women in my counseling practice never to do, and I do mean never. I gave up control of our finances and had no idea what our financial status was apart from our everyday lifestyle. I had done this for several reasons. One, I didn't want to make waves. Two, I hoped he had more knowledge than I did in terms of investments. It never occurred to me that I should worry about it. After all, we were in the same boat, weren't we?

The harpy kicked in again, this time bellowing that I'd better check it out. There is nothing like a good survival scare to get a body, however depressed, into motion. The only problem was that all our financial records were kept at his business office. I couldn't let him know how suspicious I was, thanks to the attorney, newly and secretly hired, who exhorted me to keep quiet until I got my hands on the financial records. The harpy cackled her agreement. The bitch was back. I had been one of those wives who held titular corporate offices in the family business. The office building was fitted with an alarm system that consistently went off for no discernible reason and annoyed the neighbors and I had a key so I could take care of that problem in my husband's absence. I had returned his key to him when we finished our solitary and separate trips, but I had had a spare made for future absences. I looked at the key daily and thought about it for a while.

Finally, I decided that on nights when I was certain he was at the summer cabin, I would take up a new career. I became a cat burglar. Of course, I had legal access to the office and our financial records, so I wasn't really a burglar, but the drama of it all kicked in and I went for it. Please remember cracked and crazed.

I decided the best time to cat burgle was around one or two o'clock in the morning. I parked the car in a dark spot at the back of the building, and dressed all in black (yes, really), I let myself in to the office and proceeded with a routine I developed over several visits. Blinds down and closed. Only rear office lights on. A quick rustle through the file cabinet that held all our financial records. And then the tedious chore of copying documents on paper I brought along so the office supply would not be noticeably smaller. An hour or so, no longer, then lights out. Blinds back up. And I was gone, like the spies say, in the wind.

It was during one of those forays that I stumbled over the proof—love letters, tucked in with the financial records. That was the night that I fell way past the event horizon and into the black hole. It's one thing to have suspicions, to be uneasy and uncertain, to question, even to go looking. It's entirely another to fall into the pudding of the proof, a slimy, sloppy, gooey place where drowning occurs. And so I did, for one night. Drown. The night I stayed up and read every single letter. The night I read they had discussed leaving their respective spouses for each other. The night I read how lucky they felt for having this rare and unusual love, this great passion. The night I read about their activities and realized many of my memories had to be realigned to fit the facts, not his lies. I felt like puking, but I didn't. Instead, I grieved the loss of my marriage, and I grieved for my then-husband because I knew that the light of romantic love had blinded him to any reality. Romantic love feels great. I can recommend the experience. But as a friend of mine once observed, it lasts approximately ninety days; on the ninety-first day the first load of reality arrives like an unwelcome relative. For people who are unfaithful, that drug-induced high with their new partners can last until their current marriage breaks up. I'm no expert (who is?), but I believe that long-term marriages contain a combination of intermittent romantic love (no one can sustain that initial level over many years), friendship, spirituality, and what I call a commitment to the commitment. When it gets rough (and it always does), there has to be a mutual agreement to

hang in there at least long enough to work through it—one way or another—
before moving on to someone else.

The craziness didn't stop. Soon after my discovery of the infidelity, my car
was in the shop for repairs and I acquired a loaner car. Driving home I realized
no one would recognize the car, "no one" being my then-husband and his new
honey. An irresistible urge to find them together overwhelmed me. I had
copies of their letters so I didn't need further proof, but I had a driving, almost
physical need to see them in each other's company with my own eyes. It was
fall, it was cold, and it was raining. I created a different physical profile for myself by stuffing my hair under a stocking cap and wearing nondescript clothes.
I headed out to find them that evening. My ex had been spending a lot of time
at our summer cabin trying to find himself and his space, so I figured they
would probably go there for privacy. I went to his office building and skulked
around outside trying to determine if he'd left. I had the half-baked notion of
following him. Skulking around his office wasn't easy because the building
was isolated and located in a large open space and there was no place to park
unnoticed. After making endless loops driving around, I realized I had missed
him. I headed out for the summer cabin, which was located, with a few other
cabins, down a dead-end gravel road. Occupants of the cabins could hear cars
coming half a mile away, so just to be on the safe side I parked a mile away and
slogged through the rain and mud and, did I mention, the dark of night, like a
postal carrier determined to let nothing stay her course. Of course no one was
there. When you're crazed, no one is ever where they're supposed to be.

Demoralized, I headed for home and . . . there he was. He'd decided to
spend that night at our house. As I dragged my sorry butt in out of the weather,
dripping wet, he just stared at me. And at the "new car" sitting in the carport.
I explained about the car being serviced and mumbled something about my
disheveled self. I needn't have worried. He was so uninterested in me I could
have said I just returned from a rough flight to the moon in the shuttle and he
would have nodded, uh-huhed and disappeared somewhere in the house still,
no doubt, trying to find his space.

After that dark and stormy night (I felt like Snoopy on top of his doghouse,
writing the quintessential novel), I told my husband it would only be courte-
ous to let me know when he planned on spending the night or nights at the
house. After all, I couldn't barge in on him at the cabin, could I? (When had
I become so good at walking the balance beam of the slippery moral line?) He
agreed, and I swallowed my hypocrisy whole.

After that episode, somehow I returned to semi-sanity, bucked up, and resolved to patch our marriage back together. Why throw away sixteen years of

marriage? Wasn't that worth saving? I shoved the ever-present and vocally abusive harpy back in her cell and told her to shut up. I found a marriage counselor and made an appointment.

The counseling turned out to be exit counseling, or what is termed "counseling for closure," because after two sessions I realized he wasn't thinking about leaving, he'd already left the building. Exit counseling exists for the sole purpose of letting the couple disengage in a civilized fashion, that is, encouraging them to do an autopsy on their relationship and to make peace with the fact that it is over. At its best, it helps prevent acrimonious divorces and custody battles. I didn't want to flog a deceased relationship into tatters. However, I had a few things to say, so I requested he stay for two more sessions so I could unload everything I had on my chest, which was considerable. That's when I discovered he'd forgotten all about his threatening conversation in the early weeks of our marriage. I was dumbfounded. And angry, mostly with myself because I also remembered I'd said at that time he might be the one we should worry about. One day I may learn to listen to that small voice and thereby avert disaster. That was not one of those days. I also requested he stay through the holiday season, a request he readily agreed to. I suspect he was feeling merciful because it was plain that I was unraveling just a tad around the edges. However, I rallied because . . . drum roll . . . I knew something he didn't know. I knew his secret and he didn't know I knew it. This was the four-month period in which I morphed into Wonder Woman. I was strong. I was invincible. Hear me roar. I was still just a bit cracked.

In that state, I decided to throw myself a good-bye party because I was determined that sometime after the holidays were over I would move out of our house to a larger city some distance away from our small town. That decision came from not wanting to live alone in an isolated rural setting, which was where our house was located. I thought that I would probably never see our joint married friends again and I wanted a last time together. It was a different kind of farewell party because nobody except me knew it *was* a farewell party. My soon-to-be-ex and I smiled, served, circulated, hosted, poured drinks, refreshed drinks, made small and big talk and otherwise looked like the glowing golden couple all our friends perceived us to be. I had a really good time. I said good-bye in my head, noticed all the small things, and was, as the Zen folks say, fully in the moment. It's hard to describe the powerful feelings that ensue when you're the only person in the room who knows what's really happening. When I told some of those people after my husband and I separated what had gone down (I was surprised some of them actually remained my friends), most of them were astonished. Some sensed something was wrong, just not the details. Some thought it was a hoot I threw myself an anonymous farewell party. I had such a good time I decided to do it again, this time at my husband's annual Christmas party in mid-December. I'd lost about thirty pounds during the previous three months (stress, anxiety, and depression are better than amphetamines for weight loss) and, if I do say so myself, I was looking pretty good. I owned, but previously could not get into, a stunning red silk Anne Klein suit, which now fit. I wore a sexy black lace teddy underneath the jacket, slinky stockings, and high-heeled shoes. I looked hot. More to the point, I felt hot. I should mention here that no one dressed up for this annual Christmas party, but I didn't care. I wanted all those people, including the other woman, to remember the boss's soon-to-be-ex-wife the night she looked like a million bucks in that red suit, before she disappeared in a puff of smoke. I don't know that any of them remember me at all, of course, but I know they noticed me that night.

Christmas was pretty dismal because we weren't telling the family anything. Going through the motions was difficult. Fortunately, there were no children to worry about. That left New Year's Eve, which was simply a disaster. It had been my favorite holiday after Christmas because it was one of the few times we dressed up and went dancing. Or at least, we watched other people dance because my one, my all, my everything didn't like to dance and toward the end of our marriage took to a flat refusal when I suggested it. I admit I should have thought ahead to the midnight event, but I didn't. I had not expected a kiss, but I thought a friendly hug would have been civilized considering we were with two other couples. Instead, he abandoned me in the middle of the festivities and took a chair by a column in the ballroom, chin on his chest, deep in thought. I stood like the ninny I was, alone in the middle of the room, flabbergasted. And furious. Don't love me anymore? OK. Want your own space? OK. Humiliate me in public in front of friends? I don't *think* so. Happily, everyone was so caught up in kissing each other no one noticed our complete lack of contact. It was one of those clarifying moments when you know absolutely what comes next and what you have to do. I took control of my future and later that night I told him he'd made it clear to me it was time I moved on. He probably wondered what took me so long. By January 15 I was out and in an interim apartment. I was in that apartment for a year and a half while the divorce ground down to its inevitable end. I stayed with the therapist as I tried to get over beating myself up for being a failure and to come to terms with what my part was in the demise of the marriage. In addition, I read like a mad woman everything I could get my hands on that dealt with my current predicament. I found a great deal of reading material, but there were only a few things that resonated with me. I can recommend with enthusiasm the four books referenced at the end of this essay, which includes the book I co-authored on how to journal your way through the process.

My life has moved on, as lives always do. Being single and older ain't for sissies. Dating? Help me. The entire singles' scene seems to be geared toward the younger set. Being dumped at sixteen is different from being dumped at fifty-two. When you're young the possibilities for recovery are endless, and the next romance is usually just around the corner. The percentages for finding a significant other begin to shrink exponentially as we age, or at least they have for me. Maybe I'm pickier than I was at sixteen, maybe I'm more jaded, or maybe I'm not as desirable to the opposite sex as I once was. The thought of living in my future alone isn't always happy, but I have friends, a couple of careers, and a life. I gave up daydreaming that my ex-husband had been drugged and was struggling to free himself from his new relationship. I tried very hard to fight the notion that I'm terminally special and therefore impossible to give up, which alternated with feelings of ineptitude and worthlessness. Finding the balance has been my goal.

The final act to my relationship came about eight years after the official fizzle when my ex-husband asked me to help him obtain an annulment through the Catholic Church. Since neither one of us was Catholic, but his new significant other was, I figured a marriage was in the near future. It was the last straw. Although by that time I had moved away geographically, I realized that our every communication raised the specter of the marriage, a ghost that clung to me like the clutching vegetation of a swamp-thing. I didn't want to help him at all, and according to the Catholic Church precepts, I discovered he could obtain the annulment without any assistance from me. However, what he wanted was to do it the easy way (which meant he needed my help). While fuming to a friend one day she asked me if I wanted him to go away. I said, emphatically, yes. Then, she said, why don't you just give him what he wants? She had a point. But I had one, too, and that was that my voice was going to be heard in the process, the voice I'd lost in order to keep the peace. I told him what I remembered about my first divorce, and then told him I was severing all communication with him. We had no children to co-parent, there were no ties between us, either financial or emotional, and I did not want to talk to him, see him, e-mail him, or communicate with him in any way one more minute of my life. I cut him loose and requested, politely, that he return the favor. He tried to re-engage me several times, and then finally stopped. I haven't heard from him in almost three years, and do not know the aftermath of the annulment (which was granted). He could be married. He could be dead. What I felt then, and feel now, is a "click" of disengagement and a corresponding feeling of freedom which I can only illustrate with the feeling you get when you take a deep gulp of air after surfacing from beneath a deep body of water.

And then life had another surprise for me. The high school teenager, my prom date, my first love and first Dumper reappeared in my life—online. It was irresistible. How many times does anyone get to revisit long-ago youth with a first love? Talk about tying up loose ends. We e-mailed and exchanged current information, flirted a bit, and then delved into our memories. High school was a long time ago, and it turned out I could recall a good deal more than he did. That struck a familiar chord. I suspect, being the Dumpee, I probably wasn't important enough in his life for him to recall the details. He could scarcely recall the girl he traded me for, let alone the fact that he had thrown me over for her. I'd thought about him sometimes over the many years, wondering what had happened to him, and like many people who have been hurt, still wondering every now and then "what if?" kinds of thoughts. After a good bit of online chatter and some bodacious flirting, we arranged a face-to-face meeting. Half an hour into our "tryst" I came to an ugly conclusion . . . I didn't much like my first love. The more he talked about high school days and his current life, the more I realized he was pretty much now as he was then, except then I didn't see it. What I saw was a man concerned mostly with himself and his needs, never mind anyone else's. Worse, I saw that he was the template for many of my relationships post-high school. Worst, it had taken me all this time to figure that out. I'd like to think that sixteen-year-old hormonal levels got in the way of good judgment, but I worry that my judgment may be ingrained in my genes and/or my psyche and that I might be stuck with my flawed views.

Nevertheless, I've learned a lot during the ten years since the end of my second marriage. I've learned I can be single and not die of boredom or loneliness. I've learned that I have astonishing friends who love me for who I am, not for who they'd like me to be, the same friends who rallied around me during the worst of the worst and who, I'm convinced, saved my emotional bacon. I moved across the country on my own. I come and go as I please. I go to bed and get up when I like. I take up the entire bed at night and love it. And I've come to believe men and women look at relationships through two different prisms. Women appear to be programmed for context, men for content; that is, women look at relationships like a bowl that contains all the content necessary to make a relationship, men look at the content in the bowl as what is important, discarding the bowl as irrelevant. That any of us stay together at all is a miracle. I believe the successful couples who manage good long-term relationships are those who have learned how to see through the opposite prism as well as their own, knowing that both viewpoints are valid. I'm not sure that I have the talent (or the energy) to attempt another serious relationship, but I've also learned never to say never.

So I came full circle. I was dumped, I moved on to dumping, and at the end was dumped again. And then, in a very small way, I dumped my original dumper. There is a certain symmetry to that equation, an arithmetic satisfaction that somehow makes up for all the pain woven throughout the formula of my romantic life.

Works Cited

Estes, Clarissa Pinkola. *Women Who Run with the Wolves*. New York: Ballantine Books, 1992.

Pittman, Frank. *Private Lies: Infidelity and the Betrayal of Intimacy*. New York: W. W. Norton, 1989.

Senn, Linda, and Mary Stuart. *The Divorce Recovery Journal*. St. Louis: Pen Central Press, 1999.

Valentis, Mary, and Anne DeVane. *Female Rage: Unlocking Its Secrets, Claiming Its Power*. New York: Carol Southern Books, 1994.

The Only Life I Have

JANICE STIEBER ROUS

I t was I who came home in 2002 after being on retreat in Ireland and told my husband that I wanted out of our thirty-one-year marriage. Although he would say that I dumped him," I would not describe it that way. As the poet Mary Oliver says in her poem "Journey," I was saving the only life I have.

I was married at twenty-three. I thought that if I had a man and was married, my life would be settled; after that I could develop my career. My mom was Turkish, with very traditional ideas about women—even though she counseled me and my sister to always have our own bank accounts so we could be independent of men. My dad was Viennese and extremely chauvinistic, doubtful that women had the capacity for a profession. My parents' message was clear: first get the man, then maybe get the career.

I decided on the first date with my future husband that he was the catch for me. He was Jewish, cute, kind, and intelligent. That was all I needed to know. The rest I figured I could work with. It was all up to me, I thought. I believed my influence, help, and hard work would make him the man I wanted him to be and make the relationship what I wanted and needed. We were traditional in our attitudes toward the institution of marriage, so we were committed to staying together. He wanted us to grow older together and I believed we would. However, after my children left home it became more difficult to stay committed to the relationship. This was all I could expect from my life. The relationship was good enough. My husband's sweet nature and loving soul made him a good father and husband.

But what he had to suppress to stave off his demons had its costs. What lived inside him was a rage that I have now tapped into. All his disclaimed fury was keeping us both hostage. I was terrified of unleashing his dark shadow. It never occurred to me, however, that by always putting my children first and staying in the marriage for them, I was building up so much of my own rage and resentment that when I finally decided to leave I did it in a way that I still regret.

For decades I worked to make sense of the burning hunger inside me, pushing at me. In my dream life and my waking life I felt trapped. I imagined life without the constraints of monogamy and I was mystified by my chronic shame and self-flagellation. After thirty-one years, I still wanted to stay married so badly that I denied how lonely I was. But the more I worked on myself, the more I felt this ache. I became aware of the emptiness inside, and the longing for an intimate partner became more intense. Something happened in our thirty-one years together that robbed me of my sexuality, creativity, and sense of possibility. Our dynamic was suffocating me. To be a woman and not a child, I had to leave the home I had helped to create. At fifty-four, I knew that I could no longer live with the decision I made as a girl of twenty-three.

I chose my husband because I could not manage the wild, crazy emotions of my young adult years. They were creating chaos in my life and my imagination. I needed someone to hold me when I was scared and make a home for me since I had no idea how to do that for myself. My husband was delighted to be interior designer, cook, and grounds keeper. But, he demanded aesthetic control; he could not tolerate me buying a pillow for the couch or a shower curtain for the tub. He needed our lives to look good at all costs. Somehow for all the formal occasions we did fine. We were a handsome family with two gorgeous kids, smart, well spoken, and funny. We had the peace and tranquility of Shabbat dinners. We had Thanksgivings at his family's house in New Hampshire. It always felt like I was in someone else's movie because it was so perfect. We had everyone convinced that we were what we seemed to be. The only one I could not convince was myself.

I had never wanted to be the one to ruin my family's "perfection," but I had no choice. Something kept gnawing at me that my life was not truthful. Some part of me was out of alignment with another part. Something told me that if I did not get out and find deeper truth, I was giving up on myself, my life, and ultimately my children. I can remember vividly the moment I told my husband that I could no longer stay married. We were in the house I had bought with my own money in Maine, my dream for thirty years, and I had decided to sell it because the whole time I was there I could not stop crying. I could not say why, what the grief was that was overwhelming my every moment: Was it the kids leaving home? Was it my husband's and my individual preoccupation with making sense of our pasts? Was it our obsession with unanswered questions about our childhood drama? Was it menopause? Was it a sense of failure in our work ambitions? What and why haunted me daily. But something told me that if my house in Maine could not give me a sense of the future with this man, then perhaps there was no future at all.

I still try to understand what really happened between us. Was it betrayal, as he would like to suggest, or did we "betray" each other long ago? Am I looking to justify what I did? This is a tangled web that will take years to unknot. And so, the expression "being dumped" does not work for me. It does not take into consideration how complex the ending of a relationship is. It does not probe the dynamics of two people's psyches and uncover the covert and overt ways each used the other to avoid taking responsibility for their lives. It does not allow for the nuance and subtlety of meaning around the issues of dependency, security, and eros in a relationship.

It took me years to make this decision. At times it totally preoccupied me. I still have not stopped blaming myself. I have to face the risk of being alone in my old age, being ostracized at family gatherings, and having to be financially independent. Fear kept me with my ex-husband for years. Hardest of all was risking the loss of approval, of knowing I was a good person in everyone else's eyes, which I depended on so. I even had to risk finding real pleasure, not a compromised attempt at what I thought it looked like.

Every day is still hard. I have to center myself emotionally on waking each morning. I have to work hard not to let my emotions swing me on a pendulum. Often when I am swinging from one side to the other I need to call on friends to steady me with their reassuring words. I must walk in the woods and go to the beach. I rely on the sensual pleasures of good food, music, and essential oils. I need to paint, sing, dance, to be reminded of what I have to celebrate. Everything I feared is harder than I imagined. I cried furiously this past summer when my favorite niece was married and I was not invited. I had taught her to ride a bicycle, after all. Was it not my place there with her at the chuppah? My daughter's homecoming has to be calculated so both of her parents have time with her. My son has to negotiate his delicate separation and healthy independence while trying not to offend either parent. My mother's death took a toll on me beyond the normal pain because it came at the same time as I lost my home and my marriage. If she had been a good parent, she said, "maybe we would still be married." Is all this pain worth it? Freedom has a huge price.

I am finding who I left behind thirty-one years ago when I asked my husband to manage the wild, crazy, creative young woman I could not control. I have tools now to work with this intense energy that lives inside me. Sometimes I feel like I am dying from the pain that is being released from the past. The present is often safer when I can get quiet and find the compassion necessary to hold the grief over the loss of the unlived life.

The future is waiting to be lived. Being single at fifty-four means knowing I have to make peace with the choices I have made. I have to accept what I would have done differently had I known better. Every day I have to choose to use the tools I have, to be more conscious, gentler, more loving to the people who love me, and more loving to myself.

Observing the Cormorant

PHYLLIS BERMAN

Sleek black diver
chained to the fisherman's boat
throat-rigged so she cannot swallow.

She stands at the prow
watches for water-stir
then flies into the slim blue corridor

between the Yangtze and the sky.
She is destined to dive, catch
return with a fish in her powerful beak

and yield it to the fisherman.
Each morning, I look out from my window
while a cool sun spills over fish and boat

and tethered bird until one day
I step to my desk and write
to the man I still call husband:

. . . *I have come halfway across the world*
alone. I cannot return to what
I have left.

I write the letter three times.
Three times I tear it into pieces.
Then I write it once again

seal it in an envelope
and slip it in the mailbox
where it cannot be retrieved.

* * *

In 1985 my husband admitted that he was having an affair with a former neighbor seventeen years younger than we were (we were both fifty-seven). He did not want to end our twenty-eight-year-old marriage, but it was clear that he wanted to change the terms on which it was based. He wanted to have the marriage and wanted to have affairs as well. What followed were months of acute unhappiness and feelings of great loss alternating with brief periods of disbelief. I seemed unable to make a final break with my husband.

Then an opportunity fell at my feet, when I needed it most. I was invited to teach at Wuhan Medical School (now Tung Ji Medical University) in mainland China. I had not traveled abroad much, and when I did, it was to professional meetings in Europe where I was part of a group of people I knew. This trip was different. I traveled alone at a time when the lack of telephone connections within China made calls almost impossible, my knowledge of the language was scanty, and I had very little idea of what I would find when I arrived. It was an uncharacteristically daring step for me to take and an enormously confirming experience. I learned many things from my time in China: most important were lessons about myself, my new capacity for independence, and freedom from the need to compromise, as reflected in the poem "Observing the Cormorant."

Two

PERSPECTIVES ON BEING LEFT AND LEAVING

Trashed

CAROL BURDICK

All the stopped day
I have been dealing the past
like sticky cards,
trying to sort out,
pack, throw away.
Sheet music from the 40s,
old paperbacks with pages
missing, bridge-table sets
still virgin in their
wedding wraps, yellow
envelopes with
negatives of children
sulky in their Easter best—
trivia, tarnished treasure—
all the discarded pieces
of the daily game we played
for twenty years.
It was—ok (well,
not too bad) until I found
the dusty broken music box

you'd brought me back
"for a surprise"
fifteen years ago.
And when today
I tossed it out, it started
playing: "Traumerei"
by Schumann.
Just as if some dreams
could not give up, as if
the tune had never stopped,
the little drum went round,
the hairpin hammer hit.
The notes, precise and tinny,
filled the room.
Come to think of it,
I don't believe I ever
gave you anything you liked
the way I loved my music box.

* * *

This verse, among many others written in the year following my husband's departure for someone (he said) who reminded him of me when I was young, itemizes a few of the souvenirs from our twenty years together; the music box did come to life when I tried to discard it, but the marriage did not.

Marriage Comes and Goes but Sex Is Forever

ANNE SIMCOCK

Why is lifelong monogamy such a widely accepted goal? Is it even feasible for most of us? Aren't we setting ourselves up for disappointment when we expect it from our partners, or ourselves? And finally, if we accept that our partnership will be less than lifelong or more than monogamous, are we contributing to its decline?

I had thought that I had answered these questions before my second marriage. Based on irrefutable evidence I was not monogamous and would find it quite difficult to be so. However I was strongly dyadic. That is, I wanted to have a unique mutual bond with another person involving love, caring, trust, and many shared interests, including living together and having a family. I did not and still don't see this kind of union as being incompatible with an independent life, independent interests, individual friends, independent travel and, yes, other sexual partners. Mutually open marriages are relatively new, beginning in the twentieth century, when equal partnerships became possible. Marriages open at one end (ajar marriages), with the opening at the male end, of course have always been present.

We are not a monogamous species. Indeed lifelong monogamy is rare in nature. Konrad Lorenz just didn't catch his faithful greylag geese having EPC's (extra-pair copulations), but DNA tracing has shown that they abound in seemingly monogamous birds as well as seemingly monogamous humans. Furthermore it is not just polygamous males forcing their attentions on faithful females. Not at all. Many females play the active role, enticing the passing male to their nests.

We come from a primate line in which our nearest relatives are the chimpanzee and the bonobo (pygmy chimp). We share 98 percent of our DNA with them and both are promiscuous. We alas don't follow the charming bonobos whose social organization "make love not war" is so attractive, but have more in common with the competitive chimpanzees who have dominant males and rather aggressive sexual interactions. The social system we have evolved, with the ideal of lifelong monogamy, is rare in nature and probably unworkable because our strong inherited behavior patterns lead us toward more opportunistic mating, for both sexes. Most of us understand this. Why, then, are we so surprised when our particular union breaks up?

I understood it so well that I had suggested an open marriage to my second husband and that more or less was what we had. We were independent in many ways,; we shared a profession but kept our professional lives separate. One lot of medical meetings, hospital dinners, and staff whoopees is more than enough for any one. We had some separate interests but many in common. We usually took vacations together, later with our son. We had some separate friends and over the years other sexual partners. We rarely did couples' things. Our mutual friends were mainly single or gay or lesbian. I particularly hated the concept of "The Smiths" as an entity since it eradicated individuals, particularly the woman. In general marriage has a set of assumptions which every woman has to spend considerable and constant energy to combat. Both of us I think found coupledom oppressive and yet we really enjoyed each others' company. We still do. I thought that I had found "The Way" and was absolutely astounded when the path turned out to be mined.

Things change. We change. Shit happens. Some of the shit that happens is predictable and one of the reasons I am writing this piece is to talk about the sexual and other changes which happen with age and which drive our behavior. Perhaps you can be prepared. I was not, though I already knew some of this. I hadn't put it together because of course I had found "The Way" and preempted all of the possible problems. After all, when my partner had sexual problems I suggested he take a lover on our sailboat to work things out in a stress-free environment for a couple of weeks. Pretty cool, I thought. No one could reject a partner as understanding, flexible, and open as I, could they?

First, the sexual changes in men. Viagra and its sons have altered the picture radically but not completely. For most men these changes occur gradually, some start earlier and move faster, others have little change until their late sixties. Most are experiencing some change in the fifties. Erections become less reliable. Sometimes they inexplicably droop in medias res, sometimes they come and go, sometimes they don't happen at all. Often at their best they are not as hard as yesteryear. Orgasm takes longer. Sometimes in spite of an hour of grinding away it just won't happen. Other occasions it happens in ten seconds but this is rare.

With all of this the usual component of anxiety enters: "It won't work. I can't come. It won't stay up. Oh my God, she will laugh, leave me, tell someone, reject me, find another, Oh my God." The anxiety of course makes it worse.

Men's reaction to all this varies. Some say, "OK, my sex life is over." Some accept what is happening and operate with what is available: "So mostly it works and sometimes it doesn't but that's OK." A few, quite a few blame, the resident woman: "If you were younger, firmer, juicier, more passionate, more creative, more enthusiastic, indeed, not you, it would work." Many resident women buy into this, which is a pity because it is almost certainly not true. It is true that a new person can provide a stronger stimulus which may initially enable a better erection, but if insufficient blood is getting to the penis, the erection will not be sustained. A sexual encounter with a new and visually arousing person may result in an orgasm, of course, but the novelty stimulus soon wears off. Habituation is, alas, a universal mechanism.

I had a lover from college. We met once or twice a year for decades. Although we had many memories and some acquaintances in common from our Oxford years, the focus of our reunions was almost entirely sexual. In his late fifties he started to have difficulty maintaining his erection. His MD had said there was a drug available in the United States, not yet available in England, which could help him. My friend was convinced that his difficulty was not physical. How could a very successful alpha male have this wimpy kind of problem? No, he needed me. I had always known how to turn him on. He was going to fly over on the Concorde to get the cure from me. Now I am not going to pretend that this was not immensely flattering, though I knew it was bullshit. At fifty-eight you need all the affirmation you can get. So I showed up with a supply of Viagra. We went to bed and I used all my tricks with the predictable nonresult. Then I suggested we try the little blue pill with a room service snack. It worked so well that my friend forgot entirely the earlier failure and decided he needed the little blue pill and me. How he got weaned from the me part of the equation is another story. The me was pure fantasy. Although obviously I was the same age as he, in his mind I was the sexy undergraduate who had captured his virginity. It was no different from when real twenty-year-olds occupy the fantasies of aging males. I did not look twenty, I looked my age. Twenty-year-olds look twenty but present other difficulties for a fifty-eight-year-old to relate to, so another kind of fantasy has to take place.

What this does illustrate is that no matter what the fantasy, the purely physical is of major importance in some of the problems of the aging lover.

For the orgasm problem there are many answers. The best is that if one does not orgasm one can keep going, the source of an ancient Chinese myth of the aging perpetual lover. Myth it may be but there is some truth to it. I have experienced in my lovers utter panic and depression at the inability to orgasm, acceptance and delight from lovers who have realized that they can now keep going indefinitely, and a somewhat bewildered adaptation from a lover who said that all his life he had orgasmed rarely but found that women were so upset by this that he had to fake it. He said that the great thing for him about getting older was that his contemporaries were now experiencing the same problem he had all his life. Women lovers in his age group were as a result more understanding and less likely to interpret his lack of orgasm as a personal affront. Some men, though, cannot adapt to the decrease in frequency of orgasm, feeling that if they have not come, the sex had no value.

You may note that I mostly use personal experiences for my anecdotes. One of the advantages of the open lifestyle is that I have had a lot of these. But the main reason for using them is because I know that what people tell their psychiatrists—and I have to assume me as well—is not, really not, the truth. I had a patient who was the wife of a physician who was alcoholic but recovered. She was unhappy because they had no sex. He would try, she said, but could not get an erection. He was seeing a colleague of mine and we conferred, with everyone's agreement, of course. My colleague told me that the physician was having an affair with a much younger woman, which was frequently and happily consummated. Chance brought his lover to my door. Her concern was that she was having an affair with an older man, a physician, and she wanted to know if the history of alcoholism could be the reason for his impotence because he had told her it was due to her inexperience. This kind of circumstance has been repeated many times. Colleagues confer and chance and geography bring related people to us. The motivation to dissemble in the very sensitive issues of sex is enormous.

Libido is, believe it or not, even more complex than erection and orgasm. Both of these are influenced by the most important sex organ, the brain, but also depend on the state of the blood vessels and the peripheral nerves. Libido is only lodged in the head, or is it? Most of us have experienced wide swings of libido in our lifetime. The death of someone close, the end of an affair, loss of a job, extreme work pressures can sometimes eliminate sexual thoughts and fantasies entirely. A new relationship, a warm beach, a vacation, music, or even a different hairstyle and sex is everywhere all the time. But many of the influences on libido take place outside awareness. Remember adolescence, where everything was sex with an occasional brief hiatus during key exams or a critical game. Clearly that was related to the same hormonal storm that produced the pimples and the pubic hair. Levels of testosterone do change over time and for most men levels are lower during the fifties than the twenties though still within the normal range, whatever that really means functionally. There is also a decrease in the frequency of sexual thoughts, fantasies, and masturbation. Frequency of intercourse itself is not a good measure since it is dependent on many extra-libido factors even in men. It is obviously difficult to know how much of the loss of interest in sex with a partner is due to physiological changes causing global loss of libido, boredom with the same old routine, or trouble in the relationship. Whatever the cause, having a new sexual partner can indeed perk up the libido for a while.

One of the startling examples of neurochemically induced decreases in libido is that caused by antidepressants, particularly the selective serotonin reuptake inhibitors, Prozac and sons of Prozac. One patient described his feelings after stopping the medication as "being myself again, a person with sexual desires." Another said that he, subtly at first, began to notice women in the street, then had fleeting sexual fantasies before finally emerging with a full inner sexual life as was the norm for him and for most of us. This switching on and off of libido has also been noticed by men on supplementary testosterone. Those I am familiar with are getting testosterone by injection or patch to prevent the muscle wasting that accompanies HIV infection. They report clear changes in desire related to dose and sometimes a drop in fantasies and thoughts as the time for the next treatment nears. One man said, "It's as if the injection makes you a different person." Another older man said that he had welcomed the diminution of desire as he aged, feeling that it gave him time to focus on his writing, but reluctantly accepted its resurgence as an inevitable side effect of his treatment. Libido is so complexly influenced and variable in one person over time as well as from person to person that any general statement is likely to be immediately refuted. Generally, though, as they age, men spend less time in sexual thoughts and fantasies, masturbate less frequently, and, if they are honest, often experience a general decrease in sexual interest.

What I am describing is a change over time, not a loss. Older men can be wonderful lovers. Less driven, less focused on orgasm, more leisurely, pausing as an erection subsides to talk and caress, continuing sometimes slowly and gently, much more interested in pleasing their partners than counting how many orgasms they "gave" them, and above all, accepting whatever is given or wanted without critique. But this can't happen until the man has accepted the changes in himself. Some men do this and it is wonderful. Others respond to the same changes with denial, defensiveness, anger, blaming, desperation, depression, and frantic efforts to alter the direction of time.

It is a complicating factor that these changes in sexual response usually occur at a time when other changes—physical, social, occupational—are also happening. Children are becoming sexual and starting out on a life of their own full of promise and expectation at a time when one's own expectations have flattened out. The last promotion happened some time ago and there will be no more. The steady upward trend has stopped in all spheres except age itself and one is facing at best more of the same and at worst decline and constriction. It is not surprising that the suicide rate is highest in men in their fifties and sixties. The options to change the situation are limited. Changing the occupational situation at this age is not easy and unlikely to be advantageous, children will become adults, and time will march on. The one thing that can be changed other than oneself is one's partner. The man is occupationally and socially at his height and may for this reason be sexually desirable, especially to women who are below him on the occupational ladder—students, interns, secretaries, assistants. The stimuli for a change of partner at this stage are so ubiquitous that what is surprising is that it doesn't happen more often.

Obviously there is a downside to such a change and there are some positive reasons for remaining with one's partner. Nonetheless, many times men do change their partner and it does seem to me from the vantage point of sixteen years on that I would have wanted to be more psychologically prepared for the possibility. It does of course raise a question that I asked at the beginning of this essay: how much does being prepared help to bring it about? I don't know, but understanding that this point is reached at some time for most men whether it is discussed or not, or whether the outcome is being cut loose or not, rather than being an exceptional circumstance that could not happen to you, has to be useful at least in shaping more thoughtful responses.

Of course many men deal with this traumatic time with other adaptations. Those who can assume the generative role do best. I have been very touched by some of my colleagues who take enormous pains to nurture their students and take great pride in their successes. They will themselves step back to allow the younger person to have the limelight and will often mentor someone to eventually take over their own position. (This is quite different from the empty boasting that one hears in cell phone conversations everywhere about children's SAT scores, college admissions, grade point averages, which is generally pointing to the wonderful superiority of one's genes.) There are unquestionably many other adaptations which do not involve getting rid of the resident woman, but since this is the focus, I want to look now at some of the changes which are happening to women themselves at middle age, as I had to look at myself.

The sense of having reached the limit of one's occupational achievement and of facing an inevitable decline does not seem to happen in the same way for women. The prospect of retirement, for example, seems to be much less threatening for us. When I announced that I was retiring at sixty-five many of my male colleagues asked me anxiously what I was going to do with my time, how could I stand not being a doctor, could I afford it? All of my female colleagues understood perfectly. In my early fifties, when I was cut loose, I was loving my professional life, and though my rise was leveling off, there was no sense of feeling, "So this is it. This is as far as I will go"—thoughts which were preoccupying some male contemporaries. These thoughts have little to do with where one actually is but more with a sense of one's own particular ladder having no more rungs. It may be that for women in my generation merely being on the ladder at all was enough; perhaps this attitude will change. If it does, it will be unfortunate since it brings much discontent. Perhaps other factors such as children, grandchildren, mentoring assume greater importance for us.

Contented as we may be in our professional lives in our fifties, it is an age at which sexual self-esteem is not high. Everything around us says we are sexual nonentities. Men no longer turn when we pass. We enter a room to deafening indifference. Clothes are made with somebody else, quite else, in mind. The women in the ads are our daughters, except of course for the ads for antidepressants in the psychiatric journals, where we have a prominent role. Two comments from friends, close friends, sum it up. One, a gay man, a friend of many years, had gone to a wedding, which he had hated. He described the women at his table as "postmenopausal, you know what I mean." Noticing my face he then spent a great deal of time and ingenuity explaining that I was not that kind of postmenopausal. What he meant was asexual and embittered. Another friend, a psychiatrist, ten years older than I, said, "No man really gets sexually turned on by a woman much over forty," citing his years of analyzing male patients. This comment was in the context of a patient we had both seen and the atmosphere was collegial. I think he forgot who I was, for he is not an insensitive man, but there is no question that this was his conviction as well as his personal experience (he had found, after years of searching and celibacy, a woman thirty-five years his junior). My experience is that this is definitely not true of all men, though it is probably true that our sexual fantasies, male and female, involve bodies less tainted with age and living than our own.

I believe that for women the cultural attitudes toward us as we age are more important than our perception of our own bodies and the physiological changes we experience. The mechanical problems, drying of the vagina, loss of lubrication with sex, thinning of the vaginal wall can be helped by local estrogen now that hormone replacement therapy has been discredited. The decrease in libido which happens for many of us can be helped by testosterone cream, which also prevents atrophy of the clitoris. The FDA, in a stunningly sexist decision, refused to approve the testosterone patch for women on the grounds that although the experimental group reported increase in sexual feelings, they did not actually have increased intercourse. All participants were married and since frequency of intercourse is governed almost entirely by the male, this was hardly relevant, but it was enough for the FDA. Who would want all these sexually desirous postmenopausal women around anyway?

I have been rather brief about the physiological changes in women but I urge all women to find a good, open-minded female gynecologist and discuss your concerns with her. The reason for the brevity is that although understanding and dealing with these changes is important for us, our behavior is driven much, much more by our perception of being sexually second rate. It is this perception that I hope to change.

From what friends tell me of the usual ways in which older women get to meet men, I can see how it would precipitate one right into a Prozac ad: the lone paunchy male surrounded by twenty women at a mixer, the carefully arranged dinner party followed by no telephone call, desperately "letting your friends know you are available," as if they didn't, the hopeful cruise on which you meet some wonderful women just like you and so on. When I was cut loose I was fifty-three. I was very busy. I was running a large clinic, had a heavy lecture schedule around the United States, and was president elect of my medical society. I was also writing a book. For several months these activities swept me along mindlessly and sexlessly. Then it was New Year's Eve and I was alone, miserable, and extremely horny. For the first time in my life I made a list of resolutions. There was not a great deal else to do. After all, we have been conditioned to believe that New Year's Eve is not like any other night, so reading seemed inappropriate, the television, unused generally and ancient, was in the blizzard mode, the gym was closed, and my son, home for the vacation, had gone off rather worriedly to a party. He told me last year when he, himself, was getting married that he had been really concerned then that I was so involved with work that I was going to be spending all my New Year's Eves alone, which made him feel responsible for my well-being. He also told me how relieved he was the next vacation when I was off spending my weekends with various lovers. I had no idea. To me he was the typical eighteen-year-old totally absorbed in his own exciting life in which I was a mere shadow on the periphery.

My resolutions were practical. I was going to put an ad in the *New York Review of Books* (this was 1989, no Internet) and I was going to get a face-lift. Oddly I had little feminist anguish about this. I could see how I was coming to resemble my Uncle Arthur. It seemed obvious that dating would be easier without wattles. It was, I suppose, a measure of my cognitive disarray that I had been reading some self-help books on divorce. I generally find self-help akin to astrology in its methods, providing generic descriptions of personalities and problems with obvious, easy, and often wrong answers in a prose that makes my bottom twitch. One, however, had suggested a group, which was a good idea. I found an eight-week, nontherapy group for the newly separated at the local YMHA. The group was useful. Here were twelve people (ten women) over forty whose marriages had recently ended mostly on their partner's initiative. The stories were different and the same. Seeing the ways one did not want to go was extremely useful, fighting over money, bitterness, self-pity, vindictiveness, demonizing the other, all so unattractive when watched in others but so easy to fall into oneself.

There was one woman who was beginning to think about the future rather than bewailing the past and we became friends for a while. We both had mates who thought that their sexual problems were due to our age and could only be resolved by a younger model. That neither actually had the improved sex object in hand only made the rejection worse. We had to get over the inevitable feeling of being dehumanized by being looked at as used bags of flesh past our sell-by date and the humiliation and the unfairness of it all. So many of us have this ineradicable feeling that life should be like cricket with rules and an umpire ensuring fair play, and by this analysis, it certainly is unfair that middle-aged men get a much greater sexual choice than middle-aged women. On the other hand we had it better during adolescence and early adult life. My generation of men, coming of age in the fifties, had generally sexually bleak lives as young men unless they married early, which had other problems. I, in contrast, had a wonderful time as the only girl in the advanced science classes in high school and with ten men to every one woman in college and even more in medical school. This was oddly and quite irrationally comforting.

Mary and I were very different. When she was down she would take to her bed with a romance novel and Oreos, occasionally chocolate marshmallows, and weep. I would go to the gym, throw weights around, and swear. Hers was the more adaptive response since she only got indigestion while I sometimes got injured. Mary was attractive and quite charming which helped me to accept that the rejection was not a reflection of our lack of sexual appeal nor were our mates' perceptions necessarily how others might view us. We agreed to eliminate sentences beginning "All men . . ." and also those referring to the past beginning "I wish that I had . . ."

Mary was going to put her ad in *New York Magazine*. My initial effort for the *New York Review of Books* read:

> It shouldn't be so hard to find
> A man who's sexy, thoughtful, kind.
> I'm fifty-three and passing fair
> In fetching shape, and good repair.
> For sex or friendship, hikes or tea,
> Take the plunge and write to me.

My ads were often raunchier later on as I gained confidence, but this one drew over fifty replies. The least successful ad I wrote was one where I tried to conform to the deadly format of solemn statistics, overblown personal charms, and romantic aspirations which characterized most of the personals, just to see what it would produce. Very little, it turns out, so why do they keep on doing it?

Mary got about thirty responses to her cheery, unrhymed ad. We sifted through the letters and prepared to face the dating world. It was the first time either of us had done this and it was fun. Eliminating the letters from prison, the barely literate, the formulaic, those who wished to tie us up and whip us, the ones with sick/frigid/nonunderstanding wives and one that began, eerily, "confident women like you often secretly desire a stern disciplinarian—" I wound up with twelve interesting replies which I decided were worth a phone call. Five remained after long conversations. I remember one reject whose letter had been quite sparkling (maybe someone else wrote it) who said on the phone that after ten years of psychoanalysis his psychiatrist felt he was ready to "seek a mate." Not me. With the first of the lucky five I set up a meeting in a coffee shop. Ambivalence does not begin to describe how I felt as I tarted myself up for the first "date." For decades I had struggled to be judged by my intellect and competence and I knew that the most important, if not the only, thing that counted now in being accepted was my looks, and that the 38 DD that had been such an infuriating barrier to being taken seriously in the past was now an asset. And of course behind the anger at having to tart up was the fear that I would not look good enough. I would like to believe that out there is a real feminist who, sailing out for her first date at fifty-three, would not have these degrading feelings. I would love to meet her.

Mary and I compared our experiences. How ludicrous our anxieties had been. Both men had understated their age by at least twenty years and considerably overestimated their charms, though perhaps we all do. They were both,

of course, very eager to meet again. I had been so preoccupied with acceptance and being rejected that it had not occurred to me that men would lie
about their age and that in fact I would be the one, for the most part, doing the
rejecting. I hope I was kind. The step had been taken and the lesson learned,
however, and it was easy after that. Like swimming in the English Channel; it's
great once you get in.

For the next two years I dated through the ads. It is labor intensive, but I became expert. However carefully one screens, that first meeting is always unpredictable. It is the flesh, the physical presence, that changes everything. I
met some delightful men, some awful men, some pathetic men and a couple
who met a psychiatric diagnosis, one poor fellow with early Alzheimer's and
one who was clearly in a hypomanic phase with a history (I asked) of bipolar
disorder. Within five minutes of meeting, actually less but I want to appear
thoughtful, one knows if there is any possibility, which is why the first meeting
should be coffee and not dinner. I went out beyond that first encounter with
perhaps a dozen men in those two years, some only a few times, others for
longer. Sex was usually after one or at most two meetings. I was horny and also
this was important information. I was looking for a sexual partner or partners
after all, so if the sex was lousy in a way that was unlikely to improve I needed
to know about it before developing any significant attachment. Unfortunately
intellectual and sexual compatibility are not linked. There were a couple of really good lovers and a few acceptable but not inspired. Several were terrible,
not because of erection problems but because they deeply did not know what
to do and thought they did. My age group mostly missed the sexual revolution
and it shows. Nevertheless I met some quite delightful people who could easily have become sexual friends if not my primary partner, but the major difficulty that emerged over time was, in spite of initial protestations to the
contrary, the desire for a monogamous relationship and/or cohabitation. Then
I met Don. He was perfect. A polymath who wrote erotic Westerns and worked
as a senior editor for a publisher of dubious books on nutrition and health,
Don could do the Saturday crossword puzzle in the *New York Times* (the most
difficult) in four minutes, compose funny limericks while washing up, and
play a fiendish Scrabble game. He was also an enthusiastic and inventive lover.
His initial reply to my ad (my seventh) began: "I live in an odd shaped house
in Croton with an ill tempered cat named Grace." I was charmed, and remained so for several years, by his curiosity and inventiveness.

Mary had by this time met Paul, an accountant turned artist, and was in
love. Paul was extremely handsome as well as five years younger than she, and
this was very helpful for her self-esteem, which had been wrecked by the quite
cold-blooded rejection she had received from her husband of almost thirty

years. Although our friendship being mainly situational attenuated with time, we have had occasional contacts. Somewhat to my surprise their relationship has continued with apparent success. I supposed that she had been too fixed on demonstrating to her world and especially her ex-husband that she was still an attractive woman and that this had directed her choice. Rejections on the basis of undesirability due to age are so crushing that the need to prove to our-selves and especially to others that someone obviously desirable considers us worthy of sexual attention can lead to bad selections. By way of confession I too had fallen in love shortly after my separation, with a man who was wildly unsuitable for me, conventional, domineering, jealous, very competitive with me, and truthfully not awfully bright. Somehow after eight weeks of delirium I had come to my senses one afternoon as he was telling me exactly why my furniture was incorrectly placed and my couch should be retired, unsolicited comments on a matter in which I had little interest. As I listened to him with new ears, quiet hormones, and some intellectual distance, I thought of all the reasons, mostly bad, that had led me to be captivated by this man. Shamefully, the fact that he was younger than I and good looking were among them. I am glad it happened and that I awoke and I am also glad that in Mary's case what-ever the reasons for the initial attraction, it has been a successful relationship for her.

Don and I had an exciting time together for seven years until his death. His other lover, Marilyn, and I became and have remained close friends. We were able to be mutually supportive at his unexpected death. Her daughter and I were with her when she had surgery for colon cancer. We see each other as often as geography permits. Don and I discovered a group supporting open re-lationships that was not a swing club. I have nothing against recreational sex and have certainly done just that on some memorable occasions, but I look for ongoing friendships in which sex plays an important but not necessarily central role. This group was founded in 1973 by some beneficiaries of the sexual rev-olution. Mostly young professionals, lawyers, doctors, academics, teachers, they wanted to promote sexual freedom and humanitarian values. There were so-cial events, hiking, museum visits, wine tasting, and of course parties where people could meet others who shared their values and find partners who were not monogamous. There were many such groups in the seventies but most did not survive through the eighties with its change of mores and particularly the specter of AIDS. This group did survive, numbering currently about three hundred and with some of its early members still around, now in their fifties, sixties, and even seventies. I have found enduring friendships with both men and women in this group. I still have a very satisfying sexual friendship with a man I met through the group in 1994, eleven years ago, and a close friend-ship with his partner with whom I traveled to Peru last year. I met my current partner (G) at the annual dinner dance five years ago.

After Don died I went through a period of mourning which was very differ-ent from the angry misery which lasted, fortunately attenuating, for at least a year after my divorce. This was quieter, mellow and not about me in the same way. It was about losing someone who had added a unique dimension to my life which would not be replaced. Ours was the first relationship that I have had which was just what I wanted, completely open, completely free, and yet strongly bonded. I did not think that I would ever have it again and part of the mourning was for the loss of that ideal. I still miss Don for his very original self but against all odds and my own expectations, G and I found each other. I am not using his name since he is still working in a position where, in the current social climate, membership in an open relationship group would be profes-sional death. It is odd that we who value honesty in all our dealings, especially our sexual encounters, are much more stigmatized than those who deliber-ately deceive their partners to whom they have promised lifelong monogamy. When people talk about their extramarital affairs, they are usually greeted with complicit empathy or at worst understanding disapproval. When I say I have three lovers whom my partner knows, likes, and respects, most otherwise quite liberal people are appalled. Sometimes there is titillation and envy which usu-ally subsides when I point out that my partner also has other lovers, one of whom is a good friend of mine.

When I went to my fortieth college reunion some years ago, God, garden-ing, and grandchildren were the themes. (This in a college that had produced Margaret Thatcher and Indira Gandhi.) There were some other interests of course but there was a definite feeling that sensual life was over. For me, my sexual life pervades and enriches everything else and within that life there is a network of friends and lovers who share not just our bodies but our ideas and principles. I have no idea how long this can continue and it does not matter because today my life is exciting, challenging, and fun.

I wanted to write this not to proselytize for the open life but because being cut loose can be an opportunity to create for yourself a life that you have always wanted but somehow had not achieved. Painful and wrenching as it was, I find myself today oddly grateful for the experience.

Lost Love

The Nature of Romantic Rejection

HELEN FISHER

> "Parting is all we need to know of hell."
> — EMILY DICKINSON

Fires run through my body—the pain of loving you. Pain runs through my body with the fires of my love for you. Sickness wanders my body with my love for you. Pain like a boil about to burst with my love for you. Consumed by fire with my love for you. I remember what you said to me. I am thinking of your love for me. I am torn by your love for me. Pain and more pain. Where are you going with my love? I'm told you will go from here. I am told you will leave me here. My body is numb with grief. Remember what I've said, my love. Goodbye, my love, goodbye." This poem, recited by an anonymous Kwakuitl Indian of southern Alaska to a missionary in 1896, captures the excruciating pain of lost love.[1]

Thousands of men and women in other cultures have left evidence of their despair. An Aztec native left these melancholy words in the sixteenth century, "Now I know / why my father / would go out / and cry / in the rain." An eighth-century Japanese poet wrote, "I look at the hand you held, and the ache is hard to bear." And Edna St. Vincent Millay scribed these wrenching lines, "Sweet love, sweet thorn, when lightly to my heart / I took your thrust, whereby I since am slain, / And lie disheveled in the grass apart, / A sodden thing bedrenched by tears and rain."

People around the world have also told anthropologists about their suffering.

A forsaken Chinese woman confided, "I can't bear life. All my interests in life have disappeared." A scorned Polynesian woman moaned, "I was lonely and really sad and I cried. I stopped eating and didn't sleep well; I couldn't keep my mind on my work." Up the Sepik River in New Guinea rejected men compose tragic love songs called "*namai*," songs about marriages that "might have been." And in India, brokenhearted men and women have formed a club, The Society for the Study of Broken Hearts. Each year, on the third of May, they celebrate National Broken Hearts Day, swapping stories and consoling one another.

From the ancient Sumerians, Aztecs, and Hindus to contemporary African Pygmies, Australian Aborigines, and Arctic Eskimos, people in over 150 societies have left songs, stories, accounts, myths, and legends recounting the anguish of lost love. It seems that at some point in life, just about everyone feels the emptiness, hopelessness, fear, and fury that romantic rejection creates. In fact, among college students at Case Western Reserve, 93 percent of both sexes reported that they had been spurned by someone they adored; 95 percent also said they had rejected someone who was deeply in love with them.

A Multipart Study of Romantic Love

The degrees and shades of this fierce malaise are probably as varied as human beings. Yet psychiatrists and neuroscientists currently divide romantic rejection into two general phases: protest and resignation/despair. During the protest phase, the deserted lover tries obsessively to win back the departing mate. Alas, their romantic passion also intensifies. And most abandoned men and women feel rage as well as love. Then, as resignation sets in, the discarded lover gives up and often slips into depression triggered by despair. These two phases of romantic rejection, I will maintain, are caused by the activity of several conjoining brain systems. Among them is dopamine; this natural stimulant plays a key role.

I hypothesize this because in 1996 I embarked on a multipart study of romantic love. First I canvassed the psychological literature on romantic love, culling those traits, symptoms or conditions that were mentioned repeatedly.

Being in Love

Romantic love begins as a man or woman starts to feel that another is unique; the sweetheart takes on special meaning. The lover then starts to focus his/her attention on the beloved. Lovers can list what they don't like about their sweetheart, but they minimize these traits and aggrandize those that they adore. As Chaucer wrote, "love is blynd." The lover feels euphoria when things are going well and swings into despair when the relationship has a setback. Adversity heightens the lover's passion. Lovers feel intense energy too; some hardly eat or sleep. And they become emotionally dependent on the relationship, reordering their daily priorities to remain in contact with their sweetheart and experiencing separation anxiety when apart.

Lovers are also sexually and emotionally possessive. They feel powerful empathy for their amour; indeed, many would die for him or her. And they think obsessively about the beloved. The fourth-century Chinese poet Tzu Yeh wrote of this, "How can I not think of you." And an anonymous eighth-century Japanese poet moaned, "My longing has no time when it ceases." But perhaps most important, the lover craves emotional union with his or her sweetheart. Indeed, the lover is intensely motivated to win this prize—at almost any cost. As Walt Whitman declared, "I would stake all for you."

Last, all these feelings of romantic passion are involuntary and exceedingly difficult to control. As Stendhal wrote, "Love is like a fever; it comes and goes quite independently of the will."

Questionnaire on Romantic Love

After establishing these core components of romantic love, I designed a questionnaire using these traits and administered it to 437 Americans at and around Rutgers University (New Jersey) and New York City and to 402 Japanese at the University of Tokyo.

The results were what you might predict. Age, gender, sexual orientation, religious affiliation, ethnic background: none of these variables made much difference. For example, on 82 percent of the statements, people over age forty-five reported being just as passionate about their beloved as those under age twenty-five. Heterosexuals and homosexuals gave similar responses on 86 percent of the questions. On 87 percent of the queries, American men and women responded virtually alike. Race and religious affiliation were not factors either. The greatest differences were between the Americans and the Japanese. On most of the questions where they showed statistically significant variations, however, one nationality simply expressed somewhat greater romantic passion.

I became convinced from these questionnaires and other literature on romantic love that this passion is a human universal. This madness must be deeply embedded in the human brain.

The Chemistry of Love

Then I launched an investigation into the brain circuitry associated with human romantic love. Using functional magnetic resonance imaging (fMRI),

I and my colleagues, neuroscientist Lucy Brown at the Albert Einstein College of Medicine and psychologist Dr. Arthur Aron at the State University of New York at Stony Brook, first studied the brain activity of seven men and ten women who had "just fallen madly in love"(Aron et al. 2005). Participants reported being in love an average of 7.4 months (median=7; range 1–17 months), and they ranged in age from eighteen to twenty-six.

The experiment consisted of four tasks: each subject looked at a photograph of his/her beloved and then at one of an emotionally neutral acquaintance, interspersed with a distraction task to cleanse the mind of romantic passion. In this case the task consisted of looking at a large number, such as 8,241, and mentally counting backwards from this number in increments of seven. Hence each participant looked at the positive stimulus for thirty seconds; then counted backward for forty seconds; then looked at the neutral photograph for thirty seconds, then counted backward for twenty seconds. This process (or its reverse) was repeated six times; the experiment lasted about twelve minutes.

The results told us much about the brain in love. Most important, when participants looked at the photo of their beloved, they showed increased activity in a tiny factory in the midbrain known as the Ventral Tegmental Area (VTA), as well as in regions of a much larger organ located near the center of the head, the caudate nucleus. The VTA is rich in cells that produce and distribute dopamine to many brain areas, including the caudate nucleus. And in the right proportions and quantities, dopamine can produce feelings of ecstasy, as well as focused attention, enormous energy, and intense motivation to win a reward. In fact, the VTA and the caudate are both part of the brain's "reward system," the network that controls general arousal, sensations of pleasure, focused attention, and goal-oriented behaviors.

The Drive to Love

These data suggest something important about romantic love. Because early-stage intense romantic passion activates the VTA and caudate nucleus, rather than emotion centers of the brain, I came to believe this madness is a fundamental human mating drive.

Neuroscientist Donald Pfaff defines a drive as a neural state that energizes and directs behavior to acquire a particular biological "need" to survive or reproduce. Like drives, romantic attraction is tenacious; if you love someone in the morning, you will love them in the afternoon. Emotions, on the other hand, come and go across the day. Like drives, romantic love is focused on a *specific* reward, the beloved; emotions are linked instead to a variety of objects and ideas. Like drives, romantic love is not associated with any particular facial expression; all of the primary emotions (such as anger, fear, joy, and disgust) have stereotypic facial poses. Like drives, romantic love is exceedingly difficult to control; it is harder to curb thirst, for example, than to control anger. And like all drives, romantic love is associated with elevated activity of dopamine in the brain.

Drives lie along a continuum. Some, like thirst and the need for warmth, cannot be extinguished until satisfied. The sex drive, hunger, and the maternal instinct can often be redirected, even quelled. Falling in love is evidently stronger than the sex drive because when one's sexual advances are rejected, people do not kill themselves or someone else. Rejected lovers, on the contrary, sometimes stalk, commit suicide or homicide, or experience severe depression, even physical pain. Indeed, a recent neuroimaging study indicates that emotional pain induced by social exclusion affects some of the same brain regions as does physical pain (Eisenberger et al. 2003). So the pain that many rejected lovers report is real.

To understand more about the suffering of romantic rejection, I and my colleauges put a second group of subjects into the brain scanner: eleven women and six men who had recently been spurned by their romantic partner. We used the same protocol. Each looked at a photo of their rejecting mate and an emotionally neutral individual, interspersed with the count-back distraction task. This study is still in progress. But the psychological literature on rejection, and some preliminary findings from this study, suggest that dopamine (as well as other chemicals) is also associated with the agony of lost love.

The Protest Response

When a man or woman first realizes that their partner is ending the relationship, some deny the truth. The rupture is too horrible to comprehend. But as the hours or days go by, they come to face the fact: he or she is leaving.

With this realization, the abandoned partner generally becomes intensely restless. They reminisce, searching for clues to what went wrong and how to patch up the crumbling partnership. They think continually about him or her. And they protest. Spurned lovers take extraordinary, often dangerous, even humiliating measures to reconnect with their beloved, revisiting mutual haunts, phoning day and night, writing letters or incessantly e-mailing. They make dramatic entrances into a beloved's home or place of work, then storm out, only to return and renew their appeal for reconciliation. Most become so focused on this missing partner that everything reminds them of their sweetheart. As poet Kenneth Fearing put it, "tonight you are in my hair and eyes, /

And every street light that our taxi passes shows me / you again, still you." Their obsession: reunion. So they relentlessly seek the slightest sign of hope. Psychiatrists Thomas Lewis, Fari Amini, and Richard Lannon maintain that this protest response is a basic mammalian mechanism that activates when any kind of social bond is ruptured. They use the example of the puppy. When you remove a puppy from its mother and put it in the kitchen by itself, it begins to pace. Frantically it combs the floor, scratches at the door, leaps at the walls, and barks and whines in protest. Baby rats that are isolated from their mother hardly sleep, their brain arousal is so intense. So these psychiatrists believe this protest reaction is associated with elevated activity of dopamine, as well as the closely related neurotransmitter norepinephrine. Rising activity of these cate-cholamines, they say, serves to increase alertness and stimulate the abandoned individual to search and call for help.

Their hypothesis may turn out to be correct. Preliminary results from our brain scanning study of rejected people suggest that regions of the caudate nucleus are involved in romantic suffering, and these regions are associated with the activity of dopamine (Fisher et al. 2005). This dopamine activity, in combination with many other brain chemicals, could contribute to the abandoned lover's motivation to protest.

A related brain chemical kicks into action as one gets dumped: cortisol. Any kind of severe stress stimulates the adrenal cortex to synthesize and release this hormone. Cortisol then activates myriad brain and bodily systems to ameliorate the trauma. Among these circuits, the immune system revs up to fight disease. Despite this bodily readiness, disappointed lovers tend to get sore throats and colds. But this short-term stress reaction also triggers production of dopamine and norepinephrine—which most likely also contributes to the protest response.

Frustration Attraction

Alas, along with the stress and impulse to protest, abandoned lovers also feel another powerful sensation: renewed passion. Terence, the Roman dramatist, once wrote of this: "The less my hope, the hotter my love." Indeed, rejection heightens feelings of romantic passion, what I call "frustration attraction." And this seemingly odd reaction also has a biological correlate: when an expected reward is delayed in coming, dopamine-producing neurons in the brain's reward system *prolong* their activities.

How ironic: as the adored one slips away, the very chemical that contributes to feelings of romantic love becomes even more potent, creating protest and romantic passion—and impelling the abandoned lover to try with all his/her might to secure the deserting mate.

Abandonment Rage

The impulse to protest, the stress, and the heightened romantic ardor that abandoned men and women experience all make sense to me. Rejecting people often feel deeply guilty about causing the breakup. So if the discarded partner earnestly pursues, the rejecter is likely to reconsider and return. Many do, at least temporarily. Protest sometimes works.

But why do jilted lovers get so angry? Even when the deserting mate honors his or her responsibilities as a friend (and often co-parent) and leaves the relationship with compassion and honesty, many rejected people swing violently from feelings of heartbreak to utter fury. English poet John Lyly commented on this phenomenon in 1579, saying, "As the best wine doth make the sharpest vinegar, / so the deepest love turneth to the deadliest hate." Psychologist Reid Meloy calls this reaction "abandonment rage." I use the term "love hatred" as well.

Why does passionate love turn to hate and rage? Because love and hate/rage are connected in the brain. The primary rage system is closely linked to centers in the prefrontal cortex that anticipate rewards. And animal studies have shown how intimately these reward and rage circuits are intertwined. Just pet a cat to stimulate its reward circuits and hear it purr; then remove your hand and feel it bite. This common response to unfulfilled expectations is known as "frustration-aggression." In short, when people and other animals begin to realize that an expected reward is in jeopardy, even unattainable, these centers in the prefrontal cortex signal lower regions associated with rage—and trigger fury.

This anger is not always directed at the lost reward, however. An enraged monkey may vent his ire on a subordinate monkey rather than attack a superior. In the same way, a rejected lover may kick a chair, throw a glass, or get angry at a friend rather than strike an errant sweetheart with words or fists. But this brain link between love and hate/rage helps explain why crimes of passion—such as stalking, homicide, and suicide—are so common around the world. When an attachment is ruptured, the brain can easily turn romantic love to fury. The opposite of love is not hate, but indifference.

In fact, love and hate have much in common. Both are associated with bodily and mental arousal. Both produce excessive energy. Both drive one to obsessively focus one's attention on the beloved. Both generate goal-directed behaviors. And both cause intense yearning, either for union with a sweetheart or for revenge against a rejecting partner.

But rage stresses the heart, raises blood pressure, and suppresses the immune system. Why did our ancestors evolve brain links that enable us to hate the one we cherish? Psychiatrist John Bowlby argued in the 1960s that the anger that accompanies the loss of a loved one is part of nature's biological design to regain the lost attachment figure. Undoubtedly abandonment rage sometimes serves this purpose. But fury is not a likeable trait; I can't imagine it often entices a lover to return. So I have come to think that abandonment rage evolved for another purpose: to drive disappointed lovers to *extricate* themselves from dead-end matches and resume their quest for love in greener pastures.

Abandonment rage most likely also motivates people to fight for the welfare of their children. This occurs frequently in divorce proceedings. Otherwise well-adjusted men and women become diabolical to acquire custody of and resources for their young. In fact, an American judge who presides over trials of violent criminals reports that he is much more worried about his personal safety during divorce proceedings, particularly when child custody is an issue. He and other judges have even installed panic buttons in their chambers in case arguing spouses become violent.

But despite this fury, abandonment rage does not extinguish romantic love. In a study of 124 dating couples, psychologists Bruce Ellis and Neil Malamuth found that romantic love and feelings of hate/rage can operate simultaneously. Hence, you can be terribly angry at a rejecting sweetheart, but still very much in love.

Resignation and Despair

Eventually, however, all these feelings wane. The focused attention on the failing partnership; the drive to win back the beloved; the showdowns; even the rage: for most disappointed lovers, all dissipate. The abandoned person is now spent. As the eighth-century Chinese Poet, Li Po, wrote of this, "I am exhausted by longing."

Then the rejected individuals must deal with new forms of torture—hopelessness and despair. They toss in bed and cry or just sit woodenly and gaze into a void. Perhaps they feel an occasional urge to renew pursuit or a passing flash of anger. But generally they feel deep melancholy, what is known as the "despair response." In a study of 114 men and women who had been rejected within the past eight weeks, some 40 percent experienced "clinically measurable depression"; of these, 12 percent displayed moderate to severe depression. People also die of a broken heart. They expire from heart attacks or strokes caused by their depression.

Men and women tend to handle love-sadness differently. Men are often more dependent on their romantic partners, probably because men, as a rule, have fewer ties to relatives and friends. Perhaps because of this, despairing men are more likely to turn to alcohol, drugs, or reckless driving than to their kin or friends. Moreover, men are less likely to reveal their pain. And men are three to four times more likely than women to commit suicide after a love affair has decayed. As poet John Dryden put it, "dying is a pleasure, / when living is a pain."

Rejected women sob, lose weight or eat too much, sleep too much or not at all, lose interest in sex, become unable to concentrate, have trouble remembering commonplace daily things, withdraw socially, and contemplate suicide. Some write out their grievances. And most women talk for hours on the phone with any sympathetic ear, retelling all. Although this chatter can give a woman some relief, these replays of shattered dreams often backfire. As she dwells on the dead relationship, she can inadvertently retraumatize herself.

This second phase of rejection—resignation coupled with despair—is well documented in other species. Infant mammals suffer terribly when they are separated from their mothers. As you recall, when you isolate the puppy in the kitchen, at first it protests. Eventually, however, it curls up in a corner in a despondent heap. Abandoned infant monkeys suck on their fingers or their toes, clasp themselves, and often curl into a fetal position and rock.

The feeling of despair has been associated with several different networks in the mammalian brain. But among them are the brain's reward system and its fuel: dopamine. As the abandoned partner gradually realizes that the reward will never come, the dopamine-making cells in the midbrain *decrease* their activity. And diminishing activity of dopamine produces lethargy, despondency, and depression. The stress system contributes. As mentioned, short-term stress activates the production of dopamine and norepinephrine and suppresses serotonin. But as the stress wears on, it drives the activity of all these potent substances down below normal—producing profound depression.

Evolution of the Despair Response

Like abandonment rage, the despair response seems counterproductive. Why waste precious time and energy crying? But scientists now believe that the depression that otherwise psychologically healthy people experience when abandoned may have evolved as a coping mechanism. Perhaps, some maintain, it originally emerged to enable abandoned infant mammals to conserve their stamina, to discourage them from wandering until their mother returns, and to keep them quiet and thus protected from predators. Others suggest that the high metabolic and social costs of depression are actually its benefits: depression is an honest, believable signal to others that something is desperately wrong, that the depressed person genuinely needs help.

Aeschylus, the classical Greek dramatist, saw another merit to depression. As he proclaimed in *Agamemnon*, "He who learns must suffer. And even in our sleep, pain that cannot forget falls drop by drop upon the heart, and in our own despair, against our will, comes wisdom to us by the awful grace of god." Depression gives insight. In fact, mildly depressed people make clearer assessments of themselves and others. But even severe, prolonged depression can push a person to accept unhappy facts, make decisions, and resolve conflicts that will ultimately promote their survival and ability to reproduce. The pain of rejection probably steers the abandoned individual away from making similar bad choices in the future, too.

Not everyone suffers from abandonment to the same degree, of course. How we react to rejection depends on many forces. Our upbringing makes an enormous difference. Some people make secure attachments as children and have the self-esteem and resilience to overcome a romantic setback relatively quickly. Others grow up in loveless homes fraught with tension, chaos, or rejection, leaving them clingy and defenseless. As we venture through life, we develop new feelings of competence or incompetence, different sorts of romantic expectations, and different coping mechanisms that also affect how we weather lost love. Some people have more mating opportunities than others, so some more easily mitigate their feelings with amorous distractions. And some people are simply biologically less angry, less depressed, more self-confident, and more relaxed about life in general and romantic rejection in particular.

Still, we humans are intricately wired to suffer when we have been spurned. Most men and women can vividly remember the bitter details of their distress at a breakup—even decades after the turmoil has defused. For good evolutionary reasons. Those who love and mate and breed will pass on their genes toward eternity, while those who lose in love and sex and reproduction will ultimately die out. Jilted men and women have wasted priceless reproductive time and energy. And their reproductive future has been jeopardized—along with their social alliances, personal happiness, self-esteem, and reputation. So to avoid genetic oblivion, you and I have evolved intensely powerful reactions to desertion, including the protest response, frustration-attraction, abandonment rage, and despair.

Crimes of Passion

"We must in tears / Unwind a love knit up in many years. / In this last kiss I here surrender thee / Back to thyself. / Lo thou again art free." Poet Henry King was able to let a departing lover go. Some people find this impossible to do. And the sexes tend to vary in the ways they handle their urge to protest, their rage, and their despair.

Men stalk; they are far more likely than women to obsessively follow a departing lover and threaten or harass her. Some shower her with vile or entreating messages. Some steal her valuables or personal items, such as underwear. Some follow with their car. Others loiter near her home or place of work to jeer or plead. In one study of American college students, 34 percent of women said they had been followed or harassed by a man they had rejected. And one out of twelve American women will be stalked by a man at some point in her life, usually a former spouse or lover. In fact, every year over a million American women are stalked; 59 percent are stalked by a boyfriend, husband, former spouse, or live-in partner. Eight out of ten are physically assaulted by their stalker as well. And five independent investigators on three continents report that in some 55 percent to 89 percent of cases, stalkers became violent (Meloy and Fisher in press). Most are men. Men kill, too. About 32 percent of all female murder victims in the United States die at the hands of a spouse, ex-spouse, boyfriend, or ex-boyfriend; but experts believe the true numbers may be as high as 50 percent to 70 percent. Men commit the vast majority of spousal homicides in all other countries as well.

Women are far less likely to maim or murder when they have been abandoned. They tend to berate themselves for their own inadequacies and try to lure and seduce instead, hoping to recapture their mate's affection and rebuild the relationship. Women are also more likely to try to talk things over and understand the problems. But when all this fails, some women stalk. In 1997 about 370,000 American men reported being stalked; most were between the ages of eighteen and thirty-nine, men of reproductive age. Unlike males, many female stalkers have other mental problems. Like males, female stalkers send e-mails or letters, phone ceaselessly, or appear unexpectedly as they obsessively follow a departed mate. Women also kill rejecting lovers. But far fewer take this drastic step. In 1998, only 4 percent of male homicide victims were killed by a former or current female partner.

Like love, hate is blind. For some, no form of violence is too extreme. And this violence is probably influenced, in least in part, by brain chemistry. As you recall, when lovers are first rejected, they protest—a reaction that is most likely accompanied by soaring activity of dopamine and norepinephrine. These stimulants probably give the stalker, batterer, and murderer their focus, energy, and motivation. But rising activity of dopamine also *reduces* the activity of serotonin in the brain. And low activity of serotonin is associated with impulsive violence against others.

Stalkers and murderers are responsible for their mayhem, of course. Humanity has evolved sophisticated brain mechanisms for *curbing* murderous impulses. Nevertheless, we carry within us a "fatal reflex," as psychologist William James called our human ferocity. And some abandoned men and women do not contain it: they stalk, batter, even slaughter their jilting sweethearts.

Love Suicide

Others kill themselves. Humans are the only creatures on earth who commit violent suicide in high numbers. It is difficult to obtain accurate accounts of why healthy people kill themselves; solid statistics are lacking. Loss of money, power, status, or respect and/or the realization that one will never achieve a long-sought goal can drive a person to quit this life. But most men and women don't have a lot of money, power, prestige, or goals they can't attain. They do, however, fall desperately in love. And romantic love is associated with high activity of dopamine—a *brain substance that drives down the activity of serotonin*. Low activity of serotonin is associated with suicide. I suspect many who kill themselves do so over lost love. For centuries, the Japanese even glorified this act, regarding "love suicide" as an honorable statement of one's devotion.

Attempted love suicide may even have been adaptive in ancestral times. Many suicidal women fail to kill themselves. Psychiatrists now believe these cases are examples of an extreme strategy that abandoned women use to manipulate a rejecting mate into returning to the relationship. Alas, many mistakenly do kill themselves. And suicide is unquestionably maladaptive. For these unfortunate men and women the drive to love triumphs over their will to live.

Ageless Love

"How cruel, you say. But did I not warn you? Shall I count for you love's ways? Fear, jealousy, revenge—pain. They all belong to love's innocent game." These words come across the centuries from the Celtic legend of Tristan and Iseult. I often think of them as I walk through archeological museums and look at the beads, pots, and arrowheads that lie in the display cases. All the men and women who made these precious objects must have loved and lost at some point in their lives. Romantic love evolved millions of years ago to enable our forebears to focus their courtship energy on a particular mate, form a pair-bond, and conceive a child. This drive is deeply embedded in the human brain. And I suspect just about everyone who has ever lived has felt the despair of romantic rejection.

But we are creatures with an elegant array of adaptive mechanisms, and among them are persistence and hope. The vast majority of us eventually recover from lost love, renew our quest, and fall in love again. And today we have the time to do it. Men and women are living longer. Anthropologists believe the natural human life-span has not changed in at least a million years. But today far more people survive infancy, infectious childhood diseases, accidents, and childbirth. So many more live into old age. In 1900, only 4 percent of Americans were over age sixty-five; today 11 percent survive to this age; by 2030 some 20 percent of all Americans will be over sixty-five; by 2050, 15 percent to 19 percent of the world population will be over age sixty-five as well. Many older people now live alone, too, rather than with their children. And many are healthy. In fact, some demographers say we should begin to think of middle-age as extending to age eighty-five because 40 percent of men and women at that age are fully functional. Humanity is gaining time to love.

Technology is helping. Testosterone creams, Viagra, estrogen replacement therapy, and a host of other innovations, from plastic surgery and hip replacements to unguents and clothing of every imaginable texture, shape, and style, help men and women attract a mate, even in old age. And they are doing it. One friend of mine fell in love again at age ninety-two. He wife had died five years before and he became enchanted with a longtime friend of the family. His only concern was that she was a younger woman, aged seventy-six. Interestingly, in a study of 255 people aged sixteen to sixty, scientists found no overall difference in the intensity of romantic passion. The only difference was that aging people did more varied and imaginative things together.

This primordial brain mechanism can be triggered at any age. One only needs to make oneself available. Then, with some luck, one can soar with romantic passion, what the classical Greeks called the "madness of the gods."

Note

1. References for all quotes and facts in this article can be found in Helen Fisher, *Why We Love: The Nature and Chemistry of Romantic Love* (New York: Henry Holt, 2004), except where other references are indicated.

Works Cited

Aron, A., H. Fisher, D. J. Mashek, G. Strong, H. F. Li, and L. L. Brown. "Reward, Motivation, and Emotion Systems Associated with Early-Stage Intense Romantic Love: An fMRI Study." *Journal of Neurophysiology* 94 (2005):327–337.

Eisenberger, N.I., M. D. Lieberman, and K. D. Williams. "Does Rejection Hurt? An fMRI Study of Social Exclusion." *Science* 302 (2003):290–292.

Fisher, H., A. Aron, D. J. Mashek, G. Strong, H. F. Li, and L. L. Brown. "Motivation and Emotion Systems Associated with Romantic Love Following Rejection: An fMRI Study." Paper presented at the Society for Neuroscience annual meeting, Washington, D.C., November 15, 2005.

Meloy, J. R., and H. Fisher. "A Neurobiological Theory of Stalking." *Journal of Forensic Sciences* (in press).

Leaking Affections

A Socio-psychoanalytic View

CATHERINE B. SILVER

After twenty years of marriage and two grown children, Elsie finds herself alone and suicidal in a large apartment, her husband Irving having left her and everything they had shared for a younger woman. Using the case of Elsie, a patient of mine, as a starting point, I am proposing a reflection on being dismissed, pushed out, let go abruptly or, in a word, dumped. Dumping is conceptualized as a speech-act that is the expression of feelings through action. It reflects a communication gap, a void that overwhelms a relationship, bringing about a sense of inner terror that is expressed through embodied actions and performed in unconscious ways inside and outside of the relationship. Dumping is the hidden psychic work of two people who have been in love, raised children, taken care of each other, and finally are confronted with a feeling of "overproximity," a psychic condition in which silence and fear of closeness take over.[1] I am not talking here about a mutual agreement to separate or get a divorce. I am talking about one spouse or partner leaving the family abruptly after many years together. Being dumped is a psychic trauma that can happen either to a woman or to a man and is usually the source of great anxiety, suffering, questioning of self, even suicidal thoughts. Being dumped connotes being sacrificed to an unconscious drama, the last stage of a long and often unrecognized process of small withdrawals, emotional leakages, cuts into the fabric of a relationship bleeding to psychic death. I want to discuss the mechanisms that bring about this unexpected disavowal and rejection of the (M)Other in intimate and long-term relationships. I use the formulation

(M)Other to reflect the fact that the mother is also an Other, and that mother and the Other are psychically and unconsciously linked throughout life.

The Process of Cutting Loose

Life is organized around oscillations of attachments and separations, fear of engulfment and fear of loss creating a movement with its own psychic dynamic. Being dumped is among the most traumatic of separations/losses in adulthood because it is a unilateral action, forced by one of the partners on the other. The verb *to dump* has been used to describe the disposal of dangerous materials or dead bodies, often illegally. The elements of danger and deadness are combined in dumping of both material objects and human beings. Monique, the main character in Simone de Beauvoir's *The Woman Destroyed*, expressed her feelings after being abandoned in the following terms: "Now, I am a dead woman. A dead woman who still has years to drag-out. How many?"[2] While the final act may appear abrupt, the dumping process is one of leaking affections over many years until the last, abrupt, physical, and brutal withdrawal. The leaking of affections is a slow process that takes the aliveness out of a relationship through growing fragmentation of the self and increased generalized anxiety.[3] These psychic losses happen so gradually that they often are not experienced as losses but as small inconveniences to be endured. Men and women continue to go through their normal routines, rationalizing the feelings of estrangement and deadness that are taking over. One is too busy with children, career, and family to pay much attention. As part of being cut loose one of the partners comes to experience the (M)Other as disappointing, dangerous, to be disposed of, while the other partner feels distant or oblivious to the situation.[4] In the end the inside of the couple's relationship has been drained of emotional connectedness and libidinal energy, hollowed out like a tree ready to break.

The process underlying this drifting apart has a subtle and dense quality for both parties. A slow but increasing emotional distance infiltrates the relationship like a poison that cannot be smelled or tasted, creating what Michael Eigen called "damaged bonds."[5] The process of detachment and inner panic, which precedes the final act of dumping, encompasses unfulfilled needs and unexpressed fears about not being loved, taken care of, or simply recognized enough. In the end these feelings turn into accusations, transforming the perception of the partner into a castrating and dangerous (M)Other.

Ironically, the person who comes to be dumped often lives within her/his bubble without much awareness of what is going on, busy with life preoccupations. When the final abandonment occurs, when the silence is shattered by torment and tears, the unspeakable has been performed. The will/negativity of one person breaks up the embodied psychic life of the relationship. The person who is dumped often reacts with surprise and bewilderment, bringing a sense of unreality to a much-too-real situation. Quoting Monique in Simone de Beauvoir's essay: "My head was filled with confusion. I thought I knew what kind of person I was. What kind of person he was. And all at once, I no longer recognize us, neither him nor me" (193). After the initial shock of being cut loose, the traumatic experience of loss needs to be digested and a sense of self-worth gradually recovered. The difficult work of reflexivity starts with questions about shame and betrayal, questions that reawaken deep psychic traumas. Monique describes the feeling of disillusionment in the following way: "Ah, I was so proud of us as a pair—a model pair. We proved that love would last without growing weary. How often had I stood-up for total faithfulness! Shattered, the ideal pair! All that is left is a husband who deceives his wife and an abandoned wife who is lied to" (166).

Let me illustrate further the psychic responses to being cut loose. Ariela, a patient from my therapy practice, had been dumped by her boyfriend after a decade together. She had been the driving force in the relationship, the one who could be relied upon, financially responsible and willing to sacrifice herself for the sake of the couple. Her boyfriend left her suddenly and without warning, refusing to have any contact with her whatsoever. After the initial shock, it took her over a year to regain enough psychic balance to start dealing with her feelings of betrayal and anger. But having gained a growing sense of self-worth, new feelings of disorientation and psychic dizziness emerged. "How could this have happened without me being aware of it?" "How could he have lied so much without my noticing it?" "Am I such a fool?" "Did I let it happen?" "Did I collude with him?"

Ariela needed to explain to herself her own blindness and failure to decipher the terrible drama as it had been prepared and enacted, and her naïvety and blind trust in her boyfriend. The realizations of having been duped, misled, and lied to, touched feelings of self-punishment that took the form of self-accusatory attacks. With more therapeutic work, Ariela was able to go beyond these feelings of shame and anger and confront her unconscious desires, wishes, and fantasies that had led her to repeat/relive past traumas. Her childhood trauma of having been abandoned and manipulated to satisfy her mother's emotional needs—that is, denied a separate identity—had created deep psychic wounds around which her sense of self became organized. In her adult years she experienced an unconscious conflict between her search for the unconditional love that she never received as a child and the feeling of not deserving the love that she so much needed. This conflict led to situations where she ended up being abandoned or dumped, thus repeating the original trauma of her childhood. These vignettes point to the role of early emotional injuries in the cutting loose process.

Narcissistic Injury and Fear of Abandonment

The shortage of emotional sustenance and the lack of emotional breathing space in children can endanger individuals' sense of aliveness in their adult lives. Injuries to the self, stemming from the lack of recognition and affective connectedness, can lead to a search for attachments outside the immediate family, through greater involvement with peers, school, work, grandchildren, and friends as well as immersion in worlds of fantasy. Being cut loose reawakens emotional injuries that the infant experienced in the separation process from the (M)Other. The need to be admired, to feel special, to be cared for, is an important part of the development of the self through what Freud called primary narcissism, which helps in the separation process.[6] Adults who did not receive enough early emotional sustenance as children are likely to carry within them narcissistic wounds. They become detached from (M)Other and invest their libidinal and emotional energy back into the ego as a form of auto-affection. This process of turning inward makes it increasingly difficult to identify with and link up with significant others.

The conflagration of the mother's love and the fear of abandonment in children are repeated in adult life in an unconscious search for lost loved objects. This dynamic, it has been argued, is different for female and male. Both genders have to separate from an early state of plenitude and oneness with the mother's body and accede to a world of representation, symbolization, and relatedness. Without delving into psychoanalytic theories of gender development, whether from a pre-Oedipal or Oedipal point of view, "mothering" affects boys and girls differently because the links to the mother and the separation process create different narcissistic wounds.[7] (M)Others push the male infant to separate physically and emotionally with greater force than the female infant.[8] The infant girl remains ambivalently attached to the (M)Other throughout her life. For Julia Kristeva, women do not split mother's image into sublime and terrifying objects the way men do and consequently stay to a greater extent emotionally involved with her ideal/fantasized image all through life.[9] Women also retain, to a greater extent, access to sources of caring since they are more likely to experience childbearing, childrearing and other forms of caring and relatedness. Indeed, women are more likely to take care of elderly parents or sick relatives and more likely to be found in the "helping" professions.

The fear of castration pushes the infant to solve the Oedipus drama,[10] enter into the symbolic world of language, and internalize social expectations through the eyes of the (M)Other.[11] For Kristeva, the dynamics of separation additionally take the form of identification with a pre-Oedipal father, not only the stern Father of the Law, but a loving father that she calls the "Imaginary Father."[12] In our discussion of narcissistic injury an emotionally present and loving father/partner mediates the tension between attachment and fear of abandonment by the (M)Other. Many of the women and men who experienced dumping reported growing up in families where the emotional safety net of having a loving father did not exist. The women that I talked to, unlike the men, wished to be different from (M)Other yet stay attached and identified with her, oscillating between positive and negative identifications. Men reported searching for women who could fulfill a motherly role while being weary of mother's engulfing and castrating powers. Men were looking for women who could take care of their needs for food, order, cleanliness, sex, and even beauty without too many emotional demands.

A mother's projection of her own unfulfilled needs and wishes onto the child as well as the simultaneous push toward separation creates the first conflict between need for love and fear of abandonment. Dumping someone is certainly an act of fear, aggressiveness, and symbolic violence. When an individual dumps a partner she/he expresses narcissistic rage comparable to a child's tantrum. A man I talked to mentioned that his wife lives in a self-contained world that he enters intermittently but does not understand; after being married for a decade he felt that he no longer was cherished, loved, or desired as much as he wanted to be, increasing the emotional distance and de-sexualization of the relationship. These feelings led the husband to think of his wife/partner as a "sister" or a "close friend." By putting sexual distance the husband coped with his underlying aggressive rage. Most of the men who dumped their wives described them as encroaching, critical, and possessive. In contrast, women's views of their own needs were quite different from the way men perceived them. Women expressed their desire for successful men who could exhibit maternal tendencies and their frustration at the lack of nurturing qualities in men whose vision of masculinity and success pre-empted them.

Analyzing the mutual dependence in marriages, one can argue that each partner needed the (M)Other to provide admiration and approval and simultaneously hated the expression of these unacceptable needs. Dependence on the (M)Other and the resentment, hostility, and aggression that such dependence breeds is often acted out with the partner. Each partner only sees a polarized and persecuting version of what is feared inside themselves. This mutual and fantasied dependence on the M(Other) and the fears that it provokes are shaped by sociocultural contexts.

The Expression of Narcissistic Needs across Cultural Contexts

Early gender differences in modes of attachment and the expression of narcissistic and sexual desires are shaped by linguistic, normative, familial, and institutional structures which are all culturally and historically grounded. For most adults, familial arrangements provide arenas in which to fulfill emotional, sexual, and erotic needs. But there are additional legal and institutional arrangements to satisfy these needs through access, for example, to multiple wives, mistresses, and concubines.[13] These arrangements are found across centuries, countries, and religions. Despite their variety, these legal and religious systems have several commonalities: they organize men's lives rather than women's; they tend to favor higher social classes; and they add to the size of the patriarchal household. The possession of several wives and/or concubines traditionally increased men's wealth, status, pleasure, sexuality, and procreative power, while decreasing the fear of aging and death. Today, these patterns are still found in modified forms and create systems of gender inequalities in access to erotic and sexual pleasures.

In countries like France and Japan, there is a wider acceptance for men of intimate, erotic, and sexual relationships outside of marriage. France has a well-known tradition of mistresses, who in the past have received legal and social recognition. Today, the male head of a bourgeois household can maintain a private space (*garçonnière*) where he pursues intimate encounters with the knowledge, if not acceptance, of his wife. Erotic encounters are positioned differently from sexual/reproductive ones.

Among Japanese managerial classes, erotic and emotional connectedness can be enhanced by visits after work to "hostess clubs." These "clubs" provide physical and emotional spaces where men spend a few hours with women whom they pay to boost their ego. They can regress to being childlike, getting motherly indulgence, ego support, and sexual excitement without having the responsibility of a real commitment or a full sexual encounter. In these "clubs" men can feel important and taken care of:

> Males become so attached to their mothers in their pre-adult years that they either can't duplicate this closeness with a wife or sexualize the structure of the mother-son attachment, enacting the relationship with a paid-for woman more easily than with a spouse. The emphasis is how men need to be taken care of, treated indulgently, and flattered.[14]

In these in-between zones, neither private nor public, Japanese men can get emotional gratification of intimacy and sexual play. The emphasis is not on sexual consummation but on erotic pleasure. Their wives, however, are expected to get gratification from their devotion, indulgence, and sacrifice in raising children and preparing sons for success in arduous educational exams. Emotional distance and desexualization of the marital relationship occurs within a work-family system based on a family wage that prioritizes the husband's work and legitimizes his absence in the socialization process of the children. The situation of "fatherless"[15] families in Japan provides women emotional control over their children, especially the sons, who become intensely attached and guilty about (M)Other's love and sacrifice for them. Wives compensate for their physical and emotional isolation from their husbands by displacing of affection onto their children, especially the boys.[16] These arrangements greatly penalize women and limit their options outside the home.

While there are no statistics on dumping, there are statistics on divorce rates. Japan has one of the lowest divorce rates in the industrialized world, but equally important it has one of the lowest birth rates and the largest increase over a decade in numbers of single women.[17] The low birth rate, a great concern for policy makers, could be seen as an unconscious "feminist revenge" against a socioeconomic system that gives so little occupational choice and emotional support to married women. The family structure and institutional arrangements in Japan around gender relations and the family-work nexus make it improbable that physical separation can occur. However, emotional dumping and withdrawal occur in daily family life without any disruption, supporting the demands of the work-family system in the name of the greater good of family and community.

In the United States in 2001 41 percent of all marriages ended in divorce.[18] Unlike France and Japan, the United States does not legitimize nor encourage zones of intimacy and sexual/erotic play in addition to married life.[19] While the family as an institution holds a central role in American society by providing a privileged place for the socialization and nurturance of children, the workplace has become an increasingly significant arena where sexual fantasies and emotional needs of adults are expressed and gratified. Men and women express fantasies and project emotional needs onto others and onto the work organization itself. In the workplace, desire for care, attention, and the expression of sexual desires are acted out in organizational contexts where numerous young, bright, and ambitious men and women are available and ready to fill the nurturance gap of middle-aged managerial officers. Gender difference reappears in the workplace in the ways narcissistic needs are structured and re-sponded to within a knowledge-power nexus that favors the organizational and symbolic world of male heterosexual power. Women lose socially, econom-ically, and emotionally in all the arrangements discussed above. While the tra-ditional legal structures of sexual inequalities around the family no longer exist in modern Western nations, the unconscious wish for multiple wives/partners and erotic gratification outside marriage constitutes a widespread state of mind and provides a psychic framework within which to analyze dumping.

Fantasies of Multiple Wives/Partners

A professional woman that I interviewed recalled that in the 1970s she was labeled, with other young female professionals, "office wives." They were ex-pected to provide emotional support and admiration to the boss as part of their regular job. Clinical cases show that men's fantasies involve a desire to be taken care of by several (M)Others, illustrating Freud's observation that the psychic world tends toward satisfaction through fantasy against an outside world which gradually imposes the reality principle on the individual.[20]

On occasion I have heard male patients described their fantasies of living in harems or having multiples wives/partners that would ensure a continuous and plentiful source of physical care and emotional nourishment. Other men that I interviewed had similar fantasies; some of them stayed with their desires while others acted them out. Fantasizing about other women as M(Others) can work in several directions: erotic and sexual desire can be channeled and diffused within socially acceptable frameworks or they can be expressed through acting-out by having affairs or cutting loose from the partner. As Freud's discovered, anxiety regarding the infant's fear and anger at the loss of mother's breast is defended against through hallucinations and fantasies.[21] Aggressive fantasies of devouring, mutilating, and destroying the breast be-come projected onto individuals, situations, and/or organizations before being re-introjected into the ego, bringing about a paranoiac self.[22] The fantasy of multiple partners is a metaphor and compromise formation for an uncon-scious desire to simultaneously destroy and regain the original love object.

Fantasies of escape are also likely to erupt when reality becomes too dis-appointing, painful, or unreal. Love between partners starts as an all-encompassing feeling of symbiosis, sometimes described as an oceanic feeling of togetherness. Partners experience each other as ONE through the eyes of the Other's desire. Over the years love becomes disjointed; it no longer in-volves the whole person but gets attached to an individual's objectified attrib-utes and/or skills. When these emotional shifts occur the partner has become

instrumentalized and is no longer experienced as able to fulfill sexual excitement, romance, beauty, and intellectual challenges. At this point feelings regarding the partner become highly ambivalent, underscored judgments of
inadequacy and disappointment. These views of the Other bring about desperate attempts by the recipient of such projections to regain feelings of safety,
union, and sharing through defensive responses: "Tell me that you love me!"
"Don't you love me anymore?" "I need to hear you say you love me a thousand
times!" and the like. By the time reassurances are verbally expressed the phan-
tasmatic frame of the relationship has shifted. The tangible reality has not yet
changed, yet an emotional shift has occurred that discloses feelings of distance
and depersonalization making loving more unreal and cutting loose more
likely. The social structure of gender inequalities creates the framework by
which the loss of access to sources of gratification and pleasure outside the
home is likely to impact men and women differently.

Unlike the middle-aged men, the women I talked to did not express clear desire for multiple husbands or lovers. Sexual desire played a role but it was more
muted and diffused. They reported fantasizing about meeting other men but
also experiencing women as companions, sexual partners, and close friends.
Their fantasies expressed wishes of sharing ideas, activities, and time; getting
involved in reciprocal relationships rather than simple sexual encounters.[23]
These fantasies of men and women for additional partners helped fill in the gap
between emotional and erotic needs and supplies, a gap that increases with age.

Aging and the Dumping Process

Aging is a creative process accompanied by a sense of drift, loss, and grief
that goes together with fears of the fragmenting body becoming less socially
and sexually valued over time, especially for women. Today older women are
still at an economic and social disadvantage compared to men, making them
more careful about leaving a relationship. For most women aging also means
a humiliating process of gradual sexual disqualification based on a double
standard; as Susan Sontag expressed it: "Growing older is mainly an ordeal of
the imagination—a moral disease, a social pathology—intrinsic to it is the
dreary panic of middle-aged men whose 'achievements' seem paltry, who feel
stuck on the job ladder, or fear being pushed off by someone else younger."[24]

The fear of death and bodily fragmentation bring about a variety of responses: from projection of negative feelings onto others, to fantasies of multiple partners, creative searches, and cutting loose the (M)Other. The need
for emotional supplies, like connectedness and emotional sustenance, increases with age while the sense of selfhood is redefined. Growing older takes

individuals by surprise unless they have the ability to imagine old age, something that younger people and most adults cannot easily do.[25]

When being cut loose occurs among older individuals, it opens more widely earlier psychic wounds. The trauma of loss and betrayal is intensified for older women who are left behind with limited social and financial options. The following dream of a middle-aged female patient expresses the fear of being abandoned for younger women:

> "I was inside a tall building with an elevator. I was looking for my husband when the door of the elevator opened. The elevator was very crowded and I saw him standing at the very back. It was so crowded that I could not get in. As the doors started to close, a young woman pushed her way in. Her knapsack got caught in the door and fell to the floor. She picked it up, kept the doors open and pushed her way back. The doors closed. I was left out, feeling abandoned and powerless, following with my eyes the ascent of the elevator that was taking my husband away."

Her associations to the dream revealed her sexual anxiety at losing her husband to younger women, something that she was not fully aware of. In her associations she blamed herself for not being young, aggressive, strong, and sexy enough to keep her husband interested in her and yet expressed her wish to be daring and exciting. The issues of power relations emerged with the feeling that older women are powerless and childlike. They have to compete unfairly to be included and noticed.

With age, sexuality and libidinal needs change, bringing the tactile body, not just sex, to the center of embodied selves. The space where two bodies touch is a space where it is possible to be a part of and yet distinct from the (M)Other, a space that brings together and separates at the same time. Among older people this transitional space creates new forms of intimacy that redefine a sense of self within a relationship: "Our sense of being real in our bodies, especially aging bodies comes from being touched."[26] Dumping means losing the intimate and physical contact that affects our psychic body; it puts in question our social reality. The need for a tactile body and physical touch are experienced differently by older men and women. The middle-aged women I talked to crave this type of connectedness as part of a relationship that reinforces feelings of safety and intimacy.[27] Among the middle-aged men I talked to, fear of bodily fragmentation was more likely to bring out the expression of narcissistic rage. As some psychoanalysts have shown, the fear of fragmentation can be greater than the fear of death. Freud described in "A Disturbance of

Memory on the Acropolis"[28] how he experienced old age and suffering as punishment and a second castration. The fear of castration and loss among older men could explain their greater need for nurturance and reassurance as well as their desire for younger women. As the double standard applies to love relationships, older males are allowed, if not encouraged, to be with and marry much younger women. Freud did surround himself with younger women in addition to his wife, Martha Bernays: Minna Bernays, Marie Bonaparte, and Lou Andreas-Salome (his muse), and of course his daughter Anna Freud.

The middle-aged women that I talked to and who survived being dumped experienced aging as a challenge, a space for change and creativity despite fears of loneliness and changing body image. Their remarks illustrate that psychoanalysts who have talked about fragmentation in old age and the disintegrating of the body have been predominantly male. Female psychoanalysts have a different view of the aging process that stresses change and creativity.[29]

The combination of fear of castration, bodily fragmentation, and death among older individuals, especially men, can further account for the symbolic violence of the dumping process. At this point in life differentials in power and social status between men and women are overshadowed by fear of illness, pain, and social isolation. The self emerges in the mirror stage of infant development through the illusion of bodily unity, the acquisition of language, the entry into the symbolic order and creating a sense of identity through Other's desires.[30] Older individuals experience the reverse process, going from a sense of wholeness to a fear of disintegration and death. Misrecognition of the self in the mirror of old age is likely to occur when the gaze of the (M)Other fails to sustain the illusion of wholeness, when one's selfhood is questioned anew. Renewed aggressive wishes and paranoid fears are likely to be expressed and translated into the search for younger gazes.

Compared to men, women develop greater independence and assertiveness as they age; they become more dominant and forceful in what is called "postmenopausal zest." Among older people a crossover occurs, with women becoming more assertive and independent and men more mellow and dependent.[31] This asymmetrical situation, however, increases rather than decreases men's insecurities and fears; they often perceive this change as a loss of increasingly needed attention and sustenance. Despite the original devastating impact of being cut loose, the women that I interviewed were likely to invent new lives for themselves.

At a time when social support and emotional rewards are decreasing and when younger generations are pushing ahead, the gap between narcissistic needs and narcissistic supplies among older people increases. Fears and anxieties stimulate phantasms and breaks from reality creating the conditions for potential abandonment unless shared experiences of connectedness and caring work within relationships are explored and encouraged.

Countering the Leaking of Affections

The dumping process has a certain feel of unreality so well captured by Woody Allen's movie *Interiors*. In the movie an older man announces casually at dinner, surrounded by his wife and grown children, that he is leaving the family and starting a new life with a younger woman. From that point on we witness the unfolding of a Greek drama that shows the breaking-up of psychic structures, the struggle to make sense of an unreal situation, the pull of madness that ends in suicide and the destruction of all potential new beginnings. As expressed in *Interiors*, depersonalization, deadening silences, and a sense of meaninglessness are part and parcel of the dumping process. While the movie dramatizes to an extreme the process of depersonalization, in real life the leaking of affections and the silencing of discourse also destroy the emotional space between individuals. In a feeling void becoming real to oneself and others becomes increasingly difficult. The depersonalization that is part of cutting loose entails a lack of libidinal investment in one's body and body image as well as a deadly inner silence that gets filled with phantasms and ghosts. In such a void words become deadening silences rather than a source of connectedness. To use Michael Eigen's formulation: "When words are used to evacuate rather than to build meaning, meaning is murdered."[32]

There are ways to counter the leaking of affections and the psychic deadness that ensues. The gap between narcissistic desire for emotional sustenance, affection, and recognition and narcissistic supplies needs to be narrowed. Social support from family members and friends as well as fantasies can provide important safety valves when confronted with a sense of depersonalization. They can introduce some breathing space. However, it is creative work through the use of touch, language, and imagination that can gradually restore a world of inner meaning and a sense of aliveness between partners that was shattered in the dumping process. After being cut loose, taking the emotional risk of "becoming" creates the excitement and psychic energy of feeling alive.

Acknowledgments

I want to acknowledge the time, patience, and caring of my friends Nan Bauer-Maglin, Sam Bacharach, Henri Grinberg, and Les Max for their feedback and editorial suggestions; Kirsten Christiansen for her editorial work; as well as my patients for their invaluable insights that guided the writing of this paper.

Notes

1. Slavoj Žižek, "Love Thy Neighbor? No, Thanks!" in *The Psychoanalysis of Race*, ed. Christopher Lane (New York: Columbia University Press, 1998), 154–175.

2. Simone de Beauvoir, *The Woman Destroyed*, trans. Patrick O'Brian (New York: Putnam, 1967), 253. Subsequent citations to this work appear in the text.

3. The generalized anxiety is responded to by defense mechanisms like splitting, whereby the object of identification is split into a "good" and a "bad" object. Melanie Klein, "Our Adult World and Its Roots in Infancy," in *Envy, Gratitude, and Other Works, 1946–1963,* (London: Hogarth Press, 1984), 247–263.

4. In this paper I use the terms *dumping* and *being cut loose* to describe the traumatic process of forced separation in adult relationships. They are used interchangeably but point to different aspects of the process.

5. Michael Eigen, *Damaged Bonds* (London: Karnac, 2001).

6. Sigmund Freud, "On Narcissism: An Introduction," in *Standard Edition*, vol. 14 (London: Hogarth Press, 1914), 69–102.

7. I use the term "mothering" to express a pattern of relatedness between mother and child that can be applied to a variety of people whether they are the actual mother or not.

8. Nancy Chodorow, *Feminism and Psychoanalytic Theory* (New Haven: Yale University Press, 1989).

9. Julia Kristeva, *New Maladies of the Soul* (New York: Columbia University Press, 1995).

10. Sigmund Freud, "Three Essays on the Theory of Sexuality," in *Standard Edition*, vol. 7 (1905), 136–149.

11. Jacques Lacan, "The Ego and the Other," in *The Seminar of Jacques Lacan, Book 1: Freud's Papers on Technique, 1953–1954*, ed. Jacques-Alain Miller (New York: W. W. Norton, 1988), 38–51.

12. Julia Kristeva, *Tales of Love* (New York: Columbia University Press, 1987), 133.

13. Going back to the early stories of the Bible, the patriarchs had several wives and concubines, Sarah and Hagar being the most famous ones. Jesus had two wives in the form of Madonna and Magdalena. Freud with his wife and his wife's sister Minna Bernays, and the American President Thomas Jefferson and his African American slave are additional cases. There have been quite a number of situations where men actually had several full families across continents or in different parts of the country: a recent and prominent example being Prince Berhard of the Netherlands, whose second family was discovered after his death in 2004 (*International Herald Tribune*, Dec. 15, 2004). The French have/had a tradition of

having a mistress for whom kings built magnificent houses (Hotels) and provided with financial support. Today, French presidents still have their "second wife." In today's world, religious prescriptions for multiple wives are present among Mormons sects, some Islamic societies and in tribal lands across the world.

14. Anne Allison, *Sexuality, Pleasure and Corporate Masculinity in a Tokyo Hostess Club* (Chicago: University of Chicago Press, 1994), 136–137.

15. By "fatherless" families I am referring to the fact that the father is absent from the socialization process, not that there is no father in the family. If anything, families are organized around the father as patriarchal institutions.

16. Allan Roland, *In Search of Self in India and Japan: Toward a Cross-Cultural Psychology* (Princeton, N.J.: Princeton University Press, 1988).

17. Harry C. Katz and Owen Darbishire, *Convergence and Divergences: Worldwide Changes in Employment Systems* (Ithaca, N.Y.: ILR Press and Cornell University, 2000).

18. Rose M. Keider, "Fertility and Family Statistics," *New York Times*, April 19, 2005.

19. Following the Japanese lead, erotic clubs are opening up in large American cities. However, unlike the Japanese clubs, the American erotic clubs welcome both men and women, providing each gender with a separate and special space of erotic experiences.

20. Sigmund Freud, "Two Principles of Mental Functioning," in *Standard Edition*, vol. 12 (1911), 215–227.

21. Sigmund Freud, "A Child Is Being Beaten," in *Standard Edition*, vol. 17 (1919), 175–195.

22. Melanie Klein, "On the Development of Mental Functioning," in *Envy, Gratitude, and Other Works, 1946–1963* (London: Hogarth, 1984).

23. Elisabeth Young-Bruehl, "Beyond the Female Homosexual," *Studies in Gender and Sexuality* 1(1) (2000), 97–124.

24. Susan Sontag, "The Double Standard of Aging," in *The Other Within Us: Feminist Explorations of Women and Aging*, ed. Marilyn Pearsall (Boulder, Colo.: Westview Press, 1997), 19–20.

25. Haim Hazan, *Old Age Construction and Deconstructions* (Cambridge: Cambridge University Press, 1994).

26. Kathleen Woodward, *Aging and Its Discontents* (Bloomington: Indiana University Press, 1991), 174.

27. The Japanese have a term for the need to be taken care of in that way; they call it "amae." Takeo Doi, *The Anatomy of Dependence* (Tokyo: Kodansha, 1973).

28. Sigmund Freud, "A Disturbance of Memory on the Acropolis," in *Standard Edition*, vol. 22 (1936), 238–248.

29. Catherine Silver, "Gendered Identities in Old Age: Toward (De)Gendering," *Journal of Aging Studies* 17 (2003), 379–397.

30. Jacques Lacan, "The Mirror Stage as Formation of the Function of the I," in *The Seminar of Jacques Lacan, Book 1*, 1–8.

31. D. L. Gutmann, "Psychoanalysis and Aging: A Developmental View," in *Adulthood and the Aging Process*, ed. I. G. Stanley and G. M. Pollock (Washington, D.C.: NIMH, 1980), 489–517.

32. Michael Eigen, *Psychic Deadness* (London: Jason Aronson, 1996), 47.

What's Really Going On Here?

The Therapist's Perspective

Marilyn Ogus Katz

The woman reaches for a tissue from the box next to her chair in the psychologist's office. "I don't understand how this can be happening," she says, her voice quavering as she dabs at her eyes. "We don't fight. For the past year, we've barely spoken. He turns on the television as soon as he comes home and doesn't come to bed until I pretend to be asleep. We've been married for twenty-four years and we've had our ups and downs, but this feels different." The woman pauses, but her therapist remains silent and within a moment she continues. "I keep waiting for him to ask for a divorce," she says, allowing her deepest fear to surface. "Maybe there's someone else. I feel like a failure." Unless the psychologist helps this patient examine her reactions and engage her husband in sustaining the relationship, she may have begun the long and painful process that often characterizes the collapse of a long-term marriage.

While many American marriages end in divorce and, in recent decades, our culture has considered dissolution an acceptable response to marital unhappiness, marriage still shapes the identity of women who came of age in the mid-twentieth century and remains a central value of their lives and measure of their success. The fact that the husband who leaves for a younger woman has become a cliché makes it no less, and possibly more, painful for his wife. Recently, in defiance of traditional expectations, some newly independent women are also cutting loose in midlife from what they see as confining, or even destructive, relationships. But regardless of who ultimately initiates the divorce, interviews with eighteen social workers, psychologists, and psychiatrists who treat both couples and older women indicate a complex and nuanced reality. These therapists define a multiplicity of issues and events that bedevil marriages at midlife, often leading to the anguish and rage of divorce, but also to the opportunity for growth.*

Training and inclination may cause them to stress different causalities. Those trained in psychoanalysis and developmental psychology often focus on those issues that linger from early childhood; others with medical expertise are quick to identify and treat clinical depression and other mental disorders in one or both partners; some with a cognitive and behavioral approach work to change negative into neutral thinking and destructive into positive behavior; and still others with a political and social orientation blame the culture that has conditioned women's responses to marriage and divorce. Yet, despite somewhat different emphases, they define remarkably similar problems, effects, and recommendations for treatment.

Unlike some other issues they may encounter in their practice, those involving marriage generally resonate in their personal lives. One psychiatrist asserts that therapy can actually be harmful if the therapist has gone through a bitter divorce and projects that situation on to the patient. Another therapist, whose ex-husband had been unfaithful, admitted that a patient upset her so much she couldn't control her reactions and sought supervision to ensure she didn't undermine the treatment. But almost all reveal their personal stance toward marriage when they begin. One psychiatrist who treats couples declares his prejudice in favor of marriage in an early session. A social worker explains to the couples she treats: "I don't believe in divorce, but I don't believe in martyrs. Sooner or later, though, if you want a long-term relationship, you will have to fix yourself. You can do it within this relationship with hard work and commitment or you can begin a new relationship and the personality traits that caused friction before will do so again. The problem is that if you end this relationship, there will be other victims, a society that supported your marriage, family, friends, even co-workers." She hopes her statement will give the couple an incentive to work on their marriage. Another therapist, though, questions the societal assumption that people should stay married until they die and that a marriage should be saved at all cost to the individual. "Sometimes," he said, "divorce is like pulling the plug on a dying patient." Still another places acceptance of divorce in a broader societal perspective: "In the seventies, we experienced an epidemic of friends breaking up. If the marriage was not working, it was a respectable way to get out of it. It is cultural; if you are allowed to do it, you do it."

---

*Therapists are not named and cases have been disguised to protect confidentiality.

How Individual Pathology Destroys Marriages

Whether a partner's behavior results from unresolved issues from childhood or is the manifestation of a mental illness, it will create marital chaos. Several therapists described problems that arise when husbands and wives project early childhood conflicts into the marriage. One social worker called this a failure to complete developmental tasks. She added, "Partners . . . may behave toward the spouse as though he or she were the parent." Another explained that even in well-functioning marriages, "we tend to marry people with the personality traits of one or both of our parents. It's as though we want to get it right this time." In the case described at the beginning of this essay, the woman reacted to her husband's withdrawal as though he were an authoritarian parent who had the right to judge her harshly; like a child, she refused to speak up and waited for him to make a decision about her fate.

Therapy offers an opportunity for the couple or individual to examine the inappropriateness of childlike reactions to adult situations. A social worker described a client who couldn't tolerate her husband's outside interests and his social involvement. "She needed to understand that she was feeling abandoned just as she had when her mother spent mysterious times away during her early childhood, times when the mother, unbeknownst to the child, was hospitalized for nonexistent ailments. When her husband pursued his interests, the woman experienced the same abandonment and insecurity she had known as a child. She needed to withdraw early from her mother, who was too intrusive and too laden with anxiety to give her enough positive feedback. As a result, she hadn't developed a good or complete separate self."

A psychiatrist who treats both couples and individuals cited a current case in which both husband and wife remained flawed from childhood and never abandoned infantile ways of dealing with frustration. "They have temper tantrums at home and in my office. After every session, I feel I am in kindergarten," he sighed. "Yet their personality types demand they relate to each other this way." This psychiatrist, who had been determined to help the couple save their marriage, finally began to believe, after two years, that the best he could do was to lead them to what he called "an amicable divorce." A psychoanalyst described one patient who failed to separate from her parents, and now has difficulty setting boundaries with her grown children. As a result, the woman was shocked when her second husband balked about paying college tuition; she refused to recognize his resentment at having to support her children despite their father's financial capability. This analyst also speaks of the significance of a history of loss; thus, she asks patients for a genetic history as well as a history of their relationship with both mother and father. "Early traumas can be catalysts in therapy," she explained. "You can always make changes if you are inclined and curious enough to do so."

As a consequence of incomplete developmental tasks, one partner may be, in the therapist's estimation, unusually self-involved and needy. When anxious or in pain, these partners will seek outside themselves for solace rather than look within. A social worker discussed such a case: "I treated one younger woman who met her husband at law school, but was also in love with another guy. She married the first for stability, but kept comparing her husband to the other man. She complained that her husband didn't give her what she needed emotionally. She began having an affair with the other guy, a writer who never worked nor married and still lives with his mother. He was a fantasy for her, a free spirit who satisfied her. She kept harassing her husband for what he didn't give her, and eventually, her husband found someone else." She concluded, "No marriage can provide everything you need. You have friends, other family, and your work."

While self-involvement may be occasional and situational, in some patients it may be an indication of narcissism, a personality disorder in which patients relate every relationship and situation to themselves. A narcissistic person often possesses the charm and excitement to attract a partner; however, the inability to acknowledge the other's needs often destroys the partnership.

Undiagnosed mental disorders in one or both partners may also contribute to serious marital dysfunction. A psychiatrist named untreated depression as a major trigger of discord. "From my perspective," he said, "when a marriage fails, I look for an untreated depression in one member of the couple. A depressed person can neither take nor give love. The mate feels bad because he or she is powerless. In a couple, you must ask whether there is pathology in one person, whether a mental disorder is contributing to the dysfunction. I advise medication as well as therapy." Treating the depression or mental disorder in a spouse through medication and therapy changes the dynamic in the marriage and often opens the possibility for building a stronger relationship.

What Happens at Midlife

Many therapists identified particular problems that surface for couples after many years of marriage. They speak of husbands and wives who stop listening to one another and develop instead what one called "a culture of silence." While this may be a refusal to hear the other's immediate desires, one psychologist pointed to a more profound source: "Both men and women are afraid of becoming overwhelmed by one another's *fears*," she said. A spouse's continual worries about health, finances, and the behavior of grown children may be terrifying and therefore better left unheard and unacknowledged. Worries intensify as couples reach their late forties and fifties and become increasingly aware of their mortality. When the stronger partner who plays the role of stabilizer in the marriage expresses fears and anxieties, the partner who had depended upon that strength finds it especially difficult to listen.

Social workers and pastoral counselors in one group practice viewed the actual break-up of a marriage as part of a progression. Marriages go through a variety of transitions that often culminate at midlife with the departure of children or disappointment in them, the acceleration of untreated alcoholism, or the sudden loss of financial security. Over the years, the assumptions of the marriage may have changed, as one partner or the other developed in unexpected and different ways. Most common in the therapists' practice is the man who becomes wealthy and powerful and believes he has literally "earned" the right to a younger and more exciting woman than the one who supported him through those early years. Many men feel threatened by evidence of their wives aging and harbor a fantasy that they will be able to attract someone else. A social worker explained, "The husband is scared to death of dying and keeps himself very fit. He thinks, if I don't do it now, it will be too late." Another put it succinctly: "At midlife, there is a kind of searching. You have no idea what you want, but sense your spouse won't go along with it."

Unlike couples who complain about the gradual loss of romance in their marriages, others who married for more practical reasons now wonder what they missed. One couple claimed they'd been best friends as young adults, had never really been in love, and now hunger for that experience. "The relationship feels insufficient," their therapist said. "At midlife, they want to have all the endorphins." If they have lived pragmatically, absorbed in the economic and emotional details of managing a family, they may have difficulty making the transition once their children leave home. A colleague in the group practice spoke about marriages that have "shelved" pleasures, putting off sex, travel, or looking good for one another. "In the office, he's eloquent, interesting," one of her clients complained. "Why is the best of him getting siphoned off?"

By midlife many women have forged successful careers but may still behave as dependents within their marriages. According to some therapists, the institution itself seems to foster dependency in women. One psychologist cited the case of a woman who makes an extraordinary salary in the business world, but whose college professor husband excludes her from decision making. Another career woman in her practice, married for forty years, said she was glad she'd kept her therapy appointment, but it was only because her husband had reminded her to do so. "Oh, he always reminds me of my appointments. He keeps my date book," she explained. While he intimidates her, she also wants him to take care of her. The therapist was encouraged when in a recent session, after claiming her husband really didn't like her, the woman closed by saying, "Let's talk about why I don't like myself." While she will probably remain in the marriage, therapy is beginning to help her become more confident and less dependent on her husband.

Sometimes it is only at midlife that men and women accept their own sexual orientation and acknowledge that they are actually gay. In earlier decades, they might have had a secret life, but now, with greater self-revelation and acceptance, the number of people who come out has increased. One psychologist believes society offers little support for those couples who divorce after one declares a different sexual orientation. They too need help to remain connected both as a couple and as a family.

A psychiatrist cautioned against viewing midlife as a singular transition. "I don't believe in midlife crisis," he exclaimed. "What is midlife? Forty? Fifty? There are many adult life crises; a thirty-year-old may suddenly realize that he or she hates the career he or she has chosen." Our culture doesn't always recognize the need otherwise healthy people have for professional help during all of these transitions, whether they be premarital, pre- and post-pregnancy, or midlife.

Why Infidelity Can Be Cause, Symptom, and Catalyst

Several therapists observed that when marriages are in trouble and the couples resist help, it is as if they had actually designated one person to be unfaithful. A social worker commented, "They are not smart enough to find a therapist, so they elect one member in the relationship to have an affair." In these cases, the affair becomes symptomatic of deeper issues in the marriage.

But men sometimes choose another woman in the belief they are ensuring the continuity of their lives. Particularly when men fear aging, an affair with a younger woman reaffirms their virility, strength, and youth. A social worker remarked, "For men in their fifties—powerful, wealthy men—the world is their oyster." Another observed, "It is wonderful to have the rejuvenation of a love; there are men who confuse that with change in their lives. But let's face it," she added. "The new love does keep them younger. Women are more likely to look for rejuvenation in a career or a cause or even in changing their faces or bodies through surgery."

While middle-aged men typically have affairs with younger women, therapists say they are seeing more and more women who initiate affairs. A psychologist observed, "Now that more women have power and money, they are doing what men have traditionally done, gone out and found younger and exciting men." They may consider leaving their husbands, but, interestingly, many hang on, even though they remain ambivalent and conflicted. The marriage gives them a base from which to stray. One woman she treats began to have sex with other men and her husband knew it. "She made a video of herself dancing in the nude and sent it to her male admirers. Yet, her husband won't leave and is waiting for her craziness to pass." This psychologist observed that some women even seek affairs with contemporaries to keep their marriages together. "Different people satisfy different needs," she explained. A psychoanalyst mentioned a patient who is so involved in an affair with an old boyfriend that she is in denial that her marriage is about to fall apart. In fact, she wants a third child and hopes, after two daughters, that it will be a boy. "She has a difficult time being monogamous. She is a tough cookie, very bright, articulate, feels like she has the therapy lingo down pat. But language becomes an impediment to feelings." Another patient is married to a man she loves, but who also repels her physically. She has taken a lover. "She and her husband have been together for fifty years. Her lover has other lovers. He is a sex machine," her therapist commented. "In therapy, she came to understand that her husband also puts her down, as do her two children, and she must deal with all three of them. Once I realized she wouldn't leave her husband, I helped her confront him. She comes to me for reinforcement. She needs to tell him, 'listen to what you said.'" For this therapist, as for many interviewed, the woman's adultery was less important than the intimidation she suffered in the marriage. While the woman might continue her affair, she will have a better marriage as a result of challenging her husband.

A social worker refuses to treat a couple when she knows or suspects one to be involved with someone else. "I am treating the relationship, not one person or the other. My patient is the marriage. And I cannot treat the marriage if there is a third person in the room," she says. In such cases she sees the husband and wife separately to offer each an opportunity for greater honesty. In her experience, men and women react differently when they learn a spouse is involved with someone else. "When a woman discovers her husband is having an affair, she reacts most to the dishonesty," she said. "She wants to know, 'did you talk to her about us, tell her about me?' She is deeply hurt that another woman, a stranger, knows all about her, while she knows nothing about her husband's lover." The social worker contrasted this to the husband's reaction when he discovers his wife has been having an affair. "For many men, the major concern is that she had sex with someone else. He wants to know, 'Where? Was it in the car? Was he better than I am? Did he have a bigger penis?'"

While many consider fidelity a basis for a long-term marriage, and the discovery of an affair may destroy a marriage, experience also shows that many marriages survive affairs and even endure them. In fact, some therapists claim that those marriages without a strong sexual component may even owe their survival to the affairs themselves. Suspending judgment, they listen to the details of each story and decide the direction of treatment. Sometimes, this means helping the betrayed partner recognize his or her contribution to the circumstances that led to the affair. At other times, the fault is not within the marriage, but within the partner who chose an affair instead of addressing his or her personal midlife problems. Then, identifying those problems becomes the work of therapy. In some cases, patients must confront marital frustrations that are irrelevant to the infidelity. Thus, discovery of an affair can become the occasion and catalyst for serious and productive therapy.

Renegotiating the Marriage

Responding to these issues of later life, social workers, psychologists and psychiatrists encourage couples to find different ways to communicate. Through therapy, the couple learns structured behaviors to develop tenderness toward one another, both emotionally and sexually. "Once you begin to listen to each other again, a lot of feeling returns," a psychologist observed. "When you share your fears with one another, you become kinder."

During this process, the therapists insist both partners assume responsibility for the marriage. "No matter what the picture," one explained, "a woman owns 50 percent of the relationship. She must work on the piece that was her own issue, rather than avoid it and become overwhelmed by bitterness. A woman has just as much power. She may not leave, but she may be dumping the man emotionally." Another social worker gave an example from his practice: "When the man threatened to leave for a younger woman, a really showy blonde, his wife realized that she had actually been abusing him, treating him like a loyal puppy throughout the marriage." Only then did she begin changing her behavior.

Therapists also urge their clients to find occasions to infuse later life with romance. "It is a developmental failure not to work to redesign your marriage," a therapist concluded. "It is possible to fall in love four different times with the same woman." Her colleague added that a long-term relationship itself may become a serial marriage and that as the couple renegotiate, they recognize the possibility of changing even long-standing patterns. Several therapists commented that if husbands and wives can navigate these middle years and enter their late sixties and seventies together, they generally learn to value their shared history and become more tolerant and tender while they face death, not as an abstraction, but, as they themselves age and parents and friends become ill and die, as a reality in their daily lives.

Cutting Loose

When all efforts to secure the marriage fail, divorce may finally be precipitated by an external event, the death of a parent, the loss of a job, the youngest child leaving home, a serious illness. These events lead people to reassess their life choices. A psychiatrist who works with cancer survivors gave examples of two women who decided that living more fully and freely in the shadow of their illness demanded that they face the inadequacies of their marriages and divorce their husbands.

One psychiatrist asks practical questions: "When I work with patients who are considering splitting up, I listen for clues. Does the person have a support system? What fantasies do they have about splitting up? What are their friends saying? Does a parent oppose the split? This can be very important."

Two therapists asserted they sometimes use their authority as professionals to help the patient make the decision to leave. One claimed she needs to be more directive with those who are less self-reflective. She also uses her authority to help women leave husbands who are abusive or alcoholic, when leaving becomes a necessity for the woman's health and safety. The other described a woman who was dominated by her parents and whose husband married her as a source of income. "My role as a therapist is to make absolutely clear that she must kick him out. As a respected authority figure I can help her feel her own authority and act against the authority of her husband, her parents, and the society. I see it as expunging the dybbuk and freeing the woman. Because of her background, she chose a dominating man, but she developed the strength to get rid of him." As he spoke about this patient, the psychiatrist speculated that treatment helped her develop a successful independent life, even if she remained too damaged to sustain a successful relationship.

Again, several therapists generalized about the differences between men and women in initiating a split. "I have never known a man to leave unless there was someone else in his life," a social worker commented. "Younger people divorce for other reasons, but usually an older man will go to something or someone." Exploring this further, another agreed, adding, "He will say the reason is that the wife spends too much money or that he needs space, but he actually has a replacement in place." She contrasts this with older women, who leave because they have moved forward professionally and the marriage no longer satisfies them, or, if they are more traditional, once the children have grown would rather be alone than with someone they have come to despise. Putting it simply, one psychologist said, "It is, after all, difficult for a woman to find another man. It is easier for men to leave; women have to be desperately unhappy."

Some, men in particular will make quiet plans and then confront their wives with the decision. One woman was taken by surprise. Her husband had decided to sell their apartment and rent, giving various financial reasons, but only after the apartment was sold, did he tell her he was taking his half of the proceeds and moving on. A therapist explained, "Sometimes men don't know how to leave. One man planned it all out and then sprung it on his wife. When you are with someone who is abusive, you do it in a quiet way in order to get out." But when partners seem shocked by what appears to them a unilateral decision, it indicates the degree to which they have chosen to insulate themselves from the feelings of their partners and the realities of their marriage.

Assessing the Damages

Not surprisingly, women often respond to divorce with excruciating pain at the assault upon their identity and self-esteem, grief over loss of both the past and the future, regression into childhood feelings of abandonment, and unmitigated rage at their victimization. Some become clinically depressed. Shame and humiliation exacerbate these feelings. Yet, one psychiatrist asserts that everyone reacts to life crises differently. "How you respond to this trauma reflects how you usually defend and deal with issues. There is a broad spectrum of responses depending on the person. The best analogy is that after an injury, some individuals have a barely noticeable scar, while others develop keloids. After the end of a marriage some find strength and affirm how precious life is, while others become almost nonfunctional." Another agreed, "The woman may say, 'I will never trust anyone again,' but if she trusted before, she will again. That is the best predictor of how she is going to heal."

LOSING IDENTITY

Every therapist interviewed described divorce as a powerful assault on a woman's identity. The blow to self-esteem leads her to question who she is, how she looks physically, and how she appears to others. Circumstances may compound these insecurities: One therapist explained, "The woman knows he left her for a woman bartender, a crossing guard, or she gave up her career and he left her for a colleague and all she's got is that she parented. She believes her husband thinks she's fat, not interesting, too devoted to the children. She's not a sexual being. The bottom line is that the person who knows her best doesn't want her." This extraordinarily painful realization may last months and even years. One psychiatrist counters by helping the patient understand that "when someone doesn't want you, it reflects more upon them than on you. It is not related to your being fat or ugly. When someone stops caring, it is almost always not your problem."

Only after the marriage has ended do women begin to recognize how much of their identity has been shaped by long years of responding and reacting to someone else. It takes time and hard work to disengage and shape a separate self.

EXPERIENCING LOSS

The end of a long-term marriage represents a profound loss of both the past and the future. Women find themselves revising their entire marital history. If the marriage ended with infidelity, the woman has to develop a better sense of who her partner was. "What she thought about her marriage wasn't true," the therapist explained. "Her husband, for example, may have had another life. She may begin by wondering what the new person saw in her husband and then recognize she actually didn't want to change her life in the ways he wanted." According to one social worker, in order to sustain a marriage, "You often have to convince yourself that your partner is brighter and more sensitive than he really is. Now you have to revise that assessment in the light of what happened."

Divorce is also a loss of the imagined future, the golden years the woman took for granted. One psychiatrist called this "a foreshortening of the future." Like death, divorce leads women through the stages of grief. Some experience a depression, a numbing and emptiness, and an inability to function. "You have lost a friend, a helper, and a lover," a social worker observed. A psychiatrist distinguishes between what he considers appropriate grieving and extreme symptoms that may indicate a clinical depression. An antidepressant allows some of these women to return to what he called "a baseline of grieving" that will then respond to therapy.

STRUGGLING AGAINST REGRESSION

As a concomitant of grief, some divorced women regress to childhood feelings of abandonment, particularly when they've experienced losses in the past. "It stirs up so much from early life," a social worker commented; "a body in the house, in bed, makes the woman feel secure and now she goes so far back in her development that it is a primitive need." A woman may relive an early trauma and become infantile, as if she were helpless and hopeless with no resources, even when she really is accomplished and attractive. One therapist told the story of a woman who called her grown son from the supermarket because she wasn't sure whether or not she should buy a quart of milk. "You don't drink milk," he reminded her. Another offered the example of a woman who felt abandoned, even though she had initiated the separation. "She was dissatisfied with herself all along and made all kinds of changes in her activities while still married, never satisfied, and then decided on the final change. She ended up drinking and using drugs and her treatment is still ongoing."

When therapists see regression, they help patients make a realistic assessment of their skills. A social worker described the process: "You try to get someone to resist regressing. When a patient says 'I can't manage,' you point out that she is responding as if she were a child and not an adult. You tell her, 'You need to remember you are an adult. You can learn to handle it. The first thing to work through, though, is what the divorce meant and how you responded to it.'" In therapy, a patient may discover, for example, that she allowed herself to be taken advantage of all of her life. "Women who don't revisit the past remain in an area of dissatisfaction, embracing the role of victim," the social worker concluded. What the therapist does, a psychoanalyst explained, "is to listen for replays, for reactions that were inappropriate in the marriage, without stressing their inappropriateness. You explore the notable experiences and what they were like, the emptiness caused by being abandoned. When the patient is ready, you explore the ways in which the spouse didn't suit her and what she wants for the future."

WORKING THROUGH RAGE

Many women reeling from these losses often react with incredible rage and the therapist must accept that anger and help the patient work through it. "A woman can't move on until the rage has abated," one therapist said, adding, "This can take up to two years." One enraged woman stalked her ex-husband, parking in front of his apartment, tapping into his telephone account, wanting to hear all the details of his affair, no matter how painful. Her therapist said, "She sometimes punishes herself with visions of the other woman, seeing him stroke her hair, seeing them in bed, torturing herself. 'I can't believe he's not coming home,' she'll say." In therapy, the woman realized that rage had led her to a form of self-abuse. She had to look at what her therapist called "her own shadow side."

Some women take up the cause of victimhood and band together with others around their anger. They talk about the break-up with family, friends, and children. They bond with their girlfriends and paint their husbands as villains.

They hold on to bitterness, sometimes for years. They seek revenge by making serious and sometimes unrealistic financial demands upon their husbands. Others get on with their lives after the original blow and can look at the experience objectively. "I am not critical of either path," one therapist commented. "Women who feel they are wronged can take strength from it." Another agreed that anger may empower women appropriately: "They need to be angry. It can be practical when they go to a lawyer to be sufficiently pissed off to make demands. I feel my role is to help them use this anger to advocate for themselves." She added that women should not take responsibility for what is not their fault, physical abuse or untreated alcoholism, for example, or even a blatant affair. "They should be angry about an affair," she explained. "This may make the husband feel guilty and sometimes guilt leads to responsible behavior." Thus, a certain degree of anger may propel a woman forward into necessary action.

BATTLING SHAME

Not surprisingly, shame and humiliation exacerbate reactions to divorce. "This generation of women was basically trained to be married and have children," said a psychologist. Thus, the end of a marriage feels like a public admission of failure. These women generally had parents who remained married regardless of the strains, and they cherished this expectation for themselves. "Women feel responsible for the survival of a marriage. And society holds them responsible when it fails," explained one psychologist, who believes shame is the salient element in women's reactions to most life situations. "Shame becomes a cover for feelings of helplessness; everything grows out of that," she said, noting that in her own practice she concentrates on freeing her woman patients from the societal expectations they have internalized. The psychoanalyst spoke of a patient who was not only devastated when her husband left, but also experienced severe embarrassment because he left her for a woman who was far less accomplished. A social worker who practices in a suburban town emphasized the importance of image for her patients. "You spend lots of energy trying to make your marriage look good to the community," she said. Women suffer, according to another, "a change in social status, some[what] real and to some degree exaggerated. Divorce gives women a sense of lost respectability, loss of social freedom and social life, and loss of benefits, both financial and in self-worth." But for one psychiatrist, shame is an issue not only for women, but also for men. "It affects anyone who has high standards about what should be. This kind of person is going to be more concerned about embarrassment and the public quality of divorce."

WINNING HIM BACK

Even after the initiation of divorce proceedings, a few women direct their energies toward getting their husbands back and sometimes even succeed. A social worker described such a case: "This woman's husband left her for another woman. He had been a philanderer and she was not completely surprised, but she fought to get him back in every way. Her friends told her to get rid of him. They got into family therapy. It took about a year, but now they are back together." The explanation, according to the therapist, is that the woman was willing to change dramatically. "She became more open, funny, and charming. She began to see humor even in herself. This helped her see things about him that infuriate her. He is anxious, shy, retiring, passive-aggressive. She got him into therapy. She truly loves him, even though she was angry. She understands now that in leaving her he was acting out; she knew it and put up with it." Another social worker described a case where the effort to win the husband back failed but succeeded in allowing the patient to get on with her life. "The husband left on Christmas Eve. She made it difficult for him, calling him, asking to have dinner, changing her appearance. Her own actions made her feel stronger. As she got to know the reasons her husband left, she realized that he was very shallow. She knew there was no way she could get him to return, but she wasn't able to put closure on it until she tried. She went on to do extremely well and have another life." This social worker added her own observation that the effort to win a husband back may work if he made the gesture of leaving in a spontaneous and irrational way. Then, she suggested, it may be necessary for a woman to refuse to take "no" for an answer. "At midlife, men require comfort," the therapist argued, "and they are sometimes relieved to return to the familiar."

Occasionally, women do their own acting out in response to the shock of divorce. A woman may behave recklessly or impulsively for a while, in the absence of a standard by which to measure herself. One patient began having an affair with her gardener, and that helped ease the pain for a time. "He was a better lover and showed her that there were other men out there. It was briefly ego building." But, her therapist shrugged and laughed, "It was like fast food."

Responding to Grown Children

In this age group, most women have grown children and, even though they themselves are in pain, they must also deal with the reactions of their sons and daughters. In a sense, a marriage with children is never really over. One therapist advised that children need to understand how much unhappiness led to the decision. But many issues upset children in their late teens, and even twenties and thirties. Public shame disturbs them, particularly if they took pride in having an intact family while they watched the divorces of so many parents of friends. Like their mothers, they feel they must revise family history. With finances disputed, they worry about the future and may be caught in ugly arguments, such as who will pay their tuitions. Victimized and angry women can poison their children, or, at the very least, find solace in children agreeing with them. Therapists discover they must sometimes help women resist rallying children to their cause and alienating them from their fathers. Other women behave as helpless children themselves and give their children inappropriate custodial roles.

"Instead of celebrating the major events of their grown children's lives at graduation, at weddings, couples refuse to speak to one another and make the children miserable," one social worker commented. Another remembered a dispute about who would walk the child down the aisle. Attending a child's wedding alone can be painful, especially if the ex-husband arrives with his new partner or wife, reminding the woman that he can not only start over again, but possibly begin a new family. This therapist suggests to her client that she consider inviting an escort to family weddings and other public events.

Sometimes a woman sees traits of her ex-husband in her grown children and reacts with disproportionate anger. Here therapy can be helpful in identifying and changing behavior. A social worker gave an example of a woman whose thirty-year-old son insisted on reading a magazine while she was talking to him, much as his father had done for years. However, the woman had learned through therapy not to react to the son the way she had to the father. "Instead, she told the young man, 'It feels as though you're not interested in what I have to say.' The son immediately put down the magazine and apologized for his habit of doing two things at once."

One social worker said she had seen situations in which both parents forged a healthier, more involved relationship with their children, even if the overburdened mother feels resentful at times. She commented, "Each parent takes on roles they had never filled."

Moving On

While most transitions in our culture are accompanied by ceremonies, such as christenings, weddings, and funerals, we have no ceremonies to mark a divorce. One therapist described a friend who invented a ritual to put closure on her marriage. She called one morning and asked the therapist to join her on a climb to the top of a nearby mountain. "I want to have a ceremony for my divorce," the friend explained. When they reached the summit, she spoke about her marriage and what went wrong and why her efforts didn't work out; she also talked about her plans for the future. "Then she attached her husband's photograph to a rock and threw it over the side of the mountain." The therapist felt this invented ceremony helped the woman begin to create a new life.

As the patient gradually recovers, she must ask herself serious questions about the value of her marriage. "The best you can do is to learn that your husband was not destructive, not harmful, not toxic," a psychiatrist suggests. "You begin to ask was this ever a good enough marriage?"

As they help their patients move on from pain and bitterness, all of the therapists spoke of the importance of rebuilding self-esteem in the aftermath of divorce, one calling it "the major work" of treatment, particularly when the divorce was not the patient's choice. She theorized that most women in this age group came into their self-esteem later than most men, perhaps in their thirties and forties, and concluded that this might make them less secure in their identity when they divorce. Another noted that some married too young and without a sense of who they were. Many also spent their lives accommodating to their husband and children and have never asked themselves what they really want. After the divorce, the simplest decisions may be difficult for them.

Obviously, a career may help a woman adjust by giving her the opportunity to be herself, make significant choices, and demonstrate her strength within a larger community. "A career can be ego boosting," one social worker said. "You go some place and you are confident. In day-to-day life, you don't get perks, but when you walk into your office, you become empowered. Anything familiar boosts self-esteem." But all therapists advise women to tap into their strengths. One speaks about building up competencies, while another suggests her patients reconnect with early passions and interests. "What did you love to do as a kid?" she asks them. One of her patients returned to art through jewelry making, another went to law school, and a third became a social worker. With the support of therapy, her patients found their own abilities and discovered that outside the constraints of a difficult marriage, they were freer to exercise them.

Newly divorced women need supportive communities as they make more deliberate social decisions, discover who their friends really are, and condense their friendship circle. As one therapist said, "A single woman in society still has a very difficult time. Families become involved in their own lives and are not sensitive to the woman. Even if you have close friends rallying around you, you find yourself alone a lot. It is difficult to be invited to a big event and know you have to go alone. The answer seems to be to develop a new social life." Women often reconnect with old girlfriends or seek out other divorced women and widows to help them navigate a coupled world and provide them with different perspectives, activities, and opportunities.

While therapists speak of divorce as an opportunity for growth, several cautioned those who expect a new relationship with a man. "The odds are against them," one psychiatrist put it bluntly. A social worker added, "She is fifty-eight and men her age are not going out with fifty-eight-year-olds. This is reality," she stressed, as she spoke with a group of male colleagues, "and not a depressive stance." For some women, it is difficult to be without a man. "I help my patient make a distinction between wanting a man and needing a man," a psychologist explained, but another therapist noted that if the individual is suffering, the desire for a companion can become a major need. "Studies do show that those with companions live longer, healthier, and fuller lives," he observed. A psychoanalyst cautions her patients against what she calls "repetition-compulsion," seeking a relationship similar to the one that did not work out. Many women try the Internet and ask friends to introduce them to available men, but dating itself can be fraught with unexpected difficulty. A therapist commented, "When an older woman starts dating, she feels like a teenager; sometimes she goes back to being eighteen, with all the excitement and thrills. But she discovers the old rules don't pertain. For example, the woman might have to deal with a grown child who still lives at home. She has to consider whether and when to bring her lover into the household." She added that sexual issues may become the subject of therapy as women adjust to aging bodies and responses. "You find ways to accommodate and discover what works. You speak more honestly to your doctors, to your partner." The honesty itself often leads to a better relationship than the woman has ever experienced. For some, this might mean developing a new kind of relationship, what one psychologist labeled an arrangement of "Wednesdays and weekends" that meets the woman's current needs by giving her more independence than she had within her marriage. Sometimes, she added, less frequent contact even ensures greater and continued excitement in the relationship.

A psychiatrist warns his patients against becoming involved with someone too soon. "The person who is hurting needs a different kind of mate than they will later," he explained. "I tell patients to wait. I had one patient who left his wife and found a soul mate immediately. My concern was that leaving may be appropriate if there is not much there, and another person makes it easier to leave. But I tell them to take their time and give themselves a longer chance to adjust. This isn't based on scientific studies; it is based on my judgments, my life experience. There is no rule about how you do this." Studies do show that after divorce men do better financially but women do better emotionally. Some theorize that because women generally can't find relationships as quickly, they are forced to go through a longer, more effective process of healing.

Whether or not new relationships work out, single life begins to take on a pattern, and a woman may begin to see some of the disadvantages of marriage. She enjoys doing what she wants when she wants to do it, and may even realize she is better off alone. She begins to celebrate her growth. One social worker suggested, "Being in charge of one's own security may bring with it a great surge of strength." While the therapist must address the psychodynamic issues of the past that have been ignited by the loss, the substantial work of therapy involves helping the patient create this new life and learn to be comfortable as a single woman, through work, activities with single and married friends, and contemplative and productive time alone. As the patient gradually recovers, the therapist offers practical advice, using professional experience and personal wisdom to become both a coach and a guide.

With the help of her therapist, the woman begins her own spiritual and psychological journey and moves on from grief. One described that process: "She asks herself who she was in the course of the marriage and what she needs to do to become a whole person. She internalizes a part of what her husband gave her. She grapples with financial realities successfully. She no longer takes 'being dumped' as her new identity. The woman who continues to see herself as a victim will remain victimized and draw similar women to her side. She will make that her world and allow the act of divorce to have the power to define her, but," he concluded, "you can't forgive until you empower yourself."

Divorce Is Economic Suicide

NANCY DAILEY

Warning: *Park your emotions here before reading further.*

I sound this warning with the best of intentions. I mean to educate, not offend or put you on the defensive. I am neutral about divorce. However, our society and our economic system are not. Too often, the "emotional noise" swirling around divorce shuts down our ability to hear or recognize the realities of this legal and economic act of uncoupling. There is no denying that divorce is an intense, emotional life experience. But more importantly, it will cause a complete meltdown of your financial life.

Divorce is economic suicide for women. Divorce may be the solution to a problem marriage but marriage is the only sanctioned path to financial security in old age. Quite literally, when you divorce in later life you are jumping from the frying pan into the fire. The socioeconomic outcomes of divorce are repeatedly documented in the media, in the academic literature, in chat rooms. This is not new news. Yet, as many marriages continue to end in divorce, there is no real conversation or public discourse about what women need to do to survive the economic ruin that parallels divorce.

I can almost hear you saying: "What about wealthy women?" Yes, they are the exception. However, the number of wealthy women who can claim divorce as an economic windfall is minuscule compared to the millions of women who experience economic suicide. I am not going to spend any time here with this exception to the rule. Besides, there are many, many stockbrokers, financial planners, insurance agents, estate planners, and lawyers ready, willing, and able to provide wealthy divorcées with advice.

TABLE 1: YOUR DEMOGRAPHIC DNA:
FACTORS THAT PREDICT YOUR FINANCIAL HEALTH

Work: What's your earning power?	We're working girls, working mothers, working women. Yet, we've had lots of interruptions due to child care, elder care, or other life events. We have chosen or been forced to make career compromises throughout our work life. Bottom line: we'll work, on average, ten years less than men. Because of this, many, many of us will be surprised to learn, at retirement, that we will earn more Social Security as a spouse than on our own personal work record (which is why the ten-year mark of a marriage is critical for Social Security earnings).
Education: What's your occupation power?	Economists and sociologists call it "human capital." It's the investment we make in ourselves, not just our money portfolios. Because of the kind of work women do—more service work than manufacturing or physical labor work—the only real way to increase our "human capital" is through education. Investing in your occupation, whether with a college degree or specific job or technical skills, is an important path to long-term financial security. Women with college degrees and strong job skills have more occupation power because they have the option to work more years, to stay in the job market (to make up for time lost because of family interruptions), to save longer for their retirement.

Family:
What's your
    relationship
    power?
	Women are the purveyors of "social currency." It's what sociologists refer to as the ability "to make things happen." Women make things happen in their families. We now need to use our social currency to change the conversation about caregiving. Why? America is aging. By 2030, when all baby boomers will be aged 65+, they will represent 20 percent of the population. Who will provide care for this huge group of elderly? Women will, particularly the "young-old," women aged 55–65. Women will be asked to leave the labor force to care for a parent, a spouse, a sibling, an uncle, a grandparent, a grandchild, just when they need to build their own retirement nest egg.

TABLE 1: (CONTINUED)

Marriage: What's your economic power?	Two can save easier than one. That's an economic fact even the most skilled divorce lawyer cannot overcome. Married women are the least likely to fall into poverty. Divorced women are the most likely to fall into poverty. Marriage is society's institution for personal wealth creation. Divorce for women is economic suicide.
Money: What's your financial power?	Amazingly, talking about money is still quite taboo in our society. The result is that many women remain functionally illiterate when it comes to personal finances. Money is a complex subject. We must learn about money, what to do with it, how to manage it, how to invest it. We're getting better but we still have a long way to go. The more you learn, the more you're worth!

Here are six stories of real divorced women and what they are doing or not doing to secure their financial future as they move into later life. All of the stories concern middle-aged divorced women. Some remarried successfully, some chose a path of employment security, some neglected their financial lives, some made the right choices knowingly or not, and some repeatedly made the wrong choices. Is there any way to predict who will escape the economic downfall caused by divorce? From my extensive research, I have developed a predictive index that measures how secure women will be in later life.[1] It is based on socioeconomic factors that shape financial health: work, education, marriage, family, and money—a woman's demographicDNA.[2]

Just as a woman's biological makeup (family history, DNA, etc.) plays a major role in her health and well-being over a lifetime, her demographicDNA determines her financial health in old age. As you read these stories, look for the predictive variables and think about how they affect the woman's long-term financial security.

Adele

Adele was three years old when she lost her family to the concentration camps of World War II. She grew up in postwar Germany knowing scarcity and self-reliance. After a handsome American GI offered marriage, she found herself in Miami, speaking English with a heavy accent but thrilled to be in America. Trouble began when her husband was discharged from the army and decided to return to college to finish his degree and Adele was pregnant. To keep them financially afloat, a few months after her daughter was born, Adele went to work as a hairdresser, a skill she had learned at school in Germany. European hair salons were the rage in Miami at the time and she did well, thanks to her accent and skills. Adele quickly became the sole provider of the family, increasing her work hours to full time.

One day Adele came home from work to find her husband and her daughter gone. For the next six years she hunted for her daughter up and down the East Coast and in Canada. Adele filed for divorce and received full custody from the Florida courts but that didn't help much when she couldn't find her ex-husband or child. Adele moved to the Washington, D.C., area and struck up a friendship with a neighbor who was a public health nurse. It was this nurse (using her investigative skills in tracking down highly contagious disease carriers) who found Adele's ex-husband and eight-year-old daughter living in Georgia. Adele had been separated from her daughter for six years.

Adele spent the next ten years trying to make it up to her daughter. But as the sole breadwinner she had to work long hours. She opened her own hair salon in Bethesda, Maryland, and bought her first home in a good neighborhood where her daughter went to good schools. She lived frugally. Adele remarried in her early forties. Alan was a real estate attorney working for the federal Justice Department.

Now sixty-two, Adele is reaping the benefits from her remarriage and her home ownership. She did not sell her first home when she married Alan. She rented it for eighteen years. Then, she insisted that she and Alan live in the house for two years so they could avoid paying capital gains taxes, which were significant. She earned $500,000 (tax free) on her little house, which is now part of her retirement savings. As the spouse of a federal retiree, Adele will also have good health insurance coverage as she ages.

She and Alan have just finished building a million-dollar retirement home on Hilton Head Island in South Carolina. Adele is still cutting hair for her long-time clients even though she really doesn't need the money.

Adele's demographicDNA gives her a predictive score of 85/100.

Molly

In her mid-thirties, Molly moved to rural Virginia with her husband and one-year-old son. The idea was to leave the commuter nightmare of city life for a more rustic, slower pace. They were going to start a home-based business and home school their son. It lasted about one year.

Divorce left Molly literally stranded in the countryside. At the time, the real estate market was in a slump and selling the house at a loss, if it would sell, was not an option. In the divorce settlement, she opted to keep the house. She would have to get a job and put her son in public school. Her dream of a rustic heaven vaporized, Molly faced reality and applied for a job at the local post office.

The irony isn't lost on Molly. Fifteen years as a postal carrier on a rural route may not be a commuter nightmare but it takes its toll on the creative spirit. Audiobooks are Molly's companions along her route. She wants to send her son to college and have retirement savings. This job lets her have both.

Molly has no plans to remarry. The house that was such a liability at the time of her divorce has turned out to be an investment plan. The rural county she lives in has become a victim of urban sprawl and is fast becoming a bedroom community. Molly's house has appreciated two-and-a-half times its purchase price.

Molly's demographicDNA gives her a predictive score of 65/100.

Paula

Two marriages, two divorces, two children, too little time to make corrections. Her first marriage was a youthful mistake. She was sure her second marriage was the real thing. Neither marriage hit the ten-year mark. This will prove to be a serious financial regret in her old age.

Paula earned a PhD in her late twenties and began the tenure track at a southern university. Time for children as well as relocation for her husband's career advancement took Paula off the tenure path. She carved out a professional life of part-time university teaching and part-time clinical practice at a local hospital. It worked well while the kids were young. But it was a bad place to be when her second divorce was finalized. She was not making enough to support herself. Her portion of the proceeds from the sale of the family house let Paula make the down payment on her town house. Her ex-husband continues to make child support payments and is an attentive father, but he has remarried and has two toddlers.

While highly educated, Paula never put into place any long-term financial security plans. Her financial struggle started the day of her divorce and hasn't abated even though she filed for bankruptcy. Now fifty-three years old, Paula is very pessimistic about her financial future. To make things worse, the hospital had cutbacks and her program was eliminated. She now needs to look for new employment and it has been two months since her last severance check. She took a loan from her small retirement savings plan to cover expenses her unemployment check doesn't. Now she really has no savings. Her even bigger concern is what she will do for health insurance.

Paula's demographicDNA gives her a predictive score of 20/100.

Diane

Diane married and was a mother by age twenty-one. Today she has been divorced for thirty years. Her only child is now in graduate school. Diane would have remarried but never found the right man at the right time.

Her ex-husband has been an absentee father, but he did provide child support as ordered by the divorce agreement. That allowed Diane to divert some of her earnings to savings early in her work life.

Shortly after her divorce, Diane took a secretarial job with a well-known global financial services company. Diane worked hard, moving up the ranks to senior vice-president. She has been a very successful stockbroker, advising clients on investing their money. She now has a loyal client following. Diane invested heavily in her professional development, learning and stretching herself, taking advantage of on-the-job training opportunities and learning from others in the business. She has ridden the economic highs and lows of the stock market and the highs and lows of working in the male-dominated financial services industry.

As she moves into her mid-fifties, she does have a big regret. Diane never graduated from college. Her lack of a college degree always made her feel insecure, working with others who were far more credentialed. Being a single mom with a demanding job, she never had the time to go to college. She is determined to get her college degree when she retires.

Diane practiced what she preached. She took her own advice about creating, managing, and protecting wealth. Not only has she made nice investments but with the lengthy tenure with her employer, she participated in all the savings options they offered, including a 401k retirement plan, an employee stock option plan, and a deferred-compensation plan. She feels that she has prepared for her older years. She is more concerned about getting bored in retirement so she is looking forward to going to college. She is also hoping that her son will make her a grandmother sooner rather than later.

Diane's demographicDNA gives her a predictive score of 65/100.

Roberta

Roberta's marriage lasted for about ten years. She went to nursing school, then worked to put her husband through college. She really wanted children, but her husband kept delaying the decision. Finally, when she turned thirty-three, she realized she was not going to have children with this man. They divorced, and since both of them had invested heavily in their educations, assets were little. Both walked away with $5,000 from the sale of their town home.

Job security was never a problem for Roberta since she is an RN. She could always get a job. But she had little in the way of savings and she did not contribute to a retirement plan. She wanted to own her own home but never got around to taking the action needed to secure the financing. As she approached forty, Roberta started thinking of becoming a single mother. But then she met Brad. Brad was ten years older and had two teenage children from his first marriage. He was not interested in having any more children. Roberta married Brad when she was forty-two. She is happy with her decision.

Brad is a physician with privileges at the hospital where Roberta works. They have a full social life and Roberta looks forward to being a step-grandmother when the time comes. She is spending more and more of her time caring for her elderly parents, who live about thirty miles from her home. Roberta is an only child.

Roberta's demographicDNA gives her a predictive score of 75/100.

Ellen

Ellen married for the first time when she was thirty-five years old and had her only child at age forty. She has been a legal secretary in Washington, D.C., her entire working life, changing employers every five to seven years when she got fed up with working with big egos. Ellen has a hefty commute each day.

Ellen and her husband filed for bankruptcy early in their marriage but didn't entirely learn the lesson of not using credit cards. Every few years, she found herself sitting in front of a credit counselor working to eliminate credit card debt. Saving for retirement has never been on her radar.

Her husband, several years younger than Ellen, asked for a divorce last year after more than twenty years of marriage. The divorce was just finalized. One financial decision they made did prove fruitful. Their town house had appreciated significantly over the twenty years of their marriage. Ellen walked away with $35,000. This is her total savings. Now that she is fifty-seven, divorced, and beginning to experience health problems, she is getting very anxious. She has one brother who lives nearby, but they are somewhat estranged over his handling of their mother's estate. Ellen just learned that she will not inherit anything from her mother. The entire estate went to pay nursing home bills and taxes. She has strong suspicions about how her brother handled the estate. Her son, now seventeen, is a high school dropout and drifts in and out of her life. Ellen knows he has a drug problem. She knows she will be caring for him over the next few years just when she should be saving as much as she can for her old age.

Ellen cannot afford not to work. Her salary as a legal secretary is quite good but living expenses as a single person in the metro area are high. Her rent alone is twice as much as the mortgage payment she used to share with her ex-husband. She will need to buy a new car soon. She keeps asking herself how she got to this place of insecurity and financial anxiety. She finds herself using credit cards far too often.

Ellen's demographicDNA gives her a predictive score of 40/100.

Divorce in Later Life Is Risky Business

Clearly, Adele and Roberta, the remarried women, are in a far more secure financial position as they move into their later years. Molly and Diane, not remarried, are still at risk but they have made a solid foundation for their future. Paula and Ellen, the recently divorced, are the most vulnerable and at risk. Paula's situation is particularly troublesome because she has no savings or immediate job prospects and she never met the ten-year marriage requirement for Social Security. Ellen has some savings, and if she stays healthy and continues full-time work for the next ten years, she may greatly improve her financial future. But those are two really big ifs.

Let's look at Table 2, which illustrates the demographicDNA scores for the women in the stories. If you were to plot on a chart the demographicDNA scores of a hundred divorced women, it would look like a bell-shaped curve. There would be a small group of women, the fortunate few, who would score 80 and above (Adele). There would be a small group of women who would score in the real danger zone of 20 and below (Paula). The majority of divorced women would fall somewhere in the middle, as Molly, Diane, Ellen, and Roberta did. However, if you plot women who divorce in later life (fifty-years-old-plus), the curve would skew heavily to scores of 40 or less, like Ellen and Paula.

The Reality: Fear of Bag Lady Status Is Justified

Society's promise goes something like this: if you invest in job skills and/or in your education and work throughout your adult life in the paid labor market, you will be entitled to security and leisure in old age. The catch is, for women, you have to stay married. Or, you have to make Herculean efforts to create financial security for yourself. From a financial viewpoint, divorce in later life is far worse than becoming a widow. Among women sixty-five and older, widows have almost 50 percent higher average

TABLE 2: REAL DIVORCED WOMEN: DEMOGRAPHIC DNA
SCORES OF THE WOMEN IN THE STORIES

	Adele	Molly	Paula	Diane	Roberta	Ellen
Are you working full time (more than 35 hours per week)?	no	yes	no	yes	yes	yes
Do you have and/or are you contributing to retirement savings?	yes	yes	no	yes	yes	yes
Do you have a four-year college degree?	no	no	yes	no	yes	no
Are you buying or do you own your home?	yes	yes	yes	yes	yes	no
Are you married?	yes	no	no	no	yes	no
Do you have older relatives—parents, in-laws, siblings, aunts, uncles, etc.	no	yes	yes	yes	yes	no
Do you anticipate providing care for older relatives (financial or help with day-to-day activities)?	no	yes	yes	yes	yes	no
demographic DNA score	85	65	20	65	75	40

Note: This table does not contain the entire assessment questionnaire. It lists only the first level of questions. Depending on the response to the primary question, respondents may be asked to answer other questions to derive the actual score.

wealth holdings than divorcées. In other words, the majority of divorcées are asset poor, indicating small marital dissolution settlements.[3] The most vulnerable of divorced women will be those who have not met the ten-year marriage requirement. These women are not eligible for spousal benefits, which are often greater than those earned on a woman's own employment record.[4]

Ask a baby boom woman "what is your greatest fear of growing old?" and you'll probably hear the quick retort "becoming a bag lady." Does divorce in later life inherently catapult you into bag lady status? While most baby boom women don't really believe they will become bag ladies, many harbor the negative fantasy. Almost 30 percent of baby boom women (and 25 percent of baby boom men) have experienced divorce.[5] Divorce causes a confluence of status change—social, economic, employment, housing, financial—therefore, the bag lady metaphor is playing well these days.

Our current economic system was built on the social norm of an enduring marriage. Divorce almost always compromises a woman's financial health. The closer a woman is to her retirement years at the time of divorce, the more vivid the bag lady nightmare becomes. In 2000, more than 17 percent of baby boomers were divorced or separated. Of this group, more women (56 percent) than men (44 percent) were divorced or separated.[6] Now, it is true that most people who divorce remarry (about 75 percent), but there is a clear relationship between age and remarriage. The younger you are at the time of divorce, the greater the probability of remarriage, most likely within three years. However, the inverse is also true—the older you are at the time of divorce, the less likely remarriage will occur. The probability of marriage or remarriage is less than 20 percent for women aged fifty and older.[7]

Today, nearly 25 percent of divorced women aged sixty-five and older live in poverty.[8] As baby boom women join their mothers and older sisters in retirement, the number of divorced women in poverty will swell. In 2002, 82 percent of divorced baby boom women had personal earnings of less than $40,000 annually; 15 percent earned between $40,000 and $74,999, and a tiny 2.5 percent made $75,000 or more.[9] Women who have access to pensions, employer retirement savings plans, and health insurances, generally women in professional jobs, will enjoy a secure retirement. But the overwhelming number of divorced baby boom women will be working to fend off the reality of becoming a "bag lady."

Baby boom women and the feminist movement rejected dependence and sought independence—through education, paid work, and pursuits outside of the home, within our marriages or through divorce. But the overwhelming majority of divorced women have learned that financial independence and security are elusive goal. Divorced or separated women are three times more likely to file for bankruptcy than married women.[10] Without marriage, our social roles of mother and caregiver preclude long-term financial independence.

So is "bag lady" status inevitable for women who divorce in later life? No, but time is running out. You have to recalibrate your assumptions about the later part of your life and make informed decisions about the realities of life in old age. What are the real assumptions you should make and what kind of strategic action should you take today?

TABLE 3: RECALIBRATE YOUR ASSUMPTIONS AND TAKE STRATEGIC ACTION FOR YOUR FINANCIAL HEALTH

Assumption	Strategic Action
1. Your home is your best investment. You will need to convert it to cash as your savings dwindle. Many divorced women will, out of necessity, be bag ladies. The difference is their bags will be suitcases with wheels. Divorced women are most likely to live with children, relatives, or friends during old age to minimize living expenses and maximize disposable income.	Resist the urge to take equity out of your home. Your house is your primary savings. While the U.S. economy is experiencing historic low interest rates, consider selling your house at as high a price possible and then safely invest your capital gains. Make your home work for you today. Rent your home and consider living with family members or friends. Put any profit in retirement savings. Check with a tax adviser first.
2. You will live a long time. You will outlive your savings. Your Social Security checks will be critical to pay basic living expenses.	Verify your Social Security earnings. Go to *http://www.ssa.gov/mystatement/*. Do the math yourself or have someone at the Social Security office figure out if you can earn more filing as a spouse or filing under your own employment record.
3. You will work outside the home well into your sixties because you have no choice.	Make sure you like what you are doing or at least are getting well paid for doing it.
4. You will have chronic health conditions that will limit working past seventy years of age unless you can do work requiring high skill or higher education.	Inventory your job skills, education, and career network. Consider developing new skills or brush up on job skills that you will be able to use if your mobility or health declines.
5. Relationships are your key assets and liabilities. You need to consciously manage a matrix of personal relationships that can make or break your financial security—with your parents, your children, your friends, your siblings, your extended family. Women's financial lives are different from men's because we are the primary caregivers for children and the elderly. Your personal relationships are a huge influence on your financial health.	Manage the expectations of your family. Initiate crucial conversations with family members who may be expecting you to provide elder care or child care as you age. Ask yourself: "Can I afford not to get paid for the work I will be doing?" If you choose to provide elder care or child care, negotiate the terms with your family so that you are financially protected.

TABLE 3: (CONTINUED)

Assumption	Strategic Action
6. The more you learn, the more you are worth.	You must stay actively involved in all aspects of your financial health—saving, spending, investing, and protecting your future. Today, personal finance is complex. With so many options and choices, you will probably need financial guidance ranging from tax advice to retirement planning to insurance coverage. No matter how challenging (or boring) learning about money and finances can be, you must not delegate or ignore responsibility for your personal finances.

Marriage remains the number one predictor of a woman's financial security at any stage of her adult life. If you are divorced, are thinking about getting divorced, or have no choice but to get divorced, you need to clearly understand the economic implications of your marital status as a divorced woman. The odds are stacked against you. Divorce in later life is economic suicide for women.

Notes

1. My first book, *When Baby Boom Women Retire* (Westport, Conn.: Praeger, 1998), outlined the key variables which determine a woman's economic security.

2. DemographicDNA is a trademark registered under Dr. Dailey.

3. S. J. Haider, A. Jacknowitz, and R. F. Schoeni, "The Economic Status of Elderly Divorced Women," Working Paper 2003–046, University of Michigan Retirement Research Center, May 2003.

4. B. A. Butrica and H. M. Iams, "Divorced Women at Retirement: Projections of Economic Well-Being in the Near Future—Statistical Data Included," *Social Security Bulletin*, 63, no. 3, Fall 2000.

5. *Marital Status of People 15 Years and Over, by Age, Sex, Personal Earnings, Race, and Hispanic Origin*, March 2000, U.S. Census Bureau.

6. J. Fields and L. M. Casper, "America's Families and Living Arrangements, Population Characteristics," *Current Population Reports*, June 2001.

7. R. M. Kreider and J. M. Fields, "Number, Timing, Duration of Marriages and Divorces: 1996," *Current Population Reports*, February 2002.

8. Haider et al., "The Economic Status of Elderly Divorced Women."

9. *Marital Status of People 15 Years and Over, by Age, Sex, Personal Earnings, Race, and Hispanic Origin*, March 2002, U.S. Census Bureau.

10. E. Warren and A. Tyagi, *The Two-Income Trap* (New York: Basic Books, 2003).

Single Women at Midlife

The Always, Already Dumped

NANCY BERKE

> A single life is a happy life
> A single life is lovely.
> I am single and no man's wife
> And no man can control me.
> —Appalachian folk song

As a single woman in my forties, I am an expert on getting dumped. I understand the experience of being dumped because I live it every day. If *dumped* is a term we use as an angry response to being left—being left alone— then those of us who live singly are leftovers, products of the dump, refuse. While some singles recycle and others settle into peaceful coexistence with their coupled brethren, the increasing number of people who live alone is becoming an unsightly reminder that the couple, although it is still privileged, is no longer the exclusive social experience of American life. *Dumped* is a powerful word. It suggests some kind of exile or separation. It is a rent in the social fabric which represents coupling as the most worthwhile human relationship.

To be dumped is certainly not just the province of the recently separated or divorced. If a woman is ever-single at midlife, her experience of being dumped is far more existential. She must bear the social insult of having something wrong with her because she never "settled down" with anyone. Not only have lovers dumped her, but so has society dumped its judgment on her. The midlife single woman, to use post-modernist parlance, is "always already" dumped. If we pay attention to the quantitative research favored by the corporate-driven media, she is too old to be eligible for any offers of love that might be still available as she enters the twilight of her sexual attractiveness. If we apply a cultural interpretation to the Bernie Siegel school of self-healing, she has probably done something to ensure or *deserve* her singular status. Perhaps by her narcissism, or her drivenness, or her feminism, or her pickiness, or her perfectionism, or her countercultural kinkiness, she has destroyed whatever possibility she had of finding happiness with a member of the opposite (or same) sex.[1]

This always already dumped status to which I refer denotes the pressure that the single woman feels to become part of a socially sanctioned unit—the couple. Couples symbolically remind the singular outsider that she is a social misfit, a failure at societal convention, a threatening loner in an increasingly politically terrified world. While many a woman who is single at midlife will argue that she is happy alone (although social science steadfastly tries to undermine this singular satisfaction with suspect studies and statistics), she exists within a social space that has defined her solo status as a kind of deviance. From the midlife single woman's perspective, Simone de Beauvior's famous comment in *The Second Sex* that woman is other takes on new meaning: if woman is other, then the older single woman is *really* other.

Unlike the older woman who is dumped by her long-term partner and must deal for the very first time with being on her own, the always already dumped has had years of preparation for becoming an older single woman. Perhaps her attempts at partnership have been thwarted. Or she may just desire to reinvent her life outside the socially sanctioned couple. While her choice to remain single may be satisfying, it is always under the scrutiny of the patriarchal panopticon, whose high beams follow her everywhere with the stenciled pronouncement, "Aren't you lonely without a mate?"

Even though a woman may choose not to pursue a particular relationship, her choices are always already determined through complex, socially mediated circumstances. In fact, it would take several Proustian volumes to explore an ever-single woman's subterranean decision making with regard to the vicissitudes of her romantic history. "Was I born to be single or have circumstances made me this way?" she asks herself. When the actress Mae West declared, "I'm single because I was born that way," she imbued singleness with a prurient edge. As a sex goddess of Hollywood's golden age, she could make herself more appealing by alluding to her singular status. Yet will this same coy suggestion be appreciated when it casually drops off the less-than-sultry lips of the ordinary midlife single woman?

Influenced by Simone de Beauvoir, later feminists observe that one is not born a single woman, rather one becomes one. Propped up by an uncontested patriarchal social undercurrent, which remains in place even after thirty years of feminism, coupling is the representative social ideal. A woman measures her attractiveness, her confidence, her overall personal success based on whether or not she is in a sexual partnership. The coupled culture dictates a woman's experiences, her sense of self, her capabilities, her acceptable and unacceptable behaviors. Everything from her consumer activities to her sexuality is measured against the coupled world in terms of how much it deviates from the coupled "norm."

Thirty years after feminism, the older single woman's sexuality continues to be as puzzling to the older single woman as it does to the couple-centric culture that surrounds her. Why, for example, does it still seem odd to the average passive observer of our popular culture that a single woman over forty-five could describe herself as sexually active? In an informal poll I took among middle-aged *Sex and the City* viewers, Samantha Jones was everyone's least favorite character. Her midlife determination to remain single and to get laid made her the least "realistic" member of the quartet, not to mention the most "shallow." This is not to say that there is no support for women's midlife lustiness. Recent films like *Never Again* and *Something's Got to Give* attempt to show the midlife single female's curiosity and appetite. Yet there is no real discourse about midlife sex outside of marriage and coupling.[2] While it is assumed that a man's sexuality runs constant through the life course, a woman's continued inscription within biology erases her sexuality once she is no longer fecund.

What do women in the always already dumped category face when they attempt to follow the cultural mandate to couple? Imagine that you have spent your twenties and thirties contemplating a life left over from the good old days of counterculture, civil rights, and feminism. You envisioned innovative frontiers beyond the coupled world of your parents; you wanted to search out alternatives to relationships that were stifling rather than fulfilling, repressed rather than liberating, soul deadening rather than soul savoring. You discovered that there were alternative avenues on which to stroll. If you came of age in the nineteen-seventies, the texts of your time, *Zen and the Art of Motorcycle Maintenance*, *At the Edge of History*, Marge Piercy's novels, even the decade-earlier *Golden Notebook*, and rediscovered feminist classics like *Daughter of Earth*, mapped out a different set of social ideas and gave the old ones a nap. The traditional version of love that equals marriage, children, and the happily-ever-after started to look stale and silly. What is more, if you grew up watching films like Ken Loach and David Mercer's *Family Life*, you knew damn well that the traditional nuclear family created schizophrenics out of all of us.[3] You wanted your freedom; you wanted meaningful intimacy, you craved a sex life that was as vastly and intensely interesting as the intellectual life you were pursuing.

Then came midlife. Your relationships — sexual, intellectual, and otherwise — have come and gone, but you managed to do one thing about which you are still gleefully proud. You embraced the open road, studied, traveled, experimented, lived each day with a sense of wonderment, lived righteously, lived recklessly, and confronted the contradictions. Most significantly, you managed not to couple like mom and dad. One problem remains, however. There is now a serious backlash against the social, political, and cultural values which formed your processes of social dissent. For the last twenty-five years, the dreams and desires about which you grew up singing have been shattering steadily. You suffered through what sociologist Stanley Aronowitz once spoke of as the Reagan-Bush– era declaration of war against 1968. We are still feeling its fallout. At middle age, you find yourself single in a married world. Or so it seems. We don't really live in a married world if four in ten U.S. marriages end in divorce. Moreover, there are 86 million Americans who are currently single. That is a sizeable proportion of our national population, yet the way the media plays it and the government legislates it, one would think that single people did not exist.

Even in late capitalist society, a woman is still less likely to be viewed as independent when compared to a man. As a result, the single woman, who is by the fact of her everyday existence independent, is rendered invisible. Thus, the single woman is dumped by virtue of her absence from the cultural mainstream that associates women with the relational worlds of coupling. As Bella dePaola and Wendy Morris contend, the ideology of intensive coupling is so pervasive that the myriad worlds in which the single person lives are imperceptible. These authors suggest that it is the "ideology of marriage and family" that dictates certain cultural norms which create an assumption that "just about everyone wants to marry, and just about everyone does."[4] This principle also creates the supposition that the desire for a sexual partnership is a universal social goal; consequently, ideology becomes accepted as fact, "a sexual partnership *is* the only truly important peer relationship."

Given this context, try to imagine what the always already dumped, midlife single woman faces when she heeds the cultural call to couple. Mind you, some women are lucky. They are successful at midlife coupling. Perhaps they are the same women who were successful at adolescent coupling. I speak, however, for those women who continue to follow their bliss, as it were, into middle age, realizing that coupling isn't everything and that solitude has its merits despite the lack of dialogue, theoretical studies, and cultural iconography about the positive effects that solitude has on a woman's life. Solitude is more than its dictionary definition—the state of being alone. I define solitude as a place designated for one's self and one's self only. This is a place, I argue, that is endangered in a cultural climate which valorizes intensive coupling over any other form of habitation. I do not mistake this solitude for the enforced solitude that many sick and elderly women face, or the solitude imposed upon incarcerated women. Instead, I suggest focusing on the merits of solitude and sisterhood. Women who at midlife are not coupled are increasingly ordinary citizens; they have their solitude and they also have their friends, colleagues, and extended families.

I am one of these women. Because I have become used to the always already dumped experience, I have learned how to navigate the waters of single life. I have learned domestic solitude. I have developed enduring friendships and cultivated a set of emotionally and intellectually satisfying networks that are intimately connected to my everyday life. Yet I must also continually deal with a marriage culture's social dumping on the single person. I am dumped on by an impervious social structure that uses coupling as a way to uphold patriarchy in order to secure traditional gender hierarchy.

British economists (and former sixties radicals) Bob Rowthorn and Paul Ormerod have recently argued that marriage as an economic arrangement is far superior to any other social lifestyle for *both* men and women.[5] Nevertheless, patriarchy is well served by the practice of intensive coupling. Men are rewarded the lion's share of coupledom's benefits. Coupling gives men wives, and wives provide emotional and domestic labor. What is more, wives offer a support system at home whether or not a man has similar support on the job.

Patriarchy's social dumping of midlife single women also makes women feel insecure about their social position. Although men sense the age pinch as do women, their pinch is more individual. Generally speaking, there is no social stigma for men as they age. The cliché of the suave, sexy older man exemplifies this truism. Despite the Mrs. Robinson chestnut about the sexy older woman seducing the much younger man, midlife is not by and large thought to be a sexy time of life for women. Consider Germaine Greer telling fifty-something women in her book *The Change* to get in touch with their "inner crones."[6] Then there are the incessant commercial reminders of menopausal changes—vaginal dryness, flagging sex drive, brittle bones, thinning hair, hot flashes, and ashy, sagging skin. What otherwise healthy, happy, and still horny middle-aged woman wouldn't feel discouraged by the cultural discourse on aging?[7] Women internalize these social messages, and as a result feel diminished and insecure. Yet, whose need is it that women appear young, sexy, confident, stylish, blond(er), slim, and well-toned? Even the midlife single woman who recognizes her status as always already dumped feels the pressures of feminine conformity.

Regardless of what we infer about the always already dumped status of the single midlife woman, it is crucial to acknowledge this representation as it relates to the culture of the couple. The socially sanctioned institution of coupling needs to be understood as a site of privilege in western society. Those who live outside of this unit are necessarily marginalized. Even though single people, especially those under thirty-five, may not feel like cultural outsiders, or may claim to enjoy the subcultural experience of their marginalization, coupling is represented as a primary, genuine, and mature social status. Single life continues to be characterized as an unhealthy alternative. Yet, how do we actually understand single life when the majority of the research, writing, and commentary that influences popular thinking is so transfixed on the experience of coupling? While it is true that single life is fraught with frustrations that are often similar to what couples endure—anger, pain, fear, moments of elation and moments of regret—because the heterosexual social unit is taken for granted as normative, there is little appreciation of uncoupled lives. We might actually learn something about the practice of intensive coupling by encountering the stories of those who are unpartnered.

While we wait for the older single woman to tell the truth about her life, which may indeed cause the world to split open, the culture of the couple persists.[8] Because it is pervasive and pushy, it forces a tug of war with the older single woman's circumstantial solitude. It proposes that the singular outsider continue to become part of its orbit, to keep trying, *to put herself out there*. The prize is social and cultural acceptance. Whether from sexual desire, peer pressure, genuine loneliness, or occasional boredom, you find yourself ceding to this powerful social and erotic force. You laugh off the jokes about midlife dating, the Internet stories, the December-and-May fantasies, the adulterous affairs—both real and imagined. You take the dive—again; at your age, while you may be a little rusty, you are not a novice, even if you tempt fate with the knowledge that you are always already dumped.

Imagine for a moment this scenario. You are in New York City, standing near the entrance to the subway station at Union Square. You are locked in an embrace with a man who has just told you that you are not "the one." His apologies are vaguely familiar, as if the rejection had been some kind of déjà vu.

Remember, you have been there before, said good-bye to someone in some recognizable zone where the script had ended, if not with the exact same words, then with similar phrasing. You have just finished telling this person about how at your respective, similar ages you should be moving beyond the youthful pursuit of the soul mate, that elusive love to which your date, just shy of fifty, apparently still clings. You remark that the two of you should be content to have found in each other similar personal histories, similar cultural tastes and political perspectives, and well, obviously a bit of sexual chemistry—the kiss has lasted a rather long time.

As you walk down the subway stairs to catch your train home, instead of calculating how many times this has happened to you before, you are struck by the contradiction of your experience. You live within the rigidly defined boundaries of the coupled universe; you've spent most of your adult life either trying to couple, or trying to justify why coupling hasn't yet happened to you. Yet as a middle-aged woman, you are beginning to see the opportunities to couple disappear, and your singular status become a liability. Single life is for the young; coupled life is for the middle aged. Neither young nor coupled, where are you?

Once again you experience the existential angst of the always already dumped. In the post-modern world of the midlife single woman, there are no widespread truths about what it is to be single in middle age. There is no acceptable dogma for your perusal, no scripts to memorize, no defense or doctrine to prove that your experience has, if not universal relevance, then at least some kind of value for shared dialogue. Not because the chance at romantic partnership continually eludes you, but rather your inscription within the romantic social ideal, over which you have no control, has been emphasized over all other self-defining moments. While satisfying work, chosen community, and a continued pursuit of personal desires are a huge part of one's self-definition at midlife, if romance is absent, the gnawing golden halo of incompleteness shines brightly around one's head. Although no one can determine the nature and longevity of a romantic relationship, its absence suggests instability.

The scholar and author Mary Helen Washington, writing a number of years ago about her single life, offers compelling commentary on this issue: "A single woman [who] describes her life without reference to romance—no matter how rich and satisfying her life may be, no matter what she says about wonderful friends, exciting work, cultural and intellectual accomplishments—in fact, the *more* she says about these things—the more skeptical people's reactions will be."[9] Washington's observation also highlights one of the saddest aspects of contemporary western culture: the notion that an exciting romantic life is the most interesting aspect of a woman's personality. Friendships, community ties, and whatever other contributions a woman makes are subordinate to the story she might tell about her hot, new romance (or the rekindling of a marriage about to go south). Talk of her career, artistic pursuits, and hobbies can never sustain a conversation the way her love life does. To put it another way, romantic attachments, especially with men, are considered the only kind of legitimate romance. The midlife single woman could have a romance with her work, with nature, with music, with her studies, but such romance is never given the same respect.

Shortly after her fortieth birthday, the single, child-free, Grammy award–wining musician Sheryl Crow was interviewed on the television news program *Sixty Minutes*. The program delighted its viewers with a peek into Crow's celebrity lifestyle. They saw her ten-acre compound in the Hollywood Hills, her vintage sports car, her customized tour bus (where Crow was teased for making "peanut butter and jelly sandwiches"). Viewers also saw clips of her concerts, where she aped the hyper-masculinized posturing of the rock star so well: cowboy hats, mirrored shades, leather pants, electric guitars. While the program's presentation of her certainly made the midlife single woman's existence seem wildly appealing, she couldn't escape the inevitable question that marks the single woman. No amount of international stardom or financial independence, no coterie of interesting, talented friends can replace the significance placed on coupling. A voiceover by interviewer Steve Kroft sets the appropriate ideological tone, "Like most successful women of her age, she is torn between her career and her personal life, or lack thereof."[10] Then he asks, "What's missing? Anything missing?" While Crow provides the expected answer—a husband, children—she manages to squeak through a powerful challenge to the question's marriage-centric implication. "I have a different kind of life. I have a life that a lot of people would trade what they have for." Indeed.

The same question dogs the ordinary, midlife single woman. Although she might have fascinating friends, exciting work, a good relationship with her children (if she happens to be a mother), and a variety of accomplishments, she never gets to be the subject in front of a television camera. Her life of adventure, but more importantly her life of solitude, is rarely if ever scripted. The invigorating life the midlife single woman lives for herself is nowhere to be found in the cultural imagination. Her solitude, one of the greatest gifts of single life, is never romanticized the way her romances are.

The fictionalized versions of women's single life that have been cropping up in recent years in literature, television, and film present an idealized product: svelte, beautiful, ambitious *young* women who have lots of sex with handsome, well-toned, high-achieving men. These are single women, but where is the singular in their lives? We never see the joys of solitude explored (taking the dog for a stroll in the park on a misty spring afternoon). Rarely do we see the solitary intelligence in action (reading the cross-continental correspondence of two Trotskyist poets in the Berg Collection at New York Public Library). Hardly ever is the mundane detailed through the pleasures of the individual senses (cooking a lavish dinner for one, complete with candlelight and a good Mâcon-Villages, reading a wonderful novel or some Howard Zinn, enjoying a musical shuffle of Mary Lou Williams, Billie Holliday, and Patty Griffin in the background, soaking in a tub filled with Kiehl's lavender bath salts. And then coming to multiple orgasms by means of the latest high-tech gadget plucked from its pristine Toys in Babeland box). Such scenes as these, if presented at all, are fed to the public as pathetic scenarios of loneliness. With no support for the solitary life that has become part of her hard-won birthright, the single woman discovers herself in an unimaginative void that is our current couple-centric society.

What would it be like to live in a culture in which the sexual partnership is *not* looked upon as the only valid relationship? What would it be like to live in a society which embraced a view that a woman's worth is not primarily centered around her youth, beauty, fecundity, and compliance? Consider the far from conventional life of the early twentieth-century travel writer and Arabist Freya Stark (1893–1993), one of the first westerners to visit Iraq.[11] At thirty-five, the age most contemporary single women are reminded that it is their last chance to beat the convulsive ticking of their social and biological clocks, Stark went off alone to the Middle East—a journey that would last until the end of her life. Despite Stark's inevitable role as exoticizer and colonizer, her travels gave her a sense of identity and palliative solitude that eluded the majority of her generation of middle-class British women. Today we recognize the suspect role westerners played as visitors in the lands their nations colonized and that Stark used her privileged position to her political advantage.[12] Nevertheless, it is necessary to concede Stark's contradictory position. As a mature woman inside the English patriarchy, her opportunities for self-discovery and escapade were limited. Moreover, Stark lived at a time when women rarely traveled abroad by themselves. Photographs of Stark wearing Middle-Eastern male attire suggest that in order for her to cut a figure in the solitary landscape, as it were, all signs of her female gender would have to disappear.

Stark's nomadic life allowed her to live a continuous adventure when the domestic spaces of a status-quo marriage were the norm for most women. When she was on the cusp of forty and more accustomed to travel planning than wedding planning, Stark recognized the anomaly of her experience, that she had "stepped into a wider world" by not coupling: "I used to feel that I had missed the real reason for life by not marrying, and was out of the stream in a backwater as it were. But I now feel this is not so . . . we are just stepping into a wider world and need not feel lonely, except in the ways that pioneers are lonely."[13]

Confronting the pervasiveness of the ideology of marriage and family, Stark found through travel and writing a richness that equaled life's "real reason." The marriage culture that women internalize as their life's primary narrative pulls them away from dreams of seeing "a wider world." It provides them with the security of a domestic environment—a sinecure against solitude's lonely backwaters. The average woman is seldom recognized as a seeker of solitude. In fact, in the public imagination, a woman who wants to claim her own space the way that a man does is considered selfish or peculiar. Peculiar is the way my mother described a friend's daughter, who, after dropping her children off at school, would go to a diner and have a long, leisurely breakfast all by herself. What my mother didn't understand was that her friend's daughter had the freedom to enjoy solitude away from the domestic spaces constructed for women in a culture of intensive coupling,

Why does it seem strange that a woman would want her space, that a woman would crave solitude? Men want their space; *need* their space (a classic line almost every heterosexual woman has heard sometime in her life). American cultural myths extol the solitary male figure of creative discovery. Walt Whitman had his Mannahatta and his open road; Woody Guthrie, his ribbon of highways; Jack Kerouac, his Denver, San Francisco, Los Angeles, and Mexico. None had a nosy public to interrupt his idylls with questions about domestic desire.[14]

In his book *Solitude: A Return to the Self*, British psychoanalyst Anthony Storr argues against the traditional psychoanalytic view that solitary life is inherently neurotic. Yet Storr himself resorts to conventional wisdom. With the exception of Beatrix Potter, Peter Rabbit's eccentric female creator, Storr provides only male examples of the benefits of solitary life. Solitude inspires genius that is gendered male.[15] Ironically, however, one of the most significant discussions of solitude's ability to transform lives comes from the nineteenth-century women's rights activist Elizabeth Cady Stanton. Speaking of the ordinary female, Stanton maintained that a woman's self-knowledge was the key ingredient in acquiring an independent identity. Without the ability to be on her own—to sail her own vessel as Stanton put it—a woman would remain as dependent as a child.[16]

Freya Stark found her solitude of self on a slightly different kind of vessel as she rode her camel across the Egyptian desert. She made herself a modern pioneer not only because she chose travel and self-discovery over marriage, but also because she understood that solitude was *both* a choice *and* a necessity. In her words, "[Solitude] is the one deep necessity of the human spirit to which adequate recognition is never given in our codes. It is looked upon as a discipline or penance, but hardly ever as the indispensable, pleasant ingredient it is to ordinary life."

I, too, believe that solitude is a "deep necessity." Solitude means it is comfortable to spend lots of time by yourself and to live alone. According to the latest census statistics there are 26 million Americans who do so. Solitude suggests a state of mind. It confirms the right and desire to put oneself first; it confirms the right and desire to build relationships outside the prescribed heterosexual couple. It resists the judgment that people who are not in exclusive sexual partnerships are neurotic, emotional failures. Solitude is a complement to the life one leads with other people. While mainstream social science may not recognize that long-term friendships are relationships of equal value to the exclusive sexual partnership, many of us in the "always already dumped" category have friendships that are far more intimate and enduring than the marriages of our parents, or a great number of the couples that surround us daily.

After thirty years of feminism, it is still difficult to define the role of solitude in women's lives. There is scant history and little practice. Popular culture, literary culture, and the social sciences continue to frame the questions about being alone as if solitude were every woman's death sentence. As a result, it is extremely difficult to envision the positive effects of single life for women when compared with coupled culture. Why not challenge patriarchy by asking this question: If solitude benefits men, why can't it benefit women as well? Imagine the absolute freedom to pursue and develop new hobbies, interests, professional goals, or to become part of a new social movement (or to use some of that solitary time to revitalize the old ones). Just think how much easier it would be for the woman who has been dumped by her long-term partner, who leaves her marriage at midlife, who is widowed, or who, at thirty, decides never to marry, if it were genuinely socially acceptable for her to embrace solitude.

Imagine what would happen if a woman did not feel compelled to search for that complementary other half? What if she became her own complement? What if her friends, family, and community were all seen as complements? What about a fifth female friend in *Sex in the City* who isn't coupled off as the series ends? Picture her, the one off screen; consider the possibilities of her single life. She will look when it suits her and date without the aid of a computer screen. She will leave it up to fate, or go without, or shop at Toys in Babeland. Instead of worrying over what she will do without a mate, she will mentor young women to value solitude, and she will tell them that it is all right to be single, or she will encourage those who are heterosexual to date men who want an equal partnership, and who appreciate a woman's need for solitude as well.

Lately I've been missing a postcard that used to hang above the intercom panel in my apartment. In a Roy Lichtensteinesque drawing, a negligeed blonde wakes in the morning to a bold discovery. "Oh my God," a bubble-caption above her head announces, "I think I'm becoming the man I wanted to marry." Riffing on Gloria Steinem's famous second-wave comment, this postcard served to entertain a growing crop of women who chose themselves over their elusive partners, or more broadly, the elusive pursuit of love. Part of the existential bargain of being single at midlife is that those of us who have *ended up* this way are remarkably resilient. We relatively contented ones have settled into an extremely enjoyable independence. Moreover, it is important to remember that this independence is still a relatively new phenomenon for women, as well as an overwhelming privilege, when we consider how the majority of the world's women continue to live.

Being dumped is an agonizing personal trauma, but it is also relative to a culture that valorizes coupling as an unparalleled human experience. I think of that anonymous Appalachian woman responsible for the sentiment in the epigram that opens this essay, "A single life is a happy life / a single life is lovely / I am single and no man's wife / and no man can control me." The author of these words was probably not single. Perhaps her life of hardship inspired a fantasy and she embraced a dreamy-eyed moment of solitude. Some women have never had a choice to be single. Doesn't that give perspective to the woman who finds herself alone at midlife?

Notes

1. A New Haven MD and self-healing advocate, Siegel argues in a best-selling book that people get sick because they have a bad attitude. Rather than pointing to environmental toxicity as a chief source of soaring cancer rates, Siegel focuses on individual behavior. According to Siegel, "happy people don't get sick." *Love, Medicine, and Miracles* (New York: Perennial, 1990).

2. The stir caused by Jane Juska's recently published memoir about her cross-country sexual exploits at the age of sixty-six suggests how little discussion there has

been about older women's sexuality. *Round-Heeled Woman* (New York: Villard, 2003).

3. In 1971 Loach, the British TV and film director, teamed up with British dramatist Mercer to remake their BBC television drama, *In Two Minds*. Influenced by the work of Scottish psychiatrist R. D. Laing, both play and film make daring parallels between the dysfunctional family and schizophrenia.

4. Bella dePaola and Wendy Morris, "Singles in Society and in Science," *Psychological Inquiry* (2005, in press).

5. Bob Rowthorn and Paul Ormerod, "Happily Ever After," *The Observer* (UK), March 25, 2001.

6. Germaine Greer, *The Change: Women, Ageing and the Menopause* (London: Penguin, 1991).

7. I write the word *horny* with an awareness of its masculine bias. Curiously, I am unable to come up with a feminist equivalent.

8. I borrow this image from the brilliant twentieth-century feminist poet Muriel Rukeyser. In the closing couplet of a poem about the German artist Kathe Kollwitz, Rukeyser writes: "What would happen if one woman told the truth about her life? / The world would split open. 'Kathe Kollwitz,'" in *The Collected Poems of Muriel Rukeyser* (New York: McGraw-Hill, 1982).

9. Mary Helen Washington, "Working at Single Bliss," in *Women: Images and Realities: A Multicultural Anthology*, ed. Kesselman et al., 3rd ed. (New York: McGraw-Hill, 2003), 271–277.

10. "Sheryl Crow," narr. Steve Kroft, *Sixty Minutes* (New York: WCBS, July 20, 2003).

11. Stark was born in Paris to two English artists. Her fascination with the Middle East started early in her life, but she did not begin to travel there until she was in her thirties. She wrote over twenty travel books, several autobiographies, and volumes of her letters have been published. Stark studied for a time at the School of Oriental and African Studies in London. During World War I, she worked as a nurse, and she worked for the British Information Ministry during World War II. At age fifty-four, Stark married diplomat and historian Stewart Perowne, though the couple separated five years later. In 1972, she was named Dame of the British Empire.

12. A recent argument made by Efraim Karsh and Rory Miller maintains that during World War II Stark traveled to the United States as propagandist for Britain's wartime Palestine policy. The British government's White Paper held severe restrictions on Jewish immigration into Palestine, and was widely condemned throughout the Jewish world. "Freya Stark in America: Orientalism, Antisemitism, and Political Propaganda," *Journal of Contemporary History* 39, no. 3 (2004), 315–332.

13. Quoted in "The Making of a Traveler," Barbara Krieger's introduction to the Marlboro reissue of Freya Stark's *Baghdad Sketches* (1938; repr. Marlboro, Vt.: Marlboro Press, 1992), ix–xvi.

14. This idea of male solitude and the open road reminds me of how complicated the notion of solitude becomes when you add the categories of gender and race. While in this essay I make comments that in general are relevant to all midlife single women, it is important to note how certain aspects of single life are experienced differently based on race, class, and sexual orientation. For example, a few years ago, I asked one of my women's studies classes to imagine how it would be for a woman to drive across the United States by herself, which was something I had done in my early twenties. One student remarked that as a black woman she would never dream of doing such a thing. It was too dangerous.

15. Anthony Storr, *Solitude: A Return to the Self* (New York: Ballantine, 1988).

16. Elizabeth Cady Stanton, lecture delivered January 18, 1892. See *Solitude of Self* (Ashfield, Mass.: Paris Press, 2001).

Snow White and Rose Red Meet Their "Prince"

Isabella Giovanni and Annie Peacock

And Lose Him. And Meet Each Other.

Back in the days when we both thought it was possible to meet a so-called prince, or even just a decent man, we did not know each other, but we were destined to meet through the same medium that caused our common pain: the Internet.

We are not as different as we appear, though appearances do count in this tale. One of us is dark, the other fair; one is petite, the other tall, one has hazel eyes, the other brown. One of us has long hair, the other short—wait, that was not true back then; we both had long hair, but one of us has black hair and the other white. We are alike in many ways, however, and that counts, too. We are both university professors, literate and witty, more than presentable and very fit. We are also kind and honest women who value gentle and honorable friends. We had both been in long-term relationships, and although they ended badly, we still believed such a partnership was the ideal.

We would both rather be alone, however, than with a jerk. We are smart, educated, middle-aged New Yorkers. We are not easily duped.

So there was this prince. Actually, he was a frog, but since neither of us had seen a prince in a very long time, he didn't look too bad, in spite of not being nearly as tall or as handsome as he claimed, or as honest, as we were to discover.

Rose: He wrote to me after seeing my profile on Craig's List, some time in the early spring. I had never tried Internet dating and had just posted my profile and preferences. He described himself as an architect and said he was separated. There were no pictures on the list, but he was very eager to meet. He wanted to see me right away. We had a pleasant dinner, during which he talked incessantly. I was not overwhelmed, but I thought it was worth it to try. He seemed to have all the characteristics I was looking for. He was bright, interesting, attractive enough, and personable. One odd note: he pulled out his driver's license and asked me if I wanted to confirm his identity. This should have been a warning sign, but I laughed. It suggests he had been meeting other women who were more savvy—or suspicious—than I was. The turning point for me was when he walked me back to my building and asked, "How did I do?" He must have sensed that I wasn't entirely convinced. I found his question endearing and warmed to him. It all seemed so easy!

Snow: I met him through Match.com, a month or so later than you did. He saw my profile and e-mailed me his. He had no picture yet, but he said it would be up soon. He described himself as five ten or five eleven and "damned handsome." He wasn't lying about the picture; it did show up the morning before I was to meet him, but as for the rest, his face was so asymmetrical that at first I thought he might have had a stroke. I had made a commitment to meet him, so I went. When I got to the café, I glimpsed a man hanging around the front, but I walked right past him because he was a good three or four inches shorter than the Prince had said he was (and he's an architect). In fact, he was shorter than I was. I suppose he was checking me out, because a few minutes later he came in and found me at the bar.

Yes, our prince was the same man, and we dated him at the same time. And he broke up with us both at the same time too.

Paradoxically, just before this point, he had planned to spend the same period with Rose on one island resort—in New England—and with Snow on another—in Europe. Neither of us had particularly invited him, but he angled for invitations to both and went so far as to make ferry and airline reservations, reservations that would have put him in both places at the same time. Before his scheduled synchronized departure dates, he contacted each of us on our various islands and told Rose, by phone, that he had met someone and decided to be monogamous and Snow, by e-mail, that he wasn't "in love" with her (well, who is, after only a couple of months?) and that he wanted "to be in love." The abruptness of his apparently global change of heart (neither one of us had made "the cut") suggests in retrospect that his wife—from whom, we later realized, he was not really separated—must have found out about his adventures with Viagra. Neither one of us had done anything that could have tipped her off. Perhaps there was a third (fourth?) woman who did.

A Chance Encounter—Two, in Fact

A couple of months after the Prince's passion for both of us evaporated, Rose and Snow met, and that's the best part of our story. An unusual course of events tilted the normally mellow Rose into a fit of constructive anger, and she posted a profile of the Prince online that caught Snow's eye the same day— only a few hours after it appeared.

Snow: I had never looked at Craig's List before, and I wasn't even planning to look at the personals. I went there to check out real estate, because I was thinking about buying an apartment. As long as I was there, I thought I would look at what sorts of men were listed. I put in my age range and clicked. There, about three entries down, posted that very same day, was the headline, "Sleazy Married Architect, 60, Looking for You Here." As far as I knew, the Prince was separated—his story—but there had been moments of doubt. When I read the rest of the entry, I was sure it was describing him, and I also realized that the writer was not the Prince, but a woman trying to warn others about him. Rose, your description of his touching stories about his sons and his painful separation was so accurate—and so familiar—that I had no doubt. When I e-mailed you to ask if it was indeed the Prince, I already knew what you would say.

Rose: I hadn't thought of warning anyone till that day. I was going to a chain store uptown, made a wrong turn, and decided to go to the midtown store. Because of construction, I couldn't find the entrance and walked past it three times. The fourth time, I turned back: there, in an alcove of the construction site on one of Manhattan's busiest sidewalks, stood the Prince, talking on his cell phone, obviously to his wife. I rubbed my eyes. Then I tapped him on the shoulder, and he did a classic double take. After politely waiting for him to complete his conversation, I confronted him with his dishonesty and the brutal way he handled the breakup. He said, "Everything I told you was true." Everything Snow and I found out put the lie to that.

After Rose and Snow met, we decided we had learned so much that we should let the Prince know what we had discovered about the world and about him, so we wrote him a letter together. Although we could not enjoy seeing his reaction, we could gleefully imagine his confusion and anxiety, perhaps even some embarrassment, at our shared itemization of his various performances, to say nothing of his wonder at how we might know each other and for how long. What magic did we possess? Something better than his potions, perhaps? How does an aging prince feel when he realizes that his secret has been discovered? We will never know.

What Did the Princesses Learn?

Well, if a prince is really a frog, he needs more than one princess to spin his tales to, and a little magic, too, to cast his spells, supplied in modern times by the Internet and pharmaceuticals, rather than stardust.

How do you tell if a prince is a frog? You pay attention to every warning sign. In retrospect, we ignored many. While this may sound very familiar, some would-be princes are very good at concealing the warnings.

Have you ever seen a frog shoot his tongue out to catch his prey? Well, modern would-be princes sometimes use technology to ensnare their prey, but real princesses with good hearts can also use technology—with a bit of chance and magic added—to find each other, to heal themselves, and spread warnings about lusty, mean old frogs to other princesses throughout the land.

Sometimes fairy tales end happily without a prince, especially when princesses learn two important lessons: they can overcome adversity without a prince and, second, a true friend is much better than a phony frog.

Snow: Sometimes I felt uncomfortable with him. I sensed a kind of insincerity, a canned quality to what he said, but because he was also slightly awkward in a way I found sort of charming, I chose to attribute it to nerves rather than prevarication.

Rose: I too felt uncomfortable sometimes. I didn't exactly ignore the red flags, but I chose to give him a chance.

Snow: It did bother me that he seemed to be available only Tuesdays, Wednesdays, and Thursdays and that I didn't have his office number. Was he available to you only those days too?

Rose: Yes, but he said he was responsible for his son on weekends. And then there was his Manhattan apartment closet: two shirts, two towels, and a pair of flip-flops. Hello! There were also his tales of his "open" first marriage.

By the way, did he try to avoid using condoms with you?

Snow: Did he! When I finally went to his apartment, after putting him off for several weeks, he said he had bought a box of condoms that very day and gotten home to discover that it was empty! The story was so ridiculous I almost believed it. Of course, I had condoms in my bag.

Rose: Yes, it's especially amusing since he was so concerned that the women he was seeing be drug- and disease-free. I guess it makes sense, since he was already planning to risk not using protection.

We will never know how much of what he told us each was the truth or whether he was genuinely seeking a legal separation. We believed him because he seemed to be a committed and loving father. On the other hand, we now know that, like some other men his age, he was recklessly pursuing at least the two of us, trying every device to avoid using condoms—even though he himself had herpes and never volunteered the information. We also know that, like many people with a guilty conscience, he suspected his princesses of doing the very thing he was doing: avoiding safe sex and using sex-enhancing drugs. He asked us many of the questions we should have asked him.

We have wondered how two intelligent women let themselves be taken in.

Rose: We were out of practice. We had been in long-term relationships and tried to make them work. We were faithful partners, and we forgot what dating was like. We lost our edge. We would never have fallen for such transparent lies when we were in our dating twenties.

Snow: Yes, and even some married men seem to stay in practice, obviously, but I also think we were duped by our own expectations. We assumed that someone who appeared to be like us, a bright, well-educated man with lovely taste and wide interests, who talked as if he had high moral standards, would in fact be lovely and honorable in his behavior. We couldn't imagine that someone who seemed to be our equal in intellect, aesthetics—and even ethics, to hear him talk—would be so shallow and shoddy and dishonest and so careless with our well-being and his own. I also think we were both impressed that he was not looking for a younger woman. There's a lesson here for older women, though: listen the way you did when you were twenty-five.

There are three miracles in this story, but the Prince is not one of them: the chance encounter between Rose and the Prince on one of New York's busiest streets that enabled her to confront him and precipitated her warning to other women; the chance click that took Snow to that site that very day; and the friendship that developed between Rose and Snow, enabling them to heal and grow and enrich their lives with true friendship. Princesses, take warning. Be wise, be strong, and don't discount the healing power of a good talk, a good laugh, and a good friend.

Left Alone

Deserted by Death or Divorce

MERLE FROSCHL

Nearly half of women over age sixty are left alone. Widows make up 38.6 percent of women over age sixty; divorced women make up 8.6 percent; and women who are separated, 1.2 percent.[1] In *Widow to Widow*, Genevieve Davis Ginsburg argues that widows and divorcées should not be lumped together under such titles as "Single Again" and "Women Alone."[2] On the other hand, in a recent *Law and Order* episode, a widowed mother responds to her grown daughter, who has just been cut loose, that "loss is loss."

My own experience as a widow in her sixties—and that of female friends of similar age who are widowed, divorced, or dealing with a broken relationship—lead me to agree with the widowed mother on *Law and Order*. Loss *is* loss. Yet the similarities and differences are worth noting.

Both the widow and the divorced woman are learning new roles. For a woman over age sixty this can be especially daunting. Each day, every occasion—whether birthday, holiday, or dinner party—is a rehearsal in being a woman alone. As with all new roles, sometimes what you try on fits, sometimes it doesn't. It's all about taking chances at a time when you thought those kinds of risks were long past.

The differences emerge from the basic fact that widows and divorcées are separated from their partners in starkly different ways. There is no element of choice for a widow. The decision is final. As John Robertson and Betty Utterback state in *Suddenly Single*, death is "socially acceptable in the widowed because the loss is obvious."[3] Divorce is another matter. It is often assumed that the separation is what at least one partner wants. The other partner may not want to let go, holding out hope that the decision isn't final.

Ultimately, widows tend to remember the best of times; divorced women, the worst.[4] The issue, however, is not about whose loss or pain is greater, but about what widows, divorcées, and women in the throes of being cut loose can learn from the experience and from each other. As Beth Maccauley (Jessica Lange), a recent widow in the 1990 film *Men Don't Leave*, tells her young son, "Heartbreak is life educating us."

What's in a Name?

In 1934, Hollywood offered charming but unrealistic images of widows and divorced women. There was *The Merry Widow*, starring Jeanette MacDonald and Maurice Chevalier (in the 1952 version it was Lana Turner and Fernando Lamas), and *The Gay Divorcée*, starring Fred Astaire and Ginger Rogers.

"Merry" is hardly the image that comes to mind for the word *widow*. Genevieve Davis Ginsburg says that the word itself is so dreadful as to have no synonym. But it does have a color: black.[5] When one thinks of a widow, what usually comes to mind is an older woman, grieving and sorrowful. The tendency to equate widows with the elderly may stem from the fact that so many of the elderly are women (three-quarters of the people over age seventy are female).[6]

It is not a given that the divorced woman, like the widow, will evoke pity. As unfair as it may be, she might be viewed with a critical eye—what was her role in the separation, was she not a "good enough" partner? Though the picture of a divorcée is more diverse than that of the widow, "gay" is not the predominant picture. Yet despite differing images, there is a commonality in name: someone divorced or separated from her husband is called a "grass widow."

Bereavement and Betrayal

It is generally accepted that both the widow and the divorced woman need to go through a period of mourning. Whether young or old, women left alone are united by grief. Descriptions of the stages of grief are influenced in the main by the work on death and dying of Elisabeth Kübler-Ross. They include denial and isolation, anger, bargaining, depression, and acceptance.[7] As frightening as it is, the widowed and the divorced woman must fully experience all the stages. As the shock sets in, heart-pounding, breath-gasping anxiety attacks are normal. Yet there is a great deal of social pressure to "move on" Given the sex-role stereotype of the macho male, men may feel even greater pressure to be stoic, to bear up and leave their emotions behind.

A normal grieving process can take years, and it is rare to go through the procedure in lockstep. One step forward and two steps back are more likely as the stages of grief return in waves at unpredictable moments. In addressing the grieving process, J. William Worden, a psychotherapist and researcher, defines four "tasks" of mourning that can apply to all women who have been left alone. He advises that it is necessary to: 1) accept the reality of the loss, 2) experience the pain of grief, 3) adjust to the new environment, and 4) withdraw emotional energy and reinvest in another relationship.[8] The last task can be particularly intimidating for older women, for whom the idea of dating and being a "girl" friend seem almost ridiculous.

The sense of betrayal is greater for the divorced woman, who is often dealing with issues of trust with her partner. She may feel more abandoned as friends, and perhaps family, take sides. The divorced or separated woman might see her friends, like her possessions, divided. The divorce of an older woman may confuse and embarrass her grown children who wonder why now, after all these years? In comparison, friends of the widow rally around. At first, food, flowers, and concern abound. However, even for the widow the rallying around can be short lived. It is a sobering moment when the last mourner leaves.

Transition as Opportunity

Loss, whether for the widow, divorcée, or separated woman, is devastating and life altering. For this reason, the newly left woman should not be hasty in making additional changes. Decisions such as getting a job, selling the family home, or throwing away clothes can be postponed.

In *The Way of Transition*, William Bridges makes a distinction between change and transition, which is critical for both the widow and divorced woman.[9] He describes change as a situational shift. Losing a loved one through death or divorce is a change. Transition is the process of letting go of the way things used to be and then taking hold of the way they subsequently become.

In between the letting go and the new beginning, there is a chaotic period that every woman who has been left alone will recognize. Bridges calls it the neutral zone: "A low-pressure area, where all kinds of heavy weather is drawn into the vacuum left by the loss."[10]

As difficult as it seems, this neutral zone can be an opportunity, an outlet for creativity. It can provide the space to discover or create a new way of being and a new identity.[11] This will not happen overnight, and each widow's and divorced woman's timetable is unique to her. Age also is a variable. For example, if remarriage is an issue, women in their twenties have about the same chance of remarriage as men. By age sixty, however, there are only twenty-seven single men to one hundred single women.[12] The chances of an older woman remarrying are further reduced by the fact that men have a far wider age range from which to choose potential partners than do women.

But choice is not limited to replacing one partner with another. It is true that older women must challenge society's equation of youth and beauty, combat the stereotype of the genderless and sexless older woman,[13] and face health issues that may come with aging. But there are still vast opportunities to discover the person buried under so many layers of daughter, wife, or mother.[14]

The older widow's and divorcée's future is uncharted territory. It can include becoming independent, learning new skills, taking unimagined risks. An expanded circle of friends will take effort, but ultimately can be rewarding. The challenge lies in accepting these possibilities; in realizing that life doesn't necessarily have to be better or worse to be different. The loss will always be part of you, but the future holds the gains.

Notes

1. Thank you to Nancy Dailey for assembling these statistics from the *Current Population Survey* (Washington, D.C.: U.S. Bureau of the Census, 2000) in a personal communication.

2. Genevieve Davis Ginsburg, *Widow to Widow: Thoughtful, Practical Ideas for Rebuilding Your Life*, rev. ed. (Cambridge, Mass.: Fisher Books, 1997), 101.

3. John Robertson and Betty Utterback, *Suddenly Single: Learning to Start Over through the Experience of Others* (New York: Simon and Schuster, 1986), 51.

4. Discussed in Ginsburg, *Widow to Widow*, 2, 168.

5. Ibid., 3.

6. Ibid., 4.

7. Elisabeth Kübler-Ross, *On Death and Dying: What the Dying Have to Teach Doctors, Nurses, Clergy and Their Own Families* (New York: Collier Books, 1969).

8. J. William Worden, *Grief Counseling and Grief Therapy*, as reported in Robertson and Utterback, *Suddenly Single*, 149.

9. William Bridges, *The Way of Transition: Embracing Life's Most Difficult Moments* (Cambridge, Mass.: Perseus Publishing, 2001).

10. Ibid., 156.

11. Ibid., 45.

12. Reported in Robertson and Utterback, *Suddenly Single*, 196.

13. Margaret Urban Walter, *Mother Time: Women, Aging, and Ethics* (Lanham, Md.: Rowman and Littlefield, 2000), 3.

14. Ginsburg, *Widow to Widow*, 139.

Splitsville

Break-up Literature

Nan Bauer-Maglin

David Denby, in a review of the movie *We Don't Live Here Anymore*, says he is "wary of domestic drama." The reason for his wariness, he says, is, that "there's too much of it around—on television, on the stage, and at home. Who wants more? Movies devoted to marriage and family . . . have to be absolutely right in texture and nuance, the way *Shoot the Moon* was twenty-two years ago, or they fall into nagging banality."[1]

Writing in the *New York Times Book Review*, Laura Miller makes a related point: "It is hard to make the case that adultery—or for that matter the implacable obligations and virginity taboos . . . —still packs the punch it did back in the day [the mid-nineteenth century]." She asks: "What can replace adultery in the modern secular novel?"[2] This is a good question. Nonetheless, it appears that writers of the modern secular novel feel that even without a religious notion of sin and evil and despite our acceptance of sexuality and its various expressions, adultery is still a potent subject for fiction. This is true, for example, for Anne Taylor Fleming, who wrote *Marriage: A Duet*, two unrelated novellas (*A Married Woman* and *A Married Man*) about the effects of adultery on a wife and on a husband. She said in an interview: "We always think of marriage as this thing, this solid big thing, but it's the most amazing, volatile, complicated arrangement. . . . A chance wound or remark can send a 25-year-married heart reeling with rage. . . . I wanted to capture that, the depth of feelings engendered by marriage. There is nothing like it. It's not like parenthood, where there are blood ties and obligations. Marriage is voluntary.

You sign on and you have to keep signing on, as it were. And then where there is infidelity, the wounds, the shattering—it can be immense."[3]

For me and many women (and some men) I know, coming out of our own private dramas, seeing domestic dramas on the page and screen helps us feel less alone, helps us get insight into our own situation. That is why William Nicholson wrote *The Retreat from Moscow: A Play about a Family*. When he was a young adult, his father left home, leaving his mother "broken in half." He wrote the play in order to "tidy up the mess of life, to impose meaning on the meaningless. . . . I am trying, clumsily, to reach the truth of my life. . . . I write to strip away these lies, and say, Look, this is how it really is. . . . I'm trying to tell the truth about the pain of living badly."[4] And we read for just the same reasons: to tidy up the mess of life. Some "real life" stories are hard to talk about, are mostly kept secret, are felt to be private (especially when they are about infidelity, being dumped and divorced), so fictional stories come to fill in the silences. Talking about the collection of stories in *Dumped*, editor B. Delores Max says that "what makes these stories so fulfilling and so disturbing at the same time is that they are as like life as any real story you know. In real life, though, in the thick of heartache, in the chaos of grief, it is often impossible to make sense of anything. But because these are works of fiction, controlled by their authors, precisely crafted, they contain the keen insight and wisdom we all desire."[5] Max hopes the reader will find "solace and truth" in these stories.

Let me share with you some of the contemporary literature about breakups I read to keep me company during my own breakup. From many works, I have selected about two dozen, listed in the chart in the appendix to this essay. While I will touch on all of these books, some I will concentrate on. The chart also will help you follow the discussion as I refer to so many husbands, wives, and the other women/men.[6]

To make sense of it all, I have broken down these breaking-up stories into the following categories: men who leave; women who leave; the bourgeois marriage/the home is not a haven; pain and anger; the other woman; and reconciliation or letting go and moving on. I am especially interested in the depiction of older men and women in long-term relationships that undergo a dissolution or near dissolution. Surprisingly for me, I found several books by men to be the most profound and meticulous about documenting the process of splitting up: Hanif Kureishi's *Intimacy*, A. B. Yehoshua's *A Late Divorce*, and William Nicholson's *The Retreat from Moscow*. The women were particularly good in describing the pain.

While each story is different, there are similarities: stories echo each other in some fashion because they participate in literary history and literary convention, and because they are stories of our lives, which also echo each other.[7] "You know how uncanny it is that there are so many similarities in the way men dump women? The things they say, the words they use, the order in which everything unfolds," says Jane (aka Dr. Marie) Goodall, self-styled sexual behaviorist, in Laura Zigman's *Animal Husbandry* (243). As individual as we are, we are similar in ways as our lives participate in overlapping contexts (legal/social, cultural, historical, and bio-psychological).[8] One thing to note is that these stories are most often told in the voice of or from the perspective of one partner (except for *A Late Divorce*, in which the husband and wife as well as the adult children and their partners narrate different chapters), so they necessarily give a lopsided picture of the events. And they are lopsided in another way: they are mostly stories of men who leave and the older women who are left.

Men Who Leave

In Elizabeth Buchan's *Revenge of the Middle-Aged Woman*, Nathan Lloyd, age fifty-one, tells Rose, age forty-seven, that he's in love with someone else with whom he has been having an affair for about a year. He needs "freedom," "air," and "space" from their twenty-five-year marriage: "I feel imprisoned by the walls" (58). He says Rose never loved him as he loved her, whereas Minty, Rose's twenty-nine-year-old assistant, loves him in the way he has always wished to be loved. Minty's joie-de-vivre is what draws him: "Minty reminds me of how you were before . . . before we all changed. Became middle-aged, I suppose" (137). In *Acting Out*, by Benilde Little, after about fourteen years together and three children, Jay Robinson leaves Ina, both now in their early forties, for a "younger, thinner, better-credentialed woman, who he'd met at a traffic light" (4), but he says "it's not about her. . . . I just had to get out, or I was going to lose it" (141). Jay says he is not happy, that Ina is "not who I married" (9), that he does not know her anymore. Each has become a different person (although he does not dwell on his changes—only on hers): he is driven to make money in his real estate business, and she is no longer an artist type but instead a super mom. Passionate sex and passionate talk have become things of the past.

In *A Married Woman (A Duet)*, by Anne Taylor Fleming, after twenty-seven years of marriage, William Betts starts a "transgenerationally provocative" (71) affair with April, a friend of their daughter, a woman half his age. Despite his silence, Caroline Betts has intuited it and watches her husband closely for all the signs, from his crumpled shirt to his weight loss to his nightly pacing, preparing internally for his departure: "she was already thinking ahead to the nights when he wouldn't be there" (31). Saying that he cannot stand it anymore, that it is destroying them, William leaves for a weekend, to sort things out. His leaving is not like other times he had left, to go on a fishing trip with his buddies or to take their daughter to look at colleges; this has an "intimation of permanence" (35).

After thirty-three years of marriage, Edward first informs his son and then his wife, Alice (in her late fifties, like Edward), that he is leaving the marriage (*The Retreat from Moscow*). What has happened is that he has fallen in love with Angela, the divorced mother of one of his students at the boys' school where he teaches history. "I didn't mean it to happen. It was an accident," he says (31). But now that it has happened, he is in touch with what he has been missing: "I was a sleeper in my own marriage." Angela's touch made him weep; he says life has been returned to him and that "all those years ago, I got on the wrong train"—referring to when and where Alice and he first met. With Angela, "it is easy." There are "no demands. No expectations. Just love" (61). All Edward wants is to do his crossword puzzle without any interruptions, without any criticisms—with Angela he can.

How does one explain these departures? The men explain them as a failure of the relationship; the relationship is no longer working, no longer positive for one or both partners. The men have stayed in them as long as they could. And some of the marriages, such as the ones in *The Retreat from Moscow* and *A Late Divorce*, clearly are not working. In *The Retreat from Moscow*, Alice, desperate to connect with Edward and get some reaction out of him, in addition to her daily badgering, acts more and more "deranged," going so far as to confront him in the staff room where he teaches and stripping nude on the school's playing fields, asking him to talk to her, to look at her. In *A Late Divorce*, Yehuda Kaminka says he tried his best for the forty years of the marriage; he stayed with his wife, Naomi, until the three children were quite grown up and out of the house. The three are upset with him for leaving their mother, leaving Israel, and emigrating to the United States. The story takes places over the week before Passover five years later when Yehuda has returned to Israel in order to get a divorce, to get "rid of this bane of my life" (107) and to settle who gets the apartment they own (213).

It is hard to decipher the relationship between Naomi and Yehuda; we have reports from both husband and wife as well as the children, but we are seeing it five years after the breakup; we do not see them within their relationship. Yehuda says he stayed with Naomi until she drew a knife on him and tried to kill him (also she appears to have been stealing during this tense time); we do not know the interaction that led to that moment, after which Naomi was institutionalized. Naomi says she tried to knife Yehuda because he disappointed her. She also says (in what appears to be a dialogue with herself but may be between Yehuda and herself) that she was not trying to kill him, but that "I had only wanted to cut you loose from the desperate fear that made you want to run away, but to leave some part of you too" (290). According to the youngest son, Asa, they had been quarreling bitterly for a lot of the time he was living with them. Tsvi, the other son, calls the marriage "their hundred-year war" (212). Yehuda is now living with a middle-aged (the children call her "young") American woman, Connie, who is having his baby. One of the sons says it is all about sex;[9] Yehuda says Connie has restored him, given him "new hope," and that he has experienced an "intellectual renaissance" (126). At age sixty-four he has the strength and potential to begin again. While Yehuda understands why his children are negative about the divorce and hostile to the notion of this woman and the baby, he asks, "Did they really think that I would live out the rest of my life chained to her?" (107). He says he had always "feared her even those first years when we made love" (335). We cannot fully know if Naomi considers herself cut loose in the negative and/or positive senses of the term, and if she is "crazy" or not as her voice/voices is/are hard to read (she is in a mental hospital but is about to be discharged). Naomi claims that quite some time ago she wanted a divorce, but Yehuda was unwilling. Now, much negotiation is needed between Naomi and members of the family; but when she finally agrees go through a Jewish divorce with the three rabbis, she says that she feels peaceful: "Here I am with the divorce that I wanted, he's given me his share of the house, never again will I hear him speak to me in that overbearing manner of his that punched my life full of holes" (267). But on a more negative note, speaking to her son, "Everything is finished with . . . you say that I'm free now . . . I suppose you think that I'm eighteen years old" (271).

Yes, men do leave and men (often) do leave for legitimate reasons, but for the reader of many of these stories, the question is why now, why at such a late date, why so abruptly, and what are the men seeking? That's what Pauline in Anne Tyler's *The Amateur Marriage* wonders while breaking the news to her adult children that their father has left after thirty years of marriage: "I don't understand men in the least. I might not even like them. Can you tell me why Michael did this? And why now? Why not years and years ago, if he was so dissatisfied? Back when I was young and pretty and could have found someone else?" (194). Theirs was a working-class marriage that was begun when they were young and ignorant; it is clear that there are actually two marriage, his and hers:

> "'So what if we fight a bit? I just think that proves we have a very *spirited* marriage, a marriage with a lot of energy and passion. I think it's been a *fun* kind of marriage!' "
>
> "But he said, 'It has not been fun. . . . It has been hell.' " (175)

The repeated words or themes from the men are that they want love, they need freedom, the marriage suffocates them or is dead, and that while they are, often, seeing another (younger) woman, they most often say it is not about her. In contrast, most of the women do not want out and they seem shocked by the men's announcements.

The fictions offer other explanations for men leaving, besides the many-leveled statement that the marriage is just not working. There is the life-stage explanation and there is the men-are-animals-(literally) explanation. In Nora Ephron's *Heartburn*, long before their marriage founders on the issue of Mark's infidelity, Mark and Rachel talk about their friend Arthur's affair in the context of his eight-year-old marriage. Because Arthur is almost forty, they characterize the affair as "a passage" (138, referring to Gail Sheehy's book *Passages*) or a "midlife crisis" (139).[10] In *Open House* by Elizabeth Berg, Samantha, left by David after twenty years of marriage, labels it "early male menopause" (9); David and Samantha are both in their forties. Some, like Jane Goodall in *Animal Husbandry*, are very amusing and sardonic about the reasons for the phenomenon. Jane, age thirty, a talk show producer, takes on a research project to "explain why Ray dumped me, why Eddie dumped everyone, why Jason would undoubtedly dump Joan—why everything seemed so impossibly, inexplicably fucked up" (185–186). Jane is not an uninterested scientist: "The wanton polygamy of the male stump-tailed macaque I had just read about had made me mad" (192). Upon reading an article about the Coolidge Effect in *The Great Sex Divide* by Glenn Wilson (this is an actual book)—the need to provide bulls with multiple cows for mating as "rams and bulls are unmistakably resistant to repeating sex with the same female" (204)—Jane begins to formulate her Old-Cow–New-Cow theory about "the narcissistic behavior of the male species" (205), based on the fact that humans are animals. As she enumerates it:

> The Coolidge Effect in humans most commonly occurs when a male, after engaging in a romantic and sexual relationship with a female for a period of time—a month, three months, six months, a year or more—grows increasingly bored with his previously New Cow. In the vernacular this is usually referred to as the 'itch.' The male will then begin to sniff around, if you will, for variety and will pick from the somewhat wide selection of New Cows available to him one to his liking. Mating with this New Cow will ensue, which will promptly lead him to view the Cow he is primarily involved with as his Old Cow. In the majority of cases the male will leave the Old Cow to pursue a relationship with this New Cow, only to find, after

a varying period of time, that this New Cow has gotten Old, and he will desire variety again and so repeat this process innumerably. (248–249)

And what is astonishing to Rachel in *Heartburn* is not that the "number of
men who remain faithful is . . . so small but that there are any of them at all"
(84). One of the men in the book admits that "men never stop wanting to fuck
strangers" (140).

For whatever reasons, when men leave long-term marriages, they seem to
do so very abruptly.[11] This is not to say they have not been mulling it over for
some time. *Intimacy* is about one night in the life of a man agonizing over his
plan to leave his partner, Susan, whom he has known for ten years (living with
her for six of those ten years), and his two sons, ages three and five. We do not
know his exact age; he is middle-aged and Susan is four years younger than he.
And we do not know his name as *Intimacy* is a dialogue with himself. "I have
contemplated this rupture from all angles", he says (11). "I have wavered and
searched myself for a reason to stay" (69). He admits that "this is not my first
flight" (25) and is aware that his need to flee must be understood in the context of his relationship with his mother and his mother's and father's relationship to each other. "I imagined that with each woman I could start afresh.
There was no past. I could be a different person, if not a new one, for a time"
(21). He "used women to protect me from other people"; but "at the same
time I liked to keep my options open; desiring other women kept me from the
exposure and susceptibility of loving just one" (21). Or as he puts it, succinctly:
"The world is a skirt I want to lift up" (21); he even had a sexual encounter
during the moment Susan was giving birth.

His thoughts and feelings veer widely, from fear and anxiety to self-loathing
and from self-justification to trenchant analysis of himself and the institution
of marriage. For example, on the one hand he is critical of his pattern of exiting: "Not loving Susan I insist on seeing as a weakness, as my failure and my
responsibility. But what is the point of leaving if this failure reproduces itself
with every woman?" (53). But on the other hand, he is critical of those who
condemn him for moving on: "But why do people who are good at families
have to be smug and assume it is the only way to live, as if everybody else is in-
adequate? Why can't they be blamed for being bad at promiscuity?" (38). On
the one hand he believes he should have the right to leave a relationship that
is not satisfying. Chief among his dissatisfactions is the sense of having lost
himself, that he no longer knows his own mind, that he does not feel at home;
he is shriveling at home and he feels unrecognized (15–17). Lost in the middle of his life, most importantly, he fears a future life without love. He asks: "Is

it too much to want a tender and complete intimacy?" (64), despairing that this is all the happiness he gets. He has had enough of middle-class deferral. On the other hand, he feels "self-disgust," picturing himself among "all the other cowardly men who had fled" (68). He is not naive about the chance that his pursuit may not turn out so well; several examples are given of middle-aged men who leave marriages (for young women), only to discover it is not worth it—but then find there is no way back. He asks himself if he cannot develop his own inner sustenance for "surely you can't constantly be replacing people who don't provide what you need?" (58). He is smart enough to interrogate his notion of "liberation" (24), but still not able to shake his hunger for it.

Besides his dissatisfaction, there are differences between him and Susan that for him get in the way. The class difference between them rubs at him: he is lower middle class and she is solidly middle class. Susan is too much: she has a busy mind and is always active (he says out of desperation); she has vigor and spirit. "In some ways, it is less of everything I want" (84). Whereas Susan considers herself a feminist; he sees her as disapproving and bad tempered. He needs to break her spell over him so he no longer cares what she says; he needs to break her dominance over the children; he feels cut out of fatherhood.

They have tried couples' therapy. Susan explains his malaise (unaware that he is poised for flight) as a middle-age crisis. He does not mind being called adolescent if it means still indulging in "passion, frivolity, and childish pleasures" (81); he just does not want to be bourgeois. He wants to recapture those vibrant feelings that accompany a new relationship—a vibrancy no longer present in their relationship. While he does not think Susan is unattractive, he is conscious that "she has become middle-aged" (86). Seeing himself in a mirror while masturbating, as an aging, grey-haired man with a backache, makes him want to weep and to seek rejuvenation. He wants to become someone else, to find someone to love him in the way he wants to be loved. He thinks he has found that in Nina. He calls her a girl; he has some dread in terms of their age difference, wondering a bit facetiously, "What is wrong with maturity? Think of the conversation I could have—about literature and bitterness—with a forty-year-old!" (116). But Nina tantalizes; she stimulates his yearning (his sexuality and his zest for life); he believes he loves her. He tries to convince himself that "leaving someone isn't the worst thing you can do to them," that while "to move on is an infidelity," it also can be an "optimistic, hopeful act, guaranteeing belief in the future—a declaration that things can be not only different, but better" (11). Eyes wide open, when morning comes, he leaves.

In *The Retreat from Moscow*, Edward may or may not have been debating his departure for a while (he is very closed off—at least to his wife, but, it appears, also to himself), but certainly his fascination with the book about Napoleon's retreat from Moscow he is reading indicates that the question is now very much alive for him. According to the historical record, on the retreat from plundering Moscow, the wounded were left to freeze to death; if they fell off the wagons, nobody looked back. Quoting the diaries of men in retreat, Edward says one question came up again and again: "Am I permitted, am I entitled, to do what is necessary for my own survival" (85), even if it means letting my comrade die? Alice sees the connection right away: this is "his bloody retreat . . . ; it's alright to dump me in the snow" (52). Edward had been brought up to think of others; while he does not "mean to be cruel" (78–79), he finally wants to think of himself. And when he leaves, his complaint is that he is perceived as "the bad one," while "Alice has cornered all the suffering" (86). No one knows his side of the story.

Women Who Leave

In these fictions, mostly it is the men who initiate the dissolution of the marriage; they will be the ones to physically go, leaving the women (and sometimes the children if it is a younger marriage) in the home. Contemplating men's exits, the narrator of *Intimacy* knows judgment will follow: "It is the men who must go. They are blamed for it. . . . I understand the necessity of blame—the idea that someone could, had they the will, courage or sense of duty, have behaved otherwise" (40). Often, in these fictions, if the women leave or ask for the end of the relationship, they are responding to acts of infidelity or to some sort of abuse or lack of communication. Some only leave (emotionally or physically) for a short time. In Berg's *The Pull of the Moon*, after twenty-five years together, one day with no warning, Nan, age fifty, packs a bag and takes off; she had given Martin no indication that she was thinking of leaving. She travels cross-country, keeping a diary and writing Martin letters. She says she has lost herself (like a good many of the women in these fictions, she does not work); she accuses Martin of dominating and not responding to her. Nan, however, intends to return. Like *The Pull of the Moon*, Doris Lessing's novel *The Summer Before the Dark*, written in 1973, is not really about dumping husbands but about finding oneself and then finding how to be oneself back within the marriage. Neither story shows us the reconfigured relationship since both end with the wives about to return to the home, reversing, as it were, the exit of Norah (in Ibsen's *A Doll's House*). After twenty-five years of marriage raising three children, now, at age forty-five, Lessing's Kate Brown suddenly feels "demented" (93) when she contemplates her past and thinks about her future. While once a contented housewife, she now thinks that she and her female contemporaries are like "prisoners or slaves." Their one function was "to manage and arrange and adjust and foresee and order and bother and worry and organise. To fuss" (94). Looking in the mirror and looking inside herself, all those years now seem "like a betrayal of what she really was" (126). She is Mrs. Michael Brown and does not know who Kate is. So she takes a four-month sabbatical from the family, takes a job, takes a lover, travels, has a kind of breakdown, lives with a group of people, and does other things most respectable middle-class, middle-aged wives and mothers would not do even now. When she returns she is a changed person, as symbolized by her loose gray hair—hair that used to be manicured and colored. In Sue Miller's *While I Was Gone*, Jo Becker, age fifty-two, who had left her first husband (an early marriage), seems pretty fulfilled in her second marriage (a long-term one that has produced three girls who now live on their own) until she meets a man from her past hippie days. Her attraction to Eli Mayhew has an excitement that makes her feel like the vibrant young woman she once was; she understands why people give up long-established lives: "You read or hear every now and then of a romance starting up between middle-aged or even elderly people who knew each other years earlier. People who throw over long established, comfortable marriages or sensible lives for the chance to love again in a particular way—a way that connects them with who they used to be, with how it felt to be that person" (173). Ordinary life no longer engages her, although she still throws herself into her job as a veterinarian. Some of her feeling of "dislocation" can be attributed to her daughters leaving home, some to aging. Daniel, her minister husband, likes their comfortable, companionate marriage, whereas she wants to be "blown away"; so she pursues her attraction to Eli, absenting herself emotionally from Daniel for a short time. Marion Cole in *A Widow for One Year*, by John Irving, permanently leaves her husband, Ted, and their young daughter, but because of a very particular circumstance: the deaths of their two sons leaves her in such a state of mourning that she needs to be alone. However, her husband's constant affairs with young women who model for his drawings surely are a large factor in her departure as well. Even Jo's (*While I Was Gone*) temporary withdrawal is related to more than a middle-age crisis; there is unfinished business (a murder) from her past that she needs to resolve.

It is interesting to think about why some women stay and why some leave when their husbands have affairs. In *A Married Woman* (*A Duet*), Caroline asks herself if staying is an act of courage or cowardice, making "a silent promise that if she started hating herself—instead of him and the girl—she would leave" (33). In *Heartburn*, Rachel's friend Julie advises her to wait it out; the implication is that this is what men do; it is a stage; ignore it. Caroline stays and Rachel leaves. In the secondary plot of Stephen Carter's *The Emperor of Ocean Park*, Kimmer Garland leaves her husband, Talcott, after nine years of marriage and one child. While she says this is about his behavior and not another man, the fact is that she is having an affair with one of Talcott's students, a former well-known basketball player, who is ten years younger than she is. (Both are African American and in their forties; Talcott is a law professor and Kimmer is a law partner who is up for a judgeship.) In mulling it over, Talcott suspects Kimmer would say "that staying in this marriage a moment longer would have killed *her*, and given my antics in recent months, I could scarcely blame her" (570). While he certainly has been obsessed with the mystery related to the death of his father, a renowned conservative judge, Talcott is taking on too much of the guilt here.

Kimmer informs Talcott after nine years of marriage, and in Meg Wolitzer's *The Wife* Joan Castleman, age sixty-four, tells Joe, her husband, age seventy-one, after forty years of marriage that she wants a separation: "I am almost a senior . . . I want to go there alone" (191). Joan breaks the news in a sauna in Helsinki. They are there for Joe's award, the equivalent of the Noble Prize in literature (Joe's novels, by the way, "are populated by unhappy, unfaithful American husbands and their complicated wives" [79]). Before getting on the airplane in New York, Joan "hadn't known for certain . . . that I would leave him. I'd had fantasies over the years, little scenarios. . . . But none of these had been translated in *action*; . . . but in the past few weeks it had become too much, it was more than I'd bargained for" (79).

Why Joan did not leave earlier is the story of a whole generation of women who were born before the second wave of the women's movement: Joan became Joe's helpmate, playing the "cheerleading role of wives" (183) so common in those days (we discover in the end that she was more than helpmate: *she actually wrote Joe's novels*). One of the generation of women who "did not believe their own dreams," Joan gave up on a career of writing, but now the changes in the world have spurred her on to finally choose herself—even at this late date. At a Midwest writers' conference where her husband is flagrantly having an affair with a student, Joan breaks down in tears; up until then she had "ignored" his strayings as best she could. A partial list of "Joe's women" includes everyone from the babysitter to women at readings he gave around the country to a film producer to a young woman who worked at a grocery in Chinatown. Knowing her mother to be miserable, Joan's daughter asks why she does not leave her father; Joan answers the question by denying that she is miserable, while thinking what a good question it was: "In her [the daughter's] worldview, bad marriages were simply terminated, like unwanted pregnancies. She knew nothing about this subculture of women who stayed, . . . women who held tight because it was the thing they felt most comfortable doing" (82). Joan, married in the late 1950s when she was a college student, only knows the example of women who stayed in marriages no matter what, like Tosha Brenner, who stayed despite her husband's affairs: "Oh Joan, we have been putting up with these men for a lifetime" (166). The women were convinced that they would be lost without their husbands, and their husbands had convinced them that men could not "control" themselves; that "the long-term damage to the marriage will be insignificant compared with what it would be if we *did* control ourselves, and forced ourselves to keep our bursting needs under wraps" (206). Tosha finds a way out: she commits suicide. For Joan, Joe's affairs are a factor, but more important is that she lost her voice (figuratively and literally) and allowed herself to put up with his macho behavior. It is only after no longer hiding her despair, finally talking to three other "weary wives," that Joan Castleman can take her first step to slamming the door.

Vera Stark, in Nadine Gordimer's *None to Accompany Me*, like Joan, leaves her marriage late in life (and at the end of the novel—whereas most of the other novels begin with the partner's departure). Unlike Joan, Vera does not leave because of anything her husband, Ben, does nor for anything really missing in her marriage or missing in herself (she is a lawyer in her sixties); rather she leaves for existential and political reasons. She wants to extract herself from the bourgeois family and its getting and spending; she wants to face her final years alone: looking death in the eye and wrestling with commitment. There is a man (a black lawyer—she is white—whom she has worked closely with) she is interested in, but it is an interest of like minds; she has no expectation of or desire for an alliance. Her husband and their adult children are incredulous. It would be easier for them if she could say that there was something wrong with the marriage, but she can not lie; nor can she lie and pretend that she is unhappy alone:

> If she could lie to him before, times before, why couldn't she find it in herself to give him a lie to grasp at, now. She turned out the lights and slept, her empty house drawn up around her. (298)

> Forgive me, for I know quite well what I do. She would pour herself a stiff vodka with a prickle of tonic water and put her feet on the coffee-table elevated with stacked newspapers. . . . The evidence of personal life was around

her: but her sense was of the personal life as transitory, it is the political life that is transcendent. Sometimes, after a second drink, when the news gave way to some piece of popular music revamped from the past, Vera, too old to find a partner, danced alone, none to witness, in the living-room of her house, . . . She would stop: laughing at herself giddily. But the dancing was a rite of passage. An exaltation of solitude would come over her. It was connected with something else: a freedom; an attraction between her and a man that had no desire for the usual consummation. Ben believes their marriage was a failure. Vera sees it as stage on the way, along with others, many and different. Everyone ends up moving alone towards the self. (305–306)

For different reasons Vera and Joan choose to take on their aging years alone, without their long-term partners.

The Bourgeois Marriage/The Home Is Not a Haven

As noted already, one of the primary reasons the men say they are leaving is that they feel trapped in the marriage or that the young, affectionate, adventurous (the adjectives change somewhat according to the man) woman they married has disappeared. One of the reasons the women like Nan (*The Pull of the Moon*), who temporarily lights out for middle America, or like Vera (*None to Accompany Me*), who moves out of the family home, or like Joan (*The Wife*), who announces her intention to leave her soon-to-be-honored writer-husband after so many years, leave is that they feel that the structure and weight of the institution of marriage has constricted them or will constrict them in their next stage of life. And sometimes even women who have been "discarded," once they recover from the shock and awe, like Ina in *Acting Out*, see that they also have been choked by the institution: "I guess that's why people leave marriages, have affairs—they meet somebody else who fills in where the spouse used to be before he or she got so preoccupied with running all the stuff they thought they were building for each other—the career, house, the kids, getting the dog to the vet" (100–101). Ina feels compelled to be a super mom, not only because she wants to be more involved and hands on than her own mother (who was a teacher and a painter), but also, as part of the black middle class, both she and Jay feel the pressure to, first of all, combat racist stereotypes (for example by having the best house and best behaved children in their New York suburb), and, second, to keep up with the black bourgeoisie and the expectations of "Howardites," again by having the best house and the most accomplished children. "My kids are my life," Ina says (118). She and Jay were sucked into "the social whirlpool" (130): Jay worked long hours, played golf, and loved networking at parties mostly among "business and law shakers and wannabes" (131). They neglected each other, and Ina now realizes that she neglected herself. "I was once free and curious and . . . I felt fulfilled. Then it just all changed and I opted for an easy way, for life in the box. . . . Edit the artist out and get your hair done" (80).

Even Rachel Smastat (*Heartburn*), who did not give up her career as a cookbook writer, says that in marriage life sort of stops: "One thing I have never understood is how to work it so that when you're married things keep happening to you. Things happen to you when you're single. You meet new men, you travel alone, you learn new tricks, you read Trollope, you try sushi, you buy nightgowns, you shave your legs. Then you get married, and the hair grows in. I love the everydayness of marriage, I love figuring out what's for dinner and where to hang the pictures and do we owe the Richardsons, but life does tend to slow to a crawl" (21).

A few of the stories raise a critical eyebrow at monogamy, interrogating the heterosexual institution of marriage. In *Intimacy*, the narrator's young, gay friend, Ian, remarks that he "never understood all the fuss you straights make about infidelity. It's only fucking" (22). Martin ("Martin's Letter to Nan" in *Ordinary Life*), whose wife, Nan, has left him temporarily, wonders if monogamy is a good idea (95). Likewise in Alice Munro's "The Spanish Lady" in *Dumped*, the wife concludes that "monogamy is not a natural condition for men and women" (5); this conclusion, written in a discarded letter to her husband of twenty-one years who has gone off with their mutual friend Margaret, is never communicated. David, in Jane Smiley's *The Age of Grief*, is not critical of the institution; in fact he wants to tie down his wife, who he pictures as a hot air balloon, with the details of daily life, hoping she will not be pulled away by her awakened desires: "The more weight we could hang on her, in terms of children, houses, belongings, foodstuffs, office equipment, and debts, the harder it would be for her to gain altitude" (144). Dana and David Hurst have been together for thirteen years, married for ten years with three young girls, having met in dental school before that. He wishes it were not the 1990s but rather the 1950s, when fidelity was valued and divorce was mostly unthinkable. In *Intimacy* the narrator also understands how his desire to leave is related to the time he lives in: if these were the fifties "separation wouldn't have occurred to a lower-middle class couple" (51). But his generation are the children of "consumerism and the inheritors of the freedoms won by our seditious elders in the late sixties" (58). Marriage is no longer endured as one endures a bad job; his parents for example, were "loyal and faithful to one another [but] [d]isloyal and unfaithful to themselves" (50).

The house is often the symbol of the relationship, and most often it is the site of contention in the divorce. Kimberly Freeman (see note 8) observes that "In the divorce novel, the house is both a place that smothers romanticism and a place that cradles societal values. . . . Divorce disrupts domestic space, and consequently, the boundaries between public and private" (139). When Dominique Browning, editor of *House and Garden*, divorced, she wrote that her "sense of home fell apart. And so, too did my house. The rooms looked ravaged, sacked as they were of furniture, art, books, the memories of a life constructed with someone else; everything fallen into disrepair. . . . It was . . . my house—disheveled, lonely-looking, pale, and crumbling—that showed the symptoms of my uneasiness in my new life."[12] In *The Age of Grief*, the husband hides out overnight in the yard of the country house because he does not want the confession and confrontation (learning his wife is involved with another man) that would take place if they were both inside. Likewise in *A Late Divorce*, the house is the container of the marriage: Speaking to his son Tvsi, Yehuda says "those last years I was hardly there. I was imprisoned with her in the house. Every time I went out was a production. But you've forgotten all that, and now you blame me for trying to salvage what's still left of my life" (121). Now separated and clearly moving toward a permanent dissolution to their marriage, Talcott (*The Emperor of Ocean Park*), standing outside of his once-cozy Victorian, sees that "a home that once housed a family and now holds only its shards is like a beach whose sand has eroded to rock—retaining only the name, and none of the reason for the name" (623). And the house is what needs to be divided or given up in the divorce. Tvsi explains that his father has finally "grasped what he should have understood long ago . . . that is, that if he wants his freedom he has to let her have the whole apartment" (213). In *Revenge of the Middle Aged Woman*, Nathan wants to buy Rose out of her half of their house. Rose identifies with the house (she is the wife of the house—a housewife) and the garden; it is where over "the hours, the years . . . happily and inventively, . . . [m]y hands bore a reminder of hours of polishing and brushing, my back the burden of carrying my children up and down its stairs, the king-size double bed the two dents where Nathan and I had slept for so long. . . . In the past, I had struggled to put the house and garden into order, to render clean and fresh my family's dwelling place. I had struggled to put myself into order. Perhaps there is nothing quite so strong as sublimated passion, the one forced underground, which pulses with a secret life" (298). During the divorce process in Jill Hoffman's *Jilted*, Douglas and Joy divide the books: he is allowed to take Freud but not Dickens; they both want the set of Jane Austen. Even though Joy initiated the breakup, losing the house was like losing a part of her self: "I went crazy when I had to sell the apartment. The views had become part of me, like my limbs" (162). Ironically, and contrary to what Nathan says, he is not looking for freedom but to restore the status quo in that house, but with a younger woman. Likewise the husband in *Heartburn* immediately looks to buy a house (four bedrooms) with Thelma, an acquaintance of his and Rachel's, who has her own children.

Pain and Anger

Upon learning that her husband wants out, Ina (*Acting Out*) says that her world was "punctured, upturned and I'd been crushed inside" (49). In these stories, the shock of that first announcement by the partner, and the subsequent process of separation and the dismantling of the structures of a joint life leading to divorce, are depicted as gut wrenching. The pain of learning that one's partner is having an affair, of the betrayal, seems almost as profound as the pain of a complete breakup. Candida (in Margaret Drabble's *The Seven Sisters*) says that "he has done me such wrong that I don't know how to read him, how to speak to him, . . . how to think of him any more. . . . He is like a hole cut in my side" (160). I wonder if the pain is more profound in relation to the length of the relationship? Is the pain more profound when the breakup comes out of the blue? Is the pain more profound for older women than for older men—given the limited prospects older women have for finding another mate? And is the pain worse when a woman is left for a younger woman than for a woman her own age or for no woman at all or is it just the opposite? There is obviously no way to compare or measure pain. What is true is that the psychological pain that the women experience in these novels is deeply and thoroughly embodied in the physical.

In *A Married Woman* (*Marriage: A Duet*), when William walks out the door, leaving, he says, to figure things out, we do not know if he will return. Caroline lies very still, frozen, paralyzed "as if something, some part of her, might shatter if she moved" (35). Rather than get up and begin the day, she wants to remain in a fetal curl: "in every curve and crevasse of it [her body] there was a specific and graphic sense of abandonment, as if the parts themselves—hands, crotch, armpits—were each registering the loss, singing their own individual lamentations" (37). In *Jilted*, Joy leaves her husband for another man, who is married. The other man then dumps her. While not a particularly sympathetic character, Joy does manage to embody the hurt of being jilted: "When you are jilted, it is with a jolt. You fall off the balcony of your dreams and land on the cement, the concrete sidewalk is covered with his cruelty. You can't go back to sleep. Sleep has no miracles up its sleeve" (157). In "The Spanish Lady," the deserted wife howls in pain: "I put my arm across my open mouth and to stop the pain I bite it, I bite my arm" (10).

In two of the novels, the blow of the loss is compounded by other vulnerabilities. In *Heartburn*, the marriage is Rachel's second, and she is seven months pregnant when her husband says he is exiting. She is suffering from "Compound heartburn. Double-digit heartburn. Terminal heartburn" (61). In *Revenge of the Middle-Aged Woman*, Rose is not only dismissed as a wife; she is simultaneously fired from her job as book reviewer; Minty, the age of her daughter, is given both jobs. Both the husband and the boss say it is time for new, young blood. Having lost all, Rose is "crushed by the weight of grief and despair" (108).

Even when the relationship is problematic, the shock of the departure and the loss of the companion are physically devastating, as in *Open House*. Married for twenty years, Samantha acknowledges that things were bad for a long time before David left. Nevertheless, she says "I miss him. I can feel loneliness in me like circulation; as constant and as irrefutable" (34). When the abandoned body and the aging body fuse, the weight of the pain feels so unbearable that suicide is contemplated by more than one of the women. Samantha says, "I am not a girl. I am a woman coming into middle age who has had the rug pulled out from her. And I am trying to reorient myself and I haven't yet. . . . I push pain away all day, and the moment I put my arms down it walks into me and has a seat" (139).

Alice in *The Retreat from Moscow* is shocked that Edward has stopped loving her; she assumed the constancy of his love despite her repeated criticisms of him. Alice calls him a "traitor" and a "murderer" (44). Repeating the refrain "I am old" (47 and 60), she wants to die, as waking alone in the morning hurts too much. She describes to her son what "it's like to be a left woman": "It's not just the loneliness. It's being poorer. It's not being respected by other people. It's being pitied and avoided. It's going to church more than you used to. It's watching TV more than you used to. It's waking up in the morning and not bothering to dress, because there's no one to see. It's making a meal and not eating it, because there's no one to eat it with. It's not doing your hair or your face, because there's no one to look nice for. It's getting a pet and loving it too much. It's slowly feeling yourself turn into a batty, old crone who talks to herself. And worst of it is, you don't die" (79).

The older woman who is left has to face the implications of age on many levels. Fighting the overlapping sexism and ageism in society is hard enough when one has a partner, but when an older woman is deserted, it is even harder not to feel unattractive. Samantha in *Open House* adopts the male gaze as she looks at her forty-two-year-old body: "I don't blame David for leaving me, I would like to leave me, too. . . . Gray hair is popping out all over my head. I have become intimately acquainted with cellulite" (18–19). Rose (*Revenge of the Middle-Aged Wife*) "weeps, wildly, convulsed from head to foot" (21); looking in the mirror, she does not see a young, happy woman, but an older woman, with blue veins in her legs and "dark, troubled circles under her eyes" (89). She is asked, "Would your husband's leaving have been less awful for you if the woman had been older rather than younger?" (213) Would Rose and the others still be so rejecting of their aging bodies if that were the case? I suspect the answer is both yes and no. The competition of older women with younger women is intense in these circumstances, in spite of one's feminism. Rose imagines that her children are commiserating, "Poor Mum, he's left her for a younger woman" (70).

As has been noted, breakups at any point in a relationship are painful. However, in a long-term relationship the partners assume that they will grow old together, retire together, and walk into the sunset together. Losing that (and often losing the financial security that goes along with that scenario) causes profound pain (and fear) and underscores a woman's age. If a woman wants another partner, the statistics of finding an older, eligible male are against her. In New York there are, according to Rachel (*Heartburn*), "two hundred single women to every straight single man, packs of Amazons roaming the streets looking in vain for someone genuinely eligible and self-supporting who didn't mind a little cellulite" (68). The narrator in *Intimacy* acknowledges that his partner Susan is in for a hard time: "After I am gone, there will be devastation. A lone middle-aged woman with kids doesn't have much cachet" (62). Samantha in *Open House* wonders, "How can there ever be another lover?" (40). Not only would his body be the wrong body—not be the body of your husband—but your body is an old body: flabby stomach and gray pubic hair.

For a man, being left when he is old and expecting the final years together can be just as upsetting. When Joan (*The Wife*) tells her husband she is leaving, he is confused not only as to why she did not tell him she was miserable for forty years, but also about why she cannot see all that they have: the history, the children, real estate, friends, et cetera. He does not want to be alone "at this point in my life . . . I'm an old man" (207–208). Unlike the older women who leave or are left who have little hope of finding another man, Joan knows that there will be "younger women skimming by who would approach his overstuffed body with awe" (209). However, he does not get to experience a new relationship, nor the pain, the loneliness, the self-criticism and the self-examination (facing the aging body) that so many of the women who have been left know so well; instead, he dies.

The men are just as hurt as the women when they learn—often abruptly—that the women are having affairs or plan to leave the marriage. Some "beg" the woman not to leave, trying to respond to her complaints. In Berg's story "White Dwarf" (*Ordinary Life*), Phyllis wants out of her marriage; she especially dislikes her husband's silence; she wants to be talked to. She has a brief affair. Sensing her withdrawal, George pleads: "Please don't leave me" (128). Because he finally manages to tell her a story about himself, that is, to talk to her, her hope for their marriage is renewed. "Martin's Letter to Nan" (*Ordinary Life*) is one long letter to Nan, his fifty-year-old wife, who has run off to find herself. While he tells her what "pisses" him off about their marriage (especially her need to talk about everything) and complains that she has never said what's wrong, he also tells her that while he does look at "beautiful girls," he is not interested in "skinny, miserable, navel-gazing twenty-year-olds" (89), but rather he misses her and wants her to come home: "I will be glad to see your familiar face, to take your familiar hand, to lie down with you on the bed we picked out together so many years ago" (97). Because this is not about a partner who left for another person, reconciliation might be easier. Even so, when Nan decides to turn around and return, she expresses her worry that because of his hurt and anger and her sudden disappearance, he will not accept her back: "I know there is a chance you'll be angry with me, Martin. Outraged, even, and wanting to sit in your den and sulk as soon as you see me. But there's also a chance that you'll be glad I left, and glad I returned" (*The Pull of the Moon*, 270).

Silence is the preferred mode of some men for dealing with a partner who seems discontented. Even before Kimmer (*The Emperor of Ocean Park*) declares she is leaving, Talcott suspects she is having an affair and is wounded by her distancing of him. Watching her sleep, he longs to be close to her: "I know the despair of the stateless refugee, praying that he might, against all expectations, reach once more his war-torn home, a cold, unfriendly territory from which he has been excluded" (365). He considers waking her, arguing and "begging" his "way back to my homeland"; however, fearing rejection and allowing a family trait of not expressing feelings to kick in, he turns away. In *The Age of Grief,* because Dana's attention appears to be straying from home, David suspects that she is having an affair; however, he hopes that as long as it is not put in words, it will not become something they both have to deal with. He is afraid that if they talk about it, the discussion will mushroom into the inevitable: separation, divorce—the end of the marriage. He is speechless: "If there was not this subject between us, I could have talked about the news, our friends, the office, our daughters, but now I could say nothing" (210). When Dana goes missing for two days, he is frantic, taking care of the three girls and the dental practice. When she returns, they have a brief interchange: "Well, are you leaving or staying? Staying. Are you sure? . . . She nodded. . . . We were married again" (213 and 209). We, the readers, expect them to reconcile, but at this point they do not speak about "it." Similarly, in *While I Was Gone*, Daniel wishes that Jo would keep her attraction to another man secret, but Jo spills the beans (part of the reason she does not keep it secret is a murder and her need to go to the police). Once told, Daniel cannot stop thinking about it.

As has been noted by many psychologists, women have classically turned anger inward, which leads to depression. Most of the women in these stories do just that. Candida (in *The Seven Sisters*) admits to revengeful feelings: after her husband's "dalliance became common knowledge," she felt "secret delight in his public guilt" (19). Some of the women are able to voice their anger, as in William Trevor's "Access to the Children" (*Dumped*), in which Malcolmson asks Elizabeth, his ex-wife, if he can return to her and the children, after, as he admits to himself, "he played the pins with a flat-chested American nymphomaniac and predator" (30; he left his family for a woman he had met on a train). Enraged, Elizabeth says no: "He'd destroyed her as a wife, he'd insulted her, he left her to bleed and she had called him a murderer" (36). Alice in *The Retreat from Moscow* also calls her husband a murderer.

And some of the women (and men) go even further—they act on their anger. In *Heartburn*, Rachel makes an elaborate dinner party supposedly to celebrate their reunion after her husband's abortive attempt at setting up house with another woman. For desert, she throws a key lime pie in his face and declares that she is leaving. In *Open House*, Samantha sews both the fly of David's boxer shorts and the tops of his fancy socks shut (10); he had moved out abruptly and she knows he will be back for his clothes. In "Making Arrangements" (*Dumped*) by Elizabeth Bowen, the husband's revenge ("a wild kind of justice," 272) is an escalation of the sewing of the boxer shorts. Margery, who was younger than her husband and who has left for a young man, writes a letter to her husband asking for her clothes to be sent. He takes revenge on her dresses—fancy silks, chiffons, and velvets, as they are an upper-class couple—by madly ripping them up with his hands. He then carefully packs the fragments in a trunk to be sent to Margery. Whereas some act out in small and understandable ways, others go a bit too far. In Roald Dahl's "Lamb to Slaughter" (*Dumped*), the wife takes revenge with a leg of lamb. Out of the blue, the husband tells his contented wife that marriage is over. Unable to take this knowledge in, she hopes that a good dinner will right their marriage, so she cheerfully announces her cooking plans. The husband, not interested in the pretense, says he is going out. While he stands looking out of the window, she comes up on him, hitts him with the frozen leg of lamb and kills him. Later she giggles as she and the investigating police share the cooked lamb roast. As Jane Goodall (*Animal Husbandry*) knows, Old Cow rage cannot really be alleviated: "Nothing short of death of the beloved Bull could do it" (218). Nonetheless, publishing her theory in men's and women's magazines under the name of Dr. Marie Goodall can bring some "revenge and relief" (223). In addition, Jane writes up a brief against Ray Brown to sue for compensatory and punitive damages which she assess at $1,593,333.89. Whether she actually brings this to court is not the issue in *Animal Husbandry*; the expressing of just venom is.

The Other Woman

Back in the day of the women's liberation movement, we had many long conversations about sisterhood; one of them was about competition between women over men (or over women for that matter). Rose (*Revenge of the Middle-Aged Woman*) observes Minty's and other young women's "hard, confident bod[ies]" in the gym's changing room: their bodies "were not yet slackening and disobedient, and the gap between their desires and what was returned had not yet widened to be impossible. Perhaps that was what Nathan was trying to redeem" (109–110). As Rachel observes in *Heartburn*, "It is hard to compete with *anyone* new in the sack if you're the spouse who's been around for years" (53). Desire in long-term relationships is not the lust of new relationships—whether that new woman is younger or older.

The women who have been ditched in these fictions are generally not conflicted as to their feelings about the other woman: they are just furious. Rachel (*Heartburn*) hates Thelma, but because she no longer believes in "that mystical sisterly loyalty" (190), she does not blame her. In *Acting Out*, the ferocity of Ina's feeling against the other woman is attributed to the biological need to protect one's children. On Christmas day when Julie, the girlfriend, rings their doorbell, Ina flies into a "hormone-induced," "primal" rage against this female interloper who has come into her territory: "I was the mother mammal in the woods who'd been left alone, abandoned by her mate" (146). For black women, the other woman often is not only younger but not black. Kayreen, an acquaintance of Ina's, attests to this: her husband ran off with a twenty-two-year-old blond and her brother left his wife of twenty years for a "younger model." Talking about the dearth of eligible black men, she exclaims, "But some folks are still managing to find somebody to marry. I just went to two weddings, both forty-five-year-old black men gettin' married for the first time. . . . *Mmm-hmph*, both married other—Indian, Asian, Latino, whatever. One is fifteen years his junior" (128).

What we watch with Rose is her growing ability to "see" and to revise her opinion of the other woman: At first she wavers between seeing Minty as ignorant and seeing her as cruel, egocentric, and opportunistic: "Minty had no idea of the indescribable pain she had caused—or perhaps she had" (280). Later on, when, against Rose's wishes, Minty shows up at her daughter's wedding, Rose decides for the sake of her daughter that she should not make a scene. At the same time Rose is acting in her own interest, not just her daughter's; she wants to free herself both from the despair over being dumped and her obsession with Minty: "It should add up to something greater than a mundane preoccupation with the other woman. . . . However bloody, however hard, I knew must pull the darkness and anger out of myself, and toss them away" (287). In the end, Rose realizes that Minty is not happy (she has the husband and now the house, but she too loses the job and she is beginning to sour on the whole marriage/family scene). The "floozy" and "the middle-aged discarded wife," Rose realizes, "shared more than divided us" (292).

And how does the other woman view all this? Most feel no compunction about stepping into the wife's shoes, except retroactively as in *The Wife*. Now leaving Joe after forty years together, Joan was once the other woman. It is too late for her to go back in time and apologize: "*Sorry* I wanted to say to her. . . . *Sorry for ruining your lives*" (155). In the heat of the moment, when Joe, the professor, had wanted her, the student, she had not had any understanding of how his wife felt (they had a young baby), how the story Joe told her of their marriage was one sided, and how willfully destructive his and her desires were. But now, at age sixty-four, watching her husband have dalliances with admiring (mostly younger) women, she faults herself for not being able to fully see all sides back then. Then she "had only heard Joe talking bitterly about the ways in which his wife denied him love. . . . I'd always thought Carol was off kilter but maybe she was just furious" (155).

One of the ironies in these triangles is that it is often the "betrayed" woman who keeps the other woman alive in memory, whereas the man might have moved on. In *A Married Woman* (*A Duet*), after the husband and wife reconcile, the husband's girlfriend is killed in an accident. Caroline, the wife, regularly summons up the story of the husband's betrayal, in which the girl is a major character, even though the affair is over and she is dead. Many years later, sitting beside her dying husband's hospital bed, the story is vividly reviewed once again. It is hard to erase from memory those words that so many of the men say when they walk: I (husband) don't—or never—loved you (wife), rather I love her (other woman). Rachel wants Mark (*Heartburn*) back, but wants "him to say he never loved her. I want him to say he must have been crazy" (74). But what if the dumper cannot say "I never loved her"?

Reconciliation or Letting Go and Moving On

In *A Married Woman* (*A Duet*) and in *Acting Out*, when the husbands say they're "home . . . for good" (57), the wives are willing to live with that. To be helpful, William bought Caroline (*A Married Woman*) the book *Getting Over Adultery*; she read one page of it and then tossed it away. "They would grow old together. . . . They groped their way back into a marriage, but it was not the old marriage, it was a new one" (58). Caroline did not want to know how damaged William's heart was (the extent of his loss in letting go of the young woman) as her heart was damaged as well. At his deathbed, after a forty-year marriage, she is still able to relive that painful period. While he is comatose, she by his side wonders what "long-held shards of resentment or long-withheld assertions of love" (6) were being voiced by incipient widows throughout the hospital. Caroline lets loose with both emotions. Likewise for Ina and Jay (*Acting Out*), their innocence, especially about the sacredness of the vows they had made to each other, was certainly lost. Ina realizes that she has a choice: "I could be pissed at him forever and blame him for screwing up the perfect image on the Christmas card. I could be suspicious every time I couldn't find him, or I could thank him for forcing me to find the person [herself] that had been missing for a long time" (275). And despite the terrible pain, she is grateful that they had made something new and "amazing out of the relationship" (275).

Daniel (*While I Was Gone*) is quite wounded by Jo's betrayal (that she did not sleep with the other man is not the issue). However, his only act of anger is to throw a tomato at her; mostly he keeps his distance from her. Jo knows she needs to be patient and accept "the deep moat of silence" now between them. "I saw that I couldn't, for the moment, try to change things with him. That when I did, I would inevitably do it in my own unwelcome way, and that would only make things worse. . . . I would sweep too much of his pain aside, because I so wanted it to be over" (294). It is difficult for Daniel to discard his self-protective shell, to give up the hardness in himself, to forgive and to cross over and back to their relationship. They will have to remake "what it means to be together, to touch each other, to love" (334).

Some people, like David (*A Duet: A Married Man*), get stuck and cannot move on. David cannot get over even a momentary transgression (a one-night affair, which his wife, Marcia, regrets but does not hide from him), much less a full-fledged dumping. David is heartbroken; he feels "exiled from his happiness" (164). An especially involved father to their two sons, he goes through the motions of daily life seeing "how you come to live in your marriage and outside of it at the same time, tethered by hurt, disappointment, habit" (117). Nothing seems to help: pills, therapy, recovery groups—as David calls it, the "surreal world of self help" (154). According to Dr. Lou, whom David and Marcia consult, it has been found that "it takes longer for men to get over adultery than for women" (154). True for David, as he cannot be "cajoled out of . . . rage and grief" (162). "Unmoored, overwhelmed" (164), unable to bear Marcia's betrayal, in the end he self-destructs. In *Heartburn*, Rachel, like David in *A Married Man*, feels as if repair is unlikely, but then again the damage to Rachel by all measurements is much greater. She has been abandoned for another woman, left to give birth to the baby alone. Rachel believes that when marriages break, "even when you glue it back together it's always going to have been horribly broken." What has been lost or set askew is your view of "a piece of your past. The infidelity itself is small potatoes compared to the low-level brain damage that results when a whole chunk of your life turns out to have been completely different from what you thought it was" (72). Mark does return, but Rachel decides to get out: "I am no beauty, and I'm getting on in years, and I have just enough money to last me sixty days, and I am terrified of being alone, and I can't bear the idea of divorce, but I would rather die than sit here and pretend it's okay, I would rather die than sit here figuring out how to get you to love me again, . . . anticipating the next betrayal and worrying about whether my poor, beat-up middle-aged body with its Caesarean scars will ever turn you on again." Rachel cannot stand the rage and "feeling like a victim" (219).

Letting go of the old relationship and letting go of the victim status take time and work; the process is compared by Raymond Carver in the short story "Fever" (*Dumped*) to getting over a serious illness. Ed's wife of eight years leaves him for a colleague; terribly distraught, he is left with two children. He falls ill. After talking deliriously about how they planned to grow old together, Ed emerges from the fever having completed his mourning over his wife. Ed can now move on. Alice in *The Retreat from Moscow* is also devastated at the ending of her marriage, but at some point she manages to reluctantly say: "I suppose I'll go on" (100); what she means is that she won't carry out her plan of killing herself in front of Edward at his "love nest." She does become more connected to the world (whereas she appears not to have worked during the marriage, instead putting together—but never completing—an anthology of her favorite poems); she now volunteers for an AIDS help-line where she feels somewhat comforted by the fact that men are left by men as well: "So we [she and the gay men] talk about what it's like and how men are all selfish pigs, and how is one to cope" (90). Ed ("Fever") recovers fully; Alice will never recover entirely; of course his relationship was of short duration whereas hers was for most of her adult lifetime.

Why do some women and men never recover from being dumped, while others do? Ina (*Acting Out*), who reacted to the loss of her husband so deeply the she had to take Prozac, explains why she knows that being crushed permanently was not "an option" for her. That (being crushed permanently or not), she said, was the difference between black and white women. Black women historically had no man to fall back on. The ability to go on, "that kind of will was born in my bones, just as my big thighs, thick hair and bad teeth were" (219). It is interesting that Caroline (*A Duet: A Married Woman*) and Ina (*Acting Out*) take their husbands back after they pursue other women; but that for Daniel (*While I Was Gone*) and especially David (*A Duet: A Married Man*), even a momentary or partial betrayal seems almost unforgivable. Are the women better able to forgive and reconcile? Is it because the women have different or more realistic expectations of long-term relationships? Or is it because of the uneven supply and demand?

For some of the women being cut loose has a transformative effect. Some make personality or life changes and subsequently reunite with their husbands: Ina, who gave up her work when she married (*Acting Out*), gets a photography job and puts her mothering role in perspective. Some women transform themselves and find other, better partners. Samantha, who also never worked while married (*Open House*), is sent out by an employment agency to a series of jobs: telephone solicitor, construction worker (because she goes by the name Sam, the company thought she would be a man), purveyor of cheese samples in a supermarket. When her husband, David, asks to move back, she is tempted by not having to "worry about retirement planning" or about growing "old alone and demented in some filthy apartment with a chair by the window" (216), but she rejects the notion. She says no to him way before she realizes that the ungainly, somewhat reclusive, definitely not middle-class, bearish King is a man she should and could love. Like Samantha, Rose (*Revenge of the Middle-Aged Woman*) says no, when Nathan, her husband, weeps about his wrong choices.

And some women decide that they do not necessarily need nor particularly want partners; rather their first priority is saying yes to their new selves as Candida Wilton, the central character in *The Seven Sisters*, does. Most of her adult life had been passed in the English countryside, where she played out her role as the dutiful and conventional wife to her husband, a headmaster.

Then her husband, Andrew, fell in love with another woman, the mother of one of his students (Andrew and Candida have three grown children). After the initial shock and disorientation, sensing she is an "object of gossip and pity" in their small rural town, Candida finds a small flat in a rundown part of London. She is frightened, as she has never been alone in her adult life; nonetheless, she is delighted that she "would never have to consult the taste of others" (74). Indeed she is relieved not to be a wife: "Nobody knew of the exhilaration I felt when I realized what I would not have to live with Andrew for the rest of my life" (19). Her first years are not easy as she pushes herself to try out new things, like joining a gym and a reading group and learning to use a computer. Feeling constrained by her age, which is somewhere in the late fifties (post-menopausal), she calls herself "retired" from life, "redundant" (133): "Now I look faded and washed out. My skin is weathered, and wrinkles and crowsfeet don't look as good on a woman as they do on a man" (15). But she takes a leap (helped along by a small inheritance) that begins with throwing away her marriage ring and deciding to take a trip with six other women, tracing the steps of Aeneas. No longer feeling like the "passive victim of my own fate" (149) or "the discarded shell of a sea urchin" (207), she embraces the freedom of "the third age" (148): "I have divorced myself from Andrew and married the blue water" (162).

The women who recover the best ultimately let go of their identification with and attachment to their house (often they forced to leave the house); they too begin to see the house as symbolic of an institution that does not give life but instead fosters acquisition desires and a death of the spirit. Candida, upon downsizing from rural house to city flat, says: "I felt a relief in being so reduced. We accumulate too many objects, as we grow older. I had some hope that by stripping most of mine away, I might enter a new dimension. As a nun enters a convent in search of her god, so I entered my solitude" (54). Ina (*Acting Out*) is forced to sell her exquisite house and move into a smaller, less perfect one. Likewise Rose (*Revenge of the Middle-Aged Woman*) moves out of the house in which she and Nathan raised their children into a smaller place. Both she and Ina were forced to move for financial reasons and both, after some period of mourning, realize that the move was a good one. Vera (*None to Accompany Me*) moves to her own place, a smaller place because she wants to be alone and because like Candida she wants to eliminate many of her possessions. In *Open House* Samantha does not move, but to cover her expenses she takes on a series of roommates; by so doing, she becomes open to the varieties of human nature whereas previously she had been closed off, living in a married middle-class bubble.

Rose (*Revenge of the Middle-Aged Woman*) asks herself: "Was it possible to find recompense, meaning, connection with others amidst the mess and muddle?" (310). Out of the pain and mess and muddle, many of the women do just that: they find recompense, meaning, and connection. Curiously, many of these fictional women have been rather isolated, so getting connected to other people, especially other women, is important. Samantha, as stated above, connects with those who rent a room from her. Candida goes on a trip with six other women, who become in a sense like sisters (*The Seven Sisters*). "She frequented galleries in her loneliness, but now she is no longer alone. She is one of a company. She is with friends" (203). With one woman, an old classmate on the trip, "they weave and wander their way, merrily, nostalgically, sentimentally, arm in arm. . . . As they part they kiss one another goodnight. They would never have done a thing like that, forty years ago" (209). In addition, Candida, who was never an easy mother, reconnects with her daughters and decides to become an attentive grandmother.

Some of the stories referred to here are set in prefeminist times; some of them are set during the second wave of the women's movement; and some are set in the so-called postfeminist era, as is *Revenge of the Middle-Aged Woman*, in which Minty, Rose's husband's paramour, "had the confidence of a woman whose generation did not understand why feminism had been necessary" (95). Most of the women protagonists seem disconnected from other women and from any kind of politics, like the ten women of Kate Walbert's *Our Kind*, upper-middle-class women's college graduates who became full-time wives. All "were married in 1953. Divorced in 1976. Our grown daughters pity us; our grown sons forget us. We have grandchildren we visit from time to time" (10). Their marriages broke up: "Years ago we were led down the primrose lane, then abandoned somewhere near the carp pond" (11). They seem to feel betrayed by all men even if "we left them." The men remarried "mostly, younger women" (25). These women's formative years predated second-wave feminism so their affection and support they gave each other was not called something as intimate as friendship: "We were company, perhaps; women of a certain age with shared interests. But friends? It seemed too intimate, somehow, wrong" (82). Now, "women near the end of their lives" (16), they gather at a hospice (visiting Judy, one of the group) to hold their book club meeting; this month they are talking about Virginia Woolf's *Mrs. Dalloway*. This scene illustrates a camaraderie that clearly kept them going and would now be called sisterhood: "The few times we speak of true things it is almost unbearable, and so we do not, most, preferring to laugh" (192). Of a later generation than those women, Ina (*Acting Out*), during her college years, considered herself a "womanist" (63) and had an especially close relationship with Leelah, whom Jay convinced her to drop when they married. Immersed in her family, Ina is pretty much without women friends; or to put it more accurately, she talks to her women neighbors about innocuous things and her mother's group focuses solely on their babies. When Jay leaves, Ina reconnects with Leelah (who comes out to Ina as a lesbian—they finally talk of true things) while reconnecting with herself. It is women friends who get Rose (*Revenge of the Middle-Aged Woman*) through the worst of times. After speaking to a mutual friend, Mazarine, Vee comes to check on Rose to make sure Rose does not do harm to herself. "The knowledge that they were watching over me made me feel better" (191), says Rose.

Turning to women as friends is extremely important to these women who are left; some begin to question their attraction to men. Rachel (*Heartburn*) "contemplated lesbianism. Lesbianism has always seemed to me an extremely inventive response to the shortage of men" (63). While this is said in a smart-ass way, many heterosexual women who have been left wish somehow they could will themselves into that orientation, given how many good women there are out there. Joan (*The Wife*) wonders "what my life might have been like with another woman—a life away from men and their caterwauling and continual need for affirmation, or stroking, as though with their minds they were always deep in the Den of Iniquity, always waiting with robe belt loosely tied, wanting a woman to pull it open and make them happy" (160).

Like Candida (*The Seven Sisters*), who is somewhat older than she, Rose, after recovering from being evicted, as it were, looks forward to the older woman/postdivorce stage: "I thought of grief and its fall out, . . . and the part of my life that was over. I thought of how it was possible both to shrink and unfold, how I had experienced both, and how the unfolding at forty-eight was both joyous and unexpected. And would continue for a long time" (*Revenge of the Middle-Aged Woman*, 356). While not all women (and men) who are dumped may be able to repair themselves as well as Candida and Rose did, the novels, stories, and plays of Splitsville show us that such repair may be possible, and they comfort us with good stories while we are licking our wounds.

Notes

1. David Denby, "Husbands and Wives," *New Yorker*, August 30, 2004, The Current Cinema, 103. Having recently published a book about his own domestic drama, *American Sucker* (New York: Little, Brown, 2004), he now is surfeited. *We Don't Live Here Anymore* is based on two stories by Andre Dubus: "We Don't Live Here Anymore" and "Adultery."

2. Laura Miller, "Works for Me," *New York Times Book Review*, August 8, 2004, www.nytimes.com.

3. From "A Conversation with Anne Taylor Fleming," publicity material in review copy of *Marriage: A Duet* (New York: Hyperion Books, 2003).

4. William Nicholson, preface to *The Retreat from Moscow: A Play about a Family* (New York: Anchor Books, 2004), viii–ix.

5. B. Delores Max, ed., *Dumped: An Anthology* (New York: Grove Press, 2003), xii–xiii.

6. Elizabeth Berg, *Open House* (New York: Ballantine Books, 2001); Elizabeth Berg, *Ordinary Life* (New York: Random House, 2002; 2003); Elizabeth Berg, *The Pull of the Moon* (New York: Jove Books, 1996; 1997); Elizabeth Buchan, *Revenge of the Middle-Aged Woman* (London: Penguin Books, 2002); Stephen Carter, *The Emperor of Ocean Park* (New York: Borzoi Book/Alfred A. Knopf, 2002); Margaret Drabble, *The Seven Sisters* (New York: Harcourt, 2002); Nora Ephron, *Heartburn* (New York: Pocket Books, 1983; 1984); Anne Taylor Fleming, *Marriage: A Duet* (see above); Nadine Gordimer, *None to Accompany Me* (New York: Farrar, Straus and Giroux, 1994); Jill Hoffman, *Jilted* (New York: Simon & Schuster, 1993); John Irving, *A Widow for One Year* (New York: Ballantine Books, 1998); Hanif Kureishi, *Intimacy and Midnight All Day* (New York: Scribner Paperback Fiction/Simon & Schuster, 1998; 2001); Doris Lessing, *The Summer Before the Dark* (New York: Vintage Books, 1973; 1983); Benilde Little, *Acting Out* (New York: The Free Press, 2003); B. Delores Max, ed., *Dumped: An Anthology* (see above); Sue Miller, *While I Was Gone* (New York: Ballantine Books, 1999; 2002); William Nicholson, *The Retreat from Moscow: A Play about a Family* (see above); Jane Smiley, *The Age of Grief: A Novella and Stories* (New York: Anchor Books/Random House, 1987; 2003); Anne Tyler, *The Amateur Marriage* (New York: Alfred A. Knopf, 2004); Kate Walbert, *Our Kind* (New York: Scribner, 2004); Meg Wolitzer, *The Wife* (New York: Scribner, 2004); A. B. Yehoshua, *A Late Divorce* (San Diego: Harcourt Brace, 1984; 1993); Laura Zigman, *Animal Husbandry* (New York: The Dial Press, 1998).

There are many books I did not include in this Splitsville survey. One of note is *The Dictionary of Failed Relationships: 26 Tales of Love Gone Wrong*, ed. Meredith Brousard (New York: Three Rivers Press, 2003). I excluded this precisely because, as the editor explains: "The authors of the *Dictionary* are smart, funny, and quirky women. Youth seemed especially important at the beginning of the project, because so many of today's most prominent women writers are post-menopausal" (xv). NO COMMENT! I also did not include any stories about women leaving women. Nor did I include Philip Roth's *The Dying Animal* (New York: Vintage International, 2002, an effective rant against marriage, nor Jonathan Franzen's five sketches titled "Break Up Stories" (*New Yorker*, November 4, 2004). Carol Shields and Terri McMillan are other writers I have left out—space is largely the reason for these choices. Black writers like McMillan, Connie Briscoe, and Benilde Little are now writing novels about black women over forty, describing their complicated lives which include menopause, men in midlife crises, and divorce (Felicia R. Lee, "Pioneers Are Taking Black Chick Lit into Middle Age," *New York Times*, June 27, 2005).

7. By "we" and "our," I am mainly talking about middle-class white men and women in the United States and England.

8. For some studies of the family, love, marriage, and divorce in literature, see: Tony Tanner, *Adultery in the Novel: Contract and Transgression* (Baltimore: The Johns Hopkins University Press, 1979); Kimberly Freeman, *Love American Style: Divorce and the American Novel, 1881–1976* (New York: Routledge, 2003); Allen F. Stern, *After the Vows Were Spoken: Marriage in American Literary Realism* (Columbus: Ohio State University Press, 1984); Ann duCille, *The Coupling Convention: Sex, Text, and Tradition in Black Women's Fiction* (New York: Oxford University Press, 1993); and Debra Ann MacComb, *Tales of Liberation, Strategies of Containment: Divorce and the Representation of Womanhood in American Fiction, 1880–1920* (New York: Garland Publishing, 2000).

9. Another important aspect of many of these books is the effect on the children of the parents' affairs, separation, and/or divorce. In *The Age of Grief,* the young child Lizzie's stomachaches are a result of her internalizing the tension between her parents. In *Open House*, Samantha awkwardly tells her eleven-year-old son about the breakup, saying the usual words: that it has nothing to do with him and that sometimes people who love each other grow apart, but they both still love him. What she really wants to say is: " 'Because your father is a very, very selfish person who thinks only of himself. Always has, always will. He deserted me, Travis, just like that" (18). In *The Wife,* both children react to the lies and secrets of their parents' relationship. The troubled son David, in his twenties, who is no longer living at home, pulls a knife on his father, saying that he has kept their mother as his slave. The main theme in Avery Corman's *A Perfect Divorce* (New York: St. Martin's Press, 2004) is how unsettling divorce is on the son, who drops out of his first year of college. Adult children are not immune either, often reacting with pain and indignation. In *Revenge*, Poppy, upon learning that her father is seeing someone her own age, says: "Dad's turned into an old goat "(86) and "Who does he think he is, going after a younger woman? It's such . . . such a cliche" (111–112). In *A Late Divorce*, the father, in pursuit of divorce, asks one of the sons to intervene for him with the mother; Asa says the father is "throwing her [the mother] to the dogs" (141). In *The Retreat from Moscow*, the father makes an abrupt exit, expecting the son to come down on weekends to keep the mother company. The burden on the son is great, especially when the mother asks the son to give her permission to kill herself.

10. Gail Sheehy, *Passages: Predictable Crises of Adult Life* (New York: Dutton Books, 1978).

11. In the novel *My Phantom Husband* by Marie Darrienssecq (New York: New Press, 1999), the husband of seven years walks out to get a baguette and never

returns. He leaves no note — just vanishes. The wife waits for him, searches for him, does not know what to tell people. She descends into a kind of fugue state of pain and confusion: "When he evaporated, my husband had taken with him, as a comet carries along its tail, all the atmosphere that made him be himself; nothing of him remained except me and I was deprived of the air I once had breathed and that no one could infuse me with in his place" (135).

12. Dominique Browning, *Around the House and in the Garden: A Memoir of Heartbreak, Healing, and Home Improvement* (New York: Scribner, 2002), 11–12.

APPENDIX: A GUIDE TO SPLITSVILLE FICTION

Author	Novel	Wife and husband	Approximate length of marriage	Who leaves whom	Other woman or man	Reunited or not
Elizabeth Berg	Open House	Samantha and David	20 years	He leaves	Other woman	Not reunited
Elizabeth Berg	The Pull of the Moon	Nan and Martin	25 years	She leaves	No other man	Reunited
Elizabeth Buchan	Revenge of the Middle-Aged Woman	Rose and Nathan	25 years	He leaves	Other woman: Minty	Not reunited
Stephen Carter	The Emperor of Ocean Park	Kimmer and Talcott	9 years	She leaves	Other man: basketball player	Not reunited
Margaret Drabble	The Seven Sisters	Candida and Andrew	30 years	He leaves	Other woman	Not reunited
Nora Ephron	Heartburn	Rachel and Mark	5+ years	He leaves; later she leaves	Other woman: Thelma	Not reunited
Anne Taylor Fleming	A Married Woman (A Duet)	Caroline and William	27 years	He leaves	Other woman	Reunited
Anne Taylor Fleming	A Married Man (A Duet)	Marcia and David	5+ years	She has one-night affair	Other man	Husband has breakdown
Nadine Gordimer	None to Accompany Me	Vera and Bennet	30+ years	She leaves	Other man (a friend)	Not reunited
Jill Hoffman	Jilted	Joy and Douglas	13+ years	She leaves	Other man	Not reunited

Author	Title	Couple	Length	Who leaves	Other man/woman	Reunited
John Irving	A Widow for One Year	Marion and Ted	20+ years	She leaves	No other man	Not reunited
Hanif Kureishi	Intimacy	Susan and unnamed spouse	10 years	He leaves	Other woman: Nina	Not reunited
Doris Lessing	The Summer Before the Dark	Kate and Michael	25 years	She leaves	No other man	Reunited
Benilde Little	Acting Out	Ina and Jay	14 years	He leaves	Other woman: Julie	Reunited
Sue Miller	While I Was Gone	Jo and Daniel	20+ years	She considers leaving	Other man: Eli	Reunited
William Nicholson	The Retreat from Moscow	Alice and Edward	33 years	He leaves	Other woman: Angela	Not reunited
Jane Smiley	The Age of Grief	Dana and David	13 years	She leaves	Other man (probably)	Reunited
Anne Tyler	Amateur Marriage	Pauline and Michael	30 years	He leaves	No other woman	Not reunited
Meg Wolitzer	The Wife	Joan and Joe	40 years	She leaves	No other man	He dies
A. B. Yehoshua	A Late Divorce	Naomi and Yehuda	40 years	He leaves	Other woman: Connie	Not reunited
Laura Zigman	Animal Husbandry	Jane and Ray	Brief relationship	He leaves	Other woman	Not reunited

Note: This chart does not include the following fictions mentioned in this essay: Elizabeth Berg's stories ("Martin's Letter to Nan" and "White Dwarf") in *Ordinary Life*; the stories (Alice Munro's "The Spanish Lady," William Trevor's "Access to the Children," Elizabeth Bowen's "Making Arrangements," and Roald Dahl's "Lamb to Slaughter") in *Dumped: An Anthology*, edited by B. Delores Max; and the novel *Our Kind* by Kate Walbert, which is about a group of women.

Break-up Art

LOUISE WEINBERG

Whenfaced with the challenge of writing about being discarded from a relationship as an older woman, I submitted works of art created over ten years ago in a time of great pain and anguish. These works stand as a silent record of my tormented emotional climate at that time. The challenge became how to find a way to talk about silent stelae (archaic forms like grave markers) that resonate with their own internal intelligence and measured rhythms of language and line. At the time, I wanted to scream their passages at every person passed on streets or pressed against in subway cars' rush hour. When presented with a happy ending of newfound romance on some mindless night of TV's numbing cocoon, I wanted to shout back at the inane pronouncements and their supposed truths. My truths never mirrored reality.

Art making was a way into the raw emotion—a factory, some kind of mechanism to process human passions, not unlike a sewage treatment plant. Take the bad stuff; convert to innocuous mulch to make plants and trees grow better. The artworks were about the possibility of human adaptability and resiliency. Shoot another arrow into Saint Sebastian. Or Frida Kahlo's obsessive and tormented love for Diego. Somehow her harshly realistic/surrealistic paintings weren't the way for me. A more lyrical, hidden path suggested itself. Hide the pain in a Morse code of the heart, sign language of the deaf.

The physical act : drawing and incising into soft copper sheets molded over wood forms whose dimensions were made to correspond to my own torso. Resilient like an etching plate, each panel treated like a dry point, carving into the surface like graffiti. Each blow of the hammer driving each thorn-sharp nail into the copper's pliable surface and resistant wood below was a realization that this is not working. Each mark—I exist, I am, I am still here. Repetition a mantra against not being heard, shouting against the darkness, the bottomless abyss of anonymity. Focus on the matter at hand, on the specific task of writing about working through pain, and illuminating for others rash behavior propelled by fear of death, of fading away, of not being recognized, of not being seen, of not being felt, of not being held ever again, and closing the great gaping chasm at least temporarily.

Search for equivalencies in 1940s medical texts and first-aid lifesaving books, finding comfort in the droning sameness of language. Fascinated by the possibility of texts on human physiology as measurements for emotional states.

The necessity for a clear image in the eye.

If a sharp, clear image is not formed on the retina of the eye, serious troubles follow. The muscles in the eye keep pulling and working to try to change the shape of the lens so that the vision will be clear; in reading it is a strain on the attention to tell what letters are in the words, and, in general, it makes all work that requires close attention more difficult. This overworks and deranges the nervous system, and soon the health of the whole body is injured.[1]

Take caution. Stay out of deep waters. What to do if your emotional boat founders, leaking, sinking? How does the interior of the heart appear when in pain, when in doubt? What does the needle look like on the chart when realization sets in? How are emotional events known under the skin like powders of cadmium and lead, and in the sacs and cilia of the lungs like colorless odorless toxic gases of phosgene and carbon monoxide? How to love each nail and its fierce path. I am still here worshipping tornados, earthquakes, and tsunamis, all of the violent acts of nature's maternal earth. Barometers, measuring plate tectonics, stresses of gases and flame, molten rock, shifting restless movements. Rail against death. Shout, rant, drive the storm away with language, signs, and symbols—birds for transcendence, feathers and lunar cycles for time's eventual passage.

If you don't see clearly, you get in trouble. How to know the tender intricacies of the heart and its obscure, internal portions?

Note

1. John W. Ritchie, *Primer of Sanitation and Physiology* (Chicago: World Book Company, 1934), 327.

Unholy Matrimony

DIANA FESTA

I refuse to look at stones sprawled
on rusty grass in our garden,
fallen from the shattered cathedral
where prayer stumbled.

I find a narrow cradle for my skull
in the bend of my elbow, away
from all those women in your life
whispering through the night.

When morning comes, you cover
space like a wolf stalking its prey,
eyes narrowed, your long fingers
clutching an imaginary weapon—

our home a battlefield where
invective tears more than a sword.
This, our seventeenth anniversary,
you give me two copper pans

for the kitchen, perhaps redeemed
by a bunch of roses.

Look at it from where I stand,
the corner where I am trapped

by your chiding words, sounds
muffled only through years of
repetition. Look at the chain of
mountains around, the brittle

ice in our lives, impermeable
to sun and warmth. Let us call it
quits. In the absence of harmony,
I ask for silence.

The Chore

DIANA FESTA

Break a glass in a thousand shards,
a friend told me, watch
reflections, the clouds' instability.
Rain crushes against
the calligraphy of silence—

your lover will die.
Write on granite those words
lodged in your throat.

I paint on canvas the violence of red
round bones, not to flounder
in riddles—to let him go, and my fear.

Unhinged shutters bang against
the clapboards, insistent.
The devil demands to open,
dismantle the architecture.

I weigh the daunting task of
tossing objects in piles,
the statuette we bought in Greece,
the books he wrote—

how to erase
his name at the entrance.

* * *

My twenty-two years in a bad first marriage can perhaps be faulted to an upbringing that refuted divorce. Eventually, I did ask for, insisted on an end to
a marriage where betrayal and emotional violence were daily occurrences.
The poem "Unholy Matrimony" reflects the feeling of entrapment that dominated those years. My second marriage was very happy. When my husband
died after fifteen years with me, I felt devastated, abandoned. "The Chore"
aims at expressing my enormous sense of loss.

About the Contributors

NAN BAUER-MAGLIN is an English professor and administrator at City University of New York. She is a mother, stepmother, and grandmother, who writes about literature, women's lives, and feminist issues. She co-edited *Women and Stepfamilies: Voices of Anger and Love* (1989), *"Bad Girls/Good Girls": Women, Sex, and Power in the Nineties* (Rutgers University Press, 1996), and *Women Confronting Retirement: A Nontraditional Guide* (Rutgers University Press, 2003). She also gives talks and leads workshops on retirement. She is in two women's groups, one is twenty-seven years old and other began more recently.

SUSAN BECKER (a pseudonym) is a retired academic who specialized in women's studies. Today she is retrained as a massage therapist, amateur jazz pianist, and avid tennis player and runs a nonprofit recording studio out of her house. Her essay is based on selections from a full-length manuscript that she is currently completing. She lives abroad.

NANCY BERKE is an assistant professor of English at LaGuardia Community College, City University of New York, where she teaches courses in writing and American studies. In addition to publishing essays on modern poetry, politics and literature, and women's writing, she is the author of *Women Poets on the Left* (2001). Currently she is working on a cultural study of single women.

PHYLLIS BERMAN retired from university teaching and research in psychology and child development more than a decade ago. She has been writing poetry since then. Her poems have been published in journals and magazines. Two of her chapbooks have been published: *Moongate* (2002), which includes the poem "Observing the Cormorant," and *After the Diagnosis: My Brother's Story* (2005). She no longer does long-distance traveling, but lives in Maryland where she participates in poetry study groups. She and her ex-husband have become friends of a sort, who share an interest in politics and in five grandchildren ranging from age five to sixteen.

CAROL BURDICK has held many jobs. She wound up with a teaching career in which her classrooms contained a range of elementary school, high school, college, graduate school, and Elderhostel students. She is partially responsible for three children and four grandchildren, and completely responsible for words which have been published in magazines, papers, and three books: *Destination Unknown* (verse), *Stop Calling Me Mr. Darling!*, and *Woman Alone*. She currently lives (with two formerly stray dogs) on eighty acres in the southwestern New York State hills in a pondside, self-designed home where the deck becomes a dock.

NANCY DAILEY helps educate women and their financial advisors about retirement and life economics at her Web site, www.WomensMoney.com. She is a sociologist and the author of the first work to be dedicated to the study of retirement for baby boom women, *When Baby Boom Women Retire* (1998). Her book received the 1998 Outstanding Academic Book of the Year Award from the Academic Librarians Association. Dailey co-authored the essay "Baby Boom Women: The Generation of Firsts" in *Women Confronting Retirement: A Nontraditional Guide* (2003). She continues to contribute articles and essays to journals and online publications to promote financial literacy and education for women. She is married, has three sons, and lives in the Virginia Piedmont region.

PAGE DOUGHERTY DELANO's poetry collection *No One with a Past Is Safe* was published in 2002; her work has appeared widely in journals such as *Prairie Schooner, Agni, American Voice, Notre Dame Review,* and *Amicus,* and in the anthologies *Perfect in their Art,* about boxing, an anthology of war poetry, and *TriQuarterly New Writers.* In addition to a poetry manuscript in progress, *National Bed,* she is also working on a collaborative memoir, about 1970s political activism. Her academic writing explores the role of American women in the public sphere during World War II. She teaches English at Borough of Manhattan Community College, City University of New York.

DIANA FESTA was brought up in Italy and studied at American universities. As a professor of French literature at the City University of New York, she published four books in literary criticism and was awarded the Guizot Prize by the French Academy. She is also a trained psychotherapist with a private practice. She is the author of four poetry books, *Arches to the West, Ice Sparrow, Thresholds,* and

Bedrock. She has published numerous poems and articles in various reviews. Her honors include a Guggenheim Fellowship, poetry prizes, and honorable mentions.

HELEN FISHER is a visiting research professor and member of the Center for Human Evolutionary Studies in the Department of Anthropology at Rutgers University. She has written four books: *Why We Love: The Nature and Chemistry of Romantic Love* (2004;12 foreign language editions); *The First Sex: The Natural Talents of Women and How They Are Changing the World* (1999; 14 foreign language editions); *Anatomy of Love: The Natural History of Mating, Marriage, and Why We Stray* (1992; 18 foreign language editions); and *The Sex Contract: The Evolution of Human Behavior* (1982; 7 foreign language editions). Other publications include articles in the *Journal of Comparative Neurology*, *Journal of Neurophysiology*, *Journal of Forensic Sciences*, *Neuroendocrinology Letters*, *Archives of Sexual Behavior*, and *Journal of NIH Research*, and various books. She has been on the national lecture circuit since 1983, and for her work in communicating anthropology to the public and scientists in other disciplines, she has received the American Anthropological Association's Distinguished Service Award.

MERLE FROSCHL, since the 1970s, has been developing curricular and teacher training models that foster equality of opportunity for students regardless of gender, race/ethnicity, disability, or level of family income. Currently, she is co-director of the Educational Equity Center at the Academy for Educational Development (AED). She is the author of numerous articles and books, the most recent of which is *The Anti-Bullying and Teasing Book*. She has a BS in journalism from Syracuse University and is a graduate of the Institute for Not-for-Profit Management at Columbia University. Now a widow, she was married for forty years and has a son, daughter, and two grandchildren.

ISABELLA GIOVANNI (a pseudonym), a k a Rose, is a professor at a major university. She is also a writer and a film maker, who marvels at how chance rules life.

MARGIE KAPLAN, the mother of two wonderfully special young adult women, was born and raised and has spent most of her life in the New York metropolitan area. For almost thirty years, since college, graduate school, and analytic training, she has had a private psychoanalytic psychotherapy practice treating adults, couples, and groups. Additionally, she has been teaching courses in both psychology and human services on the adjunct faculty at Borough of Manhattan Community College, City University of New York. She teaches as well at Manhattan's 92nd Street Y, creating courses regarding healthy development and relationships. With a circle of friends and family and her partner of nine years, Margie revels in free time at her country home swimming and enjoying sports and the beauty of nature.

MARILYN OGUS KATZ served as dean of studies at Sarah Lawrence College for sixteen years, having previously taught literature and writing at State University of New York College at Purchase. Widowed in her fifties after a long marriage, she was forced to develop a single and independent life. When she experienced her recent retirement as yet another loss, she struggled to shape a new identity as an editor and writer of both fiction and nonfiction. Katz has published articles on literature and the teaching of writing, on issues in higher education, and on the concerns of older women. She is a contributor to *Women Confronting Retirement: A Non-Traditional Guide*. Currently, she is assisting her companion, poet George Petty, with *Hiking the New Jersey Highlands: The Wilderness in Your Backyard* (2006), an interest she only discovered in her sixties. At the same time, she is completing final revisions on *The Lyrics to the Bridge* (working title), a novel about the coming of age of a fifty-six-year-old woman.

MARITA LOPEZ-MENA received her BA in literature from Bard College. She has a twenty- five-year career in nonprofit management and development working for museums, the environment, and healthcare. In 1980 she became the founding executive director of the Hudson River Maritime Museum in Kingston, New York, and returning to museums most recently served as development counsel for the American Museum in Britain. She currently writes for local publications and is intent upon launching a writing career. Lopez-Mena lives in Woodstock, New York, where she entertains visits from her three children and beloved grandchildren, Andre, Lucien, and Henry Freligh.

HARRIET LURIA received her doctorate from Teachers College, Columbia University, and is an associate professor in the Department of English, Hunter College, City University of New York. She teaches courses in the structure of modern English, gender, language and literature, women and the metropolis, and the city as text. Her research and teaching interests are in the areas of application of linguistics to teaching, gender and text, and women and literacy. She is the author of *Ideas in Context: Strategies for College Reading*, workplace literacy studies, and co-editor of *Language and Linguistics in Context: Readings and Applications for Teachers*.

OCTAVIA NEVINS (a pseudonym) teaches, writes, does yoga, enjoys her women friends, and is very interested in this/the next chapter of her life.

SUE O'SULLIVAN was born in the United States in 1941 and has lived mainly in London, England, since 1962, with a four-year sojourn in Australia in the 1990s. She moved from the feminist magazine *Spare Rib* in the early 1980s to Sheba Feminist Publishers until the early 1990s, and has remained involved in feminist, radical, and then lesbian projects around sexuality and sexual health for over thirty years, with an emphasis on women and HIV/AIDS since the late 1980s. She is the author and editor of a number of books; currently she edits *ICW News*, the newsletter of the International Community of Women Living with HIV/AIDS.

ANNIE PEACOCK (a pseudonym), a k a Snow, is a translator, a writer, and a college English professor specializing in twentieth-century poetry. Her varied past includes careers in advertising and fashion. She is also an accomplished carpenter and brews her own beer. She found her calling as an academic late in life, but considers it her best career and best self. She is more or less permanently settled in New York City, having lived in eight states in the United States and four countries in Europe. She speaks several languages fluently, but wishes she were a better interpreter of the language of love.

DIANE RAYMOND is a professor of philosophy and women's studies at Simmons College in Boston, where she has been since 1985. She has been the dean of the College of Arts and Sciences since 2002. She is the author of *Existentialism and the Philosophical Tradition*, co-author (with Warren Blumenfeld) of *Looking at Gay and Lesbian Life*, and editor of *Sexual Politics and Popular Culture*. In addition, she has written numerous articles in the fields of cultural studies, feminist theory, and ethics. She is the mother of a thirty-one-year-old daughter.

JANICE STIEBER ROUS teaches the Alexander Technique and is the creator of Body Dialogue, a mind body practice. She leads retreats for women redefining themselves in the second half of life. Also, she has initiated numerous programs in the field of Jewish education. Janice is the mother of two grown children.

ZOHRA SAED was born in Afghanistan and lived in Saudi Arabia before immigrating with her family at the age of five to the United States. She is co-editing the anthology *Drop by Drop We Make a River: Afghan American Experiences of War, Exile, and Return* with Lida Abdul (forthcoming). Saed received her MFA in poetry at Brooklyn College (2000) and is a doctoral student in English at he Graduate Center of the City University of New York. She teaches at Hunter College, where she has initiated courses on literature and film from the West Asian diaspora.

CATHERINE B. SILVER is a professor of sociology at Brooklyn College and the Graduate Center, City University of New York, where she was also the director of the Center for the Study Women and Society and the Women's Studies Certificate Program. She received her master's in sociology from the Sorbonne (Paris) and her PhD from Columbia University (New York). She is a psychoanalyst and faculty member at the National Psychological Association for Psychoanalysis. She is on the boards of *The Psychoanalytic Review* and *International Forum of*

Psychoanalysis. She has written books and articles on issues of gender, aging, and organizations. Her approach is cross-cultural and socio-psychoanalytic.

LAURIE SILVER grew up in New York City, still lives there, and has been writing for as long as she can remember; she is currently working on a fictionalized memoir. Laurie has a smart, beautiful teenage daughter who may someday speak without disdain, a dog who is far cuter than he is bright, and a gym membership that isn't holding its breath. Now that she has some perspective, Laurie finds herself delighted to be divorced and starting over. She would like to thank her amazing circle of friends for their continued love and support.

ANNE SIMCOCK (maiden name) was born in London, England, in 1935. She graduated in medicine from Oxford University, then came to New York City for training in psychiatry and neurology. She did research in psychopharmacology and worked with patients addicted to drugs and alcohol. She has written extensively in her professional field. She lives in Greenwich Village, New York, and has one son, who is married, and a non-live-in partner.

MARY STUART retired from an active psychotherapy practice and entered into the teaching profession; she now teaches psychology at a local private university. In her spare time she writes poetry, nonfiction, and fiction; her current project is putting the finishing touches on her novel, the first in a mystery series set in various deserts around the world. She resides in Phoenix, Arizona.

LOUISE WEINBERG is an artist working in photography and mixed media, and an independent curator/art consultant located in Long Island City, New York. She has had eight solo exhibitions of her work and has participated in over 150 invitational and juried group exhibitions both nationally and internationally. Weinberg has won numerous awards for her photography and mixed media works, which have been published in eight books and many exhibition catalogues.

NAOMI WORONOV is the author of *China Through My Window*, an anecdotal account of the two years she spent teaching English language and literature in Hangzhou. She also published two English-as-a-second-language texts in China that have sold more than two million copies. Her articles have appeared in *New York*, *Dance*, *Publishers' Weekly*, *The Chronicle of Higher Education*, and other publications. She taught English at Borough of Manhattan Community College, City University of New York, from 1965 to 1995 and on a two-year Fulbright in Nitra, Czechoslovakia, and in Bratislava, Slovakia.